# OUTSTANDING ACCLAIM FOR
## CARLTON STOWERS

TURN THE PAGE FOR MORE CRITICAL PRAISE . . .

"Stowers doesn't lecture or pretend to have all the answers; he just tells the story ... and shows how people can be blinded by love and also how perseverance can ultimately prevail."

—*Glamour*

"[A] masterful chronicle of a troubling case."     —*Booklist*

"[Stowers] has a flair for his craft, and his sense of story commands attention."     —*Fort Worth Star-Telegram*

"Stowers illustrates the great difficulty in proving infant murder, in which scientific evidence is not always conclusive."

—*Library Journal*

## OPEN SECRETS

"OPEN SECRETS is one of the most remarkable true crime books I've ever read. Every answer leads to a question; this is murder in the house of mirrors. Carlton Stowers is brilliant as he peels away the layers of a truly fascinating killer—and of the dedicated detective who finally discovered the 'mirror' with the real reflection . . . It held me captive to the last page."

—Ann Rule

"No one writes true crime like Carlton Stowers. OPEN SECRETS is a masterpiece of murder and betrayal, Texas-style."

—Faye Kellerman, author of *Grievous Son*

# CARELESS
## *Whispers*

# CARLTON STOWERS

St. Martin's Paperbacks

Lyrics from "Careless Whisper" by George Michael and Andrew Ridgeley. Copyright © 1984 by Morrison-Leahy Music Ltd. Published in the U.S.A. by Chappell & Co., Inc. International Copyright Secured. ALL RIGHTS RESERVED. Used by permission.

CARELESS WHISPER

Copyright © 1986 by Carlton Stowers.
Postscript copyright © 2001 by Carlton Stowers.

Cover photograph of police by Rod Aydelotte, *Waco Tribune-Herald*. Photograph of David Spence courtesy McLennan County Sheriff's Department.

ISBN: 0-312-97704-2
EAN: 9780312-97704-7

Printed in the United States of America

Previously published by Taylor Publishing Company
Pocket Books edition / December 1987
St. Martin's Paperbacks edition / January 2001

St. Martin's Paperbacks are published by St. Martin's Press, 175 Fifth Avenue, New York, NY 10010.

10 9 8 7 6 5 4

*To the memory of*
*Jill Montgomery, Raylene Rice, and Kenneth Franks*

# Preface

It was an April evening in 1984, one of those times ideal for sitting in the backyard and sipping iced tea, reflecting on old times with a high school buddy I hadn't seen in almost twenty years. I had managed, off and on, to keep track of Ned Butler through his mother; thus I knew that he was working in the District Attorney's office in McLennan County, but we hadn't so much as exchanged Christmas cards in two decades. Then, suddenly he called to say he was at the airport. I insisted that he stop by before driving on to Waco.

Only after we had replayed several memorable football games, making a concerted effort to convince each other that we were better than we actually had been, and sworn mightily against various young ladies back there in Abilene who had seen fit to jilt us in favor of classmates better-heeled and more handsome, did the discussion get around to the manner in which we were earning our respective livelihoods.

As I recall, I offered up several lame excuses for the fact none of my books had won prizes or places on the bestseller lists, and, in turn, Ned told me about a case he was currently preparing for trial.

I had been in California during that time in the summer of 1982 when the crime which came to be known as the Lake Waco Murders occurred, yet I remembered reading newspaper accounts of the brutal killings. The more Ned talked of the trial that was upcoming, the more fascinated I became. Before he left that evening I had committed myself to visiting the McLennan County courthouse. It would be interesting, I decided, to watch Ned Butler prosecute a case.

"Who knows?" Ned said, smiling as he backed out of the driveway well after midnight. "You might get so interested in the case you'll want to write a book about it."

The purpose of Ned Butler's surprise visit is now very clear. He had stopped by to plant an idea and for that I am immeasurably grateful. Over the last two years his offhand suggestion has caused me to explore the minds of murderers, to learn how the legal community reacts to such criminals, and to devote two years to seeking out the true story of what must be regarded as one of the most bizarre and complicated crimes ever committed.

Were it not for people like Ned Butler, this book would have been an impossible task. He and a number of others graciously saw fit to spend a great deal of time providing answers and insights that would eventually make me comfortable with my subject. In return, they asked only that I write an honest, truthful book.

The dangers of acknowledging those who have been helpful is obvious: despite the best of intentions, there are going to be those whose names are inadvertently left out. Thus I begin this list with an apology. Too, there are those who, for a variety of reasons, were willing to help but asked that they remain anonymous. To them, the thank-you is just as loud and heartfelt as it is to the ones here named.

Prosecutors and defense lawyers, adversaries inside the courtroom (and sometimes outside as well), were generous with their time: District Attorney Vic Feazell (and his wife Berni), administrative assistant John Ben Sutter, the aforementioned Ned Butler (and his wife, Carla), assistant D.A. Pat Murphy, Dave Deaconson, and DeAnna Fitzgerald; and attorneys Dick McCall, Jack Holcomb, David Anderson, Rod Goble, Claude Giles, Lisa Donaldson, Guy Cox, Bill Vance, Walter (Skip) Reaves, Hayes Fuller, and Russ Hunt.

Waco Police Chief Larry Scott provided much-needed help, as did Detectives Ramon Salinas and Dennis Baier. The same must be said for McLennan County Sheriff Jack Harwell and Captain Dan Weyenberg. Thanks, too, to Deputy Constable Gene Thorpe; William Johnston, Waco Police Department legal advisor; and Jack Daniels of the Methodist Home.

Tommy Witherspoon of the *Waco Tribune-Herald* generously shared information, as did television reporters Marilyn Moritz and Paul Gately. A gracious nod is also due the photographers whose names are carried alongside the photographs used.

Dr. Homer Campbell and James Ebert were engaging dinner companions on more than one occasion and finally managed to explain the basic principles of forensic odontology to me. Dr.

Jerry Vale was also a patient helper. And the visits Dr. M. F. G. Gilliland allowed me were valuable and appreciated.

Among those who graciously shared personal remembrances were Karen Hufstetler, Gene Deal, Gayle Kelley, Christine Juhl, Patty Pick, Dana Diamond, Patti Deis, Penny McNutt, Pat Torres, Bobby Brim, Lou Booker, Linda Hedrick, Karen Cannon, and Dorothy and Ojeda Miles.

Special thanks is due families of the victims: Nancy Shaw, Rod Montgomery, Brad and Gloria Montgomery, Jan and Robert Thompson, Richard Franks, Sandra Sadler, and Kay Sanders.

For background on Waco's colorful history I am indebted to Patricia Ward Wallace and her excellent book, *Waco: Texas Crossroads*.

Pat Stowers, the lady of the house, not only encouraged me during the research and writing; she was a dedicated note-taker on days when it wasn't possible for me to be in the courtroom, arranged files, ran errands, read rambling first drafts, and offered valued criticisms. And if there is an editor more caring and dedicated to her task than Freddie Goff, I have not made her acquaintance. Her suggestions were immeasurably beneficial, her enthusiasm most appreciated.

Finally, if this book contains the message I hope it does, a great deal of the credit is due Deputy Sheriff Truman Simons. A man who has shied from publicity throughout his long and impressive law enforcement career, he was helpful in ways I'll not even try to explain. Suffice it to say that without his input, his honesty, and his egoless interest in the project, the telling of the whole story would have been impossible. And the fact that his wife, Judy, warmly welcomed an intruding journalist into their lives was a far greater help than she probably realized.

One final note: All occurrences and conversations in this book are based on the recollections of at least one of the parties involved; more often, several. The dialogue herein, of course, is re-created but is as close to an exact account as the memories of my sources permit. I am comfortable the ring of truth is here.

# Author's Note

Over the course of hundreds of interviews, no one who was part of this story and who spoke to me on the record asked that their real names not be used. There were, however, those who did not wish to talk. And some members of the Waco Police Department were selective in the areas about which they would answer questions. It was my own decision to change certain names to avoid embarrassment to persons who had no direct connection to the crimes. The following are the names that have been changed: Connie Baines, Joanne Baines, Randy Baines, Marcie Blackwood, James Blankenship, Carl Casey, Donna Cawthorn, Ronnie Cole, Brenda Douglas, Jimmy Garcia, Terry Hough, Jerry Jackson, Johnny Johnston, Linda Kelton, Roger Lowe, Lou Martinez, Albert Everett Mendoza, Kyle Moore, Clint Olson, Julio Ortega, Fran Peters, Danny Powers, Kasey Rowe, Kerry Rowe, Glenda Thomas, J. D. Williams, Roy Willis, Lonnie Joe Wynn, and Ricky Young. All other names are real.

# PART ONE

For several silent minutes the police officer had stood looking down at the body of the young girl. Like the blonde, she too had been a pretty girl, with long dark brown hair. A gold necklace with a heart-shaped medallion was still around her neck, the chain broken and partially embedded in one of her wounds. She still wore blue hoop earrings and there were rings on two of her fingers. It appeared she had been gagged with her own blouse and her hands tied behind her with what was probably a strip of cloth torn from a towel. Lividity had already begun and, after trying to bend one of her toes, the officer decided she had been dead for quite some time. Ants and pillbugs were crawling over her bloodstained torso and flies had already laid their eggs in her nasal cavities. Soon, he knew, maggots would be hatching.

Her eyes remained partially open, a milky gray glaze replacing their original color. The lifeless stare of a murder victim seemed always to draw the officer's attention. The eyes were like once-sparkling marbles deprived of light: dull, nonreactive, cold.

He shook his head slightly, images of her killer forming in his mind. "God, if only I could see through your eyes," he whispered.

Still, the officer's expression did not change in the slightest. Years of investigating homicides had taught him to mask any feelings he might have. To do the job he knew the situation demanded, he had to go about his duties with an attitude some might mistake for a total lack of emotion. Fellow officers, in fact, had often remarked that they'd never known anyone less bothered by the sight of a homicide victim. Jokingly they said that he would get right down there with them, touching them, looking right at them, like he was checking a dog for fleas. Nothing seemed to affect the guy. It was the only way the officer knew to properly conduct an investigation.

While he stood there looking down at the girl's body, his

*hands buried in the hip pockets of his trousers, the Captain walked up and placed a hand on his shoulder. Neither spoke for a moment, then the Captain shook his head. "I've seen some rough ones, but never anything like this," he said. "Nothing like what they did to these poor kids. Bastards didn't leave them a shred of dignity. Not a bit. I think that's what bothers me the most." There were tears in his eyes as he spoke.*

*"It bothers me, too, Captain," the officer said. He took a deep breath. "It bothers me a helluva lot."*

1

For most of the day construction worker Sidney Smith and his brother-in-law Joseph Chambers had been fishing along the banks of Lake Waco with little success. Several times they had moved from one location to another, hoping to find that one special spot where either the crappie or bass might be biting. Finally, weary of the unyielding heat and disappointed with their luck, Chambers suggested they call it quits, stop somewhere for a couple of beers, then go on home. But Smith was starting a new job the next day and knew he wouldn't have the opportunity to do much fishing for some time to come. He argued that it wasn't even five o'clock yet—there were still several hours of daylight remaining—and there was one other place they might try before giving up.

Several weeks earlier he had caught some nice-sized crappie in shallow water at one of the far ends of Speegleville Park. He persuaded his brother-in-law to drive over there and try just a bit longer.

To get to the Speegleville side of the lake, Smith drove out Highway Six, over the twin bridges, then took an exit to the access road which led to the entrance of the large state-maintained park that was used mostly by fishermen and campers. After entering the park, he drove his pickup a couple of miles along the winding blacktop, then turned off onto a small dirt road that led into the thickly wooded area that bordered the lake's shoreline.

It was not a road in the truest sense, just a rutted path carved out by pickup-driving fishermen, campers who wanted to set up their tents in the more isolated areas of the park, and adventurous young lovers seeking privacy for other reasons. Even with the sun still high in a cloudless sky, the shelter of trees formed a leafy umbrella over the road and made the route they were taking so shadowed that it suddenly seemed near twilight.

Chambers, who had never been in Speegleville Park before, mentioned that the place was "spooky as hell."

"A guy could get lost out here and nobody'd ever find him," he said.

Sidney Smith grinned. "We're almost there," he said. A few seconds later, the smile drained from his face.

"What the hell is that?"

He braked to a jerking stop. Less than twenty feet away, at an intersection with another makeshift road, was what appeared to be a body, its legs stretched out into one of the rutted tire paths.

For several minutes the two men sat in the cab of the pickup trying to decide whether they had happened onto someone's bad practical joke or something far more serious. It could be nothing more than a dummy, placed here to scare whoever might be passing by. If such was the case, the perpetrator had succeeded with flying colors.

"That's no dummy," Chambers finally said, breaking a silence neither realized had set in as they contemplated the situation. Smith said nothing but was mentally agreeing with his brother-in-law as he got out of the pickup and slowly walked in the direction of the outstretched body.

He didn't have to get much closer to satisfy himself that something bad had taken place. Lying beneath a small tree on the edge of the road was the motionless form of a young man. What Smith assumed to be blood was smeared across the front of the man's shirt. He also appeared to have some sort of gag tied around his mouth.

Sidney Smith had never seen a dead person before but he was certain the man was no longer alive. Still, he stared at the body for several seconds, not even blinking, trying to detect any movement. There was none.

Finally, as if awaking from a trance, he turned and ran back to the pickup. "We've got to tell somebody," he said with obvious fright in his voice. "That guy's dead."

He backed the pickup down the road until he could turn around, then headed back in the direction of the paved road. Smith knew that Gene Thorpe, a McLennan County Deputy Constable who also served as a night security guard at the park, lived in a house trailer near the marina, just a couple of miles away. He hoped Thorpe was at home.

Driving as fast as he could along the narrow park road, Smith said nothing at all until they had almost reached Thorpe's trailer. Pale and shaken, he didn't take his eyes off the road as he finally remarked on what he'd seen.

"Jesus, Joe, he was still wearing a pair of sunglasses. Laying there dead and still had sunglasses on. Damn."

Sidney Smith felt as if he was going to be sick. God, how he wished they'd quit fishing and gone home early.

Constable Thorpe, a husky, middle-aged man with an ever-present weary look, had just returned home from work and was ready to sit down and watch the evening news before having his dinner. Thus the situation presented him by the two shaken fishermen was more aggravating than alarming. Probably, he thought, some old fisherman who had gotten too much sun, had a stroke, and died. It had happened before in the brutal July heatwaves that annually visited central Texas. Thorpe had never understood why anyone would want to get out in such brain-baking heat unless it was absolutely necessary.

There was no urgency in his movements as he pulled on the cowboy boots he had just minutes earlier removed. Whatever the case, he knew he would be tied up with the matter for quite some time. Before leaving the trailer, he placed a call to the sheriff's department. "Looks like we've got some kind of questionable death out here at Speegleville," he told the dispatcher. "Better get some people out here soon as you can. I'll have somebody waiting near the entrance of the park to direct you to the site where the body was found." He hung up, frowned, and headed toward his car. Smith and Chambers climbed back into the pickup and led him to where they had made their gruesome discovery.

Thorpe's attitude changed dramatically once he arrived at the wooded area where the body lay. Clearly this was no heat stroke victim. The body was that of a teenage boy. Stab wounds were evident in the chest and there was a gag tied over the mouth. By the way the arms were stretched behind the back, Thorpe immediately assumed that the hands had been bound as well. He instructed Smith and Chambers to drive back toward the entrance to the park and lead the investigators to the scene as soon as they arrived.

As he stared down on the dead youngster, all thoughts of his late dinner and missing the six o'clock news disappeared. Somewhere, he thought to himself, there's a real crazy running loose. And despite the intense heat which made even taking a deep breath a chore, a sudden shiver ran through his body.

Patrol Sergeant Truman Simons, a seventeen-year veteran in the Waco Police Department, was a man of average build, trim, and well shy of six feet, but something about the way he carried himself gave one the impression of a much larger man. A rural heritage was still very much evident in his rough-hewn good looks, his easy laughter, and his gentle manner. His brown eyes, which matched the color of his hair and his neatly trimmed mustache, always focused squarely on whomever he was talking with, signaling a quiet self-confidence. His dress, when not in uniform, was usually jeans, boots, and a western shirt.

Simons had been working the relief shift—3:00 P.M. to 1:00 A.M.—for several weeks and had seen very little of his wife in recent days. He would still be sleeping when she left for work at the Engineering Technological Institute, and she would already be asleep when he arrived home in the early morning hours. Both would be glad when he returned to a normal schedule.

One of the things he had missed most was attending her softball games. Judy Simons was pretty and feminine—she had played the lead in several musical comedies in college—but she also had a tomboyish manner which was one of the first things that had attracted her husband. She always looked forward to the women's softball league schedule and in summers past Truman had coached her team. Eager to hear details of the previous evening's game, he drove to her office to have coffee with her after handing out beat assignments and completing his paperwork.

For Simons, patrol was, at best, boring. On occasion he enjoyed returning to it, however, just to let the cobwebs clear away after lengthy stretches in vice and intelligence or with the tactical squad. Working patrol was his pressure valve, a way to step away from the demands of intense investigations for a time. But always he would tire of the duty quickly, and he had gained a reputation for spending unauthorized time looking into cases that didn't fall within his job description.

In the minds of many in the department, including some of

his superiors, Truman Simons was something of a renegade. He had a remarkable record for solving cases, many of them turned over to him by fellow investigators weary of running into blind alleys. But there were whispered suggestions that perhaps he didn't always make his cases by the book. "I don't know how he does it," Bob Fortune, a detective with the Waco Police, once told a fellow investigator after Simons had solved a particularly complex series of rapes, "and I don't want to know." His innuendo was clear.

When Simons worked vice, a record number of arrests and convictions were tallied. And if he found that a fellow officer was involved in some manner of illegal activity, he wasn't the least bit hesitant to call it to a commander's attention. Once he arrested a fellow officer he caught drilling a safe, and he noticed afterward that several on the force were suddenly far less friendly than before. Another time when he was working on a heroin investigation, several prostitutes told him of repeated instances where a particular officer had forced them to provide him drugs and have sex with him or be arrested. After gathering enough information to satisfy himself that the accusations were valid, that the officer was in fact using dope on duty and getting what in police parlance is referred to as "badge pussy," Simons reported his findings to the officer's superior. Several days later the accused officer confronted him and insisted he had gotten some bad information. Simons showed him the notes he had taken during interviews with the prostitutes.

"Look," the officer said to Simons, "I'll promise you it won't ever happen again. What do you say we forget it this time? You know I'm a good cop." Simons told him he had serious doubts about that.

Eventually the matter was dropped. The officer was allowed to remain on the force and he wasted little time spreading the word through the department that Simons had given him a bad rap and was not a man to be trusted. A year later that same officer was indicted on twenty-one counts of burglary.

Truman Simons eventually came to the decision that he really didn't like cops. Too many were there simply for the misguided feeling of authority the job afforded them. He developed a growing dislike for the department's tangled bureaucracy. When he had strong suspicions that a fellow policeman had killed a prisoner in the city jail, he began looking into the matter but was soon told to forget about it or find another job. The brotherhood that he felt was supposed to exist among officers was nothing more than a television-inspired myth. The truth was, he seemed to get along better with the whores and pimps and drug pushers, people who were supposed to be his adversaries, than he did with most of his colleagues.

Sometimes, he felt, his attitude toward the police worked to his advantage. In a way it actually helped him when he was dealing with criminals who also felt that most cops were assholes, not to be trusted. Recently, though, he had been giving considerable thought to the direction his own career was heading.

An academic rebel, Truman Simons had joined the Air Force at a time when his peers were finishing their junior year of high school. There he had earned his graduate equivalency diploma, but once his four-year hitch was up he entertained no desire to attend college. Instead, he worked briefly for his father as a mechanic, then served as shop foreman at the Ford Tractor plant before hearing on the radio one day that the Waco Police Department was looking for recruits. With no serious interest in or understanding of law enforcement, he decided to look into it.

From a group of one hundred taking the Civil Service exam, Simons was one of eight applicants called in for interviews. Later, he was one of two hired.

Despite the fact that at age twenty-five he had been the youngest member of the department ever to make sergeant, he still held that rank at forty. Those moving up to lieutenant were the ones who had college diplomas framed and hanging behind their desks and were continually enrolling in law enforcement courses across town at Baylor University. To Simons this was a waste of time and money. He had seen more than one good police officer ruined by too much education. Crimes, he strongly felt, were solved by hard work and long hours out on the street, not by reading textbooks.

Besides, he had no ambition to advance to the rank of lieutenant. It was a desk job, and he could not imagine himself off the streets, not mingling with the people.

Simons had just pulled out of the parking lot following the brief visit with his wife when the dispatcher put out the call. It was just minutes after 6:00 P.M. Beat officer Brian Reynolds, special investigator Jimmy Wilcox, and Sergeant Simons were asked to respond. The dispatcher's request for three officers was an immediate indication that something out of the ordinary had occurred. When a special investigator—the officer who carries the equipment necessary for crime scene photography, measurement, and fingerprinting—is summoned, it is a good bet that violence has taken place.

Even before the dispatcher informed him that they were to meet members of the sheriff's department at Speegleville Park and investigate a questionable death, Simons had a good idea what kind of case they would be working. He immediately began figuring out the shortest route to the lakeside park.

He had driven only a few blocks when a call from Brian Reynolds came over his radio, asking his location. Reynolds said he wanted to meet briefly with Simons before proceeding to the park.

Minutes later, Simons turned into a 7-Eleven store parking lot at the intersection of Highway Six and Bosque Avenue. Reynolds was already there, waiting in his car. Pulling up beside him, Simons rolled down the window to talk.

"Sarge," Reynolds said, "what do you think we've got out there?" He appeared nervous.

Simons was amused. It was common knowledge that Reynolds had an almost fearful dislike for any kind of investigative work that involved dead bodies. "Brian, it's pretty hard to tell until we get out there," he said. "It could be a suicide or maybe some old fisherman who fell out with a heart attack. I just don't know."

"The dispatcher said the sheriff's unit was already on the way there," Reynolds replied. "Think maybe we ought to let them work it?" Reynolds was obviously anxious to find a way to avoid the trip to Speegleville.

Simons smiled. "Look, Brian, I think the best thing for us to do is just run on out there and see what we've got. If it's something I think we ought to let the sheriff's people work, we'll let 'em have it. But if it falls within our jurisdiction, we're going to have to work it." He rolled up his window, ending the conversation, and pulled back onto the highway with Reynolds following him.

As they neared the Twin Bridges which led to the exit to the park, Jimmy Wilcox and Detective Ramon Salinas pulled in

behind them. Minutes later the waiting pickup led all four cars
to the edge of the wooded area where the body had been found.

Even as he stepped out of his patrol car Simons could see that
the investigation was going to be a problem. Several television
reporters who must have been monitoring the police radio were
already milling around, along with three or four sheriff's deputies, several constables, and some of the park's employees.
Simons noticed that one had brought his young son with him,
a boy no older than nine or ten. He shook his head in disbelief.
The whole scene already had a carnival atmosphere about it.
Standing in the road, Simons could see that the body was that
of a boy, probably in his late teens, wearing jeans, tennis shoes,
and a bloodstained orange shirt. He got down on his hands and
knees and crawled under the low-hanging branches to get a
closer look at the victim. He quickly determined that multiple
stab wounds had been inflicted to the chest area. As he stared
at the lifeless form, he tried to imagine the horror the youngster
had experienced before dying.

He looked up to see Ramon Salinas holding out a Polaroid
photograph. "Take a look at this," Salinas said. Still crouched
beneath the tree, Simons looked first at the picture, then back
at the youngster. In the photo, the boy was wearing the same
clothes, same orange Izod shirt, jeans, same sunglasses, that he
had on now. It was almost as though the picture had been taken
just before the boy was killed.

Simons handed the picture back to Salinas. "It's the same
kid," he said.

"We've had a missing persons report on him since early this
morning," Salinas said. "He was supposed to be with a couple
of young girls from Waxahachie. Nobody's seen or heard from
them since last night."

Simons crawled from beneath the tree and instructed the deputies and constables standing nearby to begin searching the area
for any other bodies. Since no one else seemed eager to take
charge of the investigation, he would.

He was still looking at the body of the young man, feeling
the arms in an attempt to determine how long he'd been dead,
when he heard a shout. Approximately twenty-five yards away,
in the underbrush on the other side of the fishing trail, lay the
nude body of a young girl. Simons hurried over and found a

scene even more disturbing than the one he had just left. The girl, a pretty blonde, had a piece of red and white cloth tied around her mouth and a bra tied to her right ankle. She too had been stabbed repeatedly. And somewhere close, Simons knew, there was one more.

Looking around, he saw the knee of the other girl, just visible above the weeds. Hurrying to her side, he found that she too was nude, bound and gagged. There was a great deal more blood on her body and evidence of more stab wounds than had been visible on the other bodies. Her throat had also been cut.

The missing teenagers—Kenneth Franks, Raylene Rice, and Jill Montgomery—had been found.

The discovery of the bodies had stirred a beehive of activity among the officers and onlookers. Suddenly, Simons realized, people were milling around all over the area, attempting to get a look at the bodies. Already enraged by the violent deaths that had occurred, he yelled at Brian Reynolds: "Get everybody the hell out of here. I don't want anyone around the bodies until we've had a chance to check everything out."

A television cameraman standing near where Kenneth Franks' body had been found began to argue that he had a job to do. Simons glared first at him, then at Reynolds. "If the sonuvabitch won't leave, arrest him," he snapped. "I want everybody back away from here. Now!" The cameraman grumbled, then retreated with the others.

As Simons turned his attention back to the bodies, a myriad of questions raced through his mind. There was no indication in the areas where the bodies were found that a struggle had taken place. No leaves were disturbed, no limbs broken. Only near where Jill Montgomery's body lay was there even the slightest evidence anyone had been there. The top stalk of a dead sunflower had been snapped off and on it there appeared to be bloodstains. In all likelihood, the victims had been killed elsewhere, then their bodies dumped where they had been discovered. In carrying Jill's body to where it was found, the killer could have brushed against the sunflower. But why would a killer—or, more probably, killers—not simply dump all the bodies in the same place, be done with it, and get the hell away from there?

By placing Kenneth Franks in a position where he could be

easily found, then leaving the girls in separate, more isolated spots, was someone playing some kind of demented game with them?

Nothing made sense. How could the boy have managed to keep his sunglasses on after what he'd obviously been through? A package of cigarettes was still in place, tucked under the left sleeve of his shirt. His faded red and white bandanna headband was neatly in place, as if it, like the sunglasses, had been placed there after his death. *What kind of animal did these kids run into?* Simons wondered. *What the hell's going on here?*

He considered the possibility that the murders were the work of a psychopathic killer, someone who had ended the lives of three young kids just for kicks. Probably not. Despite the violent nature of the crimes, experience had taught him that if a psychopath had been involved in what amounted to nothing more than a thrill killing, at least one of the bodies would likely have been more mutilated. The others would have been killed simply to eliminate witnesses.

Even the possibility that it was just a sex crime didn't seem likely. If someone had been looking for a rape victim, he wouldn't have sought out two girls who were obviously in the company of a boy. The parks around Lake Waco, unfortunately, offered too many opportunities to abduct a single girl, or even two girls without a male companion.

Was it, as some of the investigators were already suggesting, the result of some kind of drug deal gone sour? No, he thought, it seemed more than that.

As Simons considered such questions, all the while searching the area for any evidence that might have been left behind, he turned in the direction of where Raylene Rice's body lay and saw a park ranger placing a blanket over the girl's body. He'd already covered the boy. Once again Simons was shouting:

"Get that damn blanket away from her."

The ranger looked up, startled, then angry. "Look, man, there's a lot of people wandering around out here and these girls don't have any clothes on. Seems to me the least we could do is cover them. Besides, you're not on city property out here, and I'm not all that sure you got a right to be in charge."

"Until somebody tells me different," Simons said, "I *am* in charge and I don't want those bodies covered with anything until we've done what we have to do. If they don't want to look at them, they can get the hell out of here. You take your damn blankets and put them back in your pickup and just stay out of the way. Just get your ass out of here and let us do our job."

Simons' anger was directed not so much at the ranger as it was at the very real possibility that he had already compounded the problems the investigators were likely to have with evidence in the case. In a murder investigation, one of the things lab technicians are asked to do is to determine whether there are any foreign hair samples or fibers on the body. By placing the blankets over Kenneth and Raylene, the park ranger had almost assured the technicians of finding hair and fibers that had nothing to do with the case.

The whole thing, Simons thought, was turning into a goddamn three-ring circus. Texas Rangers had arrived, as had other sheriff's deputies and police officers, more reporters and park employees. At one point there were almost forty people wandering through the area where the bodies had been found. The situation was becoming impossible.

Simons, then, was relieved when Lieutenant Marvin Horton arrived and took charge of the investigation. No longer concerning himself with a futile attempt to keep the area clear, he concentrated his full attention on the bodies.

Though he rarely discusses it with other law enforcement officers, Simons insists he's always been able to feel a certain violence in the air at the scene of a crime. It lingers, he says, like a choking residue, a grim, almost tangible reminder that on a particular spot some unspeakable evil has taken place. On several occasions, in fact, he has returned to the scene of a crime he had investigated years before, only to find the atmosphere of violence still present, as real as it had been at the time of the initial investigation.

In the darkening woods of Speegleville Park, there were no such feelings. The only thing about the case he was absolutely certain of was that the three youngsters had not been killed where their bodies were found. They had died somewhere else and were then moved. He was sure of that.

As he repeatedly went from one body to the other, vainly attempting to make sense from something as nonsensical as the murder of three young kids, he found himself drawn back to the dark-haired girl. For some reason, Jill Montgomery seemed to demand his attention more than either Raylene Rice or Kenneth Franks.

The knife cuts on her right hand indicated she had put up more of a struggle than the others. And in addition to the fatal stab wounds on her body, there were a number of more superficial cuts—torture marks—on her neck and chest. Her death had not come easily or quickly.

For reasons he could not explain, Truman Simons felt it was very likely that she had been the primary target of those who had carried out the murders. While other investigators busied themselves with such matters as collecting several Budweiser cans found on the side of the road near the bodies and searching through the high grass and scrub brush in hopes of finding a weapon, he stood for a long time looking down at her body, studying her face. Finally, making sure no one was watching, he knelt beside her and began to speak:

"I don't even know who you are," he whispered, "and I don't know how or why this happened to you. But I promise you that whoever did this is going to pay for it. This won't be just another murder in Waco, Texas. I give you my word on that. You're not going to be some little girl who was just left lying out here like this. It's not right, and I won't let it happen."

Before the emergency van from the funeral home arrived, Simons had made his way to the sides of Raylene Rice and Kenneth Franks and had made each of them the same promise. Already, he knew, he was more personally involved in the case than he should be.

Simons helped the attendants from the Connally Compton Funeral Home place the bodies into heavy black plastic bags, then assisted in carrying them to the van. The vulturous television cameras, still hovering over the scene, recorded the grim death parade for the benefit of ten o'clock newswatchers.

Over three hours had passed since he had first arrived at Speegleville and, for the first time, he was aware of the oppressive heat as they brought the bodies from the wooded area out into the more open section of the park. The slight breeze that greeted him as he stepped from the tree line felt almost cold as it hit his sweat-soaked uniform.

As the ambulance drove away, its red taillights growing smaller in the distance, Simons lifted his head toward the starlit sky, closed his eyes, and welcomed the cool breeze on his face.

But not for long. He wanted to get as far away from Speegleville Park as he could. Maybe some distance would dim the pictures of those dead kids which were still so vivid in his mind's eye.

He helped Reynolds and Wilcox load the photography equipment into the car, then told them to meet him at the police station and make their reports. As he walked toward his car, Simons looked over at Reynolds, who was clearly shaken, his face ashen.

"Brian," he said.

"Yeah, Sarge."

"I don't blame you a damn bit for not liking this kind of work."

Brian Reynolds nodded gratefully. "Thanks," he said.

Truman Simons left the station shortly after midnight, ending his shift a bit earlier than usual. Tired, dirty, and covered with chigger bites, he wanted to get home. Stepping into the parking lot, he saw the Connally Compton van pass, followed by Sergeant Fortune and Detective Salinas. The bodies were on their way to the Dallas Institute of Forensic Science where autopsies would be performed.

The knowledge of what some pathologist would have to do to the bodies of the three dead youngsters caused him further distress. Medical examiners had a job to perform, but the detached, dispassionate manner in which they dissected a human body had always bothered him. More than once during his career, he had bought time—just a couple more hours—from a pathologist to try to learn the identity of a Jane or John Doe before the autopsy was begun. Bodies of unidentified victims were routinely cut up more than those with names and histories available to the medical examiners.

At least the pathologist would know who these victims were. Still, after what they had already been through, he thought, they deserved something better than a cold stainless steel table with a drain at one end.

Usually, Simons enjoyed driving the streets of Waco in the early morning hours. He liked the peaceful quiet that settled over the city once most people were home and in bed. On this particular night, however, the silence was literally ringing in his ears. Though he fought to free his mind from thoughts of what had just transpired at the park, it was to little avail. What kind of monster could do that to someone? How were the victims' families taking the news which had no doubt by now reached them? Why do things like this have to happen? God, why?

He pounded his palm on the steering wheel as he began to cry. The emotion so carefully kept in check while performing his duty now exploded to the surface, and his shoulders heaved as tears streamed down his cheeks.

Though he embraces few of the formalities of organized religion and finds fault with much of today's ultra-conservative preachings, and while his conversation is sprinkled with street-talk profanities, Truman Simons is a man of deep, abiding Christian faith. His mother is a Bible scholar and has passed much of her knowledge and religious philosophy on to him. It is God, he says, who has enabled him to solve so many of the cases he's been involved in. He regularly calls on a verse from the Book of Matthew: "Blessed are the peacemakers; for they shall be called the children of God." For Truman, being a police officer has always been something more than a way to earn a paycheck.

As he drove, he began to pray aloud:

"I don't know anything about those kids we found out there tonight, Lord. Maybe they were good kids; maybe they had problems. But they didn't deserve what happened to them. I hope You have welcomed them into your Kingdom and have given them peace. But, Lord, it wasn't right for them to have been left out there like that, dead and exposed. I pray that You'll help us find the people who did this . . ."

With that he pushed his boot hard to the accelerator. He wanted to get home. To see his wife and his own child.

2

Richard Franks stood at the picture window of his well-kept town house, an amused smile on his face. As the nearby grandfather clock ticked rhythmically, then chimed to indicate it was a quarter to eight, he silently observed the activities of the two young girls parked in the driveway outside. Sitting in the front seat of an orange Pinto, they were sharing the rearview mirror, checking to make certain hair and makeup were in order. Primping, he called it.

The scene warmed him, causing him a brief recollection of his own teenage dating days. Upstairs, he knew his eighteen-year-old son Kenneth was going through much the same ritual.

Home for a few days from his travels as a manager for a Waco-based paint company, Richard had hoped he and his son might take in a movie that July Tuesday evening, something they had begun doing together on a fairly regular basis. It had seemed an opportune time. One of Kenneth's best friends was grounded, something about taking his parents' boat out without permission the Fourth of July weekend. (Richard Franks had not been made aware that his son had accompanied the grounded youngster on the unauthorized holiday excursion to the lake.) Another of his son's buddies had recently begun working the late shift as a cook at the Brazos Landing, a local restaurant. And, too, Kenneth's motorcycle was in the shop for repair. Without transportation or friends to hang out with, Richard thought, his son might settle for an evening in the company of the older generation. He dropped the idea quickly—without even mentioning it, in fact—when Jill Montgomery telephoned.

Jill had first called just after Richard had sent Kenneth to the Whataburger to pick up hamburgers and fries for dinner. They were just beginning their fast-food evening meal when she phoned again. She was in town, she told Kenneth, and had to get back home to Waxahachie soon. But first she wondered if he would like to meet her at the park for a little while. A girlfriend from Waxahachie, Raylene Rice, was with her. Maybe Kenneth could get someone to come along.

At shortly after 7:00 P.M. Kenneth called his friend Bobby Brim to see if perhaps the boating escapade had been forgiven and his restrictions lifted so he could join them at Koehne Park. Bobby asked his mother and was told firmly that he was going to remain grounded for the full month she and his father had prescribed. Clearly they were still angered. Returning to the phone he told Kenneth he couldn't make it.

"Good-lookin' blonde," Kenneth told his friend.

"Sorry," Bobby said, "but I'll have to pass."

Kenneth then asked his father for the use of the car. It was, after all, just over a mile up Lake Shore Drive to Koehne Park where he and Jill planned to meet. Yet he knew the answer before asking. While his father occasionally allowed him to drive his company car on short errands—like picking up the hamburgers for dinner—he had made it clear that it was not to be used for social purposes. Never hurt to ask again, though.

His father suggested that Kenneth invite the girls to come to the house. They could sit by the swimming pool or in the complex's clubroom where Kenneth's surprise birthday party had been held the previous February.

Kenneth returned to the phone, spoke briefly with Jill, then told his father that the girls were coming to pick him up. They wanted to go to Koehne where they could sit at one of the park tables and watch the sun go down over the lake.

Koehne Park, one of the half dozen public parks to be found around the shoreline of Lake Waco, was a popular hangout for teenagers in search of a place to visit with their friends, drink a little beer, or share their marijuana free from the watchful eye of adults. On one side of the park was shore-line, with a frequently busy boat-docking facility. On the other side, a small two-lane road wound around to a more secluded place generally referred to as the Circle where several concrete tables and benches were strategically located to provide visitors with a peaceful view of the lake. It was a picturesque spot. Directly across the water one could see the wooded area known as Speegleville Park, which was favored by a different, older clientele—mostly fishermen and campers. Smaller and more accessible, Koehne was the favorite of Waco's youngsters.

Because it was so handy to his home, it was a place to which

Kenneth Franks rode his motorcycle several times a week during the summer. It got him away from the house and into the company of others his age. One need only sit at the park for a while, without any real planning, to see most of his friends in a period of several hours. Since it was located at the end of Valley Mills Drive, the street most traveled by Waco youngsters with no real place to go, Koehne Park was the turn-around point of the "cruising" route.

As he emerged from his room, wearing freshly starched jeans and an orange Izod shirt which his father had recently bought for him, Kenneth asked if he might borrow a couple of dollars. Richard nodded in the direction of the table where the change his son had brought back from the purchase of the hamburgers was still lying.

"Remember," he warned, "you've got summer school tomorrow. Don't be late."

"They can't stay long," Kenneth replied as he stuffed a couple of dollar bills and some change into his pocket. "I'll be in early."

"Before midnight," his father said.

"Okay."

"See you later," Richard Franks said.

He had no reason to believe the conversation would be their last.


The relationship between Kenneth and his father was better that summer of 1982 than it had been in years. After the disruption and bitterness of a divorce, mutual antagonism over discipline problems, and the anger and frustration Kenneth initially felt about being placed in private schools away from home, most of their differences had been resolved. Kenneth had seemed to mature a great deal in recent months and he and his father had developed a friendship that even Kenneth's friends remarked on. From their viewpoint Kenneth was "lucky," his father "a pretty neat dude."

What that meant was that there was a minimum of pressure in the Franks home. Richard was admittedly liberal in his attitudes toward the habits of his son and his friends. Eager to maintain the relationship which had evolved from more tension-filled times, he had only a few rules he expected his son to follow. He was generous with his money, seeing that Kenneth wore designer clothes, had a motorcycle, and a few dollars (but not too *much* money) in his pocket. They had even, since Kenneth's eighteenth birthday, begun discussing the possibility of getting his first car.

Richard and Sandra Franks had lived in Tyler, a quiet east Texas community famous for its roses and a Heisman Trophy-winning running back named Earl Campbell. As is so often the case, few people knew the Frankses' marriage was in trouble until they actually divorced in 1975. Active in the Methodist church, financially comfortable, and the parents of two young sons, they maintained outward appearances long after things had begun to fall apart. Only a few trusted friends knew they were regularly seeing a marriage counselor for the final two years of their twelve-year marriage.

Sandra had been suspicious for some time about the activities her husband engaged in while on the road. Too many times during his Monday-to-Friday absence she had called too many motel rooms in too many towns late at night, only to hear the dull, painful rings that were never answered. Eventually Richard would admit he had been unfaithful. Not once, but on more occasions than he could remember. He had tried to do something about the problem, but the lonely temptations of the road were too strong, almost magnetic, addictive. After a few trips on which he would keep his resolution, spending long evenings in his room, reading and watching television, he would always slip back to his old habits. First he would venture into the motel bar for a couple of drinks and conversation. Before long he would find himself back to touring the nightspots he had come to know so well on his week-long route. It was a distressing weakness. Try though he might, Richard simply could not withstand the neon temptations of the road. And Sandra could not deal with the knowledge that her husband had been and was continuing to be unfaithful. She was the one who eventually filed for divorce.

While many who knew the couple were surprised that the Frankses were splitting up, they were perhaps more surprised at the quiet, dignified manner in which the proceedings were handled. It was difficult for some to understand, but Richard Franks loved his wife and children despite his unfaithfulness. Even Sandra knew that, though she was unable to understand his constant need to seek companionship on the road. Long before she actually hired an attorney and began legal proceedings, Richard was convinced it was something she should do. He was making her unhappy. Yet for reasons he did not completely understand, he could not promise the one thing that would save the marriage. His admission was painfully honest: he didn't think he could be the faithful husband she had to have.

Even so, the separation and subsequent divorce was difficult, for Richard as well as for Sandra. Both went through painful depressions, uncertain where their lives were headed. She remained in Tyler, while Richard moved to Waco where the company for which he worked was headquartered. Gradually the hurt and anger and questions of self-worth that always accompany divorce began to ease. And after time had performed its healing process, Sandra and Richard became friends again. In the years to come, the person who would have the greatest difficulty with the divorce would be Kenneth Franks, the older of the couple's two sons.

Since the third grade, when it was first discovered that he suffered from dyslexia, Kenneth had spent his academic life in special education classes and in the company of tutors hired by his parents to help him through each agonizing school year. The frustrations which accompanied his classroom problems spilled over into his home and social life. Kenneth Franks found nothing whatever about school that he enjoyed and thus rebelled against everything associated with the authority and regimentation that was an integral part of the educational process.

Though always small for his age, he was strong and athletic and enjoyed sports. But the C's, D's, and F's which regularly appeared on his report card each six weeks prevented his ever being eligible to participate in any form of school-sponsored extracurricular activity. He hated school for the things it denied him, and for the inferior feelings it caused him.

Within the structured boundaries of school, he was something of a loner. Only when free from adult supervision and in the company of his peers did Kenneth's charm and fun-loving personality surface.

A year after the divorce, Sandra decided to take a job she had been offered in Lake Jackson, near the Gulf Coast. There she hoped to escape old memories and seek a new beginning with her sons Kenneth and Curtis. Kenneth, troubled at the thought of leaving his friends behind and worried that the distance between their new home and Waco might make it more difficult for his father to visit, was the only member of the family not excited about the relocation.

The fact that his mother had begun to see a man named Byron Sadler, himself divorced with a small daughter, added to Kenneth's problems. Only eleven at the time of his parent's divorce, he understood very little about what had happened to tear the family apart. The problems Sandra and Richard had were never discussed with him, and thus all he knew was that his mother had divorced his father. In his mind, she was the culprit and thus became the target of a deep resentment that surfaced, with increasing frequency in angry, hostile confrontations.

When Sandra married Byron Sadler the problems accelerated. Richard Franks visited with the boys in the company of Byron, pointing out that he personally liked their prospective new stepfather, trying to convince them they would be fortunate to have, in effect, two fathers. But Kenneth showed no inclination to try to fit into the new family. Never, he said, would he accept his mother's new husband.

Desperate to resolve the problems with which her son was dealing, Sandra scheduled a diagnostic evaluation at the University of Texas Medical Branch in nearby Galveston, hoping that professional advice might provide her with guidelines for dealing with her troubled youngster. All she found out was what she already knew. Despite an above-average I.Q., Kenneth was having difficulties in learning and suffered behavioral and emotional problems caused by his dyslexia and complicated by his refusal to accept his parents' divorce.

Finally, Sandra called Richard Franks and tearfully admitted she needed help. She could no longer deal with Kenneth's constant balking at her rules, his refusal even to try in school, and the hostility which seemed to be growing in intensity. Kenneth's unhappiness had spread throughout the family, she explained. She was having difficulty coping with the situation, and feared that Curtis and her new stepdaughter were being affected by the daily battles she and Kenneth were waging.

Already aware of the problems, Richard agreed that Kenneth needed a more structured environment. Because of his travel schedule and Kenneth's immaturity it would be impossible to have his son come live with him. He offered to speak with the administrator of the Methodist Home in Waco about Kenneth. During their work with youth groups of the Methodist Church while they were married, Richard and Sandra had heard numerous stories of troubled children who had been placed there with successful results. Both were therefore disappointed when officials at the Home informed them that it would be impossible to accept their son immediately. A new semester was already underway and the maximum number of students were already enrolled. Obviously, they were not the only parents dealing with a troubled child.

Realizing that the problem could not wait, Richard Franks went in search of an alternative. For a brief period of time Kenneth lived with his grandparents in rural Bowie, Texas, and for a while seemed to thrive in the new environment, even learning to play golf from his grandfather. However, it soon became obvious that the elderly couple, too many years removed from child-rearing, could not provide the supervision and discipline the youngster needed.

Thus, on January 16, 1978, Richard Franks accompanied his son to the Buckner Baptist Children's Home in Dallas. On Kenneth's enrollment form the reasons given for his placement were "conflicts between mother and son" and "need for self-contained special education." Kenneth disliked the Home from the day his father left him there until June of 1979 when, after long insisting that he was ready to adjust to the rules and routine of family life, he was allowed to return to Lake Jackson to live.

His return home would be short-lived. Truant and in and out of minor troubles, he made no headway toward adapting to life with a new family which did not include his real father. In August of 1980, Kenneth was enrolled at the Methodist Home, a sprawling collection of red brick buildings located on a 130-acre plot of land not far from downtown Waco. Established in 1890 as a mission of the Texas-New Mexico United Methodist churches, it is licensed by the Department of Human Resources to house two hundred youngsters from kindergarten to high school age. It generally operates at capacity and, as a sign of the times, there have been evergrowing waiting lists in recent years. The residents attend Waco public schools, but in all other respects it is a community within a community, staffed to serve the physical, emotional, and social needs of its residents.

The personality profile of Kenneth Franks prepared by staff personnel was much like that done on so many other youngsters entering the Home:

*Kenneth Franks is an immature, dependent adolescent battling conflicts resulting from the divorce of his parents. He is rebellious of adult authority and preoccupied with the fear of being abandoned by his parents and suffers from a deep sense of rejection.*

The first several months at the Methodist Home were difficult for Kenneth. The endless list of rules and the highly structured environment heightened his rebellion. Initially, he refused to make any academic effort and made few friends. In time, however, the frustrated youngster began to accept life at the Methodist Home. Personable and handsome, he made friends quickly once he put forth the effort to get to know his fellow students. As his popularity grew, his rebellion diminished. Actually, the Methodist Home was not all that bad. Coeducational, it had a female enrollment that made things interesting. And since he attended Waco High School, there was the added prospect of girl friends and male companions there as well.

Kenneth seemed happy to be back near his father. The Methodist Home campus was just a couple of miles from where Richard Franks lived, and almost every weekend Kenneth would secure a pass and go to stay with his father. Richard even served as chauffeur for occasional dates and regularly dropped by the Home to visit. In fact, officials of the Home found it necessary to speak with the father on several occasions about his spending too much time with his son. For them to properly carry out their plan to help Kenneth Franks mature and accept responsibility, they said, it was necessary that his ties to outside influences not be too strong.

By his second year at the Home, Kenneth had begun to show marked improvement. Though he rarely spoke of his mother to any of his friends, he proudly introduced his father to his classmates when Richard would appear on campus to pick him up for a weekend. Often when his father took him out to dinner, they would be accompanied by a girl named Gayle Kelley, who had become his best friend. A likable prankster, Kenneth earned the admiration of his fellow students and the eye-rolling frustration of administrators who tolerantly viewed his occasional mischief-making as a sign that he was growing into a more confident, self-assured young man. At Waco High School, he joined the golf team and practiced regularly even though his grades were never high enough to earn him the opportunity to travel with the team to out-of-town tournaments.

Gradually, Kenneth came to enjoy living at the Home. Despite the restrictions, it provided him a sense of independence, living away from his parents. On the other hand, the fact that he was again seeing his father regularly and talking with him on the phone several evenings each week gave him a feeling of family togetherness that had been absent since his parents' divorce.

And through his friend Gayle, he had met another girl he liked a great deal. While Gayle remained his closest friend, Jill Montgomery, a pretty brunette with flirtatious eyes and a warm, energetic smile, was something else. When he showed his father the friendship ring he had bought for her—a sign they were planning to "go steady"—Richard Franks was moved to make the fatherly suggestion that it might be more fun to date a lot of girls, to play the field. "I don't want to date anyone else," young Kenneth answered seriously. "I love her."

By the summer of 1982 the maturing of Kenneth Franks had resulted in a number of significant changes in his life. Since he had reached the age where he could make a choice about the Methodist Home, he persuaded his father to let him live with him. Pleased with the adult behavior he had begun to see in his son, Richard not only welcomed Kenneth into his home on a permanent basis but also decided it was time to discuss the subject they had so long avoided—the divorce.

Richard was aware of Kenneth's negative feelings about his mother, and had been feeling a growing sense of guilt over the matter. Deciding that his son should know the true story, Richard admitted to him that the divorce had not been Sandra's fault. He explained, in painful detail, that the divorce had actually been the result of his infidelity and his inability to change.

For several days after the discussion Richard wondered if he had made the right decision. Kenneth clearly had difficulty accepting the fact that his father had been to blame for the breakup of the family. Finally, though, he approached his father, hugged him, and said he would be able to deal with what he'd been told. Then he called his mother, told her about the conversation he had had with his father, and offered a tearful apology for the way he had acted toward her for the past several years.

It was the beginning of a renewed love between a mother and her son. And a better understanding between father and son. A weighty burden had been lifted. With the silence broken and the truth in the open, the relationship of the father, mother, and son was immediately more relaxed. In a sense, they had become a family again.

By noon on that July thirteenth Tuesday the breezeless temperature had climbed near the 100-degree mark. It was going to be another of those droning, endless summer days which Texas residents greet in late June and can expect to hang on through August and into the early weeks of September.

Kenneth Franks stood in the high school parking lot, another agonizing session of American History behind him. He was pleased that he had done reasonably well on the exam he had taken and glad that only a few more weeks of summer school remained. While most of his friends had been enjoying the luxury of sleeping late or the income from summer jobs, he had daily faced the dismal task of rising early to attend classes that would help him make up for yet another failure during the regular school year.

And now no margin of error existed. Though he was passing the course, it was imperative that he not miss another of the morning classes. Earlier in the summer he had suffered through the chills and fever of a summer cold and missed several days of school. One more absence, he had been warned, and he would automatically receive a failing grade.

To complicate his frustrations, his motorcycle had not run properly for several weeks and was being repaired. Without transportation he was forced to depend on his friend Pat Torres to pick him up at school and give him a ride home, where there was little to do but nap and listen to music. Unless he could persuade Pat to go to the lake with him.

"Naw, man, I'm gonna go home and hit the sack," Pat said as they drove toward the Franks home. "Maybe I'll give you a call later." Working the night shift at the restaurant had obviously begun taking a toll on Pat Torres. Kenneth, his books cradled in his lap, said little for the remainder of the short drive. He was clearly disappointed that his friend's only afternoon interest was sleep.

As they pulled into the driveway he sighed. "Thanks. Give me a call if you change your mind." There was no smile on his face. It had, for the most part, been a piss-poor summer.

Contributing heavily to Kenneth Franks' dark mood was the fact that Jill Montgomery had left Waco, released from the Methodist Home to return to Waxahachie and live with her mother. She planned, she had told him, to attend Waxahachie High School for her senior year.

Just the night before, he and his father had been in the car when a song on the radio had caused Kenneth to fall silent, his eyes filling with tears. Surprised at Kenneth's sudden sadness, Richard Franks asked what the problem was. "Aw, nothing," his son said. "That song just reminds me of Jill."

Therefore, that evening when Jill called to say she was in town, Richard Franks felt pleased and relieved. Seeing her, he knew, would lift his son's spirits.

# 3

Nancy Shaw, an early riser, sat in the kitchen of her house near Lake Waxahachie, sipping cautiously on her first cup of coffee and enjoying the solitude and quiet which would soon give way to the hurry of breakfast preparation. She liked that time of the day when the darkness of night was first washed away by the oyster gray pre-dawn. In the silence, before radio alarm clocks would click and awaken the frantic voice of a disc jockey giving warnings of traffic tie-ups and record-high temperatures, she liked to sit and listen to the gentler sounds that soon would be muffled by the noise of cars starting and showers hissing. From the kitchen window of her lake house she watched as redbirds and grackles flitted from tree to tree, then to the ground, foraging for their breakfast. She followed their jerky, busy movements with quiet fascination. Those few moments of peaceful awakening always felt good to her. It was "her time," a luxurious few minutes when she could be alone with her thoughts.

She had slept well the night before. In fact, she had been sleeping better for the past several days. The hostile turmoil of a recent separation from her husband—the second in their brief, stormy marriage—had finally begun to subside. And Nancy's older daughter Jill was home, showing a newly-gained enthusiasm for family life that warmed her with a tickle of anticipation for the days to come. She was, she realized as she poured herself another cup of coffee before waking the children, more optimistic about her future than she had been in a long time.

As her thoughts turned to the 7:00 A.M. car pool which would take her to downtown Dallas and her job as an administrative assistant for Placid Oil Company, she put aside her brief luxury and went in to wake her daughters. Jill, now home to stay and already talking excitedly about her upcoming senior year at Waxahachie High School, was planning a trip to Waco to pick up the final paycheck owed her for work at the Texas Rangers Hall of Fame and, as is always the case with single, working parents, Nancy Shaw had to make a number of arrangements.

Jill, it had been decided, would drive Nancy the five miles into town to the Wal-Mart parking lot where her car pool met each morning. That way Jill would have the car to take her thirteen-year-old sister, Monica, over to Nancy's sister, Jan Thompson. Jan, whom she had called the night before, had agreed to let Monica stay there until her mother returned home from work.

Uncomfortable with the idea of her seventeen-year-old daughter driving to Waco alone, Nancy had first suggested that Jill ask her older brother Brad to take her. But Brad had just taken a job as a bricklayer and said he wouldn't be able to go with her until the weekend. That wouldn't do, Jill said. Her father had driven her to Waco the previous weekend to collect her things from her dorm room at the Methodist Home. They had planned to pick up the check while they were there but had found that it was not at the Rangers museum but, instead, at the city offices which were closed weekends. Jill, then, was delighted when Raylene Rice, her best friend in Waxahachie, offered to drive them in her car.

Relieved that a resolution to the transportation problem had been found, Nancy Shaw okayed the plan and insisted that Jill pay for the gas. Several times during the day before the trip she made it clear she wanted the girls home before dark. Raylene Rice got off from her summer job at the downtown County Extension office at noon. The trip to Waco was little more than an hour's drive down Interstate 35. Even allowing time to stop and visit friends and pick up a few remaining things Jill had left at the Methodist Home, they should be home long before the Daylight Savings Time sun went down.

Time was when Nancy Shaw would not have felt comfortable allowing her daughter to make such a trip without benefit of family supervision. Now, though, things had changed. She was convinced that Jill had matured and was ready to live by the rules. It was a good feeling, one she had wondered if she would ever enjoy.

From all outward appearances, Jill Montgomery was a normal, happy small-town Texas teenager. She was crazy about rock music, loved to swim, dressed fashionably, was flirtatious and adventuresome, agreeable to secret smoking of a little grass or drinking a beer now and then. She was judged pretty by the boys in Waxahachie, her warm smile and easy laugh making up for whatever points she might have lost due to being a few pounds overweight. She had vowed to devote that summer to trimming up her already pretty figure. She was ready to put her immature, girlish days behind her and become a woman, and those last few pounds of lingering baby fat would have to go.

That she had grown up wrestling with a myriad of personal problems, battling a long-held feeling of insecurity, was something she hid well. Jill Montgomery was not one to confide her problems to others, even her most trusted friends. Thus when word spread that she was leaving Waxahachie that August of 1981 to enter the Methodist Home in Waco, many who knew her were genuinely surprised and privately wondered what sudden turn of events had occurred to prompt her parents to "send her away." The matter was even more difficult to understand for those few Jill had told she was actually "excited" about going to the Methodist Home.

Within the general population of small communities like Waxahachie, it was typically felt that only problem children, those on the verge of trouble with the law or with drug dependencies that had gotten out of hand, were sent to "homes." That, or the parents were too busy or too selfish to be bothered with their own kids. At any rate, it was a sure sign that something was seriously wrong. More than one local busybody nodded knowingly and blamed Jill's departure on the divorce of Nancy and Rod Montgomery.

There was no denying that the divorce of her parents had caused Jill Montgomery problems. She was thirteen when they separated and didn't fully understand the reasons. Few youngsters that age do. And like most children of divorce, she continued to cling lovingly to both parents long after their love for each other had faded. That her father remained in Waxahachie after the split-up helped a great deal. Though she continued to live with her mother, she saw her father several times a week and often spent entire weekends with him.

But while the divorce of her parents did undoubtedly have an effect on Jill, the truth was that it only heightened the intensity of a rebellion she had already been displaying for several years.

She had entered the first grade with a minor but, for her,

embarrassing speech problem. Rather than working to correct it, she chose to say as little as possible in class. If a teacher called on her to answer a question or recite, she would refuse, even if fully prepared to do what was asked of her. School was a daily misery, a non-ending sequence of frustrations and academic embarrassments. When it was determined that her reading difficulties were the result of dyslexia she was placed in special education classes—with good and bad results. Her grades improved but her self-esteem suffered. She didn't like being viewed as one of the "slow students." Peer pressure mounted as each school year passed, and by the time she was ready to enter the ninth grade she refused to go back to special education classes. No sooner did she return to the scholastic mainstream than her grades began to drop dramatically.

Then came the truancy problems. Her mother would leave for work, assured that her daughter was preparing for school. Later she would learn that Jill often never even left the house. Or if she did it was to join other truant youngsters at the lake or someone's house to watch daytime television and listen to records.

With school the basis of the problem, things deteriorated quickly at home. The more Jill's mother insisted she study, the less effort the frustrated youngster put forth. She made it a point to stay out beyond the curfew her mother had set. She ignored the household chores assigned her. And she told her father that she was unhappy at home and wanted to come live with him.

Concerned over his daughter's increasingly rebellious stance, and not wanting to allow her to manipulate them by playing one parent off against the other, Rod Montgomery could only suggest she try to work things out with her mother. Jill, he knew, was searching for something. What, he didn't know.

Briefly she found it in religion. A friend was a student at the local Christian Academy, a private day school which charged the parents of its students a quarterly tuition. Jill made up her mind that she wanted to leave public school and enroll at the Academy. She could get tutoring there, she told her mother. She wouldn't feel like an outcast. The classes were smaller and therefore the students advanced more rapidly. And they taught one how to better understand the Bible and live a Christian life. She had her speech down well before she approached her mother with the idea.

Nancy Shaw was desperate to see her daughter turned from her self-destructive course and to improve the quality of life at home. She was willing to consider the idea of private school and went so far as to schedule a visit with the Academy's administrators. What she learned was that the tuition was beyond her budget. Jill herself solved that problem by securing a job in the Academy's nursery after school each day to help pay for her tuition.

For the remainder of her ninth grade school year Jill Montgomery was a different youngster. Her interest in religion and the Bible bordered on the fanatical, far removed from the casual approach she had taken to Sunday School lessons at the Methodist Church. She studied late into the night and her grades improved, though not by the leaps and bounds she had expected. She read her Bible and said her prayers nightly. And she loved working with the young children in the nursery.

The following summer, however, brought another chameleon-like change. She lost interest in the Christian Academy, put her Bible away, and said she wanted to return to public school the following fall. Happy and outgoing in the company of her friends, she was sullen and withdrawn at home. Again she was balking at the rules, demanding a degree of independence generally reserved for those far older than fifteen. She and her mother quarrelled regularly. Tears often followed the angry exchanges, and there were days of icy silence. Jill again began insisting that she wanted to leave home and live with her father.

When school started that fall the problems were compounded. Still refusing the help of special education classes, Jill saw her grades fall even lower than they had before she had enrolled in the Christian Academy. She became increasingly truant.

Frustrated and weary of the nonstop tension, Nancy finally spoke with her ex-husband about the possibility of Jill living with him. She offered to give him verbal custody. Rod Montgomery agreed. Since the divorce he had only rarely seen the rebellious side of his daughter. The time she spent with him had been enjoyable, and Jill seemed relaxed and happy in his company.

Like everything else they had tried, the solution was temporary. At her father's house, Jill had expected the freedom she had tasted on weekend visits to be extended to day-to-day living. However, she soon found that her father was even more strict than her mother. In short order she returned to her mother's home. She had made a mistake, she said. She hugged her mother and once again promised to abide by the rules and try to do better in school.

"I love you, Momma," she said.

"I love you, too," Nancy Shaw replied. As badly as she wanted to believe that her daughter could—and would—gain control of her anger and frustrations and rebellious nature, she knew the promises she was hearing would, however well intended, be short-lived. "I love you so very much, and I want to see you happy. That's why we have to talk about what we need to do to help you get your life in order. I've done everything I know to do. We've got to try something else."

"I know," Jill softly answered.

From the moment the idea of her moving to the Methodist Home was mentioned, Jill Montgomery was enthusiastic. To her it was the promise of a new, exciting adventure; a way finally to escape the stifling authority of both of her parents as well as the teachers at Waxahachie High School. She saw it as her chance to enjoy the independence she was so eagerly seeking. No amount of caution about the restrictions and regimentation the Home would impose gave her cause for concern. Physically removed from the watchful eyes of her mother and father, she would be free, on her own. Even if there were rules and regulations at the Home, it would be different. She was certain she could deal with it.

Even before she and her mother paid a visit to the campus, attended several classes, and spoke with administrators, Jill was eager to make the move. What the Methodist Home offered, she confided to one of the counselors with whom she spoke, was a chance for a fresh start.

Yet the transition was not as easy as Jill had expected. In Waco, she found, the rules were far more encompassing than those she had constantly fought while at home. Rarely was she not under the watchful eye of someone in authority—teachers, counselors, house parents. When she violated a rule, a privilege was lost. And at the Methodist Home, she quickly learned, even the smallest of privileges were hard earned.

The first three months were difficult. While her grades steadily improved with the aid of tutoring and regimented study habits, Jill generally disliked life at the Home and repeatedly told her mother that she missed Waxahachie and wanted to come home.

In October she called to say she had run away. Her house parents had grounded her, she said, for something another girl had done. She hated living at the Methodist Home, she told her mother, and wasn't going back. Nancy Shaw had been warned to expect something like this and stood her ground. She insisted that her daughter return to school and at least stick it out until the end of the semester. Refusing even to tell her mother where she was, Jill hung up and placed a call to her father.

Rod Montgomery managed to convince her they needed to have a long talk. Jill told him that she and a couple of other runaways had stayed overnight at a house just a few blocks from the Methodist Home. So, driving to Waco, he met her at a fast-food restaurant where they talked for several hours. Patiently and firmly, without any anger, he explained to her that she had left herself few alternatives. Her mother, he told her, was determined that she remain at the Methodist Home. And he didn't think she was ready to try to live with him again. Her choices were simple: She could return to the Methodist Home and make the best of the situation. Or she could return to the Methodist Home and continue to be miserable. Late that afternoon he drove her back to the campus.

In a manner of speaking, it was Jill Montgomery's last roundhouse swing at the adult authority she had been resisting for so long. Back at the Home she began to make friends quickly. Pretty and personable, she attracted the attention of a number of boys and was allowed by her home parents to date several of them. Though a few of the girls judged her aloof and, noting that her clothes were nicer than those issued some less fortunate students by the Home, called her a "rich bitch," Jill soon became one of the most popular girls at the Methodist Home. Her grades continued to improve and she was given permission to travel to Waxahachie for visits most weekends. Several nights a week she would get a call from her mother and their brief long-distance talks were chatty and friendly, without past tensions.

Nancy Shaw was delighted with the progress her daughter seemed to be making. When school officials called her to suggest that it would be better if Jill did not receive calls quite so regularly or make bus trips to Waxahachie every weekend, pointing out the need for them to be in control of her daughter's life for the time being, Nancy begrudgingly agreed. If that was best for her daughter, she would do as they asked. She was too pleased with Jill's progress to question the judgment of the administrators.

Though she enjoyed the weekend trips home, Jill Montgomery was not disappointed when told she would have to remain in Waco more often. Her friend Gayle Kelley had introduced her to a boy she really liked. His name was Kenneth Franks, and her dorm parents had given her permission to date him. Her flirtations with other boys at the school ceased as she focused her attentions on Kenneth. Handsome and friendly, he was fun to be with. Jill wrote a long letter to her cousin in Waxahachie, telling her about Kenneth. She was hoping, the letter said, that he would ask her to be his steady girlfriend.

The three youngsters—Jill, Kenneth, and Gayle—soon became inseparable, spending most of their free time together. Others on the campus commented on the three-way friendship. Though Kenneth and Gayle were close, often seen at the lake together or riding along Waco Drive on Kenneth's motorcycle, there was no evidence of a romance. Gayle was dating another boy at the Home, Henry Reyes, and had told Jill she would one day marry him. Another unique aspect of the relationship was that Jill and Gayle looked enough alike to be sisters. Even some of their teachers got them confused, calling Jill "Gayle" and Gayle "Jill."

Gayle Kelley worked after school in the souvenir shop at the Texas Rangers Hall of Fame at Fort Fisher, and by the end of the year she had helped Jill get a job there, too. Jill Montgomery had never been happier. She had adjusted to life at the Methodist Home, had friends, a job, and a good relationship with her family. The move to Waco, it seemed, had worked out just as she had hoped it would.

During the final week in June of 1982, Jill asked permission to go home to Waxahachie for a weekend visit. Her brother Brad and his wife Gloria had called earlier in the week to invite her to go to Six Flags. Nancy Shaw called the Home and okayed the visit.

The weekend was pleasant and fun-filled. On Saturday Brad, Gloria, and Jill spent the day at the Arlington, Texas, amusement park. That evening they had dinner. Early Sunday morning Jill talked to Raylene Rice, the girlfriend she spent most of her time with during visits home, and they made plans to get together after church. Raylene said she would take Jill to the bus station for her return trip to Waco that afternoon as she had done so many times before.

Late that afternoon Jill walked into her mother's house, her small suitcase in hand. Surprised, Nancy Shaw glanced at her watch, knowing that the bus should have left some time ago. "What are you doing still here?" she asked. "You should be back in Waco by now."

Jill said nothing for a minute, then sat down on the couch. "I don't want to go back."

The tone of her daughter's voice immediately concerned Nancy Shaw. This was not a rebellious demand. It was more a fearful plea.

"What's the matter, honey?"

"I just don't want to go back."

"But why? What's wrong?" Tears filled Jill's eyes.

Her mother felt a knot forming in the pit of her stomach. Something was wrong. Something had changed. Suddenly. But what?

"Please let me stay," Jill said. "I just can't go back there."

"But you've been so happy . . . What about your job?"

Jill's quiet tears erupted into heaving sobs. She spoke in a frantic, pleading voice: "You can't keep throwing me around like I'm a dirty dishrag, Mother!"

Shaken by her daughter's sudden change in attitude, Nancy called officials at the Methodist Home to advise them that Jill had not yet left Waxahachie. Later that evening Rod Montgomery came over and the three talked late into the night. Jill would give no specific reason for not wanting to go back, yet her parents sensed a determination they had never seen before.

Finally, they agreed she could stay. They would try it one more time.

"But you've got to understand," Nancy Shaw told her daughter, "that the rules here haven't changed. I want to think you have."

\*     \*     \*

The home of Jan Thompson is a warm, friendly place where one need not knock before entering. Since she was a little girl Jill had spent almost as much time in her aunt's home as she had her own, often staying overnight to visit with Jana, her cousin. After Jill's parents divorced, it was to Jan she most often went with her problems. There had been a time when she had asked to live with the Thompsons. But that was before the Methodist Home; before things had apparently gotten better.

Jill had been home just over two weeks when she walked into her aunt's kitchen that morning, her sister Monica close behind. From the moment she arrived it was obvious that she was excited about the trip she would make to Waco later in the day. Although it was just after nine when Jill took her favorite place at the end of the bar which separated the kitchen and living room of the Thompson home, she wasn't surprised to see that her aunt had been up early and baked a chocolate cake—her favorite.

Jan, who had been privately concerned over the sudden decision to return home, was nonetheless pleased to see Jill. She looked upon Jill as one of her own daughters and had looked forward to spending the morning visiting with her. She listened as Jill gave an excited, detailed account of a trip she had made with Brad and Gloria to a weekend motorcycle race. Brad, she said, had crashed twice but had not been hurt. "But, man, Gloria really freaked out." She spoke of the Six Flags trip and of how happy she was to be home. She and her mother were getting along well. And she was excited about attending Waxahachie High her senior year.

Jan noticed that she was wearing her mother's senior ring. "Pretty soon," Jill said, "I'll have one of my own." She had also decided that when she graduated she was going to attend secretarial school instead of going to college. It was obvious to her aunt that Jill Montgomery had been making a lot of plans.

Jill had phoned earlier in the morning to ask if Jan could help her sew up a rip in a pair of shorts. They matched the top she wanted to wear to Waco. When Jan saw the problem, however, she realized the repair could not be done by hand. And her sewing machine was broken. Jill tried on several pairs of Jan's shorts but found nothing that suited her. They finally decided the cutoff jeans she was wearing would suffice. Jan trimmed the frayed edges while they continued to visit.

"I put in an application at the Rip's Barbecue yesterday," Jill said. "I want to get a job for the rest of the summer and save up for some school clothes." If that didn't work out, she said, she was going to try Safeway and the new Pizza Hut which had just opened.

As they talked, Jill repeatedly checked the wall clock in the kitchen. "I'm supposed to meet Raylene at twelve," she said. She explained to her aunt that she was going to Waco to pick up her check and then go by the Methodist Home. "There's a girl there who has one of my shirts and my REO Speedwagon poster," she said. Jan Thompson, not familiar with the popular rock groups of the day, privately wondered what an "Oreo Speedwagon" poster might be.

"She thinks I've forgotten about them," Jill continued, "but I haven't. She'll be surprised to see me. But I'm gonna get my stuff before I leave town."

Jan Thompson enjoyed listening to Jill talk, bubbly, so full of energy, so enthusiastic about the future. Jan sensed a new maturity in her niece. Maybe it was, after all, time for her to be back home.

As twelve o'clock neared, Monica began to plead with her sister to let her go along on the trip to Waco. Repeatedly she asked Jill, then Jan, "Why can't I go? They're coming right back. Please . . ."

"I don't think your mother would like it if I let you go without asking her," Jan said. "You had better stay here with me. Besides, there are times when big sisters don't like little sisters tagging along."

Jill kissed her aunt—a thank-you for settling the issue—and walked toward the car. Jan followed her into the front yard, giving last-minute instructions. Be careful. Be home early, like your mother said. If you have car trouble or anything call here.

"I will," Jill said.

She drove to the Waxahachie town square where she was to meet Raylene. With Raylene following, Jill drove her mother's car to the Wal-Mart parking lot, placed the keys in the glove compartment as Nancy had told her to, and climbed into her friend's orange Pinto.

At her office in Dallas, Nancy Shaw had returned from lunch. She thought about calling her sister to make sure Jill had delivered Monica and was on her way to Waco. But there was no need, really. She knew Jan would let her know if any problems had come up.

As she sat at her desk, preparing to return to work, she found herself pondering the conversation she and Jill had had the evening before. Sitting in the backyard after dinner, they had said little for quite some time, content to enjoy the subtle breeze which was finally driving the day's heat away. Nancy repeatedly caught herself staring at her daughter. Jill had spent the afternoon at the YMCA pool trying to teach several neighborhood youngsters to swim. Her hair was in rollers and her face was free of makeup. She looked somehow younger, almost fragile.

Jill finally broke the silence. "Momma," she said, "what do you do when you love someone who you know isn't good for you?"

Nancy's initial response was to treat the subject lightly. After all, she was on the verge of her second divorce. "Honey," she smiled, "I'm not exactly the best person in the world to ask." Jill didn't smile.

Her mother knew she had received a call from Kenneth Franks the previous Sunday evening. "Are you talking about Kenneth?"

"Yes."

"All I can tell you," Nancy said after a lengthy silence, "is to follow your heart and use your head." It was not, she knew, the kind of answer Jill was seeking. Neither of them pursued the subject any further.

Now at her desk she wondered if Jill would see Kenneth while she was in Waco. And would she return home with more questions? If so, Nancy thought, she would try to have better answers for her.

At the same time, Gloria Montgomery was also thinking of Jill, and something she had mentioned to no one, not even her husband. The evening after they had returned from the motorcycle races they had been in the kitchen preparing dinner while Brad showered. Jill had set the table; then rummaging idly through her purse, she had produced a yellow-handled pocketknife.

Gloria had noticed it immediately. "What in the world are you doing with that?" she had asked her sister-in-law.

"Protection," Jill had said.

\* \* \*

As the girls gassed up at a Waxahachie service station, Rod and Brad Montgomery, who had had lunch together, drove past. Jill and Raylene both smiled and waved. For no particular reason Rod looked at his watch. It was 12:50 P.M.

He was unaware of the questions which were troubling his ex-wife and daughter-in-law; questions which would forever cry for answers.

4

A puzzling uneasiness swept over Richard Franks as he awoke from a fitful sleep and tried to focus on the dial of the clock near his bed. It was 2:30 A.M. He lay there for a minute, listening for some sound that might signal him that his son had returned home while he slept. There was nothing but the soft purr of the central air conditioning unit.

Once again Richard was angry. Kenneth had promised to be in by twelve. But when one o'clock had come and gone, Richard Franks had decided to go on to bed. He would have a talk with his son in the morning and inform him he was grounded.

Climbing out of bed, he went to Kenneth's bedroom to see if he made it home during the hour and a half he had been sleeping. But Kenneth's bed was still neatly made, draped with the clothes he had changed from in preparation for the trip to the lake with Jill Montgomery and her friend.

Richard sighed wearily. The part of parenthood he disliked most was the discipline. He hated the angry confrontations that erupted from time to time. They always left him drained, feeling somehow resentful that he was forced to reprimand his son.

Certainly there had been times in the past when Kenneth had stayed out too late, even failing to come home until the following day. But that had been before they had come to a better understanding, before their relationship had grown. Richard had begun to treat his son as a man, giving him more latitude. All he had asked was that Kenneth return the trust and respect. And his son had been good about it. More than once Kenneth had called as time neared for him to be home, telling his father that he was going to be a little late for some legitimate reason. Richard could deal with that.

Now, though, the past angers were rushing back. He didn't want to return to those agonizing times when he was constantly concerned over the whereabouts of his boy.

\*     \*     \*

After the kids had left, Richard Franks, restless and finding nothing on television of interest, had decided to get out of the house for a while. He first considered a movie but finally settled on the idea of going for a drive and watching the sun set over Lake Waco. He drove down Lake Shore Drive, past the entrance of Koehne Park where the kids probably already were, and turned onto Fish Pond Road, a lazy, tree-lined avenue which runs through one of Waco's more affluent residential areas. He went to Midway Park and watched the boaters as they hurried to get in one more tour of the sprawling lake before darkness forced them to dock.

Sitting in his car, watching the activities on the lake, had a calming, almost mesmerizing effect on Richard Franks. There he could unwind, lose track of time, relax. He briefly wished he still had his own boat. But his travel schedule had made it impossible to use it very often. Just weeks earlier he had decided to sell it. Already, though, he was contemplating the purchase of another one.

It was a few minutes past midnight when he returned home to find that Kenneth had not yet arrived. Though upset, he was not really worried. No doubt the girls were well on their way back to Waxahachie. Probably already home. In all likelihood his son had met Pat Torres after his friend had gotten off work.

Richard briefly thought about driving over to Koehne Park to tell his son to get home but reconsidered and prepared for bed. Tomorrow would be time enough to confront Kenneth about his tardiness.

At four in the morning, feeling a growing mixture of concern and anger, Richard Franks dressed and went in search of his son. Driving through the pitch black of the early morning he went to Koehne Park, checking first in the area of the boat dock, then driving to the Circle. Only the sounds of summer insects broke the silence as he drove slowly past the cedar trees toward the open area where the concrete picnic tables and barbecue pits were located.

Only one car, an orange Pinto, was still parked there. On the back window was a Waxahachie High School sticker. Richard Franks drove slowly past it to make certain there was no one inside. *Damn*, he thought, *they met some other kids and left with them.*

For the next hour he drove the streets of Waco and went

from one park to another in search of the youngsters, finally arriving back at Midway Park where he himself had been earlier in the evening. There he discovered another abandoned car which had obviously been vandalized. Windows had been knocked out and the doors had been left open. Using his CB radio, he made contact with an early riser who identified himself as "Tornado" and asked him to contact the police about the abandoned car.

Richard Franks waited at Midway Park until a patrolman arrived. He explained that he was out looking for his son and had just happened on the vandalized auto. The officer thanked him, took his name and address, and listened to his brief description of Kenneth and the girls. He told Richard he would contact him if he happened to run across the kids.

Franks then drove back to Koehne to see if perhaps they had returned to the Pinto. The sun was coming up as he parked next to the car and approached it. The passenger door was unlocked and the front seat on the driver's side was pushed forward. Opening the door, Richard looked in the backseat and saw what appeared to be the leather tip of his son's key chain, concealed between the seat and the back rest. Pulling the keys from their hiding place, he felt his anger dissolve into sudden fear. Something, he knew, was terribly wrong.

Richard Franks had always advised his son that if he ever got into any kind of trouble he should quickly hide his keys. Looking at the leather strap which held Kenneth's house key and the key to his motorcycle, Richard Franks instantly knew that his son had not stayed out past curfew by choice.

He wrote a note to Kenneth, advising him to call home, placed it beneath the windshield wiper, and drove back to the house, his mind racing. It was too early in the morning to be phoning people, he thought. But he knew nothing else to do.

He woke Pat Torres's father who sleepily called his son to the phone. No, the youngster said, he had not seen Kenneth since earlier the day before. He had been tired after getting off work and had come straight home.

"Pat," Richard Franks said, "I'm worried. If there's any place you think the kids might be, please tell me."

Torres mentioned that Gayle Kelley sometimes stayed at the Northwood Apartments with Patti Deis, a girl who had once lived at the Methodist Home. Maybe they had gone over there.

He didn't know the phone number but gave Richard the address.

Patti finally answered the frantic knocking at her door and told the distressed father that she had not seen Kenneth in some time.

Richard knew he should contact the girls' parents but wasn't sure how. As he drove away from the Northwood Apartments it occurred to him that perhaps there might be something in their car that would provide him with an address or phone number. For the third time, he returned to the 1977 Pinto parked near the picnic area of Koehne.

In the glove compartment he found an address for Raymond Rice. Minutes later he was talking to another distressed father. Rice and his wife had been up much of the night, worried about their daughter. Franks then placed a call to Nancy Shaw. Despite the fact that it was just after six in the morning, she answered on the first ring. After telling her the same story he had relayed to Raylene's father, Richard Franks confided to Nancy that he was beginning to expect the worst. He was going to contact the police.

Nancy Shaw, like Richard, had spent a tense, sleepless night, angered over her daughter's not returning home by the time she had been expected. Now, though, the tone of Richard Franks' voice concerned her. Maybe he was an alarmist, she thought. Maybe he hadn't dealt with a problem teenager as often as she had. Still, she had been so certain that Jill was making a concentrated effort to abide by her rules. Jill had wanted so badly to remain in Waxahachie. She had so many plans. Risking it all by staying away all night didn't make sense. All at once, nothing made sense, and she had a sudden urge to scream.

"Please call me if you hear anything," Nancy said.

"I will," Richard said. "I think it would be a good idea for you to stay close to your phone."

Nancy Shaw's hands were shaking as she replaced the receiver. After a minute she picked it up and dialed the number of the driver of her car pool. She would not be going to work that day.

It was mid-morning when Raymond Rice called Nancy to ask if she had a photograph of Jill. Richard Franks had filed a missing persons report on the teenagers and the Waco police had requested pictures of each of them. Rice said he was leaving shortly for Waco, to pick up Raylene's car, and would take the photographs of the girls with him. Nancy said she would bring a picture to him at the funeral home where he worked.

On the dresser in Jill's room she found a snapshot Rod Montgomery had just recently taken of his daughter and Raylene. She smiled ever so faintly. Her former husband was always taking pictures but never kept any for himself. It gave him great pleasure to give them to the people he'd photographed. In the picture the girls were seated on the hood of Raylene's car, squinting slightly into the sun but smiling nonetheless. Nancy looked intently at the picture for some time. The kids looked so carefree, so happy—friends without a care in the world. For the first time that day, silent tears began to slide down Nancy Shaw's cheeks.

Despite her daughter's friendship with Raylene, Nancy had never met her parents. Yet her first encounter with Raymond Rice would be burned into her memory. Standing in the reception room of the funeral home, he focused intently on the picture she had brought. After a moment he looked at her. "Thank you," he said. He shook his head from side to side in a gesture of despair. "I can't believe this is happening."

Nancy Shaw wanted to say something that would lend some ray of optimism to the situation, words that might suggest it wasn't as bad as they both were beginning to fear. But she said nothing. Now she too was fearing the worst.

On the way back home she stopped at a convenience store to pick up some milk and lunch meat. Her younger daughter would be getting hungry and she didn't want to bother with cooking. All she wanted to do was stay by the phone, awaiting the news that Jill was safe.

Monica immediately sensed that something was troubling her mother as she walked into the house. Nancy explained that her sister and Raylene had not returned from Waco and that the police were looking for her.

"Aw, Momma, you know how Jill is," Monica said. "She's okay. She'll be back. She probably just ran into some of her friends and decided to stay there last night."

Her mother lit a cigarette with trembling hands. "Honey," she said, "I hope you're right. Please God, I hope you're right."

In Waco, Richard Franks stood near Raylene's Pinto, talking with an officer from the Waco Police Department. He had already given him all the information he had and a picture of Kenneth. He told the policeman that Raymond Rice was driving down with a photograph of the girls.

Looking out onto the calm morning water of the lake, Richard felt suddenly weak. The adrenaline which had been pumping so furiously for so long was finally giving way to an overwhelming fatigue. "Something bad has happened to those kids," he said quietly. There was a sense of resignation in his voice that surprised the officer. "I know it. Somebody took those kids away from here last night. We're going to find them lying in a ditch somewhere." Then he looked across the lake to the wooded shoreline. "Their bodies might be over there somewhere right now," he said, his voice breaking.

"I wouldn't get too upset, Mr. Franks," the officer said. "This sort of thing happens all the time. They're probably just somewhere sleeping off a drunk, that's all."

Richard Franks turned and glared at the officer. A sudden rage exploded inside him. "You're wrong," he said. He slammed his fist against the hood of the car. "You're wrong," he repeated.

Throughout the afternoon the parents waited impatiently by their telephones. In Lake Jackson, Sandra Sadler, who had received one of Richard Franks' early morning calls, stayed home from work to await news. Nancy Shaw waited in Waxahachie, never more than an arm's reach from her kitchen phone. Rod Montgomery had gone to the office, hoping work might free his mind from the worry that seemed almost suffocating, only to find that he could do nothing but sit and wait for some news. Jan Thompson had been scheduled to give an Amway demonstration that afternoon but called those she had invited and cancelled, not bothering to give any explanation.

The Rice family—Raymond, his wife Samalee, and daughter Raynell—drove to Waco to pick up Raylene's car which the police had already photographed and taken to the impound lot. Little was said during the trip.

By late evening Nancy Shaw's home had become the gathering point for all the family members. Brad and his wife were there, as was Rod Montgomery. Bernie Shaw, Nancy's estranged husband, had come directly from work.

The call came at nine-thirty.

Nancy, her face pinched with dread, heard a voice identify himself as a member of the Waxahachie Police Department. "Ma'am," he said, "I'll be at your house in just a few moments."

"What is it? Have you heard something?"

"Mrs. Shaw," the officer replied, "I'm on my way right now."

A heavy silence surrounded the room as expectant faces stared at Nancy. She stood, ashen, with the phone still in her hand. "She's dead," she whispered; then her knees buckled and she fell to the floor.

Her son helped her to the sofa. Had the caller actually said Jill was dead? Or was his mother simply assuming the worst?

"He didn't say it," she sobbed, "but I know. Jill's gone."

"You don't know that for sure," Gloria said as she placed her arm around her mother-in-law. "Let's just wait and see what he has to say when he gets here."

Nancy Shaw did not even hear her. She was already in shock.

Minutes later the police officer was at the front door, his hat removed, a solemn look on his face. "Are you Nancy Shaw?"

"Yes."

"I'm very sorry," he said, "but all three children are deceased."

The final words roared in her ears, ripping through her mind. ". . . *children are deceased.*" Deceased. Not dead, deceased. How? Why?

Even if the officer had been able to answer the questions, Nancy Shaw would not have heard him. She had fainted.

News that the bodies of the missing youngsters had been found spread quickly. District Judge Walter Smith, who lived in the same town house complex as Richard Franks, had been in touch with investigators throughout the day and had relayed reports of their progress to his neighbor. The duty of telling his friend that the body of his son had been found fell to him.

The Rices had just returned home from their trip to Waco and daughter Raynell had gone to her room and turned on the television set. Her father was just coming in from the garage when he heard her scream. Before he could make his way to his daughter's bedroom she ran toward him, hysterical. "Daddy," she said, "they said Raylene's dead." He rushed past her into the bedroom and heard the final part of the newscast describing how the bodies of his daughter, Jill Montgomery, and

Kenneth Franks had been found in a wooded park near Lake Waco.

All the way home Raymond Rice had silently feared that such a terrible thing might be possible; that he should somehow prepare himself and his family for the possibility of a telephone call from the police informing him that his daughter was dead. But never, in his most frightening imagination, would he have expected to learn of the tragedy on the ten o'clock news.

Jan Thompson had been watching the late news on another Dallas station. It, too, carried a report on the triple murder in Waco but, unlike the one Raynell Rice had been watching, the names of the victims were withheld. Yet she knew immediately that it was Jill and her friends who had been found. In a matter of seconds her phone began ringing.

Nancy Shaw would not even remember the ride to the Waxahachie hospital where an emergency room attendant gave her and Monica sedatives. It wasn't until she was being helped out of the emergency room and saw the expressions on the faces of the nurses that she knew for certain the nightmare she was living was real. Their silent, sympathetic glances told her it was true.

Back home she was put into bed. By then she recognized only faint, fuzzy images of people around her. The sedative had taken effect, making her eyelids heavy, giving her the sensation of floating weightlessly. A sudden, loud crash caused her to snap awake. She climbed from her bed and, on hands and knees, was moving toward the bedroom door, sobbing her daughter's name.

Brad Montgomery had been in a back bedroom, watching a latenight rerun of the ten o'clock news. Hearing again that his sister's body had been found, that she had been murdered, he had clenched his fist and rammed it through the wall. Cursing, he ran through the house, his father a few steps behind him. "I'm going down there and find that sonuvabitch. I'm going to find who did this and blow his fucking head off."

Rod Montgomery managed to grab his son in the front yard. They struggled briefly and both fell to the ground. "She wanted me to take her," Brad screamed. "I should have gone with her. This wouldn't have happened if I had taken her . . . Goddammit, why didn't I go?"

"It's not your fault," Rod said. "Brad, it's not your fault . . ."

They continued to wrestle for a few seconds, Brad frantically struggling to pull away from his father. Finally, he stopped and his body went limp. On their knees in the damp grass, hidden by the soft summer darkness, they put their arms around each other and wept.

# 5

The moment the elevator door opens to the basement of the Dallas County Medical Examiner's Office there is a heavy, pungent odor, unlike any other one is likely to experience. It is cloying, coppery, almost sweet, and it quickly permeates one's clothing and lingers in the nasal passages much like the nitrous oxide a patient is given in the dentist's office. One encounters it even before he walks the short distance down a narrow hall and makes a left turn into the open-spaced examining room where autopsies are performed.

Dr. Mary Gilliland, like most other pathologists, is no longer consciously aware of the odor. Only when law enforcement personnel accompanying a body to an autopsy mention it does she remember how it first affected her. There is a distinct smell attached to death, she says, that has nothing to do with chemicals or exposure or even decaying flesh. But though she has tried, she says she cannot describe it except to say it is unique, inescapable, and unforgettable.

When she arrived in the basement shortly before noon on Friday, July 15, the bodies of the three teenagers which had arrived from Waco had already been placed on the blue plastic carts and wheeled into the examining room. Already weary from a busy morning, she had skipped lunch and now knew she would face a long afternoon. Multiple deaths, the result of the same crime or disaster, were always taxing. With only the help of two lab technicians, she would conduct all three autopsies herself.

The Dallas County Medical Examiner's Office, which is located adjacent to Parkland Hospital just a few miles from downtown Dallas, not only serves the county in which it is located but performs forensic pathology for law enforcement agencies throughout north, central, and west Texas where properly equipped examining facilities are not economically feasible. Consequently, there are always too many autopsies to perform, too few medical examiners, and too little time. Though regarded as one of the premier forensic facilities in the United States, the Dallas County Medical Examiner's Office suffers the same problem other such agencies—as well as law enforcement officers—deal with on a day-to-day basis. There is simply too much crime, too much work to be done.

Little in Dr. Gilliland's personality or physical makeup would tip one off to her chosen profession. Just over five feet tall, she moves about with the quick motions of a busy wren, often talking to herself as she accompanies co-workers or visiting police officers on hurried trips through the various offices in the Medical Examiner's building. In her early thirties, she has a no no-nonsense air about her, accented by her blunt-cut hairstyle, her lace-up shoes, and large-frame glasses. She looks more like the stereotypical librarian than a medical examiner. Other women might call her "sensible," referring to her manner of dress, her hairstyle, her sparing use of makeup, the absence of jewelry.

Those who know her well speak of her engaging sense of humor, her ability to pilot her own plane to cities where she is called on to testify in trials related to her autopsy work, and the professional manner with which she carries out her job. Aware that there are those who are taken aback by the thought of a woman medical examiner, she signs her name "M. G. F. Gilliland," and insists that she be called that, or simply "Dr. Gilliland," when mentioned by members of the media. Only her close friends know her as Mary.

Professionally, she is regarded as a thorough, conscientious pathologist. Dr. Gilliland, virtually everyone working at the Dallas County Medical Examiner's Office agrees, is good at what she does.

For several minutes she walked from one cart to another, pacing, circling each, looking down on the corpses, her arms folded behind her so that she would not yield to the temptation to touch anything. First, she wanted a visual picture of what she would be dealing with on a more intimate basis for the next few hours. Simply by looking at the bodies of the victims she could, like all good pathologists, sometimes tell a great deal about the perpetrator of the crime.

In this instance, the bodies told of horrible, maniacal violence. She tried to imagine the brutality which had been inflicted on the youngsters, causing them now to be stretched lifelessly in front of her. Finally, she shook her head without comment and decided to begin her work on the young man.

Only one in five murder victims brought to the Dallas forensic lab is a woman. Here she had two young girls who had been pretty and in the bloom of life. Performing their autopsies would not be a pleasant task. That was not the primary reason, however, that she decided to direct her attention first to Kenneth Franks. Since his body was fully clothed when it arrived, his clothing had to be cataloged and prepared for analysis. Everything from the Izod shirt and denim jeans to the white socks and running shoes; the shoelaces that had bound his hands behind him, the watch (which was still keeping perfect time), his sunglasses, and the red and white bandanna headband, would be subjected to a myriad of tests. So, too, would the orange and brown terry cloth gag that had been removed from his mouth.

The dollar bill and nickel found in his pants pocket would be placed in a manila folder, along with the package of cigarettes taken from beneath the sleeve of his shirt and the small gold earring he wore in his left ear.

After inspecting all the clothing, Dr. Gilliland began her examination of the body of the young man. For a brief moment her attention was drawn to a small unprofessional tattoo on the bicep of his right arm: "K. F.," his initials. It occurred to her that he did not look like the type of person who would have been interested in a tattoo, however small and inconspicuous.

There was a total of twenty stab and cutting wounds to the chest and neck. Ten of them had reached the heart, six had penetrated the lungs, and two had punctured the liver. Any number of the wounds, she determined, could have been fatal.

What interested her most were the numerous cutting wounds, torturing slashes that did not penetrate the chest cavity. They most likely had been the first wounds inflicted, causing great pain but not life-threatening. Whoever had killed Kenneth Franks had obviously been in no hurry to have his gruesome task done. The young man was made to suffer before death finally came.

Though no weapon had accompanied the bodies, she determined that the blade of the knife used was single edged, one-half to three-fourths of an inch in width and approximately five inches long. Probably a buck knife, like that used in the majority of stabbing homicides she had helped investigate. The overall direction of the wounds was slightly downward—someone had stood over the victim while stabbing him—and from left to right. The killer, she immediately surmised, was probably left-handed.

Dr. Gilliland made note of the impressions left in the wrists by the binding shoestrings, the evidence of insect bites to parts of the body, and the fact that maggots had hatched in the nasal cavities of the victim.

Photographs were taken, then the body of Kenneth Franks was washed clean and more pictures were taken. From that point the autopsy was routine. She would find nothing out of the ordinary during her examination of the internal organs. Kenneth Franks had been a normal, healthy young man until he met his assailant. He had, she noted, eaten a hamburger and french fried potatoes at some time not long before his death.

Two hours would pass before the first autopsy was complete and Dr. Gilliland, perspiring despite the chilled temperature of the examination room, took time out for a diet soft drink. Then she turned her attention to Jill Montgomery.

When examining the body of a woman who in all probability has been sexually assaulted, Dr. Gilliland instinctively first checks the hands. In some cases, where the victim has struggled, there are defensive signs that provide valuable information. Skin fragments, perhaps scratched from the face of an assailant, are often found embedded beneath fingernails; more than once she has found hair samples tangled in a ring setting. Clearly, this young woman had fought for her life. There were deep cuts across her right hand and fingers, no doubt the result of Jill Montgomery's attempt to shield herself from her attacker's knife. However, there was no evidence of telltale skin particles or strands of hair.

An autopsy conducted on an obvious homicide victim is far different from that done on the body of someone who has died of unknown causes. Not even the simplest tests were necessary to determine the causes of death of Kenneth Franks, Jill Montgomery, and Raylene Rice. Thus Dr. Gilliland's job was more that of a detective than a doctor. What she was looking for was something, anything, that might point a finger in the direction of the person or persons who had committed the crime.

As she continued her examination that purpose became even more clearly fixed in her mind. The girl's upper body had seventeen wounds. She had been stabbed nine times in the chest, damaging the heart, liver, and lungs. There were five other "torture" cuts in the same general area. The nipple had apparently been cut away from her left breast. And her throat had been cut.

So overwhelming was the damage done by the assailant's knife that Dr. Gilliland paid little attention to what appeared to be small bruise marks on the right shoulder and left breast. They were undoubtedly further evidence of the struggle that preceded the young woman's death.

What disturbed the medical examiner most was the fact that none of the wounds, not even the gaping slash on the throat, could have resulted in a quick death. She estimated that Jill Montgomery, though probably unconscious shortly after the attack began, had lived for an hour, possibly longer, after the final wound had been administered.

Even before beginning the autopsies on the girls, Dr. Gilliland had instructed the technicians to take the standard oral, anal, and vaginal swabs for possible semen traces. Though the rape kit report would prove negative, Dr. Gilliland made note of red contusions on the wall of the vagina. She was certain the girl had been sexually violated even though there was no evidence of ejaculation.

It was an hour and a half before she completed the examination of Jill Montgomery's body. Seeing that the girl's small gold necklace, a pair of blue hoop earrings, and a 1959 high school graduation ring with the initials N. C. G. inscribed on the inner surface were placed in an evidence folder, she sighed heavily and turned away from her completed task.

During her career, Dr. Gilliland had viewed the aftermath of virtually every manner of death, and she knew this one had been slow and torturous—the worst kind. *Waco, Texas*, she thought to herself, *has a real psycho running loose.*

On the body of Raylene Rice, the medical examiner found eleven stab wounds. The lungs and left ventricle of the heart had been repeatedly penetrated, causing severe internal hemorrhage, and she had been stabbed once in the throat. Also on the neck was a wound made by a slashing motion. Like Jill, Raylene's throat had been cut. The small gold necklace she wore was still embedded in the wound.

The angles of several of the wounds indicated she probably had been stabbed while in a horizontal position. And again there was the suggestion of the left-to-right trajectory present on the other two bodies.

A red and white tank top had been tied over her mouth and a strip of beige and brown terry cloth had been used to bind her hands behind her body. Around her right ankle was a bra, tied into knots. Her toenails were painted with a maroon enamel polish.

With heavy eye makeup, dangling gold earrings, and two gold bracelets on her right wrist, she looked older than seventeen, yet she bore the mark of many young girls who were still making the frustrating transition to womanhood. Raylene Rice wore braces on her teeth.

Though the rape kit would again prove negative, there was evidence of genital injury.

It was after 5:00 P.M. when Dr. Gilliland completed her last autopsy of the day. In all, she had recorded forty-eight stab wounds on the three bodies. Removing her surgical gloves and apron, she gave final instructions to her assisting technicians and prepared to assemble the paperwork necessary to have the bodies released to the funeral homes in Waco and Waxahachie.

Nancy Shaw has little recollection of being involved in preparations for her daughter's funeral. She remembers only that she insisted on ironing the dress in which Jill would be buried, crying uncontrollably as she did so. Still in shock, she had agreed to go stay with her sister Jan for a few days. The duty of making funeral arrangements was left to Jill's father, her brother Brad, and his wife Gloria.

Rod Montgomery, a man with a penchant for detail, spent considerable time with the director of the Boze-Mitchell Funeral Home, Rev. Jay Brown of the Sardis United Methodist Church, who would conduct the chapel service, and the six pallbearers, all friends of his slain daughter, making certain that everything would go smoothly, on a timetable he had carefully planned and written out. He wanted it to be perfect. Tom Jones' "Green, Green Grass of Home," and John Denver's "Sunshine on My Shoulder," two of Jill's favorite songs, would be played.

The funeral was set for 10:00 A.M. Saturday so that Jill's school friends might be able to attend. It was Rod's decision that the casket would remain closed, a decision he and others in the family would later regret. In days to come each would remark that they would have liked to see Jill one last time before she was buried in the Sardis Cemetery, located in the picturesque Ellis County countryside just outside Waxahachie.

Services for Raylene Rice would be held at 2:00 P.M. on the same day. Though he had been in the business of arranging funeral services for many years, Raymond Rice had never contemplated the bitterly ironic difficulties of acting as funeral director for one of his own children. Many of the details he turned over to fellow workers at the Rudolph-Snyder Funeral Home and the pastor of the College Street Church of Christ who would conduct the services.

For most of the teenage population of Waxahachie it would be a long, upsetting day. Many of the youngsters had never before been exposed to the death of a friend or loved one. Now, suddenly, they would attend two funerals in one day.

Those in Waco who had been friends of both Jill Montgomery and Kenneth Franks faced a dilemma. Kenneth's funeral was also being held Saturday morning, in Waco's Wilkirson-Hatch Funeral Home Chapel. It had been arranged with the help of Sandra Sadler, Kenneth's mother, who had arrived from her home in Lake Jackson soon after Richard Franks had phoned her with the tragic news. Several youngsters from the Methodist Home were given permission to travel from Waco to Waxahachie to attend services for Jill.

Gayle Kelley had been restricted to the campus of the Methodist Home for disciplinary reasons. After a tearful plea to her home parents she was finally given permission to attend Kenneth's funeral and serve as one of the pallbearers. Bobby Brim and Pat Torres, who had been among the last to talk to Kenneth, had also been asked to serve as pallbearers.

At the Savannah Square Town Homes where Kenneth Franks had lived with his father, an American flag was flown at half mast and residents made plans to begin a fund to help police in their investigation of the murders. At Richard Franks' urging, a community move to encourage lighting and a curfew in Koehne Park was also a topic of discussion during a meeting of the home owners' association.

At Kenneth Franks' funeral, Rev. Dan Hitt, a longtime friend of Richard's parents, read from Matthew 10:28: "Fear not them which kill the body, but are not able to kill the soul; but rather fear him which is able to destroy both the soul and the body." The scripture was lost on the several officers from the Waco Police Department who attended the service, dressed in plain clothes, constantly scanning the overflow crowd in search of anyone who might look suspicious.

In Waxahachie, members of the media who had traveled from Dallas, Fort Worth, and Waco to report on the somber events marveled at the turnout for the funerals of the other two victims. "Those kids had a lot of friends," a young television cameraman remarked later as he and a woman reporter drove the short distance back to Dallas.

Experienced in covering crimes and their aftermaths, she nodded. "Yeah, but they had at least one enemy." She had covered enough funerals, talked to enough families who had felt the helpless wrath of a murder, to know to shield herself from the raw emotion encountered while covering such stories. The funerals of the two Waxahachie teenagers were the first at which she had cried in a long time.

At the Sardis Cemetery, the grave of Jill Montgomery was easily recognizable for days after the funeral, located on a hillside and covered with a rainbow of flowers. Many were left from the services; others would arrive for days after, left by anonymous friends and relatives who wished to bring their final gifts and say their good-byes in privacy. A headstone to mark the teenager's final resting place would, however, have to wait. Rod Montgomery, a man who had been making gravestones professionally for most of his adult life, would be responsible for that task. It had never occurred to him that the day might come when he would have to fashion a stone for the grave of his daughter.

# 6

The city of Waco sits at the crossroads of Texas, near the geographic center of the state, with high-tech Dallas a hundred miles to the north, politically motivated Austin the same distance to the south. But aside from the fact that Charles Alderton, an inventor by trade, came up with the formula for Dr Pepper in the back room of Morrison's Corner Drug Store back in 1885, there is little to provide Waco a unique place in Texas history.

The economy and social conscience of the city are closely tied to Baylor University, the nation's largest Baptist-sponsored college. To all the outside world, Waco is a city where Bible Belt conservatism reigns. Some would describe it as the buckle on the Belt. "Jerusalem on the Brazos," others call it.

The darker side of the city's history is well guarded and seldom mentioned outside scholarly circles. There is little reference to the fact that the one-time camping ground for the Hueco (Waco) Indians was referred to as "Six-Shooter Junction" in the lawless frontier days. Historically knowledgeable matrons would just as soon forget that the city boasted thriving legal brothels until 1917 and that in the early twenties Ku Klux Klan gatherings drew as many as 15,000, including law officers, Baylor faculty members, and students eagerly preparing themselves to spread the word of God's love. Or that Lazurus' Place, a residential eyesore hidden in one corner of town on the opposite side of the Brazos, was the only place where black residents were allowed to live. They prefer not to mention the time when a black man named Jesse Washington was found guilty of murdering a white woman and was immediately seized by a mob of irate townspeople, hanged by a chain on the Waco town square, and then burned. Later, his remains were dragged through the streets by a celebrating horseman and finally placed in a sack and hung in front of a blacksmith shop.

Leon Jaworski, the famed chief prosecutor during the Watergate hearings, spent his early days as a struggling attorney in

Waco and fell into immediate disfavor when he broke judicial tradition by vigorously representing a black defendant charged with the murder of a white. Jaworski, staunchly opposed to capital punishment, resorted to such theatrics as entering the courtroom with a dagger concealed beneath his coat and producing it with a flourish during final argument. "If you wish to kill this man," he told a stunned jury, "I suggest you get on with it right now." With that he handed the dagger to the foreman as the prosecutor railed.

Now boasting a population of just over 100,000, Waco, like most other southern cities, has progressed from the days of blatant racism and kangaroo court justice. Picturesque in its mixture of modern and antebellum architecture, it is viewed by most visitors as a city whose academic population and multitude of churches quietly protect it from the mayhem and violence that is featured so regularly on the front pages of the newspapers in Houston and Dallas.

Just beneath that surface calm, however, is a city whose crime statistics alarm the city council. Prostitution still flourishes on the east side of town where only the most adventuresome white residents venture after dark. Rumors of major drug trafficking rumble through the legal community and, just a few years ago, local authorities were investigating a prominent local citizen who was reportedly spearheading one of the nation's largest car theft rings. There was a growing list of complaints about a minister who was supposedly inviting members of his flock into his home for "special counseling" which included group sex, drugs, and porno films. And in 1982 alone there were twenty-four homicides in Waco, half of which still remain unsolved.

Word of the sadistic murders of the three teenagers at Lake Waco froze the community in fear. The headlines in the *Waco Tribune-Herald* of July 15 screamed the news:

## MAN, 2 TEEN-AGE GIRLS FOUND STABBED TO DEATH AT LAKE PARK
### POLICE SAY BODIES BOUND, GIRLS NUDE

Local television reporters gave graphic details as film of police officers and ambulance drivers carrying body bags from the Speegleville Park underbrush led off every newscast. For the next several weeks every newscast which featured a report on the lake murders was preceded by the same footage which had been filmed that night. At the Waco Police Department, where officers quickly tired of the almost nightly reminder, the footage became known as "the jungle pictures."

Predictably, parents became immediately less lenient with their teenagers' social activities, suddenly forbidding summer-night trips up and down Lake Shore Drive or to the parks they had been regularly frequenting. Coeds taking summer courses at Baylor University no longer did their afternoon sun bathing away from the campus pool. Some, with the help of boyfriends or concerned fathers, secured small handguns which they began carrying in their purses or in the glove compartments of their cars.

Many working mothers whose habit it had long been to shop at one of the malls or supermarkets that remained open late at night changed their routine to allow for necessary shopping immediately after work so they might be safely at home before dark. Even movie theater owners reported a drastic drop in evening traffic.

Crime and violence were nothing new to Waco, but this was somehow different, more frightening. It was not what the city's homicide detectives referred to as a "Saturday night beer joint killing," nor was it, apparently, the tragic end result of some domestic quarrel. The news media, which generally hinted at some kind of motive in its report of violent crimes, had not made the slightest mention of any reason for the murders. There was no indication that the victims had been prostitutes or pimps or drug pushers. If so, the public could have better understood. But there had been no hint that the murdered youngsters had ever been in any kind of trouble with the law. It simply didn't make sense. The public feared what it *didn't* know as much as what it had learned from the ten o'clock news and the morning paper.

Three youngsters were dead for no apparent reason, their bodies found in an area which many local residents found disquieting. Though there had never been any real proof, for years there had been rumors that coven meetings of Satan-worshippers were held regularly in the darkly wooded, well-hidden corners of Speegleville Park. For days after the gruesome discovery of the bodies, the telephone conversations of many Waco housewives centered around the possibility of some perverted Satanic cult being involved in the crime.

At an afternoon bridge club meeting the wife of a retired law officer confided to her fellow card players that she could not reveal her sources but she knew for a fact that the girls had been repeatedly violated with a soft drink bottle before their deaths. Her guests expressed their horror, swore secrecy, and pressed for any other information she might be able to share with them about the case.

Most residents, however, were less eager for gory details and simply discussed their fears that a homicidal maniac—some kind of demented thrill killer—was now stalking their streets, with the lake murders representing only the first of what might be a series of random summer deaths. Even veteran police officers, who had long ago ceased to make regular phone calls home to check on their wives' safety or assure them they had met with no harm during their shifts, began calling again. Some who worked the late shift began driving their squad cars well beyond their assigned patrol boundaries several times each night, making sure their families were safe.

On the night the bodies were found, Waco Police Chief Larry Scott, a tall, lanky man who seldom smiles, was at the hospital with the family of an officer who had been shot while on duty. A third operation was being performed in hopes of saving the man's life.

As he sat in the waiting area just down the hall from the operating room, sipping from a cup of coffee, he thought of the confidential words one of the doctors had just whispered to him. "It would take a thousand miracles," the surgeon had said before turning away and disappearing behind the doors which shielded Scott from his officer's fight for life.

A member of the force since 1966, Larry Scott had been named chief in 1979. Having advanced to the job through the rank and file, he was generally liked by the 172 men he commanded in spite of being demanding and often hesitant to embrace investigative ideas that had not originated in his own office. He still wore his hair in a Marine-style flattop, a topic of harmless criticism among the younger, more stylish members of the department. He was one of those chiefs who, when time permitted, would put on his uniform and ride with the patrolmen for an occasional eight-hour shift. By doing so, he would say, he could learn more about what was going on in the field than he could in weeks of reading reports and attending roll calls.

When an officer approached him in the hospital waiting room to tell him of the murder victims found in Speegleville Park, Scott's already dark mood blackened. Shaking his head and staring into his coffee, he didn't even stand. "Keep me informed," he said.

Already it had been the most stressful year of police work he had experienced since leaving the family dairy farm in nearby Bosqueville after graduating from high school. And the year was but half over. The long, hot summer, that time when tempers and the crime rate seemed always to climb with the thermometer reading, was just beginning.

The tension within his department, he was aware, had become almost unbearable even before the lake murders. There had been too many brutal killings in too short a period of time. A man had abducted two men from a convenience store, taken them onto a lonely road, forced them to lie face down, put a shotgun to the backs of their heads, and executed them. Another victim had been found in the garage of a service station, his head almost severed from his body. A young child had been found dead in his mother's clothes dryer. A rapist had been terrorizing the Baylor campus and, as usual, several prostitutes were rumored missing, perhaps the victims of foul play. It was all beginning to sound like a scenario borrowed from some sick-imagination fiction writer. Finding it increasingly harder to sleep at night, Larry Scott wondered when it all would end. Was his city moving toward the violent degradation of the larger metropolitan areas?

At Chief Scott's request, a psychologist from the Dallas Police Department had come to Waco to speak to his officers about the stress of their jobs. After hearing the psychologist speak, several Waco police officers chose to seek psychological counseling. Even Scott had been moved by the speech.

Though the Waco Police Department had no special crimes unit at the time, fourteen officers were immediately assigned to investigate the lake murders case. In a matter of days it became necessary to call in several patrolmen to assist in answering the constant stream of phone calls from people who felt they had information that might be helpful with the investigation. During the first forty-eight hours after the crime had been public knowledge, the department received an average of fifty calls per hour.

People who had been in Koehne Park on the night of July 13 called to say they had seen the three youngsters there. Second- and third-hand information was commonplace. An anonymous caller reported that a friend had told him about overhearing someone bragging of killing three kids at the lake but could provide no names. Many were convinced they had seen Raylene Rice's orange Pinto in a variety of Waco locations during the day and evening of the murders. The operator of a local miniature golf course was certain the three youngsters had been at his place early in the evening. They had rented clubs but minutes later decided they didn't want to play. He offered them "rain checks," tickets good for a round of golf at some future date, but one of the girls, a brunette, requested a refund. She was from Waxahachie, he remembered her saying, and they had no Putt-Putt course there. A woman who managed an apartment complex was sure that the girls had visited her in the afternoon, asking about renting an apartment. They had told her they would return later with the first month's deposit.

An obviously shaken caller told of picking up a black hitchhiker the night of the crime. He said the man had blood splattered on his jeans, had indicated that he had been at Lake Waco earlier in the evening, and seemed nervous, constantly looking out the back window. A woman phoned to say her young son had found a rusty butcher knife while searching for aluminum cans near the lake. She was convinced it was the murder weapon. A psychic from New York called and said, "The answer is in the trees," then quickly hung up. The owner of a Waco pawn shop reported that an older woman and a young man who looked very much like Kenneth Franks had been in his shop at around noon on the thirteenth and had hocked a camera.

Law enforcement agencies as far away as Dallas and Houston contacted Waco officials, stating that the crime bore similarities to ones they were investigating and asking for more information. The Waco Police had precious little to give.

Checking out the information coming in to them as fast as manpower would allow, they reached nothing but dead ends.

Standing in front of the coffee machine in a back room at police headquarters, one detective, weary of the constant ringing of his phone, plunged a quarter into the vending machine and punched the button with uncommon vigor. "It's got to be a goddamn drug deal that went bad," he told a fellow officer. "That's the only thing that makes sense. There'll be talk about it on the streets pretty soon. You can count on it. But we aren't gonna learn about it answering the fuckin' telephone every two minutes. Every nut in Waco wants to get in on this one."

For several days after the crime scene investigation Truman Simons endured a no-win battle against chigger bites he had incurred while crawling through the underbrush. Though not assigned to the Lake Waco murder investigation—he was working patrol and the murders would be worked by the homicide division—he spent considerable off-duty time driving through Koehne Park and Speegleville, stopping occasionally to ask people he saw if they had noticed anything unusual.

On Saturday morning, the day the funerals were being held for the three teenagers, Simons ran into Detective Ramon Salinas at the lake. They had been friends for some time, their wives playing together on the same softball team. Although Simons had reservations about the manner in which Salinas sometimes dealt with witnesses or suspects and viewed him as an officer who wasn't always as open-minded as he should be, he was still pleased that Salinas was one of those heading up the investigation. He asked about the progress of the investigation.

"We really don't have anything," Salinas said. "But right now we're looking pretty hard at the boy's father."

Simons was surprised. It was standard police procedure to look first at family members of victims as possible suspects, but the facts of this particular crime hardly fit the criteria for a domestic murder. "That doesn't really make a lot of sense, does it? Why would he wait until there were two girls with the kid if he wanted to get rid of his boy? You'd think he would have plenty of other opportunities."

"I don't know," Ramon replied. "Maybe he thought it would look better if he waited until the kid had company and then kill them all. This thing looks pretty crazy any way you approach it."

Though nothing had been said about it, Ramon Salinas knew that Simons wanted desperately to be part of the investigation.

He also knew that Simons would not become actively involved unless he was officially assigned.

"We'll solve it," Salinas said. "It's just gonna take time."

Truman Simons reflected back on the sight of the three youngsters lying dead in the wooded area across from where they were standing. He nodded. "Got to. Some crazy sonuvabitch needs to pay for this one."

With that he returned to his car, waving at Salinas as he drove away. He did not have a good feeling about the lack of progress the department was making on the case. The age-old rule of thumb among police officers is that if you don't catch a murderer within forty-eight hours of the crime, the odds of ever doing so become astronomical. Already that forty-eight hours had stretched to five days.

As Simons continued driving around the lake, not really knowing what he was looking for, a sense of frustration swept over him. Returning to Speegleville Park he again walked the area where the bodies had been found. Now only stakes marked the spots where he had first seen Kenneth Franks, Jill Montgomery, and Raylene Rice.

Even in daylight the area was foreboding, shadowed by the overhanging trees which blocked any hint of a breeze. Walking to the water's edge he could see across the lake to the Circle in Koehne Park. Ramon Salinas's car was gone. Somewhere over there, Truman Simons felt, were the answers.

Salinas had not told Simons of the fruitless leads he and other investigators had been following up on. Nor did he bother to pass on the small bits of reliable information that had been collected.

The girls had indeed picked up the check Jill Montgomery had come for. Several of Jill's check stubs had been found scattered near where the Pinto had been parked in Koehne Park the morning after the bodies had been discovered. And it had been determined that Jill had cashed a $226.05 check at a local supermarket on the afternoon of the thirteenth. Earlier in the afternoon the girls had stopped by the Rangers Hall of Fame to say hello to Lou Booker, Jill's former supervisor, and had then gone to an El Chico restaurant before calling Kenneth Franks. Beyond that there was no indication of how they had spent most of their time in Waco that day. No one at the Methodist Home could remember their stopping by. It was as if the girls had been invisible during most of their stay in town.

Contact with Waxahachie authorities who had been urged to work the case from that end only added more confusion and false leads. Someone had been sure she had seen a third party—a Mexican-American male—in the car with Jill and Raylene at about the time they were supposed to have left for Waco. One caller was sure the girls had gone to Duncanville, near Dallas, to visit a boyfriend of Raylene's earlier in the day. Another Waxahachie girl insisted they had invited her to go with them to Waco but after they had driven just a few miles she had changed her mind, remembering something she had to do, and asked that they return her to her home. Later, she admitted that for whatever reason she had fabricated the entire story.

Ronnie Roark, a former Waxahachie police officer working as a detective for the nearby Ennis Police Department, spoke with Waco Patrolman Mike Nicoletti to suggest they consider Jill's father a suspect. Still a resident of Waxahachie, Detective Roark had grown up with Rod Montgomery and had always felt he was "strange." He talked about how Rod wore his hair in a ponytail despite being forty years of age and said Rod was considered by some in town to be slightly retarded. And the word around town, Roark said, was that the divorce of Rod and Nancy Montgomery had included a bitter battle over custody of the children.

Detective Roark did not say anything to Patrolman Nicoletti about his conversation with Karen Hufstetler on the morning of July 14.

Detective Roark had gone to the Ellis County courthouse that morning and had spoken with Karen, a clerk in the County Clerk's Office, about a misplaced child support payment his ex-wife was complaining about. Karen was a friend of Roark's wife and sister-in-law, and she had seemed glad to see him. While they discussed Roark's problem with his missing check, she had seemed somehow nervous about something. Finally she had said there was something she wanted to tell him. She referred to the fact that he had once worked with Dallas psychic John Catchings on a missing persons case. "So maybe you won't think I'm crazy," Karen had said. Then she hesitantly confided to him a "vision" she had had the night before in which she had seen terrible things happening to people she didn't know, at a place she had never been. She showed him some notes she had made on a yellow legal pad, and a sketch she had made of one of the men she had seen doing the terrible things.

Roark looked at the sketch and privately thought his youngest child could have drawn a better picture. Nevertheless, he placed the piece of paper in his coat pocket and assured Karen that he would check to see if the notes she had written might fit any crimes that had recently taken place.

After the news that night carried the story about the three teenagers found murdered in Waco, Roark had received a frantic phone call from Karen. She asked him to provide the Waco Police Department with the information she had given him to see if it matched in any way the details of the crime they were investigating. Roark had assured her that he would.

Just a couple of weeks after Jill Montgomery had been buried, Nancy Shaw ran into Detective Roark while grocery shopping. He told her he was sorry about what had happened and said he had been looking into the case himself.

"I'll tell you one thing," he said, "your daughter was a fighter."

Surprised at his interest in and apparent knowledge of the case, Nancy asked what he meant. He explained he had heard that the fingers from one of Jill's hands had been severed in her apparent attempt to fight off the attacker. And from all indications, he continued, it had taken her daughter quite some time to die.

For a moment Nancy Shaw felt faint; then she broke into tears and ran from the store. Roark, left standing behind his grocery cart, shook his head, puzzled by her reaction. Hell, he had assumed she would want to know what had happened to her daughter.

There was actually very little in Waxahachie for Roark or any other local law officers to investigate. Despite a briefly circulated rumor that the girls had been killed in Waxahachie and their bodies then transported to Waco—which somehow overlooked the fact that Kenneth Franks had not been to Waxahachie and had been found dead with Jill and Raylene—the small bits of solid information that had been gathered left little doubt that the crime had taken place in Waco. And while little of it appeared promising or productive, a steady flow of information continued pouring into the Waco Police Department.

There was a brief flurry of optimism after several anonymous callers suggested that a girl named Brenda Douglas who frequented the lake parks might have some information on the murders. She had told several friends about a conversation which had supposedly taken place at Koehne Park in the early evening of July 14, the day the bodies were discovered. A man named Terry Hough had tried to pick a fight with her boyfriend and had supposedly told her and several others that he knew where three bodies, two of them young girls, had been dumped in Speegleville Park. Laughing and strongly hinting at far more knowledge than he was passing on, he said the girls had been raped and their throats had been cut.

When Ramon Salinas questioned Brenda she was certain the time of the altercation and Hough's remarks was "between eight-thirty and nine" that evening. A check with radio and television stations revealed that the earliest report of the murders had been aired at 9:15 P.M. If the time of Hough's comments proved to be correct, Salinas told fellow investigators, there was no way he could have learned of the murders from news reporters.

"Maybe," he told Lieutenant Marvin Horton, who was officially heading up the investigation, "we've finally gotten lucky."

For the next several days investigators sought out the individuals Brenda Douglas had indicated were at the park when Hough talked about the bodies at Speegleville. With each interview they conducted the story became weaker. One girl said she remembered the fight and Hough's bragging, but it had been closer to six-thirty in the evening, maybe seven. Another remembered Terry Hough trying to start a fight with Brenda's boyfriend. It had been around eleven o'clock, maybe even later. One person interviewed was positive Brenda had told her Hough had been talking about the murdered kids when she had seen him at the lake on Wednesday morning. Yet another said, yes, he remembered the incident well but it had taken place on Thursday night, not Wednesday.

Meanwhile, a check on Terry Hough's background revealed that he had, on numerous previous occasions, bragged to people about being involved in a number of murders which had been detailed by the local media. It was another dead end.

Salinas, back at his desk looking over the growing mound of paperwork related to the investigation, looked in the direction of a weary Mike Nicoletti. "Before this thing is over," he said, "I'm gonna have the name of every kid in Waco between the age of thirteen and twenty-five written down somewhere. And they're all half nuts."

Nicoletti agreed. Just after noon on July 20, one of the home parents from the Methodist Home had come to the police station with a young girl named Linda Kelton. Linda had known Kenneth Franks and Jill Montgomery, the woman explained, and felt she might have some information that could be of help.

Patrolman Nicoletti listened as the seemingly shy youngster told her story. Obviously it had not been her idea to get involved. In a voice that was little more than a whisper she told of hearing a man who ran the small convenience store across from the Methodist Home once threaten to "put Kenneth Franks in the hospital" after the two had argued. The man's name, she said, was Muneer Deeb but most of the kids called him Lucky.

"Do you remember what started the argument?" Nicoletti asked.

"I think Kenneth had ridden his motorcycle through the parking lot of the Rainbow—that's the name of Lucky's store—and cussed him or maybe shot him the finger. They didn't like each other, I know that. It had something to do with Gayle."

"Gayle?"

"Yeah, one of the girls at the Home. Gayle Kelley. She and Kenneth were good friends and Lucky didn't like that one bit. I think he wanted Gayle to be his girlfriend." With that she smiled.

"What's funny?" Nicoletti asked.

"Aw, Lucky's a little bitty guy. A lot smaller than Kenneth. I remember telling him at the time that I didn't think he was capable of putting anybody in the hospital. The idea of him even getting into a fight was pretty funny, really."

Nicoletti included his conversation with Linda Kelton in the report he filed later that day. The paperwork alone was becoming a full-time job.

The volume of information which had already been collected was out of hand. Though much of it was useless—street people calling in with hip-pocket suspects and off-the-wall rumors, frightened citizens telling of strange-acting people they had seen while boating on the lake, etc.—it was becoming impossible to assemble the information in a way that would enable each investigator to know what the other was doing. In a manner of speaking, a dozen separate investigations were going on. More than once officers would learn they were following up on the same leads, while other leads were never checked.

Lieutenant Horton, aware of the mounting confusion, gathered his investigators and instructed them to be sure they read all the reports being filed on the case daily. He didn't specify when the officers were to find time to do so.

By the second week in August the number of investigators assigned directly to the lake murders had been drastically reduced. While some continued to deal occasional attention to the case when their daily work load permitted, Detective Salinas, Lieutenant Horton, and Sergeant Bob Fortune were the only officers who continued to work the case on a full-time basis. Though reporters were told that a number of developments were being checked and that officials remained confident about apprehending the murderers, in truth the investigation was going nowhere.

Eventually the media turned its attention to other matters, asking about the lake case now and then only as an after-thought or at the urging of some editor who occasionally suggested another "follow-up" story would be in order. The reward fund, set up by a local radio station, began to earn interest. And violence in and around Waco continued. On August 10 the body of a pretty blonde named Gail Beth Bramlett was found near the railroad tracks in the suburb of Axtell. She had been shot three times.

Aside from an occasional rumor, there was little more to check out on the lake murders. One story passed on by a teacher at Waxahachie High School interested Salinas briefly. While browsing at a flea market near Dallas one weekend, the teacher had overheard two Mexican-American youngsters discussing some people in Fort Worth who said they had been involved in the murders of some kids at a lake near Waco. But after noticing her attempt to eavesdrop on their conversation, the youngsters had begun speaking in Spanish. Officially, it was nothing more than another of the ever-growing list of rumors associated with the case and was assigned no real importance.

A young woman named Donna Cawthorn hesitantly came

forward to tell of being in Koehne Park with her boyfriend on the night of the murders and seeing something suspicious. They had been parked near the Circle when she had happened to look into the rearview mirror of her boyfriend's pickup. Standing near the truck was a man who appeared to be in his late twenties, about five feet eight inches tall and 150 or so pounds, wearing a white T-shirt and blue jeans. It had been approximately eleven o'clock when she first noticed him, she said.

Frightened, she immediately called her boyfriend's attention to the intruder and he reached beneath the seat of the pickup to get a tire tool which he carried there for protection. As her boyfriend bent over to reach under the seat the man ran north in the direction of the boat ramp.

Though the boyfriend had not gotten a good look at the man, Donna Cawthorn thought she could identify him if she saw him again. She was shown a number of mug shots by police officers but found none that resembled the man she had seen that night in the park. Most of the pictures she looked at were of men with longer than usual hair and many of them wore beards or mustaches. Few appeared as clean-cut looking as the man she had described, who had short hair and neither beard nor mustache.

On September 9 Truman Simons walked past Salinas's desk and saw several reports on the lake murders. Throughout the investigation he had made it a habit to read over the reports every few days just to see how the case was progressing and, having seen nothing new for a week, he eagerly scanned the neatly typed report dated September 3.

It was little more than a recap of the findings on the case and a review of the personal items of the victims which had been returned from the forensic lab in Dallas. The final line of the report was the only surprise. "At this time," Salinas had written, "this case will be placed in the suspended file. CASE SUSPENDED."

The word "suspended" jumped from the page. Just fifty-two days had passed since they had found the bodies of Jill Montgomery, Raylene Rice, and Kenneth Franks—less than eight weeks. And for all practical purposes, the case was now being closed. Simons breathed a curse, tossed the report back onto the desk, and returned to the squad room. He had a phone call to make.

His years on the force had taught him that whenever a case was suspended and placed in the inactive file it generally meant that the only way it would ever be solved was for someone to walk into the office and confess. Once it went into the filing cabinet it was pretty well forgotten. Out of sight, out of mind.

On one hand it angered Simons that his fellow officers had chosen to give up so soon. On the other, it presented him the opportunity he had silently hoped for since that July night in Speegleville Park. Reaching for the phone, he called Chief Scott at home.

Unaware that the investigation had been closed, Scott listened silently as Simons explained that he had kept up with the case, reading reports and talking with investigators. Trying to be diplomatic, Simons suggested that a crime of such magnitude should not go unsolved and that a fresh approach to the investigation might be in order.

"What I would like to do," he explained, carefully measuring every word, "is go back over everything and see if maybe I can come up with something. Maybe somebody who hasn't been as close to the investigation, someone who hasn't been feeling all the pressures, could come up with a new idea or two."

Now talking faster, not allowing the chief time to reply, Simons emphasized that he was not second-guessing anyone who had been involved in the investigation. If allowed to work the case, he would gladly turn over any new findings to those to whom it had originally been assigned. He just felt it was too early to give up on it.

"Chief," he said, feeling as if he'd just given a courtroom final argument, "I'd really like a piece of this one."

Larry Scott was trying very hard to hide from Simons the fact that he was furious at not having been informed the case had been suspended. If it had been suggested to him he would have insisted that the investigation continue. It had long been his policy to let his administrators make decisions on such matters, but in this instance he felt that Lieutenant Horton, Salinas's supervisor, had not made the proper choice. He would discuss the matter with Horton first thing next morning.

Larry Scott's feelings toward Truman Simons had been something of a contradiction since those times when they had both worked as patrolmen. Personally, he had never really liked Simons. Why, he wasn't sure. The chemistry just wasn't there. On the other hand he admired the officer's investigative skills greatly and felt fortunate to have him on the force.

Simons was the closest thing to a real charismatic personality Larry Scott had ever encountered. Regularly he had seen new recruits, after riding with Simons for just a week or so, adopt his walk and even try to mimic his drawling speech patterns.

And no officer in the Waco Police Department had better contacts on the streets or would stick more doggedly to a case than Simons. On numerous occasions, he had taken cases on which investigators had come up empty and somehow solved them. Then he would turn the case back to the original investigating officer. One thing Truman Simons wasn't was a publicity-seeker.

As they talked, Scott thought back on several cases which Simons had solved. There had been a series of apartment-complex rapes a few years earlier which had drawn considerable heat to the department. The investigation led officers in circles, chiefly because the rapist had no apparent method of operation. He stuck to no schedule nor confined his activities to any specific geographic area. Finally, one day an officer assigned to the case approached Simons, folder in hand, and asked if he would look it over and see if he had any ideas. Later that afternoon, after reading the case file, Simons sought out the officer and suggested they take a ride.

The two officers drove through a number of Waco apartment villages, all of which looked very much alike. Simons stopped and walked around for a while in two complexes located across town from each other. After a half hour at the second stop, walking past playing children, a swimming pool, barbecue grills, and carports similar to those they had seen everywhere else, Truman returned to the car and said, "Our guy will hit one of these two apartments tonight. We need to call in some off-duty help."

It was far from the first time a detail of officers had been summoned to a stakeout on one of Simons' "hunches."

In the early morning hours, the rapist was caught climbing into the window of one of the downstairs apartments and was surrounded by a dozen police officers. Simons could not explain his premonition. Something—"a feeling"—had simply led him to believe the rapist would strike in that particular spot. Nothing more.

The following day, when one of the investigators asked him to explain how he had known, Simons insisted they had just been lucky. "Hey," he told the bewildered officer, "I was all wrong anyway. I had figured he would hit the other apartment across town."

Veteran members of the department did not find the event at all strange. They could remember a time when Simons, while investigating a drug case, had managed to secure a murder confession and had led a team of divers to the lake where a woman's body was found in an automobile submerged in sixty-five feet of water—before the victim had even so much as been reported missing.

"Truman," Scott said, "we need to solve this case. Maybe you can do it." For a moment he paused, then said, "Yeah, go ahead and take a look at the lake murders and see what you can come up with."

The chief knew there would be some ruffled egos in his department once word was out that he'd turned the case over to Simons. But, he thought, they had thrown up their hands. They had decided to suspend the investigation without first consulting him. They could damn well stew. And if Simons could pull the thing together, more power to him. "Come by the office tomorrow and we'll talk," the chief said.

There was a moment's silence before Larry Scott began to laugh quietly. "You know," he said, "I was wondering how long it would be before you came to me about this case."

Truman Simons laughed, too. He felt better than he had in weeks.

# 7

On the evening of July 13, 1982, Karen Hufstetler had been sitting quietly in the living room of her cozy apartment in the tiny community of Italy, Texas, one of the dot-on-the-map stop-offs one passes while driving southward from Dallas en route to Waco and Austin. Aside from its unusual name, Italy's lone claim to any degree of fame is the fact that former Western movie heroine Dale Evans, wife of the legendary Roy Rogers, spent much of her childhood there. Time was, in fact, when Karen's father would regularly take Dale and other members of her family fishing down on nearby Chambers Creek.

Following the failure of a six-year marriage, Karen had moved from Georgia back to the quiet, familiar farmlands of her youth with her son Carson and had taken a job in the district judge's office in nearby Waxahachie. In the almost three years that had passed since her divorce she had become comfortable with her single life, developed new friendships, and was enjoying her work. All in all, life was better than it had been in some time.

On that particular day, her work at the Ellis County court-house had been more demanding than usual. The draining summer heat which draped itself over the gently rolling central Texas terrain had become wearisomely commonplace. Time, and the people whose lives it commands, seemed locked into a lethargic slow-motion. Even the sudden cloudburst which had spilled much-needed moisture over the region a few days earlier had done little to provide relief from the oppressing, breezeless heat. Rather, it had simply added to the discomfort with the curse of rising humidity.

Once home, Karen decided to forego dinner in favor of re-laxing in front of the television for a while before preparing for bed. Normally, her first order of business upon arriving home would have been to prepare a meal, but the heat and the day's work had left her with no appetite. It was just as well, she decided. She had been trying, with little success, to lose a few pounds all summer.

Carson was away for the summer and would celebrate his eighth birthday the following day with his father and grandparents in Georgia. Part of her listlessness, Karen knew, was a byproduct of the loneliness she was feeling. She missed her little boy and was anxious for him to return.

As the last remnants of the day dimmed and the room darkened, she began to doze. The television was on but she had not even bothered to turn up the sound. Its purpose was not so much entertainment but, rather, whatever company the movement on the screen would provide.

Suddenly, for no logical reason, Karen was instantly alert. Whether she had actually fallen asleep, she could not be certain. If so, it had not been for long. Checking her watch, she saw that it was 8:45 P.M.

Then, without explanation, it was as though another television screen appeared before her. On it was a hazy image of a car filled with people, moving slowly through a wooded area which looked much like a tree-lined road near her inlaws' pond in Georgia. Karen didn't recognize anyone in the car but felt a sudden rush of anxiety.

She rose to telephone and make sure Carson was okay, wondering why a car would be traveling in the direction of the pond at that time of night. What had triggered the vision which had come to her so suddenly? Was her son among the passengers she could not yet make out? And if so, was he in danger?

Before she could dial the number, however, her questions were answered. The images continued as she crossed the room. The car moved further down the rutted dirt road and she realized it was near a lake, not a pond. Whatever she was seeing was not on the farm in Georgia. For a moment relief tempered her anxiety.

The figures in the car, three males and two females, began to come into focus. Now it was as if Karen was no longer in her own home, but, instead, traveling in the company of a group of people she had never seen before, in a place she'd never been.

Her attention momentarily focused on the girl riding in the front seat. She was brunette, pretty, looked seventeen, maybe eighteen, and was clearly frightened. The male driver had thick, shoulder-length hair, a splotchy beard, and a mustache. She was aware that he was laughing, but it was an evil, manic laughter, without humor. Karen felt an immediate dislike for him.

Though still not clearly in focus, there were two males, one who looked like an Indian, the other a white teenager, seated in the back with another girl, an attractive blonde. The driver and the Indian-looking man were drinking beer as the car made its way deeper into the wooded area.

Frightened and feeling weak, Karen returned to the recliner where she had been seated and began to concentrate. Something evil, she sensed, was happening, and the flashes she was receiving were becoming increasingly intense. She sat down and began to focus her complete attention on what was taking place.

My God, she thought, it's happening again.

From the time she was a young girl Karen Hufstetler had dealt with the gift—or the curse—of seeing and knowing things she could not explain. She had been just eight when she dreamed that a car had failed to manage the curve in the farm-to-market road in front of their rural Texas home, crashing through a ditch and into the yard. In her dream she saw a small puppy in the car with the man who was driving. The next day as the family sat eating the noon meal, her father jumped to his feet at the sound of a crash outside. Racing to the front porch, he saw that a car had torn down the fence which surrounded the front yard and crashed into a tree.

Hurrying to help the injured driver from the car, he paid little attention to his distraught daughter's insistence that he "get the dog too." Finally after her repeated pleas he appeased his daughter by opening the car door and looking beneath the seats. There, huddled beneath the driver's seat, was a shivering, frightened poodle.

"Honey, how did you know that little dog was there?" he asked.

"I just did," the little girl said.

While her family and the few friends who were aware of her abilities quickly labeled her a psychic, Karen shied away from the word. She could not, she repeatedly explained, predict the future at the drop of a hat, promising fame or fortune or success in love. Neither, for that matter, was her gift something over which she had constant control.

She was, she would admit, "sensitive" to certain things. At

times fearful of the strange abilities she possessed, she neither tried to develop them nor to profit by them. She is highly skeptical of most of those on today's rapidly growing list of "professional psychics."

In the summer of 1979 her "sensitivity" expanded and took her into a world that was both frightening and fascinating. Married and living in the southern Georgia community of Silvester, she had a vision of a black child being murdered in Atlanta. She "saw" the crime taking place in an area of the city familiar to her, and the vision was so graphically clear that she placed a long-distance call to her sister-in-law, a resident of Atlanta, and asked if she had heard anything about such a crime.

Karen described what she had seen: a young boy, probably in his early teens, had been lured into a car, taken to a particular spot, and killed in a brutal, senseless manner. "There are going to be two more murders very soon," a distraught Karen told her sister-in-law, "and they'll find the bodies close together, near a lake. I'm scared, but I don't know what to do. Maybe I'm wrong. I hope so, but please let me know if you hear anything."

It was only a matter of days before Karen's sister-in-law called to inform her that there had been a story in the *Atlanta Constitution* about two black children whose bodies had been found off Niskey Lake Road. Both were fourteen years old and their bodies had been found less than a hundred yards apart.

Thereafter, Karen called Atlanta on several occasions to tell her sister-in-law of children who would be killed or had already been killed but not yet found, giving their ages and the locations where the bodies would be found. As the visions continued, she also confided details of crimes to her husband and mother-in-law that would later be substantiated by the news reports that were beginning to appear regularly.

The entire nation had begun to share the horror of what had come to be known as the Atlanta Child Murders, a gruesome series of killings of young blacks that had the authorities baffled and residents terrorized. For Karen, however, the horror was more real, more personal than that felt by buy those who followed the tragic sequence of events in the newspapers or on the ten o'clock news. For reasons she could not explain, she was living with it constantly.

Finally, her sister-in-law contacted the Atlanta Police Department, suggesting that Karen might be able to help in the investigation. Yet even before she could fully explain the remarkable accuracy of her sister-in-law's visions she was informed that they had no interest whatsoever in talking to "another psychic."

Karen, meanwhile, wrote a biographical sketch of the man she felt was committing the crimes. The murderer, she was sure, was a Vietnam veteran who was an outpatient at the Atlanta VA hospital. While stationed in Vietnam, she felt, the man—a member of the Military Police—had seen several of his friends killed by Vietnamese children. Though generally a quiet, docile, well-liked man, it was when he had flashbacks to his Vietnam experiences that he would search out children to kill. He would wear his MP uniform, leading the children to believe he was a policeman.

In each of her visions, the killer took the children to the same spot. She was relieved that she never "saw" the actual murders.

Karen's ongoing obsession with the Atlanta murders added greatly to the difficulties she and her husband were having at the time. For some time their marriage had been falling apart and both had resigned themselves to the fact there was little hope for salvaging it. Finally, Karen decided to leave and return to Texas and begin a new life. And maybe, she thought, a move would put the recurring scenes of the horrible killings behind her.

After almost two years, a 26-year-old freelance photographer named Wayne Williams was apprehended and eventually convicted of the murders of two Atlanta blacks. Both victims were men in their twenties. Although the crimes he was tried for bore little, if any, resemblance to the murders of the black children, law enforcement agencies and the Atlanta media assured the public that the man who had so long terrorized the city had been caught. It was over; the books were closed.

By then, Karen's ordeal had also ended. The visions had ceased long before Williams' arrest. The man she felt had been doing the killings had, for some reason she could not explain, stopped. But even as she read reports of Williams' arrest and conviction she was not in the least convinced that the murderer she had so often seen in her visions had been caught.

Still, she hoped she would never again experience such a close touch with violence. Even if she did, she vowed never to discuss it with anyone. It was a vow she might have been able to keep if what she saw that July night in 1982 had not seemed so personal, so real.

As she sat in her living room, swept up in the strange, frightening vision, she was puzzled by the fact that she recognized neither the geographic locale nor any of the people. Always before there had been something, if only a setting, that was familiar. This time, however, she had no idea where it was all taking place.

She was also puzzled by the fact that she seemed to be flashing back in time. When she had first visualized the car near the lake it was dark. But now it was obviously earlier in the evening, nearing twilight, and the two girls and the teenage boy were sitting on a concrete picnic table near a lake, talking. She sensed that the pretty brunette and the boy, who looked perhaps fifteen or sixteen, were quite fond of each other.

They were a nice-looking young couple, Karen thought. The boy's hair appeared to have been recently washed and he wore jeans and a pullover shirt. The girl's hair shone in the last remnants of the setting sun and she was wearing a pair of shorts and a terry cloth top. She wore very little makeup but wore three rings on the fingers of one hand. One of them, Karen felt, had been a gift from the boy.

The other girl, a slender blonde, also dressed in shorts, was wearing more makeup than the brunette and a heavy perfume. Karen could actually smell the fragrance in the air; it was a scent she could almost recognize but did not like.

As the youngsters talked, a car approached and parked nearby. The bearded driver, whom Karen had "seen" earlier, got out, followed closely by his dark-skinned companion. As they walked toward the youngsters at the picnic table Karen got her first good "look" at the other two characters in her puzzling drama.

The driver was five feet nine or ten inches tall and stoutly built. His arms looked powerful, as if he were a weightlifter. He wore neither shirt nor shoes and his jeans were frayed at the bottom. He was drinking from a can of Budweiser and appeared to be high.

The boy at the picnic table apparently recognized him and seemed to be introducing him to the blonde. His name, Karen determined, was either Dale or Dave. The smallish man with him seemed barely mobile, staggering as he walked. Even though he wore wire-rimmed glasses, Karen was aware of a glazed look in his eyes. As the two approached the teenagers, he said nothing nor was he introduced.

Scenes then began to come in flashes. It was getting dark as the people in her vision made their way to a car. She sensed the brunette was going to get into the back seat until the bearded driver insisted she sit in the front with him. Though she was aware of the others in the car, Karen's attention seemed to focus primarily on the brunette in the front seat. Before the car reached the park entrance, the girls asked the driver to stop so they might use the public rest room which was just off the road.

None of what was taking place made any sense to Karen as she sat in her recliner. She knew none of the people and recognized nothing about the places she was visualizing. She felt as if she were intruding on a privacy which in no way concerned her. And there remained the feeling that something was not right, that there was some evil force orchestrating the entire scenario.

Then everything went blank. Sitting there, Karen wondered if it was over. Puzzled, she continued to concentrate. There must be more, she thought.

In a moment the vision returned. Though it was now dark, it was as though a high-intensity spotlight was directed on the car. She was now seeing things even more clearly than before. The car pulled into the entrance to another park and made its way toward the area where she had first seen it, the area she had mistaken for the pond in Georgia.

Once again focusing on the girl in the front, Karen was suddenly aware of a noise from the back seat. As though looking through the eyes of the girl she was so drawn to, she turned to see the Indian-looking man lean across the blonde and stab the teenage boy.

A chill swept over Karen. Her hands were clenched into fists so tight that the blood seemed to drain from them. Though she felt cold, it was as if she were gripping hot coals. She had been right: something very, very bad was happening. Somewhere, to someone. But where? And who?

Karen envisioned the car slowly rounding a bend, down a narrow road, past tangled scrub oaks which bordered on each side. Then she saw the driver get out, open the back door, and pull the body of the dead boy from the car and lay it just off the, road. The girl in front jumped from the car and began to run, stumbling and falling repeatedly in the pitch darkness.

Karen saw the driver catch up with the girl and shove her against a huge oak tree, pinning her shoulders to the trunk. He then pressed a knee to her groin and pulled away the terry cloth top she was wearing. The girl tried to fight back but was quickly knocked to the ground. Laughing and cursing, the man began dragging her back in the direction of the car.

The scene suddenly switched to the other man who had the blonde girl out of the car, standing in the road, the knife still at her throat. The driver forced the brunette to her feet, then grabbed her hair, pulling it so that she had to look straight ahead, in the direction of her terrified friend and the man holding the knife on her. She was forced to watch as a knife was plunged into the girl's throat. Karen was aware of no scream, only a horrifying gurgling sound that came after the knife had penetrated.

Again breaking from the driver's grasp, the brunette began running in the direction of the lake, through thick scrub brush which tore at her arms and legs as she ran. This time it did not take her assailant long to catch her and shove her to the ground.

From that point Karen's vision was a horrifying sequence of violence and sexual abuse. Finally, she saw the man take a ring from the girl's finger and place it in his pocket. Even with her mouth covered, the brunette managed another scream. To silence her, the man cut her throat.

As Karen envisioned the torment of the girl, a nausea welled in her stomach. It was as if she were actually feeling some of the pain the girl had endured. Still, she continued to concentrate on the tragedy which continued to unfold.

She saw the attacker sling the girl's body over his shoulder and carry her to a spot near where his companion had placed the other girl's body. He tied her hands behind her back, cut her several more times, then began to walk away, certain she was dead.

Before the driver reached the road leading to the car, however, he seemed to hear something. Karen watched him return to the girl, stab her motionless body several times, then lift her head and cut away a piece of her hair.

Thereafter, things came to Karen Hufstetler in snapshot-like flashes. She saw the two men return to the other side of the lake, to the park where they had originally picked up the three teenagers. She saw the driver walk to the water's edge, relieve himself, and throw something. Though she was not certain what it was, she was aware of a metallic sound as it hit on the rocks below.

It was well after midnight when the visions finally ended. Karen sat for some time, horrified by what her mind had forced her to witness, wondering if the tragic event had actually occurred. There was no lake, no park nearby that resembled what she had seen in her vision. She prayed that it had all been imagined, a bad nightmare. But she was certain that what she had witnessed had actually happened. To someone, somewhere. That night she did not sleep at all.

The following morning Karen Hufstetler reported to work at the courthouse in Waxahachie, drained and feeling ill. She checked through the Wednesday edition of the *Dallas Morning News* to see if any crime like the one she had envisioned had taken place. She found nothing.

No longer able to keep what she was feeling to herself, she asked one of the other secretaries if she would answer the phone and tend to customers for her for a few minutes.

"Is something wrong?" co-worker Karen East asked.

"Something awful happened last night," Karen told her. "I can't explain it. I just know it. I've got to write some things down."

On a legal pad she began to make notes of what she had experienced the night before. And even as she did, images continued coming to her. The driver she had seen in her vision just hours before was now alone, calmly walking shirtless and barefoot across a gravel parking lot. He was going to play video games. His favorite, she somehow knew, was a game called "Phoenix." She tried to draw the man she was seeing and felt frustrated by her lack of artistic ability. She could see him so clearly.

Across the street at the County Extension Office the work day had already begun. Raylene Rice, someone mentioned, was late again.

# PART TWO

*The little boy would wake in the night, certain that thousands of spiders were crawling across his bed. Large, black, and menacing, they were everywhere, coming after him from all directions. Upon awakening from his nightmare, he would scream for his mother and she would rush to his room. While her frightened, crying son stood in the corner watching, she would take the sheets and blankets from the bed, shaking them to prove to him there were no spiders. There never were, except in the boy's imagination.*

*He was six years old and the dream came often. As did the horrible face that often appeared at his bedroom window. No one else ever saw it. But he did. Looking in at him from the darkened outside, the face was that of the devil.*

*The boy came to hate the dark.*

*Even as he grew to manhood and the dream of the spiders and the face at the window disappeared, he continued to fear being alone at night. If he arrived home from a date or an evening out with friends and found that no one was in the darkened house, he wouldn't enter. Rather, he would sit in his car, waiting for his mother or his younger brother to return. Sometimes he would sleep in his car all night.*

*Feeling at ease now in the presence of the soft-spoken, friendly doctor, the man talked about a mother who had been married five times and a father whom he had seen only rarely. He spoke of his penchant for driving too fast and drinking too much; of his fear of graveyards and his frustration that he hadn't really made anything of his life.*

*Though he was now an adult he continued to live in an adolescent fantasy world. Someday, he told the doctor, he hoped to be the head of a big motion picture company earning millions of dollars. It didn't seem to occur to him that his ninth grade education prepared him for little else but the menial jobs he had worked at in recent years.*

*In many ways, the man was still a boy, still afraid. He*

described how a rush of anger would send him out of control, particularly when he was drunk or high. For instance, there was the time when, mad at his girlfriend, he had taken a hatchet to his pickup. "I just went outside, pulled it into the driveway, turned my stereo up as loud as it would go, and started really fucking up my truck. I knocked all the windows out and put dents in the doors and hood and the fenders. Tore the shit out of it."

And then, having told the story, he laughed.

The girlfriend, he explained, had caused him a lot of problems. There had been a time when he hit her regularly, but he had finally decided to stop, to try to treat her better. "It was real funny," he said. "When I was beatin' her up she was a real good girl. But when I slacked off she really got mouthy again. Turned into a real bitch."

He didn't tell the doctor about the time he had forced her to stand in front of the kitchen door so that he could throw knives at her like he had once seen a man do in a carnival act. Or how he had once placed a dog collar around her neck and forced her to spend an entire night naked in the front yard, tied to a tree by a leash. He didn't want to talk about his sexual habits and the doctor didn't press the matter.

And when the doctor asked questions that required answers that were too revealing or too embarrassing, he simply lied. Lying was something, he admitted to the doctor, he had been doing all his life.

"When you were a kid," the doctor asked, "did you ever do anything like kill an animal?"

"Naw. Oh, I might have when I was younger. Maybe a frog or something like that," he said.

A girl who grew up in the same neighborhood with him remembers differently. She recalls watching him chase stray cats through the alley near her home, seeing him catch them and disembowel them with his pocketknife.

The man had told friends how his father would return home drunk and beat him for no reason. But when the doctor asked him about this he said he could remember only one occasion when his father had even spanked him. On the other hand, he said, he had regularly watched as his father beat up his mother.

He indicated that he "believed too much" in "spirits and things" but did not go so far as to admit that he was involved in any form of organized Satan worship the way some people *had been saying. He didn't know that some things he had written had been sent to an expert on cults and devil worship for analysis. The expert had stated that the symbols were like those he'd seen associated with Satanic writing, and one of the phrases he was able to translate made reference to a "Lady of Darkness."*

*The man was twenty-five years old when he first talked with the doctor. Before their discussion was ended the doctor recognized in him a disorder of the conscience. The man, he determined, was a psychopath. He had a pathetic and lifelong history of indulging himself in immediate gratification. He seemed also to be extremely self-centered, irresponsible, incapable of loyalty and uncaring of others. He felt justified in lying when it was convenient and to his advantage.*

*Following their talk the man was returned to jail. What he dreaded most about the place was the night when the lights in the cells were turned off. "I'm always scared to go in and lay down on my bunk," he had confided to the doctor. "Sometimes I'll be sitting at the door, smoking a cigarette, and I'll look over at my bunk and start shaking—shaking like hell—thinking, what if a bloody hand reaches up and grabs me?"*

*He shook his head. "I'm always scared I'm gonna see something like that."*

*The doctor, uncomfortable in the man's presence, was glad when he was taken away.*

## 8

September 9 was the kind of pleasant, almost cool late-summer evening that beckoned the residents of Waco to venture from their air-conditioned homes and check the gasoline level in the lawn mower or sit in the backyard, enjoying the first faint signal that summer might finally be losing its hardened grip. Though fall was officially just a couple of weeks away, Texas summers always seemed to stretch until at least mid-October. But on that day a gentle breeze had arrived from the north, stirring in many a sudden enthusiasm for outdoor activity as it brought a welcomed drop in the temperature. All over the city, the break in the humid, monotonous weather caused dinners to be rushed to allow time for a drive to the lake or a walk through the neighborhood before dark.

Weary from a day of writing reports and attending meetings, Gene Deal had planned to mow his yard that evening. A parole officer for McLennan County, the former military commander often sought escape from his job in yard work. A few hours spent mowing, raking, and trimming hedges always revitalized him. At forty-two, he was a man who didn't play golf or racquetball. He was not a member of any health club nor had he surrendered to the jogging craze. There just never seemed to be the time. Working in the yard was his exercise program and he did it with enough regularity and vigor to maintain the same fit, athletic appearance he had enjoyed throughout his military career.

Sometimes, when he was lucky, he would become so involved in his task that he would briefly forget about the people whose lives he was somehow supposed to redirect toward responsible citizenship. More often, however, he found himself thinking about them as he pulled the weeds from his wife's garden or cut back the rosebushes or mulched the iris beds: the youngster back home after his first trip to the Texas Department of Corrections, frightened and overwhelmed by the changes that had taken place in just a couple of years' absence; the two-time loser who was assuring him that there would not be a third trip to prison. Daily he listened to people who came into his office with vows never again to be involved with drugs, reborn Christians who wanted to share with him the new and wonderful relationship they had developed with God while behind bars, and the few who were brave and honest enough to admit to him they were scared to death about starting over without benefit of family or job prospects. He heard a lot of stories about girlfriends who had not waited, parents who no longer welcomed sons and daughters with criminal records into their homes, and bosses who never let their people forget they were ex-cons.

Gene Deal was not one who had learned to leave his job at the office. In his years as a parole officer he had seen a lot of tears, heard a lot of cries for help. After ten years it still moved him, causing him to try to reach out. What he was doing, he felt, was important.

When around Gene Deal, a co-worker observed, you could still hear a heartbeat. He still cared about people. That wasn't always the case in his line of work. Still, he was no sucker for a sob story. For that matter, he prided himself on his ability to quickly separate those who were making a genuine effort to rebuild their lives from the manipulating con men and liars. Those who fell into the latter category were the ones who frustrated him most, and offered the greatest challenge. He had dealt with a lot of them, with too few success stories to tell.

Unlike some who had spent years in his profession, he was not one to simply sit and wait for his people—his "clients," he called them—to make their required weekly or monthly visit to his office. Despite his bulging caseload he made an effort to keep close tabs on those for whom he was responsible. He helped them find jobs, then stopped by regularly to see that they were indeed working. He visited their homes often, looking for firsthand signs of the progress they had assured him they were making in the free world. It was not unusual for Gene Deal to see a parolee two or three times a week. Or for his work days to stretch from early morning to late at night.

More than once he had been warned by fellow parole officers that he was working too hard. You can't baby-sit these people, he was told. All you can do is give them advice, then see if they keep their noses clean. They're adults. They've got to stand on their own feet. You're just there to remind them of what's waiting if they screw up again.

Deal, however, saw his role as something more. He tried to establish trusting relationships with his parolees. He firmly believed there were ex-cons who deserved the right at a second chance. And he did everything he could to see that those whose files crossed his desk got the opportunity to succeed.

Nevertheless, he was a realist. He knew some of his clients had little real chance of surviving on the outside for long. As he saw it, the greatest problem for most was the absence of support from family or friends. Those who stood alone, Gene Deal had learned, were the most likely to fall. David Wayne Spence, a young man who had first walked into his office in November of 1981, was such a case.

Spence had been paroled after serving fifteen months of a four-year sentence for the aggravated robbery of a convenience store in Fort Worth. Spence had been hesitant, almost embarrassed, to talk about the crime, so Deal had sought out the arrest report on the case. Twenty-one at the time, Spence had entered the store, threatening the cashier with a hatchet. He had gotten very little money in the robbery and was in custody within a matter of hours. It was the kind of absurd crime that parole officers, like policemen, have a good laugh over while drinking coffee. Apparently, as a holdup man David Spence had been a dismal failure.

But the trouble he was in on that September day in 1982 was far more serious. Deal received a call from the Waco Police Department, advising him that Spence had been arrested. The charge was aggravated sexual abuse.

Gene Deal was not particularly surprised, either at the fact that Spence was in trouble or, for that matter, at the nature of the charges against him.

It was the Labor Day weekend and Danny Powers, just two days past his eighteenth birthday, was enjoying the delicious kind of freedom teenagers seldom experience. His mother and father were away in Bastrop, southeast of Austin, putting the finishing touches on a new home his father was building, and his grandmother, with whom he had been living in his parents' absence, had gone down to inspect the progress.

Powers and his friend Jimmy Garcia had managed to obtain a bottle of vodka, and on Sunday evening the teenagers had spent a couple of hours at Lake Waco, drinking and listening to music on the car radio. Before dark Powers, a youngster who had little experience with hard liquor, was drunk and had been persuaded to give his car keys to Garcia who, despite having no driver's license, was far more capable of driving.

For the youngsters it had begun as one of those aimless, "cruising" evenings. They were doing nothing in particular, going nowhere special. Their only plan was to kill time and the bottle of vodka, and for a while it had been fun. But as the alcohol began to take effect the joy had gone out of the evening and their thoughts turned to home and bed. The party, begun in high spirits, was over.

As they drove from the park back toward town, an encounter with another carload of young men provided a sobering effect. While both cars were stopped at a red light, words were exchanged and briefly there was the promise of a fight. The driver of the other car stepped out, tire tool in hand, and invited Danny Powers to join him in the street. Before Powers could get out of the car, however, the light turned green and Garcia gunned the engine and sped away.

As they continued on toward Danny's grandmother's house they encountered another car. Garcia recognized one of the three men in the station wagon, whose name was Ronnie Cole. Driving was a bearded, muscular man who looked older than his companions. His tattoos and the emblems sewn on his sleeveless denim jacket gave him the appearance of a biker. The other man, who looked Hispanic, had shoulder length hair, wore wire-rimmed glasses, and was drinking from a can of Budweiser.

Garcia signaled to Cole for the other car to pull over, and they all talked for a few minutes. Powers, leaning against his car, began describing the encounter with the "tire tool-swinging sonuvabitch," wobbling slightly as he spoke.

David Spence, the driver of the station wagon, smiled. "Why don't we go find them and kick some ass?" he said.

Danny Powers, his confidence still buoyed by alcohol, quickly embraced the idea. So did Spence's friend, Gilbert Melendez. It had been a boring evening and a little ass-kicking might liven things up.

Both cars sped away in convoy, Spence taking the lead. They had driven only a few blocks when Powers' car ran out of gas. It seemed the final, crushing blow to an evening gone awry.

Suddenly the anticipation of a fight waned. Danny asked Spence to give them a ride to his grandmother's house.

Once there, Spence and his friends invited themselves into the house, carrying with them the remains of two six-packs. "I'm not supposed to have anybody here while my grandmother's gone," Powers protested.

"Ah shit, man, we're just gonna stay a few minutes," David said as he entered the house, went into the kitchen, and checked the contents of the icebox. "Besides," he said, winking at Powers, "the cops are looking for us."

Young Danny Powers, the effects of the vodka fading, began to feel uneasy about his uninvited guests.

He had good reason.

For the next half hour the loud music and shouting caused him to worry that his aunt, who lived next door, would realize he had violated his grandmother's rule by allowing guests in her house during her absence. The more he pleaded with everyone to leave, the louder they seemed to get. Having finished the beer which they brought, Spence and Melendez were drinking from a bottle of wine they found in the refrigerator.

When Ronnie Cole went into the front yard to leave, Powers followed him, trying to get him to make Spence and Melendez leave also. Garcia, now drunk, followed and began arguing with Powers.

Spence and Melendez appeared on the front porch just as Powers and Garcia began to shove each other. Finally, they thought, the fight they had been looking for was about to materialize.

"Fight him, man," Melendez said, shoving Powers in the direction of Garcia. "What's the matter? You chicken shit? You think you can't whip him? Hell, man, he ain't as big as you are. He's just a fucking kid."

Garcia, now anxious to fight, pulled a buck knife from his pocket and pointed at his friend. "I can cut you, you know."

Spence stepped forward and took the knife from Garcia. "No dirty stuff, man. Just fight the dude."

For the next few minutes a halfhearted wrestling, kicking match ensued. It was immediately obvious that neither of the youngsters was a fighter. When it broke up after Powers finally refused to continue, Garcia, nursing a slightly bleeding nose, went into the house. Danny Powers followed him into the bedroom, trying to apologize.

Suddenly, Melendez and Spence were standing next to them. Melendez swung at Powers, his fist crashing into the side of his head. He began hitting him repeatedly, the final blow knocking him onto the bed. Powers began to cry.

Spence, still holding Garcia's knife, urged Melendez on. "Maybe we ought to teach the little motherfucker to be a man," he said. Then staring wild-eyed at Powers, he said, "Take your fuckin' pants off."

"No," Powers said.

"You better do what I say, asshole, or I just might hurt you." Shaking and crying, Powers removed his jeans.

"The underwear, too," Spence demanded.

When the youngster was naked, Spence lifted him to a sitting position and Melendez slapped him across the face several times, then began choking him. Finally he shoved him back to the bed.

Spence then crawled onto the bed beside him and pressed the blade of the knife against Powers' neck. "I don't like you," he whispered through gritted teeth. "I don't like you worth a shit. I think maybe I'll cut your fucking Adams' apple out and eat it."

Danny Powers, more frightened than he'd ever been in his life, closed his eyes, feeling the sting on his face as tears rolled down over his already swollen cheeks and jaw. *They're going to kill me*, he thought. *Please, God, don't let them kill me. Please let this end.*

Jimmy Garcia, who had stood near a dresser, watching the nightmare unfold, tried to leave but was ordered not to move. There was nothing he could do but stay and watch what was happening to his friend.

"Roll your ass over," Melendez yelled at Powers after he had again slapped him. "Get down here at the end of the bed and spread the cheeks of your butt." Powers bit down on his lip to keep himself from screaming as Melendez brutally shoved a finger into his anus.

Spence then ordered him to stand up. Laughing, he pointed the knife in the direction of Powers' genitals. "You pretty proud of that little ol' prick?" he asked.

Powers, too terrified to speak, shook his head.

"I still oughta cut it off."

Now it was Melendez who was laughing as he unzipped the fly of his pants. "I'm gonna make him suck my dick."

"No," said Powers, "I can't. I won't."

Spence moved toward him, again pointing the knife. "Man, you better do what he says before I cut you."

"No," Powers again pleaded.

Without another word Spence reached across the bed and cut a deep, four-inch gash in the lower portion of the boy's leg. From that moment on Danny Powers was in shock.

Spence, alternately laughing and cursing, cut him three more times. "Do what the man told you to do or I'll kill you, I fuckin' promise."

It was then that Powers, sitting up on the bloodstained bed sheets, his chest heaving with sobs, placed his mouth over Melendez's penis. "That ain't worth shit," Melendez said. "Jack me off." Powers tried to comply.

"Hey, man, be easy," Melendez demanded, again slapping the youngster.

"Fuck, you can't do anything right," Spence said, grabbing Powers by the shoulder. "Come here."

Leading the staggering youngster into the bathroom, he forced him to his knees in front of the toilet and, grabbing him by the back of the neck, shoved his head down into the water.

Suddenly Melendez was at the doorway, pulling Spence away. "What the fuck are you trying to do?" he asked. "You're gonna kill him."

Spence lifted Powers' head from the toilet, then pushed him to the floor and kicked him in the head. Immediately more blood began to pour from a cut behind Powers' ear.

Dragged back to the bed, the teenager was forced to endure several more minutes of the insane punishment as Spence and Melendez continued their threats and hit him repeatedly.

Finally, it was over. "Okay, asshole," Spence said, "if you call the cops I'm gonna come back and kill you. Understand?"

Powers nodded.

"If they come after us," Melendez added, "here's what's gonna happen: I'm gonna take the rap for this whole fuckin' business so my bro here can come take care of your ass."

"I won't call the cops," Powers promised. There was a loud ringing in his ears and pain throbbed throughout his body. "I promise. Just leave me alone. Please, leave me alone."

He was still crying when they left, but was faintly aware of their laughter as it echoed in the night.

The following day, Detective Ramon Salinas received a call from one of his informants. The father of a kid named Danny Powers had returned from out-of-town to find his son badly beaten and cut. Word on the street was that the father was carrying a gun and looking for the people who did it.

Salinas quickly put aside his paperwork, then drove to the Powers home and talked with the father and son, learning the horrifying details of the assault. Danny, his face still badly swollen and his wounds stitched and bandaged, gave him the names and descriptions of his assailants.

"Mr. Powers," Salinas said to the outraged father, "I understand how you feel. I'd probably want to do exactly the same thing you've got in mind. But that's not the way to handle it. If your son will help us out, I'll take care of it."

Two days after Danny Powers signed an official complaint the police had David Spence and Gilbert Melendez in custody.

As Gene Deal drove toward the police station, his yard work postponed until another time, his thoughts were not on the charges which Salinas had mentioned to him on the telephone. Instead, he was once again thinking about the murders of the three teenagers at Lake Waco. It had been almost two months and there was no indication that investigators were making any progress on the case.

Now, dammit, they would have to listen to what he'd been trying to tell them about David Spence.

Unlike many Waco residents, Deal had not closely followed the progress of the lake murders investigation in the newspaper or on television. There was enough bad news in his day-to-day workload to more than satisfy his appetite for the city's darker side. However, it was impossible not to be generally aware of the most gruesome crime in modern Waco history.

When he first learned of the killings he was repulsed at the nature of the murders and saddened that the victims were nothing more than kids. Deal had a son of his own who would, in a few short years, be a teenager, and his reaction was that of most Waco parents. The possibility that some psychopath was roaming the streets where he lived both frightened and concerned him.

In recent weeks that fright and concern had grown. At first, he had not picked up on the signs. But as time went on, he was convinced he was much closer to the lake murders than he would ever have thought possible.

On the afternoon of July 21, just a week after the teenagers' bodies had been found at Speegleville Park, Deal had stopped by an apartment into which Spence and his girlfriend had just moved. David had met him in the parking lot where they talked for several minutes, then invited Deal to see his new living quarters and say hello to "his old lady."

The purpose of Deal's visit was nothing more than a check of the new address Spence had given him, so the conversation was light, chatty. Christy Juhl, the girl with whom David was living, showed Deal around the apartment, which was still in a state of disarray. They had been there only a few days, she explained. Enthusiastically, she told him of plans she had for decorating.

As Deal was preparing to leave, for some reason he did not pick up on, David and Christy began to argue. Angry words were exchanged and Christy, a sarcastic edge to her voice, mentioned something about "those two girls you were with the other night."

Spence immediately rose from the sofa and fixed a cold, menacing stare on his girlfriend. It was a look Deal had seen a number of times in the eighteen months he had been dealing with David; one which immediately signaled anyone toward whom it was directed that he was treading on David's ground and would be best advised to keep his mouth shut and mind his own business. David Spence obviously had little tolerance for anyone who disagreed with him or meddled in his private affairs.

Christy Juhl said nothing more during the parole officer's brief visit. At the time, Deal gave the incident little thought. Evidently his client was running around on his girl. A month later he began to wonder whether Christy's comment had been merely a jealous outburst—or something more.

On August 20, Gene Deal received a call from an obviously distraught Spence, asking if he could stop by later in the day.

*   *   *

David was nervous, pacing, and talking in a hurried, almost incoherent fashion. He wanted permission from Deal to leave town, something he was allowed to do only if granted proper authorization from his parole officer.

"What's the matter, David?" Deal asked. "Sit down and relax. Tell me what's going on."

"Some dudes are after me."

"Why?"

"They're just after me. I need to get out of town."

"David, that won't do. If you want help from me, you've got to tell me what's going on."

Spence paced in silence for a few seconds more, looked out the window, and finally sat down across from Deal. "I know too much about those murders out at the lake," he finally said.

Now Deal was silent, trying to absorb what Spence had just said. "Okay, look," he said, "You're going to have to let me help you. If you think you know who did those murders, then you need to go to the police."

Spence, his jaw tightening, said, "I didn't say I knew *who* did the lake murders."

"But . . ." Deal started to protest.

". . . I said I know too much *about* the lake murders."

A sudden chill swept over Gene Deal. He wasn't sure what Spence was trying to say, but disturbing questions gathered in his mind. Did David know who did the murders? Was he somehow involved? Or had he actually killed the three teenagers? He wanted badly to scream the questions at the young man sitting across from him, but he knew David Spence too well to do so. If he turned the occasion into an interrogation, David would say nothing more. Deal would get the same cold stare that had been directed at Christy Juhl.

Then suddenly, Spence was composed, calm, almost as if he had pushed some invisible button. He took a deep breath, exhaled a relieving sigh, and gazed across the room.

"David," Deal finally said, "would you let me contact the police about this?"

Spence, apparently resigned to the fact that his parole officer wasn't going to sign the necessary papers that would free him to leave town, shrugged. "It's okay with me."

Though anxious to leave, Deal remained several more

minutes, urging his client not to overreact to whatever fears he was having. Maybe what David had to say could be of help to the police. Perhaps the information he had might enable them to provide him protection from whoever it was he feared.

"Yeah, maybe you're right. Okay, I'll talk to them," Spence said.

Driving directly to the Waco Police Department, Deal realized he was shaking. Though he had nothing more to go on than the perplexing ramblings he had just heard, he could not shake a gut feeling that David Spence was somehow involved in the lake murders.

Despite years of work with lawbreakers, Deal knew few officers on the Waco police force. On occasion some had called about parolees on his caseload whom they were interested in talking with concerning various investigations. When asked, he had helped them locate a parolee. But more often than not it angered him when ex-cons were automatically viewed as suspects by investigators whose cases were going nowhere. For that reason, he generally kept his distance.

Walking into the brightly lighted police headquarters on the edge of downtown, he asked to speak with whoever was heading up the investigation of the Lake Waco murders. After a few minutes he was escorted back to the Detective Division and introduced to Ramon Salinas.

Briefly, but as thoroughly as possible, Deal told of the conversation he had just had with David Spence. "I'm not here telling you that I think he did the murders," Deal explained to the detective, "but I've got some bad feelings about David. Frankly, I think there's a very good possibility that he might have been involved in some way. He gives the impression that he knows something. And he knows I'm here. In fact, he seemed to want me to come."

"Anything else you can tell me?" Salinas asked. It was his only question during the brief conversation.

"That's about it," Deal said. "It's not much, I realize. But I just thought it was something you ought to be aware of."

Salinas stood and shook the parole officer's hand. "I appreciate your coming by," he said.

As Deal walked into the parking lot he shook his head. He sensed resentment, as though he had intruded on another's turf;

as though he had wasted the detective's time. *If that cop would get into his car and drive to David's house right now, talk to him while he's still nervous and upset, he just might come away with some information on the case*, he thought.

Salinas, however, had shown very little interest. If Gene Deal had been a betting man, he would have wagered that David would never be questioned.

He would have won.

A week later Deal received another frantic call at his office. This time it was David's mother. She was crying, and asked if he could come to her house right away.

Though he had spoken with her numerous times since becoming her son's parole officer, Gene Deal knew very little about Juanita White. She had been married four or five times, had worked alternately as a bartender and waitress in a number of Waco's less elite bars, and had never convinced him that she had any genuine interest in her son's welfare. If there was a caring mother-son relationship there, Deal had not seen it. If anything, Juanita White seemed afraid of David. By the same token, David seemed embarrassed about his mother, rarely mentioning her during their discussions.

She was still in tears when Deal arrived at the small frame house on North Fifteenth Street that morning. The house was one of a block-long row of cheap wooden structures in a neighborhood that, while not a slum, would best be described as less than ideal. One block away was an area populated by low-income blacks.

"I had to talk to someone," she said as she met him on the porch and invited him inside. "I didn't know who else to call."

In her mid-fifties, Juanita White wore her drab, gray-streaked hair shoulder length. Like David, she had piercing blue eyes, deeply recessed and dark circled. The polyester slacks and print blouse she was wearing failed to hide the fact that she was thirty or forty pounds overweight. She looked tired, and her movements were slow and listless.

Deal followed her into the tiny living room. None of the furniture matched, he noticed, but the room was neat and clean. Photographs of her children were displayed on the mantel of a mock fireplace against one wall.

"Is David in trouble?" Deal asked as they sat down.

"I don't know," she said, "but he's been acting really strange for the last few weeks. Something's wrong, bad wrong, I know that. I know David. And I know when he's in trouble."

Deal asked no more questions, choosing just to listen as Mrs. White told him how David had returned home to live a few days earlier and had been very nervous since moving back. He was drinking heavily and slept very little. When he did he would have nightmares, waking with piercing screams that frightened her.

"It's got something to do with those kids who were killed at the lake," she said. "He keeps saying that somebody's out to get him because of something he knows about those murders. Mr. Deal, I'm scared. I'm really scared." Then she broke into tears again.

She was still crying uncontrollably a few minutes later when David suddenly walked in the front door, surprised to see Deal sitting in his mother's living room. Without so much as acknowledging his parole officer's presence, he walked directly over to the chair where his mother sat and stood staring down at her with a menacing glare, saying nothing. There was a tension in the room that seemed to electrify the air.

"Your mother says you're still worried about something," Deal said.

David, his angry stare still fixed on his distraught mother, gave a quick, hostile reply: "I'm not worried about a fucking thing."

Again, Gene Deal was on the phone to the Waco Police Department, trying to reach Detective Salinas. It was the third time he had called since their first meeting. The first two calls were simply to ask if he had yet spoken with Spence. This time, however, he wanted to tell him about Mrs. White's concern. But once more the voice of a female officer took his message, promising to relay it when Salinas was free.

That night, as Deal prepared for bed, his wife could tell that he was preoccupied. They had been married long enough that she knew all the signs. He had been virtually silent during dinner and had watched television that evening with far more interest than usual. It was his way of avoiding talking about something that was weighing on his mind.

"Something's wrong," she said.

Her husband nodded. "Yeah."

"Want to talk about it?"

Without prelude he told her what had been eating at him: "I've got the guy who killed those kids out at the lake on my caseload," he said, then turned out the light.

Before going into the jail to talk with David on the night he was arrested, Deal again sought out Detective Salinas and listened as he elaborated on the charges that were being prepared. It was Spence, he was told, who had apparently done all the cutting on the teenage boy.

"Do you have the weapon?" Deal asked.

Salinas showed him the buck knife which had already been marked as evidence.

Deal looked at it. "Is there any way you can check to see if this might be the same knife used in the lake murders?"

Salinas briefly explained forensic procedures that were sometimes used to match stab wounds with a particular type blade. What he did not tell Gene Deal was that he was no longer actively investigating the lake murders.

It was almost four in the morning when Truman Simons, his night patrol shift behind him, poured coffee into a styrofoam cup, sipped from it, and looked down at the folder he had placed neatly in the center of his desk. Several minutes passed before he finally opened it and began to read through the reports that had been filed on the lake murders.

He had already read most of what had been written, but this was the first time he had seen the complete file on the investigation. As he began reading he had no real idea what he was looking for. Taking over a two-month-old case which had already been worked by several others was like putting together a jigsaw puzzle. There were a lot of pieces, but obviously nothing was in place. And he could be certain that all the pieces were not there—had they been, the case would already have been solved. Somewhere, though, he hoped he might find an unanswered question, maybe someone who had been overlooked and not interviewed. Locating a starting place would be the most difficult part.

He had read only a few pages when Sergeant Dennis Baier joined him. Simons had asked Chief Scott for one officer to help him with the reinvestigation and had indicated he would like to have Baier. Young and energetic, Baier had first come to Simons' attention when they had worked a number of narcotics cases together. A student of police work who was not only well-versed in the law but felt it should be followed to the letter, Baier was neither a clock-watcher nor a complainer.

He also seemed to understand how Simons worked. While a number of officers rolled their eyes at Simons' sometimes unorthodox methods and his occasional "hunches," Baier had seen many of those hunches result in solved cases.

Even before talking with Chief Scott, Simons had warned Baier about the likelihood that some in the department would be unhappy at having a case on which they had failed reopened.

That didn't bother him, Baier assured his soon-to-be partner. The case had to be solved, and he didn't feel that it was important who got credit for it.

On the surface theirs was an odd partnership. Country-raised Simons, the blue jeaned, flannel shirt-wearing high school dropout, and city-boy Baier, the handsome, sharp dresser who was enrolled in law enforcement and psychology courses at Baylor University; the iconoclastic police veteran stuck at the rank of sergeant and the up-and-coming young officer who followed the police manual to the letter. Simons was comfortable with his rank; Baier, on the other hand, entertained aspirations of climbing the law enforcement ladder as quickly as possible.

Yet it was their differences which had prompted Simons to ask for Baier's help. The older sergeant knew better than anyone that he sometimes tried to move too quickly with investigations, pressing eagerly ahead in situations that demanded more patience. Dennis Baier, more methodical, a detail man, would help provide a needed balance. And since Baier had not been involved in the earlier investigations, he could view things with a certain degree of detachment. Though he was only now officially on the case, Truman Simons had in effect been on it since that muggy July night in Speegleville Park.

They read the file in sequence, beginning with the first missing persons report on Kenneth Franks and finishing with Salinas's notification that the case had been suspended. Simons passed each sheet to his partner once he had completed it, occasionally making a note to himself. Neither spoke until they had finished the file.

"The only name that rings a bell with me is the Bobby Brim kid, Kenneth Franks' friend," Baier said, rubbing his eyes. "I know him. I'd like to take another run at him. Otherwise, I don't see a helluva lot here."

Simons nodded in agreement, then picked up his notebook. Patrolman Nicoletti's interview with Linda Kelton, the girl who lived at the Methodist Home, had interested him.

"That guy she mentioned," he said, "the one who runs the little grocery store out by the home, hangs around out at Skaggs a lot. In fact, I've met him. He's from Jordan or Saudi Arabia or one of those end-of-the-world places. Strange little shit."

Despite the fact that Linda Kelton had said she had heard the man named Muneer Deeb make threats against Kenneth

Franks, there was no indication in the files that any police officer had ever talked to him.

"The guy apparently knew one of the victims and probably knows a lot of the kids over at the home," Simons said. "It's a long shot, but he might be of some help."

"It's as good a place to start as any," Baier said as he stood up and stretched. "After we go home and get some sleep."

When working the midnight shift, Simons would sometimes stop by the Skaggs supermarket on Valley Mills to drink coffee with his friend Willie Tompkins, a former policeman who had recently resigned from the force after ten years to become a pastor of a small Baptist church in nearby Moody. Preaching the gospel was not enough to make financial ends meet, so Tompkins had taken a position as night security officer at the twenty-four-hour supermarket.

Simons knew that Willie, a burly black man with an easy disposition and high ambitions, had resigned from the police department more from frustration at being routinely overlooked at promotion time than from a desire to serve as a full-time minister. Responsibility to his church was simply the excuse he used to avoid burning any bridges with the department. The fact of the matter was, Willie Tompkins had been preaching for several years while still a uniformed officer. Simons privately hoped the day would come when Willie would return to police work.

On those nights when Simons stopped by to see Tompkins, the two men would sit at one of the tables near the delicatessen area, drinking coffee served by a pretty young cashier named Patty Pick. It was during one of those early morning visits that Simons had first seen Muneer Mohammed Deeb. Deeb had entered the store with two young women, sisters named Kasey and Kerry Rowe.

"You gotta watch this," Tompkins said, nodding in the direction of the girls who had already begun pushing carts down one of the aisles. "They're taking that poor little guy for every dime he's got. Just watch, they'll fill those carts up with all kinds of groceries, then he'll pick up the tab. Does it all the time. And he ain't getting much in return."

Simons glanced in their direction and furrowed his brow. "What's his problem?"

"Aw, he wants to be a big shot with the ladies. He thinks to do that you gotta flash a lot of cash. One of the girls works here. The other one, Kasey, leads him around like he has a ring in his nose. She bats her eyes and he reaches for his wallet. He's getting her a car and helps pay for her apartment and buys her all those groceries.

"And you know what she told me? She came over here after he left one night and got to making fun of Deeb and says in this real whiney little voice that she'd never even let him kiss her on the mouth. She said if anybody was gonna mess with her he'd better be ready to come up with at least a Mercedes Benz. I remember laughing at that and telling her about the best I could offer was a pizza. And even then I'd get in so much trouble with my wife that it wouldn't be worth it."

Simons directed his attention toward the woman pushing the grocery cart. He shook his head. From what he could see there was no point in her entering any beauty contests.

"The guy's a damn fool," Tompkins continued. "I've told him so to his face. I don't know; women sure can make a man crazy. Me and Patty here, we've both tried to talk to him about the way he's allowing himself to be used, but it doesn't register. He's so crazy in love with Kasey that he would give her his last dime and then go borrow some more. I can't figure it."

Simons said nothing. Long before he had met and married Judy, he had been married to a woman who, in a final fit of anger, had told him that she prayed every night when he left for work that he would get his ass blown away and save her the headache of filing for divorce. He'd had enough troubles of his own trying to understand men-women relationships.

Over the next few months, Simons had occasionally joined Tompkins and Deeb in the delicatessen for late-night coffee and conversation. Simons, who had served a military stint in Turkey and had been fascinated with some of the Eastern philosophies, urged Deeb into several discussions of the religion and customs of his homeland.

Deeb, however, always managed to direct the conversation back to the big financial plans he fantasized about. He was careful to give the impression that he had plenty of money and plans for making even more. The grocery store was just a start. One of his next investments was going to be a video game room.

Already, in fact, he and Tompkins had entered into a partnership. Willie had purchased three video games which Deeb had agreed to put in his store. The most popular of the three was called "Phoenix." Willie and Deeb were sharing the profits, fifty-fifty.

Deeb might be a high roller and a fool when it came to women, Tompkins felt, but he seemed honest. Once, he told Simons, he had shorted himself by ten dollars when he stopped by Deeb's Rainbow Drive Inn to pick up his share of the earnings from the games, and Deeb had brought the money by to him that same evening. There had never been anything in their relationship which would suggest to Tompkins that Deeb was one who might step beyond the law. Until Truman Simons and Dennis Baier paid their former fellow officer a visit late one September night.

Knowing that Deeb usually stopped by Skaggs after closing his own store at eleven, the two officers had arrived early and were waved over to the coffeepot by Tompkins. Deeb hadn't been by, he told them, but he probably would be in soon. "He doesn't miss many nights," he said. "He likes to come in and cry on Patty's shoulder about how Kasey mistreats him." He spoke loudly enough for Patty Pick, who was working behind the deli counter, to hear. She smiled and rolled her eyes. Willie signaled her to join them.

"We just thought it might be a good idea to talk with him," Simons said.

"Now that I think about it," Willie replied, "it might be. I really didn't pay much attention at the time, but right after the stories about the lake murders came out in the papers we talked about it one night. Sitting right here, I said something about how bad it was the kids had been killed. You know, just making conversation.

"And all of a sudden Deeb starts laughing about it. I mean, really laughing. He said that he was *glad* that Kenneth Franks had been killed. Said he got what he deserved. Patty was standing there and she really jumped on him, telling him it wasn't nice to talk like that about someone who had been murdered.

"After she got on his case he sort of apologized, but then said again that he really didn't care, that the boy had deserved what he got. Said he had it coming to him. He also mentioned something about knowing the two girls who had been killed; claimed they had been in his store the same day they were murdered.

"You gotta know Deeb, though. He's one of those guys who's always making outrageous statements. He gets attention that way. The guy wants to be a big shot. You know what I mean. But now that I think about it, his reaction to the whole business was pretty strange. 'Course, Deeb's always been a strange sort of guy. I just really didn't pay much attention to him. I just blew the whole thing off. Now, I'm thinking maybe I shouldn't have."

Simons ground his cigarette into an ashtray. "It's damn sure worth looking at a little closer," he said. "But I don't think we're ready to talk to Mr. Deeb just yet. I'd appreciate it if you and Patty wouldn't say anything to him about our being here, okay?"

"You got it," Willie said, the grin returning to his face. "We private citizens are always glad to cooperate with the police."

As they walked into the parking lot toward their car Simons turned to his partner. "Dennis," he said, "we're going to go home and get a good night's sleep. Then tomorrow morning we're going to hit the ground running. I think maybe we just got ourselves a game plan." Already he was making a mental list of the people they would talk with the following day.

The reaction of Muneer Deeb to the death of Kenneth Franks had added an interesting new piece to the puzzle but was hardly the kind of information one could judge as a breakthrough. Simons didn't know the young, almost baby-faced foreigner well, but he found it hard to picture him involved in an act of violence. In the first place he didn't appear to be physically capable. Small, almost frail-looking, Deeb walked with a noticeable limp. He had once told Patty Pick that his handicap was the result of an automobile running over his foot when he was just an infant.

One thing for sure, Simons thought to himself, the guy wasn't strong enough to carry the bodies of three dead kids around in the woods. Still, he had to be checked out. Simons wanted to hear what a lot of other people thought about Muneer Mohammad Deeb.

The first stop the following morning was the home of Bobby Brim. Baier explained that he and Simons had recently been assigned to the case and were going back over some of the information that had already been gathered. Again Brim explained his relationship with Kenneth Franks and retold the story of his being grounded. For that reason he hadn't gone to the park with Kenneth and the two girls that night.

"The fact you were grounded," said Baier, "just might have saved your life."

"I know that," the youngster replied.

He had thought about it a great deal since the murders, he said, but still couldn't think of anyone who might have had a reason to kill Kenneth. "It just doesn't make any sense," he said.

"You got that right," Simons said. "Sometimes cases like this don't." Then he asked the question which would, in the days to come, become something of a trademark of his investigation: "What can you tell us about a guy named Muneer Deeb?"

The question seemed to surprise Bobby. "He's this little wimpy dude who runs a store over by the Methodist Home. Now, he's someone who didn't like Kenneth, but, hey, he couldn't have pulled off something like what happened out at the lake. The guy couldn't whip his way out of a paper bag. Hell, Kenneth would have loved an excuse to kick his ass."

"What do you mean by that?" Simons asked.

"Well, they sorta had this thing going," Bobby said. "It had something to do with Gayle Kelley, one of Kenneth's best friends. I really don't know much about it but I think Deeb had the hots for her or something and Kenneth thought the guy was a creep. He was always telling Gayle to stay away from him. We used to ride through his parking lot on Kenneth's motorcycle every now and then and shoot him the finger, stuff like that. A couple of times Kenneth made fun of his limp out in front of his store and was always calling him 'Ahab.' They got into a couple of cuss fights, but that was about it. No big deal. Shit, Deeb was afraid of his own shadow. You don't think he had anything to do with the murders, do you?"

"Naw," Simons said. "We've just got a lot of names on our list and we're trying to check them all out."

"I don't know where she's living now," Bobby offered, "but you might want to talk with Gayle. She and Kenneth were good friends and she worked out at Fort Fisher with Jill."

Though neither said anything about it to the other, both Simons and Baier thought it strange that Brim's original statement to the police had included no mention of Deeb and whatever feud he might have been having with Kenneth Franks. Neither, for that matter, had the statement from Gayle Kelley. It was beginning to look as if it might be necessary to requestion everybody who had been interviewed by the original investigators.

That night, Simons and Baier returned to Skaggs in hopes of running into Kasey Rowe. Instead they encountered her sister, Kerry, and asked if she had ever heard Deeb talk of the lake murders.

"Just once," she said. "My sister and I were talking about them after it came on the news and Muneer told us we didn't need to be talking about it. He said people might think we had something to do with it."

"Did he say anything else?" Simons asked.

Kerry thought a minute. "Yeah, but it didn't make any sense. He said it was made to look like something it wasn't. And he said something about one of the girls being the sister of a girl he knew."

When the officers later found Kasey at her apartment, she had little to say. The only time she remembered hearing Deeb talk about the killings was during the same conversation her sister had referred to. When the officers questioned her about her relationship with Muneer, she admitted that he had given her gifts and money, but that they were no more than friends.

Simons studied the young woman as they talked. She was attractive, well-dressed, and had a good figure. But he hardly saw her as the stunning beauty that would cause a man to take leave of his senses. Her voice, which strung words out like slow pouring molasses, irritated him.

"From what I've heard," he said, "Deeb feels there's a little more between the two of you than friendship."

"I know," Kasey said, breaking into a smile. "He says he loves me, but I've never even let him kiss me."

Simons waited until out of the woman's earshot before saying to Baier, "If we ever need to talk to her again, she's your responsibility."

"Thanks a lot," Dennis said.

Fifteen-year-old Linda Kelton sat in one of the conference rooms at the Methodist Home, listening as Dennis Baier and Truman Simons introduced themselves. She had lived in the same unit on campus as Jill Montgomery and had known Kenneth Franks well. She had liked them both, she said. But it was neither Jill nor Kenneth the visitors had come to talk about. Miss Kelton had been the only one to mention Deeb as a possible suspect during the early stages of the investigation.

She told how she and a girlfriend named Fran Peters had spent a great deal of time at Deeb's Rainbow Drive Inn before officials at the Home had placed it off-limits. "All I know," she said, "was that just the mention of Kenneth's name would send Deeb into a rage. I remember once somebody—maybe it was Fran—mentioned Kenneth Franks and Deeb said something like, 'I'm going to put him in the hospital.' Another time, when Kenneth rode by on his motorcycle and shot him the finger, Deeb pulled a gun from under the counter and started waving it around, acting real crazy. Said he was going to do something to Kenneth that he wouldn't like."

The picture she painted of Muneer Deeb was much like what they had heard from Willie Tompkins. He liked to flirt with the young girls from the Methodist Home and encouraged their visits to his store with gifts of soft drinks, cigarettes, candy, beer, and marijuana. There were a lot of girls at the home, Linda said, who were taking advantage of his generosity.

"Did he go out with any of the girls?" Baier asked.

"Not that I know of," Linda said. "But. . . ." she fell silent.

"But, what?"

"Well, he was always asking different girls if they would marry him. He said he would pay them five hundred dollars."

"Did he ask you?"

"He asked everybody."

As they sat listening to Linda, Simons struggled with the image of Muneer Deeb as a possible suspect. The kinds of threats she described seemed more empty boasting than serious threats. He could not imagine Deeb cutting someone's throat. He did not seem to have a violent or even aggressive nature.

Simons expressed his concerns to the young girl sitting across from him. "Let's say," he said, "that Deeb was involved. A guy like that would have to have some help. Got any ideas?"

"Well, there's this biker-type dude who hangs around the store a lot," Linda said. "Real crazy and mean. He scares me. He and Deeb seem to be pretty good friends."

"What's his name?" Baier asked.

"All I know is he calls himself Chili. I don't know what his real name is. I stay away from him."

Suddenly Linda Kelton seemed nervous, anxious for the interview to end. She had tried to help, but she had no intention of admitting to them that she knew Chili all too well. A month earlier she had had her first and only date with him.

It is the policy of the Methodist Home for female residents to request permission to date, whether their boyfriend is a resident of the home or from the community. Only after a suitor is okayed by a caseworker or dorm parent is the girl allowed to leave the campus with him. And then she is required to sign out, giving the name of the person she is leaving with and where they are going. If curfew is violated even once, the relationship is no longer allowed.

There are ways, however, to circumvent the rules. If, for instance, a young man has been cleared by home officials to date a particular girl, it is generally okay if the girl invites one of her roommates to accompany her and her date. Once past that obstacle, it is easy enough to accommodate the third party with a partner who has not gone through the formal channels.

On the evening of August 10, Fran Peters had a date with a boy named Ronnie Cole and had told her roommate that he was bringing a friend. Linda, who had recently been working long hours at a summer job in the kitchen of the local VA hospital, thought the idea of a blind date sounded like fun. On the register, which both girls signed that evening, they indicated they were going out for pizza with Ronnie Cole.

Linda Kelton had reservations about her decision as soon as she slid into the front seat of the white station wagon. The driver was much older than she had expected. He was drinking from a can of Budweiser and apparently had already had several others before arriving. Though he wore dark glasses, she recognized him as the man she had seen on a number of occasions playing video games at the Rainbow Drive Inn.

"Linda," Ronnie said, "this is Chili."

Instead of going to eat, they made a stop for more beer and then drove to Cameron Park. They parked in a turnout by the side of the road and Ronnie and Fran walked toward a nearby picnic area, leaving Linda and her date sitting on the hood of the car.

Though nervous, Linda tried to make conversation. "Why don't you take those sunglasses off?" Linda asked. "It's getting dark."

"Chili doesn't want you to see his eyes," her date replied in an unfriendly voice.

"I don't like it out here," Linda said. "Let's go."

"What's the matter?"

"There are too many woods around. It scares me. This is too much like the place where some of my friends got killed."

For the first time, he laughed, then put his arm around her waist. "You wanna go in the woods with Chili? I'll protect you. Ain't nothing gonna happen to you when you're with Chili."

The way he continued to refer to himself in the third person frightened her. "I'm not going off into the woods with anybody." she said. "Why are you trying to scare me?"

"You afraid to die?" Chili asked. "You afraid of the Reaper? You shouldn't be afraid to die. Nobody should be afraid to die." He laughed again and said, "Get Chili a beer."

Linda pulled away from him and said, "Hey, I'm not your servant."

He grabbed her arm and repeated, "Get Chili a beer."

Linda was relieved when Ronnie and Fran returned to the car. Then Ronnie suggested they go to Chili's place.

For a while they all sat in the living room, drinking beer and listening to rock music which blared from the stereo. Chili appeared drunk, sullen, and refused to contribute much to the conversation.

Only when Ronnie and Fran went into the back bedroom did he move to the couch where Linda was sitting. Without a word he kissed her and began to fondle her breast. When she moved away he laughed. "You be nice to Chili," he said, "and Chili will be nice to you." He pulled her to him and kissed her again. The discomfort she had felt when she first got into the car at the Methodist Home was quickly turning to fear.

After a few minutes the others returned to the living room and walked toward the front door. "Hey, where are you going?" Linda asked. "Don't go off and leave me here."

"Don't worry, we'll be back in a few minutes," Ronnie said. Linda assumed they were going to get some marijuana.

Moments after they left, Chili was standing in front of Linda with a knife in his hand. "You be nice to Chili," he said again, rubbing the blade across her chest. "Chili doesn't want to hurt you." As he spoke, he unbuttoned her blouse and lazily stroked her nipples with the point of the knife. Then, while she stood frozen, he walked to the front door and locked it.

Grabbing her by the hair he pulled her into the bedroom, slapped her, and forced her onto the bed. As he removed his clothes he told her to get undressed.

"You're gonna get fucked bitch," he said.

Linda Kelton was crying, pleading. "Please leave me alone. Let me go. If you don't you're gonna get in a lot of trouble."

He laughed again as he climbed onto the bed. "You stupid cunt. Chili's already in a lot of trouble."

Two days passed before Linda finally confided to her roommate what had happened while she and Ronnie had been gone from the house. It was then that she showed Fran Peters the bite marks on her shoulder and breasts that had been made by the man who raped her.

# 10

There was no smile on Richard Franks' face as he opened his front door and looked out at the two officers. The events which had transpired since his son's death had prompted in him a growing resentment toward law enforcement, and he was no longer attempting to disguise his bitterness. Not only had he seen no positive results from the investigation of the deaths of Kenneth and the two girls, but he had sensed an attitude bordering on hostility from virtually every officer who had spoken with him.

That he would be viewed as a suspect had, at first, shocked him, then made him angry. He had resented being asked to take a lie detector test and had lost patience with the repeated questions about his whereabouts on the night the teenagers had disappeared. Every minute the police spent trying to determine whether or not he was involved in the murders, he knew, was time wasted.

Sandra, his ex-wife, had called him enraged after Lieutenant Marvin Horton and Detective Salinas had visited her in Lake Jackson. She said the only thing they had seemed interested in was whether she felt Richard might be capable of killing their son.

A friend had told him about overhearing a Waco police officer discussing the case at a local restaurant, explaining to his companions that it was "just a matter of time before the kid's daddy admits that he did the killings."

And there had been the anonymous telephone calls, hate-filled voices in the night insisting they knew he had killed the youngsters and urging him to confess. For a while he had considered having his number changed, but he feared if he did so some caller with valid information might not be able to reach him.

Richard Franks, then, was a man battling a number of enemies: grief and anger, frustration and disappointment. Two months had passed with no indication that the police were any closer to finding his son's killer than they had been immediately after the murders. He was beginning to lose hope.

Truman Simons had always made it a point to contact the relatives of the victims of any crime he was investigating. Nothing in the police manual demanded it, no departmental protocol required it. He simply felt the reassurance that someone was working on the case might provide some small degree of comfort. As his investigations progressed, Simons often shared with family members information other officers considered highly confidential. He couldn't tell the families everything, of course, but he felt they had a right to know as much as possible. There had been times when the anticipation of a phone call from Truman Simons was the only ray of hope crime victims had known.

So he and Dennis Baier were not there that day to question Franks on his whereabouts or to determine whether he might have had some hidden motive for killing his own son. They simply wanted to introduce themselves. If Franks had information that might help with the investigation, it would be a bonus.

A few minutes of conversation was all Simons needed to satisfy himself that Richard Franks was not a possible suspect. As he listened to the father talking about his son in a soft, almost whisper-like voice, Simons sensed an overpowering, almost crazed grief. They had talked but a few minutes before Franks was in tears.

When Simons explained that he had been in Speegleville Park the night the bodies of the youngsters had been found and told of the impact their deaths had had on him, Franks' distrust of the officers seemed suddenly to disappear. He groped for words. "I appreciate your interest," he finally said.

Simons explained that anything the father might be able to tell him about Kenneth, anything that might help him to know the youngster, would be valuable. For the next hour Richard Franks spoke of the relationship he had enjoyed with his son and listed the names of Kenneth's friends. He reflected on his divorce, told the officers about the problems of rebellion Sandra had experienced with their son, and described how living at the Methodist Home had helped Kenneth to mature.

He did not mention the fact that his son's death had driven him to the brink of insanity. He said nothing to them about his repeated trips to Koehne Park since the murders, searching for some clue, some sign that police investigators might have over-looked. Nor did he tell them about the evening when, lonely and overcome by his loss, he drove out to Speegleville to the wooded area where his son's body had been found. There, where a small wooden stake marked the spot where Kenneth had been found, he had lain down on the ground in the quiet twilight, closed his eyes, and tried to talk with his dead boy. "Son," he had said, "can you tell me what happened to you?"

Other investigators had requested to see Kenneth's room and Franks, feeling an invasion of privacy, had refused. Now, how-ever, he made the offer himself and led Simons and Baier up the stairs to his son's bedroom.

It appeared to be much as it had been that evening when Kenneth had yelled down to ask his father to tell Jill Montgom-ery and Raylene Rice he would be just another minute or two. A pair of sneakers lay on the floor at the foot of the bed. Richard went to a nightstand and picked up a box filled with letters and notes his son had kept.

Simons thumbed through them briefly; teenage love letters mostly. Several were from Jill. "Mr. Franks," he said, "I'm not sure if what's in here is any of my business."

"Mine neither," the father said, "but I've read every one of them. Several times. Kenneth had a lot of friends. A lot of peo-ple loved him. It makes me feel good to know that." There was nothing in the contents of any of the letters, he said, that sug-gested any kind of troubles or problems.

As they went back down the stairs Franks said, "If you have time there's something else I'd like for you to see." He led the officers into the den where he put a video cassette into the re-corder.

"I filmed Kenneth's birthday party last February," he said. "I thought you might like to see it."

Simons and Baier sat silently watching the home movie. Kids mugged for the camera, laughed, and danced. Several times Kenneth Franks, alive and obviously enjoying himself, came into frame.

"The party was supposed to be a surprise," Richard reflected, "but Kenneth found out about it somehow. Still, it was fun. Jill didn't come—I don't really remember why—but a lot of his friends from the Methodist Home were here. And his grandparents and little brother. It was a nice party."

Simons watched for another minute, then turned his attention to Franks. He wondered how many times he had sat in that small, darkened room, alone in his sorrow, watching that tape. He saw that tears were again sliding down the father's cheeks.

Finally the screen went blank and the officers stood, offered handshakes to their host, and assured him they would keep in touch. Both were moved by the scene in the den and felt a disquieting uneasiness in the company of such overwhelming grief.

Richard accompanied them to the door and thanked them for coming by. As they walked away he called to Simons. "I like the way you handle your business," he said. "I appreciate what you're trying to do. Please feel free to come by anytime."

"We'll stay in touch," Simons said again. Then, as he began walking away, he stopped and turned to Franks. "The pretty brunette girl who was at the birthday party," he said. "Who was she?"

Franks knew immediately who he was talking about. "She's the girl who helped me plan it. She and Kenneth were close friends. Her name is Gayle Kelley."

# 11

In mid-June of 1982, Gayle Kelley, restless and weary of the restrictions at the Methodist Home, decided to run away—again. She had done so several times since her arrival there, always staying away three or four days before deciding to return. This time, though, she was determined not to come back. She was still a month shy of her seventeenth birthday, that magic age that would free her from the Home's jurisdiction. But what difference did one month make? She was already more than ready to be on her own, free from dorm parents, case workers, and rules.

Gayle and her younger sister had moved to the Home shortly after their mother had died of a heart attack and their father had married a woman who made it clear she had no interest in raising someone else's children. The last time Gayle had seen her father was on that day in October of 1980 when he had driven her to Waco from their home in a Dallas suburb.

After she and Jill Montgomery received their weekly paychecks from the Texas Rangers Hall of Fame that Friday afternoon, Gayle confided to her friend that she was not returning to the campus. She was going to leave town for a few days, take a bus up to Grand Prairie, near Dallas, and visit some friends.

"Are you coming back to the Home when you get back?" Jill asked.

"No way," Gayle said. "I've had it with that place. When I get back I'm going to move in with Patti and get me a job. I'll call you in a few days. Just don't tell anyone where I'm going or anything, okay?"

For the rest of the afternoon they sat behind the counter at the Hall of Fame gift shop, waiting on occasional customers in need of souvenirs or postcards. Nothing more was said about Gayle's plans. Jill was not really surprised at the news that her friend was planning to leave. Or that she was thinking of moving into an apartment with Patti Deis, a girl who had once lived with them at the Methodist Home.

Jill knew Gayle was rebellious and wasn't easily dissuaded once she made one of her spur-of-the-moment decisions to do something. She had never known anyone as free-spirited as Gayle Kelley. Personable, outgoing, and not at all hesitant to speak her mind, Gayle had once eagerly accepted a dare to run through the Methodist Home campus stark naked, stopping in front of the director's house to call him into the front yard. Then there was the time when a campus security officer had stopped her and questioned her about her tardy return from a date. Gayle had winked, smiled, slapped him good-naturedly on the shoulder, and said, "None of your motherfucking business, asshole," then turned and casually walked into the dorm. Her vocabulary included more colorful and imaginative profanities than most of the male students knew.

Yet she was well-liked, one of the most popular girls on the campus. Gayle felt she had Kenneth Franks to thank for that. She had met him the first day she entered the Home and an immediate friendship was struck. The fact that Kenneth accepted her had made it easier for her to get acquainted with others on the campus. Before long, Gayle Kelley was accepted into the innermost circles of campus society.

Though she dated other boys on a fairly regular basis, it was Kenneth with whom she spent most of her free time. Even Kenneth's father had taken an immediate liking to her, often inviting her to accompany him and his son to dinner. Gayle and Kenneth dated a few times, but Gayle, who had come to view Kenneth as her best friend and most trusted confidant, suggested they would be making a mistake to stretch the friendship to something more involved.

"You're the best friend I've ever had," she told him, "and I love you for that. But I'm afraid if we tried going together and got things all complicated we'd spoil it. Let's just be friends."

Soon after that, Gayle introduced him to Jill Montgomery, a friend she had helped secure a job at the Rangers Hall of Fame. Thereafter they were, in the eyes of some, an odd threesome. Kenneth and Jill were clearly in love with each other and were soon dating steadily. At the same time there was no indication that Jill felt any jealousy toward her boyfriend's close relationship with Gayle.

At times friends would chide Kenneth about his "twin girl-friends." They looked enough alike that some thought them sisters.

While Kenneth remained her best friend and she spent a great deal of time with Jill both at work and in the dorm, Gayle had also become close friends with a girl named Patti Deis. In February of 1982, Gayle and Patti first began to hear rumors that a man who had opened a small convenience grocery just across from the Herring Avenue entrance to the Methodist Home was passing out unusual favors to girls who visited his store. Muneer Deeb, other residents were telling them, would give marijuana to girls from the Home, just for the asking. It was Gayle who suggested they pay a visit to the Rainbow Drive Inn as soon as possible.

In short order she had affected the twenty-three-year-old store owner much as she had others with whom she came in contact. Not only did he find her pretty, he admired her high spirit and her confident, outgoing manner. Before long she was clearly his favorite of all the girls who spent time in his store.

Though he asked her to go out with him on several occasions, she made it clear that she had no interest in dating him. Still, he looked forward to her visits to his store. Almost every evening, just after dinner, Gayle stopped by and talked with Deeb for a few minutes, then accompanied him to his car which was parked in back of the store. There he would roll a joint which she would take back to the dorm. It made her sleep better, Gayle told him.

For all the attention and free cigarettes and pot he showered on her, however, Gayle showed no real personal interest in the young Jordanian. Like all the young girls Deeb knew, Gayle was only using him, taking but giving nothing in return. Why not? His dope was the best she'd ever smoked.

One evening, as she sat atop the soft drink box watching a couple of men play video games, Deeb stepped from behind the counter and asked her to go out to his car with him. There he produced an ounce bag of marijuana. It was hers, he said, if she would kiss him.

"Fuck, no," Gayle said.

"Maybe you would let me kiss you," Deeb suggested.

"Fuck, no," she repeated.

"On the cheek?" he persisted.

"How about a handshake?" Gayle said, laughing.

Deeb shrugged. "Okay," he said, shaking with her and handing her the bag of marijuana.

"You know," she yelled over her shoulder as she hurried off in the direction of the Home, "you're lucky to know me."

She could hear Deeb still laughing as she reached the other side of the street. "Yeah, that's me, all right," he yelled. "Lucky."

It was a nickname that stuck. He liked it. Shortly all the girls were calling him that. It was a lot easier than referring to someone as Muneer in a part of the world where it seemed half the male population was named Billy Joe or Jim Bob.

It was Lucky whom Gayle called that afternoon she was planning to leave for Grand Prairie. She asked if he could pick her up at work and give her a ride to the downtown bus station. Without the slightest hesitation, he said he would be right there.

Though he had no idea of her plans or where she might be going, Deeb made arrangements with his partner, Karim Qasem, to close the store that evening. He planned to offer Gayle a ride not just to the bus station but to wherever she wanted to go.

When he asked, she explained that she was running away from the Methodist Home and was going to visit with friends for a few days.

"I need to go to Dallas and see my brother, anyway," he immediately said, "so I'll take you wherever you're going."

"That would be great," she said.

"Let's go," he smiled. "How long are you planning to stay?"

"A few days. Maybe a week."

"And then you will come back to Waco?"

"Yeah, I'm going to move in with Patti and find a job."

"You call me when you're ready to come home," he said, "and I'll come get you. Maybe you can go to work at the store."

"Maybe," Gayle said. Privately, she thought it was a foolish idea. Being that close to the Methodist Home, she would be immediately found and made to return. But since he was furnishing the ride, there was no point in turning him down just yet.

Deeb made most of the conversation on the two-hour trip, talking to Gayle incessantly about his plans for the future and the money his father was sending him every month. He spoke of his native Jordan and told her how he had been orphaned as an infant and found in a cardboard box by the people he now called his parents. There were eleven children in his family, he said. Someday, he hoped, they could all come to the United States where they might capitalize on the opportunities that had been afforded him.

It was as though he felt an urgent need to take advantage of the fact that finally she was his captive audience, telling her everything he could about himself, hoping to hit on something that would impress her or earn him some degree of sympathetic understanding. What Gayle Kelley heard, however, as they drove north into the darkness, were the ramblings of a pathetic, lonely man. And for the first time since she had met him she felt sorry for him.

When he left her in the driveway of her friends' house in Grand Prairie he again insisted she call him whenever she was ready to return to Waco. "Here," he said, placing several bills in her hand before she stepped out of the car. As he drove away she saw that he had given her two hundred dollars.

A week later Deeb arrived in his yellow Triumph to drive Gayle back to Waco. He seemed in better spirits than usual but talked sparingly as he drove. They were nearing Waco when he could not keep the secret any longer.

"You said you were going to live with Patti," he said.

"That's right," Gayle replied.

"I think maybe I have a better deal for you. Tomorrow I'm going to rent an apartment. It can be yours. I will pay for it. And if you want to, you can work for me at the Rainbow."

The idea of having a place of her own excited Gayle. After three years of living in a dormitory setting with twelve other girls, constantly watched over by resident adults, Deeb's offer was inviting. It wouldn't be a great idea to work that close to the Home. But, she decided, what the hell? However, she knew there had to be a catch.

"Are you planning to live there, too?" she asked.

Deeb smiled at her. "Oh, I might stay there some."

"Thanks, but no thanks."

"Why?"

"Lucky," she said, "I'm not going to go to bed with you— ever. Not even for an apartment and all the damn tea in China."

Not taking his eyes from the road, Deeb began to shake his

head and laugh heartily. "You don't have anything to worry about," he finally said. "The truth is, I can't even get it up."

For one of the few times in her life, Gayle Kelley was speechless. *My God*, she thought, *the big ladies' man, the guy who's always flirting with girls and offering them money to marry him, is impotent.*

The following day she accompanied Deeb to a Waco department store where she picked out dishes, towels, a shower curtain, and other furnishings. The bill, which Deeb paid, came to over two hundred dollars. That afternoon she moved into apartment number 144 at the Northwood Apartments, a large complex favored by young adults and students, located across from McLennan County College.

When she stopped by the Rainbow Drive Inn later that afternoon, thinking she might talk more with Deeb about the possibility of going to work there, he was speaking with a man she had never before seen. The visitor was explaining the legal wording of an insurance policy which he was obviously trying to sell. As she waited, sipping on a Coke, Deeb pointed toward her several times and she heard her name mentioned. Finally the salesman approached her with the policy form and asked her birthdate, then requested that she affix her name at the bottom of the final page. Not bothering to read it, she signed, assuming it was the standard workmen's compensation policy that most businesses take out on employees. Obviously, she thought, Deeb had been serious about the job offer.

Had she taken time to read what she was signing she would have seen that it was an accident policy which included a clause providing a twenty-thousand-dollar payment in the event of accidental death. She would also have seen that she was being listed as the common-law wife of Muneer Mohammad Deeb and that he was the beneficiary.

After the insurance salesman left, Deeb told her she could plan on going to work the following week.

This was not the first time Deeb had contemplated insurance fraud. Just a few days earlier he had asked David Spence to wreck his car for him so he could collect the insurance money. Only after Spence had agreed did Deeb find out that any payoffs from the wreckage would have gone not to him but directly to the bank which owned the title to the car.

The next day, having put her new apartment in order, Gayle

called Kenneth and invited him over. He was glad to see her but obviously upset that she had decided to leave the Methodist Home and even more disturbed that she was living in an apartment being paid for by Deeb. For most of the day he tried to persuade her to return to the Home, to finish school, and to stay away from "that asshole Arab."

Gayle and Kenneth were sitting on the floor in the living room talking when Deeb walked in unannounced late that afternoon. His face reddened at the sight of Kenneth and he clenched his teeth. Looking at Gayle, he said in his measured English, "I want to talk with you when I come back tonight after I close the store." Then, briefly focusing his attention on Kenneth, he said something in Arabic before he left, slamming the door behind him.

Kenneth went to the window and watched as Deeb sped from the parking lot. Then, turning to Gayle, he said, "This isn't going to work, you know."

"I know," Gayle said. "Help me get my stuff together so I can move it to Patti's before he comes back."

She took the new dishes and shower curtain with her.

Several times Deeb stopped by Patti Deis' apartment, searching for Gayle. On each occasion, however, either Patti or Kenneth Franks answered the door and insisted she was not there while Gayle hid in a closet. The next time Deeb saw Gayle, in fact, she was riding through the parking lot of the Rainbow with Kenneth on his motorcycle. Watching them through the window, Deeb saw young Franks shoot him the finger as they passed.

A few days later, on the Monday evening following the Fourth of July weekend, Gayle left Patti's apartment and returned to the Methodist Home. She had decided to do it for Kenneth. Reprimanded upon her return, she was immediately placed on two weeks' restriction. She could neither leave the campus nor have guests during that time period.

She was still grounded when she learned that Kenneth, Jill, and Raylene Rice had been found murdered. She heard it on the small clock radio that she kept by her bed. Kenneth's father had given it to her as a Christmas gift.

## 12

Gayle Kelley reached her seventeenth birthday on July 26 and again left the Methodist Home. Now an adult in the eyes of the school administrators, she would no longer have to worry about their trying to find her and force her to return.

A few days later James Kelley, then living in Grand Junction, Colorado, received a letter from his daughter's caseworker notifying him that she had been officially released. "Since Gayle is now seventeen," the letter read, "she is not required to return to the Methodist Home. Also, we had warned her that another runaway would result in her release. She knew exactly what she was doing. I am sorry that she has made this decision but there is nothing we nor you can do about this . . ."

Gayle again moved in with Patti Deis and both applied for waitress jobs at the International House of Pancakes. Still despondent over the deaths of their friends, they rarely left the apartment except to go to work or shop for groceries. Returning from a trip to the supermarket one day, they found that the apartment had been broken into. Though nothing seemed to be missing, the front window had been shattered and the living room furniture overturned.

Patti, initially angry at the damage done to her apartment, screamed when she went into the kitchen. There, on the counter, all the knives had been removed from the drawer and neatly laid out in a row in order of size, from the large butcher knife down to the small paring knife. Next to the knives was a note, printed on a scrap of brown paper, which read, "Sorry we missed you this time but we'll get you next time." The word "next" had been underlined. Patti read the note, wadded it up, and threw it against the wall.

"What's this all about?" Gayle asked. "Is somebody after you for something?"

"I don't know," Patti said, "but I'm going to the police."

Gayle looked at the knives, seeing the bizarre manner in

which they had been arranged. "Somebody's trying to scare you," she said.

"Well," her shaken roommate replied, "they're doing a damn good job."

When Gayle and Patti arrived at the Waco Police Department to report the incident, Patrolman Nicoletti quickly led them into one of the interview areas. He was pleasant and appeared glad to see them. "We've been looking for you two for a couple of weeks," he told them as they sat down.

"Why?" Patti asked.

He explained that he was among those working on the lake murders investigation. "You knew Kenneth Franks, didn't you?"

Gayle Kelley said nothing, but wondered why it had been so difficult for the police to find her. A call to the Methodist Home was all that would have been necessary.

For the next hour they answered questions about Kenneth and Jill, giving the officer names of people who had known each of them. They were puzzled by the fact that the officer asked so many questions about Kenneth's father. Only during the final few minutes of the interview did he express any interest at all in the break-in they had come to report.

Three days later a second break-in occurred. Patti and Gayle had returned from working the midnight-to-seven A.M. shift at the pancake house to find a sticky red substance smeared on the front door. The door, locked when they had left for work, was ajar. This time the living room had not been disturbed but the bedroom had been ransacked. Again nothing seemed to have been taken. This time Gayle telephoned the police.

Patrolman Nicoletti and Detective Salinas came to investigate. But, as before, they showed little concern over the fact that someone had again entered their apartment. Salinas, in particular, wanted only to talk about the lake murders.

Quiet by nature, Patti offered little to the conversation despite repeated questions from the detective. He strongly indicated that he was certain the murders had been drug-related and demanded to know what they knew about any drug dealings in which Kenneth Franks might have been involved.

Gayle became angry. "Ken smoked a little pot, but that's all. We don't know anything about what you're talking about," she said. "This is bullshit."

"I think you're lying," Salinas replied. "I've got a feeling you know something and I want to know what it is."

Gayle stood and glared at the officer as Salinas turned his attention to Patti. Taking her roughly by the arm he led her into the bedroom. Speaking in an angry voice, he pointed his finger at her face and said, "This is serious business and I know you're not telling me everything you know. You've been too damn quiet. Maybe if I go back downtown and get the pictures they took of those kids out at the park and show you what some sorry punk did to them, it might help you remember something."

Patti began to cry. "I don't know anything," she said. "If I did, I'd tell you."

Salinas stared at her for several seconds, then shook his head in disgust. "I ought to throw your ass in jail," he said. He turned and walked back into the living room where Nicoletti was making an attempt to calm Gayle Kelley.

"Leave her alone," Salinas said. "Let's go."

Several nights later Nicoletti stopped by the restaurant during Gayle's shift. "I just wanted to tell you that I believe you and Patti," he said as she served him a cup of coffee.

"What about your friend?"

"Detective Salinas doesn't. He thinks you're lying and that your friend is too quiet for some reason."

"You can tell him," Gayle said, "that we don't give a shit what he thinks."

Nicoletti grinned. "Maybe I'd better let you do that."

She would never get the chance. Neither Gayle nor Patti ever heard from the officers again.

The break-ins and the unsettling encounters with the police were not the only disturbing experiences the girls had in the weeks immediately following the deaths of their friends. Late one afternoon they stopped at a 7-Eleven store for cigarettes and soft drinks. Gayle went inside while Patti remained behind the wheel of the new Thunderbird her father had given her as a graduation present. When Gayle returned she saw two men leaning against the car, talking with Patti.

As she neared the car one of the men looked in her direction and told his Hispanic companion, "There's the bitch we've been looking for."

Gayle recognized the men immediately. She had seen the

Mexican-American guy hanging around the Waco High School campus where he and his brother sold pot to students. The other man she had seen several times in Deeb's store, playing video games. He dated a cashier at the Rainbow named Christy Juhl. Christy had once pointed him out to Gayle, saying that he was "her old man."

Christy had called him David. It had been the first time Gayle had heard his real name. Others in the store had always referred to him as Chili.

As she returned to the car, Gayle heard David ask, "How does it feel to live to be eighteen?"

"What?"

"Nothing," he said, grinning. "Forget it. I thought you just had a birthday."

"I'm only seventeen," she said.

"Remember me?" he asked.

She could tell he was high. "Yeah, you go with Christy."

"Not any more," he said. "You want to go out partying with me?"

"No."

He shrugged. "Well, I just thought maybe since Lucky wasn't getting any you might like to get fucked by a real man."

Gayle did not answer. Instead she turned to Patti. "Let's get out of here," she said.

A week later Gayle saw David again. She decided to stop by the Rainbow to see if Deeb was still angry with her for not having stayed in the apartment he had rented for her. If not, she thought, maybe she could talk to him about the job he had previously offered her. She was already tired of the hours and the two-dollars-an-hour pay at the pancake house.

As she approached the store David was just leaving. "I want to apologize for what I said the other day," he said. "I'd like to make it up to you. Let me take you out sometime."

Gayle gave him a cold look and again a one-word answer. "No," she said.

"What's the matter?" he asked, any trace of politeness quickly gone from his voice. "You think you're too fucking good to go out with me?"

"I just don't want to go out with you," she said as she continued on toward the entrance to the store.

As she walked away he yelled at her. "Hey, you still working the graveyard shift at the IHOP?" She didn't answer, but wondered how he knew the hours she worked. Just as she had wondered earlier how he had known about her having a birthday.

Deeb seemed glad to see her. It was as though nothing had happened. He handed her a soft drink and asked where she had been. She explained that the news of her friends' deaths had upset her a great deal and she had not felt like seeing anyone.

At first he was sympathetic. He knew, he said, how much she thought of Kenneth. "But, you know," he added, "he was asking for something like that. He had it coming." His voice was flat, emotionless.

Stunned by the observation, Gayle dropped the Coke bottle she had been drinking from. It broke as it hit the floor. Already she was turning to leave.

Deeb hurried to the door after her. "Hey, come back. I'm sorry. I was just kidding. Gayle . . ."

She didn't look back at him.

He had wanted to tell her that everything was okay about the apartment, that he had found someone to live there and take up the payments. He had told David Spence—Chili—and his girlfriend, Christy, that they could have the place.

# 13

By early September Gayle and Patti no longer talked about the murders. Both were still having difficulty putting the deaths of their friends out of their minds, but they seemed to have developed an unspoken understanding that neither would bring up the subject. They kept to themselves, working nights and staying in their apartment most days.

Several times Deeb stopped by, uninvited, just to say hello. On his first visit after upsetting Gayle at the store with his remark about Kenneth, both girls told him that if he hoped to be welcome he would never speak of the murders again. Deeb said he understood and agreed. He wanted to be their friend.

On the afternoon of September 12, Gayle answered a knock at the door and opened it to find two Waco Police officers standing there. She was immediately hostile. Simons and Baier had been warned by Nicoletti that they would not be greeted warmly.

"I've already talked to the cops," Gayle said. "I've told them everything I know. So has Patti. I'm tired of people fucking with me about all this. Just leave us alone."

She was especially wary of Truman Simons. He didn't even look like a policeman, dressed in jeans and a western style shirt. As she railed on, vividly expressing her dislike for Detective Salinas in particular and the Waco police in general, Simons listened without saying a word. Finally there was a pause in her tirade.

"You through now?" he asked.

Gayle had no reply.

"Look," he said. "I'm sorry if you've been treated badly by someone else. But you haven't given us a chance. It's our understanding that you were good friends with Kenneth Franks and Jill Montgomery. All we're trying to do is solve this case, and we need your help."

There was something about Simons' manner that calmed her,

and she let them in. Soon she was describing to them her relationship with Kenneth and Jill. The memories were rushing back and, with only a few questions from the officers, she was telling them all about how she had met Kenneth, how she and Jill had become friends, and how difficult it had been for her to cope with their deaths.

The officers had been there about thirty minutes when Simons, who had not said much during the interview, interrupted Gayle. Even while he had been listening to her, his mind had wandered back to that July night when he had crawled through the underbrush at Speegleville Park and first seen Jill Montgomery. "There's something I've been wanting to ask you since we walked in the door," he said.

"What's that?"

"Has anybody ever told you that you look a lot like Jill?"

"Yes," she answered. "At the Home people were always getting us confused. And one of the ladies out at Fort Fisher where we worked was always calling me 'Jill' and Jill 'Gayle.' Kenneth and I even got into some arguments about it. There were a few times when I felt the only reason he liked to be around me was because I looked so much like her."

Simons didn't try to explain why he had asked the question. He wasn't even sure himself.

During the conversation the girls made fleeting mention of Deeb, and Simons tried to pursue the subject without alerting them to the fact that the Jordanian store owner was the closest thing to a suspect they had. Simons had not been able to shake the gut feeling that Deeb was somehow connected to the crime. Still, all they had was the fact that he had disliked Kenneth Franks. But enough to kill him? Or have him killed? And why the two girls? Certainly it would have been easy enough to wait until Franks was alone if, in fact, he was the target.

Simons and Baier had even visited a Baylor University professor who had at one time been assigned to the Middle East by the State Department and was then teaching a course in the culture and religion of that region. He had told them that it was not unusual for families there to take the law into their own hands. If, for instance, someone had cheated a family member in a business deal or stolen a girlfriend it was very likely, almost traditional, that the offender be dealt with privately, by the family.

The placement of the teenagers' bodies in Speegleville had always puzzled Simons. The body of Kenneth Franks had been left in clear view, almost as if whoever killed him wanted him to be found. On the other hand, the bodies of the girls were better hidden. Simons had felt, from that night, that the killers were playing some kind of bizarre game. The professor listened as he described the crime scene. "I just don't know," he had said. "It all sounds very strange. And over there they do a lot of strange things. But I'm afraid I really can't help you much with this sort of thing."

Gayle finally asked the visiting officers if they considered Deeb a suspect in the case.

"At this point we don't really know," Simons said. "We're just interested in finding out a little more about him. Several people have mentioned to us that he and Kenneth Franks didn't get along."

"He didn't like Kenneth," Gayle acknowledged, "but he couldn't have done that business out at the lake. You ever seen the guy? Hell, I could whip him. He's just a little wimp."

Simons asked if Deeb had talked about the murders to her and Patti.

"For a while," she said, "until I told him I didn't want to hear about it anymore. The last time he mentioned it was when he came over here one time to apologize about something shitty he'd said about Kenneth deserving what had happened to him. We started talking about it a little then and I said something about hoping Kenneth had died quickly. Deeb started off on this business about how he didn't—how from what he'd heard Kenneth was tortured and made to die slowly. I got upset at him again and told him to leave. That was the last time he ever mentioned anything about Kenneth."

Simons wondered how Deeb might have known that the youngster had, indeed, been tortured. "Are you friends with Deeb now?" he asked.

"Sort of," Gayle said. "In fact, he's coming over to take us out to a movie tonight."

The officers asked them not to mention to Deeb that they had been there and Simons gave them his card. As they walked toward the door he extended his hand to Gayle. "Thanks for talking to us," he said. She smiled for the first time since they had arrived and shook his hand.

The movie to which Deeb took them that evening was a science-fiction film titled *Endangered Species* and dealt with the investigation of a series of mysterious mutilations of cattle somewhere in rural Colorado. A weak plot, in which a local sheriff and a retired New York policeman attempted to dissuade frightened ranchers from the belief that their herds were being assaulted by aliens from another planet, was carried along by numerous gory scenes of the dead animals. Long before the movie was over the girls had asked to leave.

As Deeb drove toward a nearby Jack-in-the-Box restaurant, Gayle and Patti were quiet. The movie had clearly upset them. They were sitting in line near the drive-in window waiting to order when Deeb asked his companions what they wanted.

"I don't want anything," Patti said.

"Me neither," Gayle said.

"What's the matter?" Deeb asked.

"That lousy movie," Gayle said. "All that damn blood. It got me to thinking about those murders at the lake." She was wondering if she would ever be able to put the imagined scenes of what had happened to her friends from her mind; if there would ever come a time when painful memories would not be triggered by something as simple as a movie.

For several seconds the car was silent except for the barely audible radio which Deeb had turned down in anticipation of giving their order. Looking straight ahead at a car whose back seat was filled with fidgety children waiting anxiously for their orders to be filled, Deeb finally spoke. "I did it," he said. He was almost whispering.

"Did what?" Patti demanded.

"I did it," he repeated. "I killed them."

"My God," Gayle said.

The ringing of the telephone in the den, the only phone in the house, finally woke Judy Simons. It was well after midnight as she made her way down the darkened hall. She didn't even bother turning on a light. Since her marriage to Truman she had answered hundreds of late-night calls after her husband had gone to sleep.

Lifting the receiver she heard the frantic voice of a young woman before she could even say hello. The caller was almost screaming into the phone. "I've got to talk to Sergeant Simons," she said, "right now. Please. It's an emergency."

Judy turned on a light and hurried back to the bedroom to wake her husband. "There's someone on the phone," she said, "and she sounds like she's in some kind of trouble."

Although he is a deep sleeper, Truman was immediately alert and hurried to the telephone. "This is Simons," he told the caller.

"This is Gayle . . . Gayle Kelley. You came by this afternoon. He did it . . . He told us he did . . . I'm scared . . ." She was talking so fast the words ran together.

"Gayle," Truman said, "I can't understand you. Calm down and talk slower. What's going on?"

"Deeb killed Kenneth," she said. Truman could hear her taking a deep breath before she continued. ". . . and he killed Jill . . . and Raylene. He did it."

"How do you know?"

"He told us, goddammit! He told Patti and me tonight. Just a little while ago. We'd gone to the movies and . . ."

Now it was Simons who was having to reign in his excitement. "You think maybe he was joking, just trying to scare you?"

"He tried to act like it afterwards," she said. "Started joking around and said he was kidding. But when he first told us he was as serious as I've ever seen anybody. The sonuvabitch wasn't joking."

Simons asked where she and Patti were and was relieved when she said they had been too scared to stay at their apartment after Deeb had let them off. They had gone to the apartment of one of Patti's friends who lived in the same complex.

"Does Deeb know where you are?"

"No."

"Okay, stay there tonight," he said. "I'll be out to talk with you first thing in the morning."

Truman Simons returned to bed but could not sleep. He was dressed and drinking coffee before the first gray of morning appeared. Growing impatient with Mother Nature's slow awakening, he wasn't going to wait much longer to call Dennis Baier.

\*    \*    \*

Gayle and Patti were both still upset as they re-created the previous evening's conversation with Deeb. It was obvious neither had slept much. Yes, they admitted to the police officers, Deeb was prone to making outrageous statements simply for the shock value. And, yes, they both knew he had lied to them about things before. Yet both steadfastly insisted he had appeared dead serious when he made the remark at the Jack-in-the-Box.

"Did he ever say he was just joking?" Baier asked.

"Yeah," Gayle said, "after he saw how upset we were. He said something like, 'I was just kidding. Don't be mad.' But, hey, I didn't think he was kidding! Not for a second."

Simons had already mapped out a plan before meeting with the girls. If Muneer Deeb really had been involved in the murders and had, for whatever reason, admitted it to them, Truman wanted to know what he was thinking now. Maybe, having realized he had talked too much, he would be nervous. Maybe he would talk even more.

"If you knew you were protected," Truman said to Gayle, "would you consider going by the store sometime today to see Deeb? See if maybe you can get him to talk about it some more?"

"No way," she said. "If he's the one who did those murders I don't want to get within a hundred miles of him."

"We'll have some people close by," Baier said. "We'd make certain you weren't in any danger. It isn't very likely he would do anything crazy in a public place, anyway."

Gayle shook her head vigorously. She looked as if she were about to cry. "I just can't believe it," she said.

"Well," Simons said, "it's gone this far. Now we've got to find out for sure."

She sighed and looked over at Patti. Her roommate did not speak, only nodded.

"Okay," Gayle finally said, "I'll go see him this afternoon."

She was relieved to find several customers in the store when she arrived at the Rainbow Drive Inn. It was nearing five o'clock and people heading home from work early were picking up loaves of bread, bags of ice, and six-packs of beer for the evening. Deeb, working behind the counter, saw Gayle as she entered and waved an indication that he would be with her in a minute.

As she stood there waiting, she wondered how she might bring up the subject of the previous night's conversation. She needn't have bothered.

"Gayle," Deeb said as he approached her, "I'm sorry about what I said last night. I was only kidding. But it was a bad joke." He then quickly changed the subject. "I'm leaving," he said.

"Leaving?"

"The bank is going to foreclose on the store," he said. "I'm going to leave the country tonight."

"But why?" Gayle asked.

"I don't know anything else to do. I'm busy trying to get things ready right now," he said, "but I want to talk to you, to explain everything before I go. Would you come back after we close?"

"At eleven?" Gayle asked.

"Make it around midnight," he said.

"I'll try," she said. She knew she had no intention of ever returning to the Rainbow Drive Inn again.

By early evening the office of Police Chief Larry Scott was filled. Simons and Baier stood near one wall, explaining the recent developments to an assembly which included the chief; Richard Carter, the department's legal advisor; and Brad Cates from the district attorney's office.

Simons reviewed the information they had collected about Deeb, beginning with their conversation with Willie Tompkins and taking the story up to Gayle Kelley's report that Deeb was making plans to leave the country that night. Even as he told his story Simons was aware that the case which had rapidly been built against the Jordanian was one of the weakest he had ever considered seeking an arrest warrant on. There were too many questions for which he had no answers.

"Right now," he admitted, "we don't have that much. This has all come together too fast to really know what we have."

Turning to the assistant D.A., he continued, "I think we've got sufficient probable cause for an arrest, but we're nowhere near having a case that would be prosecutable. All I can say is there is pretty good reason to think he's involved somehow in all this mess and if we let the little bastard get out of the country we're back to nothing."

Simons was asking for time. He knew it would be difficult to keep Deeb in jail for long on the circumstantial evidence he and his partner had collected. But by preventing his fleeing the country they might buy the necessary time to develop a more solid case. Secretly he was thinking that Deeb might even confess once arrested.

Chief Scott instructed the legal advisor to draw up an affidavit for an arrest warrant and get it to Justice of the Peace John Cabaniss.

As they waited for Cabaniss to arrive at police headquarters, Simons telephoned Ramon Salinas and Bob Fortune, asking if they could come down. It had originally been their case and Simons felt they should be involved in the arrest.

The two officers sat listening to what Simons had to say about Deeb. Fortune quickly made it clear he didn't like it. He was not at all certain they had enough to arrest him.

"I'm not real proud of what we've got, either," Truman argued, "but we're in a situation here of either going for it now and hoping we can build a stronger case, or we let the guy get off to hell and gone."

It was clear that Fortune did not share Simons' sense of urgency. "You need me?" The tone of the question rang with lack of interest.

"Dammit," Simons said, "you've spent a lot of time on this case. You and Ramon both. And you're the best interrogator we've got in the department. Hell, yes, I need you. I'd like for you to talk to this guy."

Simons found it difficult to understand the adversary stance Fortune was taking on the matter. Truman had known him since the sergeant had joined the department in the late sixties, and he admired his quick wit and dry humor. They had become friends, working a number of cases together. When Simons was single, Fortune had even lived with him briefly while searching for an apartment of his own. Simons had loaned him the money for the first month's rent.

It had bothered Truman when Chief Scott, aware of help Truman had given Fortune with numerous investigations, began to chide the sergeant about his reliance on his friend to help solve cases. And when Scott had approached Truman about overseeing a proposed major crimes unit following a series of rapes in Waco, he had begged off. The position, he felt, should go to Fortune.

Now, however, things had changed. Fortune was obviously irritated that Simons had been given the lake murders case and was making no attempt to hide the fact. That night would mark the beginning of the end of their friendship. And as time went by, Simons would find that Robert Fortune was not the only one in the department harboring ill feelings about his investigation.

# 14

When 19-year-old Dana Diamond showed up at her older brother's apartment in Waco in June of 1982, he was stern but caring as he talked to her about her aimless wanderings. She had been bumming around long enough, he said, and it was time she settled down and started thinking about her future. She could move in with him, and he would help her find a job. Eventually, he suggested, she might even want to go back to school.

Weary of fending for herself, Dana was not difficult to convince. She had been thinking of moving on to California, but now she put aside her dreams of sunny beaches and moved in with her brother.

His apartment wasn't much, just a one-room upstairs efficiency in a tiny white frame building—one room stacked over another—located behind the gravel parking lot of the Rainbow Drive Inn. It wasn't really big enough for both of them, and Dana was delighted when, after she'd been there just a month, she learned that the couple living downstairs, David Spence and Christy Juhl, were planning to move out. Muneer Deeb, the man who owned the nearby grocery, had offered to sublet them an apartment he had rented. As soon as they left, Dana Diamond moved into their room. Finally she had a place of her own.

Life had been good for Dana since she had settled in Waco. On most days she would sleep late, then walk over to the Rainbow to hang around and visit with the man everyone called Lucky. Of all the people she had met since her arrival, he was the nicest. He smiled at her, talked to her, told her how pretty she was, and never asked her to pay for anything she got from the store.

After a while, he began to ask her out. Though she didn't find him physically attractive, she finally agreed to go out for a hamburger. While they were eating he asked if she would marry him. Thinking he was joking, she laughed. But he went on to explain that he needed to marry to become an American citizen. He offered to pay her five hundred dollars. Not wanting to make him angry, she said she would think about it. She was unaware that he had made the same proposal to a number of other girls.

Though Dana gave Deeb no indication she was interested in anything beyond a friendly relationship, he became angry when she dated someone else. She became uncomfortable with his possessive attitude, and they argued about it frequently. One time a shouting match erupted, ending with Dana shoving Deeb to the ground. The argument took place in the parking lot of the store and several people saw Deeb fall. Their laughter angered him even more and he stormed off, not speaking to Dana for several days.

But, as he always did, he eventually returned to her apartment, carrying soft drinks as a peace offering, and apologized for whatever he might have said to provoke her. And Dana, like all his other female friends, was more than willing to forgive and forget and continue to take advantage of his generosity. He was, after all, harmless.

After a time, though, his attitude seemed to change. The happy, outgoing man she had first met upon her arrival in Waco often seemed to be depressed. He began complaining of not feeling well. And a temper which she had not previously seen was becoming increasingly easy to ignite.

One afternoon, several weeks after she had begun to date the man who would eventually become her husband, Deeb arrived at her apartment with an ultimatum: She would have to choose between him and the man she was dating. When she tried to explain to him that she wanted to be his friend but was in love with the other man, he became furious. "Maybe," he told her, "I ought to wait until he comes over sometime and just blow this place up. That would take care of you both."

Dana had become used to Deeb's outlandish statements and did not feel threatened. "Yeah, I suppose you've killed a lot of people," she shot back.

"Yes, I have," he yelled. "Two." Then he turned and walked back in the direction of the store. Dana picked up a rock and threw it at him. And like all their other arguments, the incident was soon forgotten.

In early September Deeb told Dana he had purchased a new Thunderbird and she agreed to accompany him on an afternoon drive. Though obviously proud of his new car, Deeb was unusually quiet as he wound through the residential areas of north Waco onto the highway leading toward the lake. Eventually, they crossed the twin bridges and turned into Speegleville Park.

Deeb drove to a small picnic area bordered by woods on one side and the lakefront on the other and stopped. For several minutes they sat in the car, only the lingering summer bird sounds breaking the silence. Finally Deeb spoke. "Dana," he said, "there's something I want to talk to you about."

She waited but he said no more. He appeared tense and more withdrawn than she had ever seen him. "Lucky, what's the matter?" she asked.

"Nothing. Nothing important." He started the engine. "I'd better get back to the store," he said.

On the night of September 13, 1982, Deeb stopped by Dana's apartment. It was almost ten o'clock and she had already gone to bed, but she let him in when he said he had something important to tell her. Appearing scared and nervous, he initially made little sense, rambling from one train of thought to another. Dana wondered if maybe he had been taking uppers. Pacing and gesturing wildly, he told her about visiting a fortune teller the day before who had warned him of bad things in his future.

"She was right, you know," he said. "The bank is taking the store away from me. I've got to leave. I'm going back to my own country. I just wanted to tell you good-bye."

Dana immediately assumed it was another of his acts, a play for her sympathy. His story, she figured, was nothing more than a ploy to persuade her to let him in and it angered her. To get him to leave she asked him to go back to the store and bring her a soft drink. As soon as he left she locked the door and returned to bed.

Truman Simons, concerned that Deeb had not been in the store when he and his fellow officers arrived, sat upright in the front seat of his unmarked car when he saw the Jordanian walking across the gravel parking lot. They had been waiting for almost an hour, the fear that Deeb might already have gotten away growing with each passing minute.

"That's him," Simons said, getting out of the car and hurrying across the street toward the Rainbow.

Deeb had not even reached the soft drink box before he felt

the handcuffs close around his wrists and heard the policeman reading him his rights.

"What's this all about?" he asked.

"You're under arrest for the murder of Kenneth Franks," Simons said.

"That's crazy," Deeb said. "I don't know what you're talking about."

Sitting in an interrogation room at the police department, Muneer Deeb was trying to avoid eye contact with the men who were asking him questions. He repeatedly insisted that he had never even heard of Kenneth Franks. Pale and perspiring, he said he knew of no instances where anyone had driven a motorcycle through the store parking lot and yelled curses or made obscene gestures.

He denied having told Patti and Gayle that he had killed the kids at the lake, saying that Gayle was probably mad at him about something and had fabricated the story in a crazy attempt to get him in trouble. Deeb was admitting to nothing.

After a while he asked that they call Willie Tompkins. Willie, he said, was his friend. He was once a policeman. Willie would tell them he could not be involved in anything like what they were talking about. Frustrated that the interrogation was yielding no results, Simons called Tompkins.

When the former police officer arrived he was briefed on what had transpired, then taken in to speak with Deeb. For the first time since his arrest, the Jordanian smiled. Hurriedly he began to explain how the police had arrested him and that he knew nothing about what they were saying.

Suddenly, in the sparsely furnished, stuffy interrogation room, Willie Tompkins was a police officer again. The easygoing manner he had always displayed during Deeb's late-night visits to Skaggs became businesslike. Sitting across from the man with whom he had shared numerous cups of coffee and hours of casual conversation, Tompkins spoke in a voice which seemed too gentle to come from such a large man. "Deeb," he said, "you're in a lot of trouble. The only way these people can help you is for you to shoot straight with them. I'm sorry about the mess you're in—I really am—but the only thing for you to do is tell them the truth. It'll be easier for you in the long run."

"Willie," Deeb said in a pleading voice, "I don't know what

they're talking about. I don't know those people who were killed."

"Wait a minute," Tompkins said. "Remember that night out at Skaggs when you told me you knew the boy who was killed and that you felt he got what he deserved? You even told Patty and me that the girls had been in your store that day. Remember that?"

Momentarily Deeb seemed angry. There was a new urgency in his voice. "Willie, I *don't* know any of them," he said. "Whose side are you on?"

Tompkins shook his head. "Deeb, are you saying I'm a liar? You know I'm a preacher. I'm not going to sit here and lie to you or anybody else. You told me you knew that boy—and the girls."

"You're mistaken," Deeb said, leaning back into his chair. "I don't know any of those people. I swear."

Willie rose, his huge frame towering over the frail-looking prisoner. He waited for a minute, hoping Deeb might say something else. Deeb only stared down at the table in front of him. He didn't even look up as Tompkins left the interrogation room.

Outside, Willie looked at Simons and shrugged. "I would have bet my life he would fall apart in a situation like this," he said. "Looks like I'm wrong. I'm afraid you've got your work cut out for you."

"Thanks for coming down," Truman said.

Simons then approached Sergeant Fortune. "We're getting nowhere with him," he said. "You're a lot better at this than I am. Want to give it a try?"

Fortune spent almost an hour with Deeb, alternately taking sips from a coffee cup and asking questions. Deeb told him no more than he had the others.

"He's not taking it," Fortune said as he approached Simons' desk.

"That's what I was afraid of."

"He said you asked him about somebody named Chili."

"Yeah," Simons said. "I was just throwing names at him. I don't even know who this Chili dude is."

"Is he a suspect in the case?"

"I don't know. Maybe. He's some guy who hangs around the store out there. When I mentioned him, Deeb said he's crazy, the kind of guy who might do something like the lake killings."

For the first time all evening, Fortune displayed a faint sign of interest. "He might be worth checking on," he said. "His name's David Spence. He's in jail right now on some kind of aggravated sex thing. Evidently he's a cutter. Big shot with a knife. In fact, it seems like his name came up a time or two when we were first looking into the lake case but I never had a chance to check him out. You put him and Deeb together somehow—then you might have something."

"Like I told you this afternoon, Bob, I think we *already* have something." Simons felt a knot of resentment forming in his stomach.

Deciding that further interrogation that night would be fruitless, Simons and Baier saw that Deeb was placed in a cell and called it a night. Both ached with fatigue as they sat in front of Baier's house for a while, talking more about the lack of interest shown by their fellow officers than the hurry-up case they had made against Deeb.

"I told you," Truman said, "the shit might get heavy before this is over."

"I know," Dennis said.

"Well, it's just starting."

While sitting in wait for Deeb to return to the store, Simons had turned off his car radio, fearful that it might draw attention to the stakeout. In the excitement of the events that followed he had forgotten to turn it back on. When he arrived home in the early morning hours Truman's wife told him the dispatcher had been trying to reach him. Deeb had apparently become quite upset and had insisted to the jailer that he be allowed to talk with Simons.

Feeling a rush of new energy, Truman drove back to the police department and had the prisoner returned to the interrogation room. But if Deeb had wanted to tell him something of value, the urge had been lost in the time lapse. By the time Truman arrived he was again calm, again saying that he knew nothing about the murder of Kenneth Franks.

"Look," Simons reasoned, "I'm not saying you killed him. I'm saying that I think you were involved. There's a difference." For several minutes he tried to explain the laws related to parties to an offense as opposed to those applying to one directly involved in a crime. Deeb listened intently, then again protested his innocence. Simons knew he was getting nowhere. He was going back home, he said, to get some sleep.

Deeb stood up, ready to be escorted back to his cell. "I didn't do it," he said again. "I don't know anything about it. But I know you want me to say I do. If you want me to, I'll lie and say I did."

Simons turned and looked at Deeb. Several times during his career he had heard the same offer made by criminals during the early stages of interrogation. In each case they had been guilty. And they had ultimately broken down and admitted their guilt. Maybe, he thought, things were moving in the right direction.

"Nope," he said, "we're not going to play it that way. But when you decide to tell me the truth, I'll be ready to listen."

As soon as word reached the newsroom of the *Waco Tribune-Herald* that a suspect had been arrested in the two-month-old lake murders case, reporters began a mad scramble to gather information on Muneer Mohammad Deeb.

Though born in Jordan, he had entered the United States through Saudi Arabia with a brother named Ali. Since his arrival in 1979, he had briefly attended both Texas State Technical Institute and McLennan County College, each time enrolling and then dropping out before the semester ended. He and a partner had opened the Rainbow Drive Inn ten months earlier.

There were quotes from a former landlady who described him as "handsome and polite and always prompt with his rent payments." Several customers and part-time employees of Deeb's store expressed their disbelief that he could even be suspected of such a horrendous act. "He's a good person," one said. "He wouldn't even kill a fly."

In his statement to the press, Police Chief Scott was careful to explain that the arrest had, by necessity, been made sooner than he and his investigators would have liked, but since they had reason to believe the suspect was planning to leave the country they had felt it necessary to move swiftly. He went on to caution reporters that the arrest had "not necessarily busted the case wide open" and that a great deal of work remained to be done before the full story of the Lake Waco murders could be told.

The story, bannered across the front page, said that Deeb was being held under $100,000 bond and that Richard McCall, son of the chancellor at Baylor University, had been retained as counsel. Nowhere in the story was there mention of the investigators who had made the case against Deeb.

When Truman Simons and Dennis Baier reported to work the following morning, several detectives and uniformed officers were already in their office eagerly awaiting details of the arrest. Lieutenant Marvin Horton, one of the original investigators on the case, was standing in the doorway of his office, which adjoined theirs, when Simons and Baier came in. He waited until they had reached their desks, then shouted across the room, "I can tell you one thing you guys did."

"What's that?" Simons replied.

"You just fucked up the whole goddamn case."

"How do you figure that?" Simons said, his body stiffening as he spoke.

"Hell, that guy didn't have anything to do with this case. You just fucked up the whole thing by arresting him, that's all."

Simons said nothing more but walked quickly to where the lieutenant stood, grabbed him by the arm, and escorted him into his own office, slamming the door behind them.

"Look," Simons said, no longer making any attempt to suppress his anger, "you've got a right to your opinion but I didn't like that little show one damn bit. You don't have any idea what we've got on this guy. And I damn sure don't see where it's up to you to determine whether we've got the right guy or not.

"The truth is, I don't give a dime's worth of shit what your opinion is. So, you just stay out of my way and I'll do you the same favor."

Simons returned to the detectives' office and motioned to Baier. "Let's go for a ride," he said. Baier, who had been in the Chief's office blowing off steam about Horton's tirade at the same time his partner had been confronting the lieutenant, eagerly accepted the opportunity to get out of the office.

While stopped at a signal light, Truman turned to glance at the driver of the car which had pulled up next to him. The driver had long hair, a skinned nose, and a black eye. He was looking back at Truman and shooting him the finger.

"That sonuvabitch," Truman said. He jumped from behind the wheel and yanked open the passenger door of the man's car. As soon as the driver saw the policeman's badge he began a profuse apology. "I'm real sorry, officer. I really am. I didn't know who you were."

"A guy can get himself kicked around a helluva lot more than it looks like you've already been if he goes around shooting the finger at the wrong people," Truman said.

"Well, sir," the man said, "you just don't understand. See, I've had a really bad day."

Truman stared at him for a second. "Bad day? You've had a bad day? Motherfucker, you don't even know what a bad day is." He slammed the door and returned to his own car. Dennis Baier was trying with little success to suppress his laughter. Truman gave him an angry look, then rocked his head back and grinned. And began to laugh himself.

"Feel better now?" Dennis asked.

"Yeah," his partner answered, "a little."

Much of the day following Deeb's arrest was spent sorting through phone messages from people whose interest in the case had suddenly been revived. Simons automatically dismissed the requests for calls to the media, searching for the names of callers who might have information that would help to solidify the case against the man now in jail.

As he thumbed through the scraps of paper his phone rang again. Nancy Shaw and Jan Thompson, the mother and aunt of Jill Montgomery, were both on the line, calling from Waxa-hachie on two extensions. A mixture of excitement and anger was clearly evident in their voices.

Simons hurriedly explained that he had just been assigned to the case for a few days. He had meant to get in touch with them, but things had moved so fast that he just had not had time. He then told them that the case against Muneer Deeb was not as solid as he would like. "I feel like we've got the right man," he said, "but there's a lot more to this than we've found out yet."

It was Jan Thompson who spoke after listening to what he had to say. Her voice was soft, almost lyrical in a rural Texas kind of way. But there was also a firmness that suggested strength and determination.

"Mr. Simons, we appreciate what you're doing, and we don't want to bother you unnecessarily. But we've been in the dark about the investigation of Jill's death for several months now.

Frankly, we haven't been pleased with the way we've been treated. We feel we have a right to know . . ."

"You have every right to know," Truman said. "I apologize for not calling you. And I promise to keep in touch as things progress."

There was a moment's silence on the line, then Jan spoke again. "Mr. Simons," she said, "God bless you."

As he replaced the receiver he tried to imagine what the two women looked like and to comprehend the agony that had absorbed them since that night two months earlier when they learned that Jill Montgomery had been murdered. He knew that in the days to come he would get to know both women well. In a manner of speaking it was one of the extraordinary rights afforded one investigating an unexplained death, that as a stranger he would be free to go to the heart of personal matters. There were times when such entree into the secret lives of others caused him discomfort. A private man himself, he understood the resentment that often followed questions which normally he would have had no right to ask. It was the only way he knew, however, to find the needed answers.

Just a week earlier, he recalled, he had read a letter to the editor of the *Waco Tribune-Herald* which had been written by Jill's aunt. It had been a moving appeal to the citizens of Waco: "There is someone, somewhere, who saw or heard something unusual that night," she had written. "This letter is directed to that someone. As a member of the family of one of the victims, I am pleading for you to come forward with your information . . ."

Truman Simons, aware that he was racing against the clock, was feeling the same sense of urgency.

After his visit to the police station to talk with Deeb the previous night, Willie Tompkins had returned to Skaggs where he and Patty Pick talked for several hours. Patty was surprised that Deeb had been arrested and found it hard to believe what the security officer was telling her. Deeb might be a braggart, might even occasionally tip-toe along the edges of the law, but she could not imagine him as a murderer.

As Willie and Patty tried to think of people who might be able to provide more information about Deeb, Patty recalled that he had once mentioned another girlfriend at a time when he was angry with Kasey. Her name was Dana Diamond and she lived in a small apartment across the parking lot from Deeb's store. Perhaps she might have seen or heard something.

The following evening, after a call from Tompkins, Simons and Baier knocked on Dana Diamond's door.

She explained to them how she had met Deeb, that he had bought her groceries occasionally and how, at one time, he had proposed marriage to her.

"Did you ever hear him make any threats against any of the people who were killed at the lake?" Simons asked.

"No, not really. But . . ."

"But, what?"

"Well," she said, "I was in the store one night right after the murders and Lucky was behind the counter, reading the paper. I guess he must have been reading about the kids having been killed. Anyway, after we had talked for a few minutes, he picked up a brown envelope and sort of waved it and said he had just missed collecting twenty thousand dollars. He said he had some kind of insurance policy on the sister of one of the girls who had been murdered."

"Did he show you the policy?" Simons asked.

"No, I just figured it was in that envelope. Really, I wasn't paying that much attention to what he was saying. I was just there to get something to drink."

As the officers drove Dana Diamond to the police station to take her statement they said little. Both, however, were feeling they had found another piece of the puzzle. There was now a motive for the crime.

## 15

Karim Qasem had come to the United States from Saudi Arabia, married Maria, a Mexican-American from south Texas, and moved into a small house across the street from Muneer Deeb in the spring of 1981. The two men soon became friends, spending evenings together sharing memories of their homelands and talking about their futures in America. Muneer enjoyed Maria's cooking and her easy, laughing manner. Sometimes he would stay after dinner, visiting until he fell asleep on the couch. Rather than wake him, Maria would get a blanket from the closet, place it gently over him as if she were tending a child, and let him spend the night.

Both men attended Texas State Technical Institute, a small business college in Waco which specialized in computer technology. Immigration regulations required them to be enrolled in school if they wished to keep their visas, but neither had any real interest in their classes. Both were more interested in grabbing a piece of the American Dream, speaking often of entering into a business partnership with money they were sure their parents would provide.

By the end of 1981 they were talking seriously about an equal partnership in a small grocery store. In mid-February of the following year they secured the lease on a building on Herring Avenue which had, at one time, housed a Zippy Food Store. With a residential area on one side, businesses on another, and the Methodist Home nearby, it seemed an ideal location. They would call it the Rainbow Drive Inn.

Initially, only Karim, Maria, and Muneer worked the long, demanding hours, taking turns opening at six each morning and closing each night at eleven. As business improved, Deeb persuaded his partner to agree to the hiring of a young woman named Christy Juhl. She was a good worker, friendly to customers and agreeable to working an occasional double shift. Maria, jealous by nature, was at first wary of the young woman, fearful that her husband might find her attractive. She was relieved when the girl's boyfriend began appearing at the store, sometimes staying through Christy's entire shift, playing video games. Maria didn't like David Spence. He often arrived barefoot and without a shirt, sometimes cursed loudly while playing the games, and got into arguments with Christy. Maria thought his nickname—Chili—was silly and refused to use it. But she found a strange kind of comfort in his presence. As long as he was around, Christy wouldn't be flirting with her husband.

Within Waco's small Muslim community, the Qasems were Muneer Deeb's closest friends as well as his business partners. However, they were not particularly upset when he was arrested because they were certain he could not be involved in such a crime and would undoubtedly be released soon.

A young man named Mahir Tumimi at first shared the Qasems' faith in Deeb, although eventually, he would wonder. Tumimi was an Israeli who had met Deeb during classes at TSTI and struck an immediate friendship with the Jordanian. He often pointed to the irony of their relationship. In their respective homelands they would have been natural enemies.

Fluent in seven languages, including Arabic, Tumimi often dropped by the Rainbow Drive Inn. Maria Qasem had always assumed he came to visit with Deeb and paid little attention to the fact that Mahir spent an increasing amount of time in the company of Christy Juhl. It came as a surprise to Maria when Christy suddenly married Tumimi after she and David Spence broke up following an argument in late July of 1982. She was not particularly surprised, however, when the new bride quit her job at the Rainbow and left town while her husband remained.

Though unlawful, it was far from uncommon for immigrant males in the United States to negotiate a convenient marriage that would provide them citizenship. Maria knew that Deeb had offered several women money to marry him. Privately, she assumed Mahir had done the same and had been more successful in finding someone agreeable to his proposal.

Truman Simons knew little about Christy Juhl when she called him from Fort Worth shortly after Deeb's arrest. Her name had been mentioned by several of those whom he had interviewed, but all he knew was that she worked at the Rainbow and was the girlfriend of David Spence.

She had telephoned Truman from Fort Worth, expressing surprise and concern over what was happening. First, her boyfriend had been jailed for aggravated sexual abuse and now Deeb had been arrested and charged with murder. Voicing an enthusiasm which puzzled him, she told Simons she had some information that might interest him and was planning to take the next bus back to Waco. He agreed to meet her at the Greyhound station at eleven o'clock that night.

When she arrived, Simons was surprised to see a well-dressed foreigner embrace her as she stepped off the bus. The officer was sure the girl was Christy Juhl; she had given him a description of herself earlier in the day, after complaining about her boyfriend being in jail.

"I'm Christy," she said to Simons, "and this is my husband, Mahir Tumimi."

Simons hoped his face didn't register his astonishment.

Tumimi accompanied the officer and Christy back to the police station where Simons spent an hour with the former Rainbow Drive Inn cashier. It was time wasted. If she knew anything about the murders or Deeb's involvement she was not saying anything. Hyper and nervous, she said nothing at all that made any sense.

Frustrated, Simons finally rose from his chair and said, "Christy, it was my understanding that you had something you wanted to tell me. Unless we had an awfully bad connection this afternoon, I heard you say you felt you could help me with this case."

"Oh, no," she said. "I just wanted to come down and find out what was going on. This whole thing just freaks me out."

Containing himself, Simons said, "Well, we're not in the business of passing out information here. We gather it. If all you want to do is 'freak out,' I suggest you go somewhere else to do it. I'm a little busy for chitchat right now."

He left the room and went to the coffee room where Mahir sat waiting.

"I hear Deeb's people are pretty upset about his being in jail," he said.

Mahir nodded.

"What are they doing?"

"I think they're looking for the people who were mentioned

in the paper," Mahir said, "the girls who say Deeb told them those things about the murders at the lake."

"I was afraid of that," Simons said. "Why don't you take your wife on home now. She's wasted enough of our time." He deliberately added a heavy emphasis to the words "wife" and "wasted."

An hour later he checked Gayle Kelley and Patti Deis into the Sheraton Hotel. "I want to get you out of town for a while," he explained. "Do either of you have out-of-town relatives you could visit?"

Gayle mentioned her grandparents in Henrietta, a small community in north Texas near Wichita Falls. "Okay, call and tell them you're coming. Don't call anyone else and don't leave this room until you hear from me. We'll get your stuff packed tomorrow," Simons said.

That night as he tried to sleep, he tossed and turned, the events of the recent days rumbling angrily through his head. He was upset at the media for printing the details of the arrest warrant, possibly placing his witnesses in danger. He was disappointed with the attitude of fellow police officers, many of whom had already begun to avoid him, obviously siding with Lieutenant Horton. He was angry with Alex Sanchez, the high school coach and part-time insurance salesman he had spoken with who had reluctantly admitted selling Deeb "some kind of policy." Sanchez recalled it as a health insurance policy. Only after checking with the local office of Southern Life and Health Insurance Company had Simons learned that Deeb had paid the first premium on an accident/injury insurance policy which included a $20,000 accidental death clause and named Deeb as beneficiary. Under the terms of the insurance contract, murder was considered "accidental death."

And he was disgusted with Christy Juhl. He was certain she knew more than she was telling, especially about the relationship between Deeb and David Spence. Working long hours in the store, it was also likely that she had heard some of Deeb's comments about Kenneth Franks. Somewhere, somehow, she was part of the puzzle. But where did she fit?

Early the next morning he spoke with Christy Juhl's mother. She was anxious to know if her daughter had told him anything about the case. She explained how Christy had returned to live at home shortly after splitting with David, nervous and behaving strangely. At any mention of the lake murders on the television or radio, Christy would become very quiet and lock herself in her room for several hours.

"Mr. Simons," the mother added, "Christy won't be honest with you. Ever since she was a little girl she's been a liar. A very convincing one, I might add."

The mother's frank admission affirmed what Simons already feared. Christy Juhl was not going to be much help.

From the moment Richard McCall was retained as Deeb's attorney he had pushed to have a polygraph test administered to his client, informing the press that Deeb was eager to take the test and prove his innocence. He also insisted that no further interrogation of Deeb be conducted unless he was present. Deeb, meanwhile, told jail officials that he was beginning a hunger strike which would not end until he was released.

The first to ask Simons when he was going to have Deeb run on the polygraph was Lieutenant Horton. "When I'm damn good and ready," Simons snapped, glaring at the man who had so suddenly become his adversary.

Simons was perplexed by Horton's attitude. He had heard from several detectives that Horton had said if any of them assisted Simons in the investigation they would soon find themselves back in uniform, working patrol.

And the day before his confrontation with the lieutenant, Simons had walked by Ramon Salinas's desk and heard him listening to a tape recording of a telephone conversation which seemed related to the murders. When Truman asked about it, Salinas nervously explained that Horton had asked him to listen to it but had said to be sure and keep it from Simons. Salinas gave the tape to Truman only after having him promise to return it immediately and not to tell Horton he had listened to it.

On the tape, a girlfriend of Christy Juhl was telling Horton that she felt Muneer Deeb was probably involved in the murders. And if Muneer was involved, the female voice continued, there was a good chance that Mahir Tumimi, Christy Juhl, and her boyfriend, a guy named Chili, were involved too.

That same afternoon, as Simons was preparing to leave, he was approached by an officer from the Crime Prevention Section who asked if he was on his way to meet the woman who had called the department's Crime Stoppers number, saying she had information about Deeb.

"I don't know what you're talking about," Simons said.

"Didn't Horton give you the message? She wouldn't give her name but gave a description and said what she would be wearing. You're supposed to meet her at the entrance to Lake Air Mall at five-thirty."

It was almost six by the time Simons and Baier reached the mall. The woman was walking toward the parking lot, preparing to leave. After the officers quickly identified themselves, she told them about a heated argument she had overheard Deeb and Christy Juhl having in the Rainbow. Deeb, obviously angry with Christy, had threatened to call the police, the woman said. "Then Christy said, 'Go ahead and call the police if you want to. Whenever they leave here, you'll be the one in the back seat, not me.' "

"Do you remember anything else she said?" Baier asked.

"Yeah," the woman said, "she told Deeb she knew enough about him and David to put them away for the rest of their lives."

Later that night, Richard Franks called Simons at home to ask about the investigation of Deeb. "I tried to call you at the office," he explained to Simons, "but you were out, so I talked with Horton. He told me there was no way Deeb was involved in Kenneth's murder, that he would be released soon."

"Did he say anything about me?" Truman asked.

"He said you were trying to make yourself into some kind of hero."

"I appreciate your honesty," Truman said.

Never during his law enforcement career had Simons been comfortable with the use of the polygraph to determine a suspect's involvement in a crime. There were too many variables, too many things left to chance. Deeb, he was convinced, was a poor candidate for such a test for the simple reason that his cultural background was light years removed from that of native Americans. His philosophies toward right and wrong, truth and untruth, might be much different from those of one raised with the morality standards of the United States. Simons knew that studies had shown that people from countries where lying did not carry the same social stigma as in the United States were more likely to be considered honest by the machine.

Thus he hoped to stall the test for as long as possible. There was a great deal more investigating to be done before he could even determine what kinds of questions to ask Deeb when such a test was given.

If the crime was as involved and complicated as he was beginning to believe, he knew he was a long way from sorting out the characters in the increasingly bizarre play. But he was beginning to see the hazy outline of a plot.

He was sure Deeb was involved in the murders but he was equally sure he had not actually committed them. The purchase of the insurance policy on Gayle Kelley hinted strongly at the possibility of a motive. To a lesser degree, so did his apparent dislike for Kenneth Franks. If Deeb had wanted Gayle and Kenneth dead, one for financial reasons and the other out of pure vengeance, he might have arranged for someone to do the killings for him. Since they bore such a physical resemblance, it also seemed possible that Jill Montgomery might have been mistaken for Gayle by the killer—killers?—Deeb had hired. If his scenario was right, Raylene Rice had been the most innocent of victims: a person who simply happened to be in the wrong place at the wrong time.

If he was right—and he was strongly beginning to feel he was—he was looking at a murder-for-hire, mistaken identity case more complicated than any he had ever encountered.

The day after their first meeting, Mahir Tumimi called Simons to ask if he might see Deeb. Since he spoke Arabic, he said, perhaps he could get a better understanding of just what his friend was involved in. "I am sure he is not the man who did those crimes," Mahir said, "and I would like to help him prove it." Simons agreed to allow the visit.

When Tumimi returned to Simons' desk after spending almost an hour with Deeb, he was grim-faced and shaken. "That," he said, "is not the Muneer Deeb I know."

"What do you mean?"

"He should be embarrassed by all of this, even frightened," Mahir said in his careful English. "But he is acting as if he is enjoying it. He seems proud that he has been arrested and is getting so much publicity. He said he is now famous. I have never seen him this way. He frightened me."

Later that afternoon Simons and Baier accompanied Gayle and Patti back to their apartment and helped them load their belongings into a U-Haul trailer. Simons gave them a hundred dollars expense money and told them to go to Henrietta. Before they left, Gayle gave him the address and telephone number of her grandparents.

The following Saturday afternoon, September 18, Muneer Deeb was given a series of polygraph tests which lasted almost three hours. Simons had been unable to stall any longer. The examiner, using a list of questions Simons had helped him compile, reported that the subject had indicated no sign of deception.

After the tests were completed, a meeting was held in Chief Scott's office. Among those attending was Felipe Reyna, the district attorney who had recently lost in his bid for a new term to a political newcomer named Vic Feazell. Chief Scott was the first to broach the subject of releasing Deeb. "Have you come up with anything since arresting him that would warrant our holding him any longer?" he asked.

Simons, sitting on the floor with his back against the wall, shook his head. His despair permeated the room. "Nothing I'm really comfortable with," he finally said.

"Well," Scott said, "you gave it a good shot. Maybe if we cut him loose he'll think he's in the clear and won't leave. That would give you time to come up with something."

"Maybe," Simons said.

"Wait a minute," Reyna said, turning toward the dejected officer. "Are you satisfied that this guy was involved in the murders?"

"I damn sure am."

"Then turn him over to the county. Hell, I've already lost the election. I'll take the heat off the police department and say we're not going to turn him loose as long as we feel he's a suspect." Even as he spoke he knew how unlikely it was the police department would agree.

"No, we've got to let him go," Truman said tracing imaginary circles in the carpet. "I hate it like hell, but we've got to let him go—for now."

The district attorney walked over to him and gripped his

shoulder. "Don't let it get you down. Stay after him. You'll get him."

Reyna then turned to Larry Scott. "I've been hearing a lot of talk about what's been going on in this office since Deeb was arrested," he said, "and I've got just one thing to say: If Truman Simons can't solve this case, it never happened."

In the hallway, Simons encountered Deeb's attorney who was passing time, awaiting the paperwork necessary for Muneer's release. He was smiling.

"Do you still consider my client a suspect?" McCall asked.

"You bet your sweet ass," Simons shot back. "I'd never have arrested him if I didn't think he was involved. And I'll tell you something else, you're going to earn your money before this is all over."

As Simons walked toward his office he was approached by one of the detectives who worked in the Offenses Against Persons section. "Sarge, can I talk to you for a minute?" he asked.

"Come on in," Simons replied.

"I was just wondering what you think about all this," the detective said.

"I think we're fixing to turn a guilty sonuvabitch loose."

"Look, we don't know each other very well," the detective said. "But if there's anything I can do to help, just let me know."

"I appreciate that," Simons said. "I haven't exactly been flooded with offers lately."

"That's what I understand. Lieutenant Horton and Sergeant Fortune both called in to find out how the test went and they seemed pretty pleased about the results. Fortune really seemed glad. He said, 'All I've got to say about it is ha-ha-ha.' Really sounded childish. It just kind of hit me wrong that they would take that kind of an attitude."

Simons managed a weary smile. "It hits me kind of wrong, too."

The detective left, quietly closing the door behind him. For several minutes Truman sat alone, replaying the incredible sequence of events that had taken place since he had asked to investigate the case. He had made more progress in a matter of days than a dozen detectives had made in two months. Yet for reasons that baffled him, everyone in the department seemed to be fighting him. Sitting there in the welcome privacy, he arrived at a decision with which he had been wrestling for some time.

*     *     *

As Karim and Maria drove Deeb from the police station Deeb repeatedly expressed his anger toward Gayle Kelley, blaming her for what had happened to him. She was one of those people, he said, who enjoy causing others problems. "You just watch. Someday she will die, too." That said, his mood lifted. Suddenly he was more carefree than either had seen him in some time.

It was over, he said. Even if the police did think he was guilty, they could not arrest him a second time for the same crime. "It's called double jeopardy," he said.

Obviously, he had picked up some faulty information about the American judicial system, since double jeopardy applies only to the retrying of an individual for the same crime and has nothing to do with arrests.

"What are you going to do now?" Maria asked.

"There are some people on my back here," Deeb said, his voice again turning serious. He mentioned no names. "I'm going to Dallas to visit some friends who will come down here and take care of things for me."

Maria and Karim, seated in the front of the car, looked at each other but said nothing. In the backseat, Deeb relaxed, drinking in the joy of freedom. He didn't know that Truman Simons, assuming he would stay in touch with Patty Pick regardless of where he went, had already persuaded her to keep him informed of Deeb's whereabouts in the days to come.

Truman Simons was in no mood to enjoy anything as he drove from the police station to a picnic marking the end of his wife's softball season, but he had promised Judy he would meet her there. By the time he arrived, the radio had announced several times that Deeb had been cleared and released.

Judy Simons had heard the reports on her way to the picnic and knew her husband would be in no mood for a party. "You okay?" she asked as he arrived.

"I've been better," he said.

Ramon Salinas, whose wife played for the same team as Judy, approached. "Sorry to hear about your man," he said. Truman detected no genuine sympathy in his fellow officer's voice.

While others ate and applauded the traditional trophy presentations, he stayed near the beer keg. As the party progressed into the night, he wondered if he was only imagining that Ramon Salinas was in higher spirits than usual throughout the evening.

"Fuck 'em all," Truman whispered to himself. He'd already had a few too many beers, but Judy, watching him, said nothing. She understood the disappointment ripping at him. She also sensed that something else was bothering him in addition to the release of Muneer Deeb. There had to be something more, and Judy Simons knew she would be hearing about it very soon.

Truman waited until Sunday evening before placing a call to Captain Dan Weyenberg of the McLennan County Sheriff's Department. A trusted friend, Weyenberg had been the chief of police in the little town of Robinson where Truman grew up. There was no other law enforcement officer in Waco whom Truman admired more. Many more times than he could remember he had gone to the sheriff's department for advice, even help, from the captain while working on a case.

He and Weyenberg talked briefly about Deeb before Truman got around to the purpose of his call.

"Captain," he said, "I'm going to quit the police department. I've had all the shit I'm going to put up with over there."

"What are you going to do?" Weyenberg asked.

"I'll go back to working on cars if I have to," Truman said, "but if you've got a place for a jailer, I'm applying. I talked with Sheriff Harwell about it a while back, but I don't think he took me seriously."

"You're talking about the bottom of the ladder, you know," Weyenberg said.

"I know," Simons said. "You got anybody else working in the jail with fourteen years experience as a supervisor?"

Weyenberg laughed. "Hardly." Then he paused. "You're serious, aren't you?"

"I sure am," Simons said. "I'm not looking for any preferential treatment. All I want is one favor."

"What's that?"

"I'd like to be allowed to continue working on this case in my spare time."

"You're sure you know what you're doing?"

"I'm sure," Truman said.

"Well, come on by and see me. We'll drink some coffee and work it out. Seems to me we could use a little more experience in the jail."

Simons hung up the telephone, knowing he had tossed aside not only a career to which he had devoted much of his adult life, but also the security and retirement benefits he considered so important to his family's future. He knew, too, that the salary he would earn as a jailer for the sheriff's department would be approximately a thousand dollars a month less than what he was earning as a police sergeant.

His wife had been sitting nearby, listening to the phone conversation. Truman searched her face for some reaction but saw none. "Someday I'll probably regret this, you know," he finally said.

Judy smiled gently. "I don't think so," she said.

# 16

It was not the first time Truman Simons had given serious thought to leaving the police department. Sensitive to the demands of the profession, he knew the importance of keeping one's emotions in check. Yet in all his years of law enforcement he had never managed to achieve that personal detachment many of his elders had assured him was necessary for survival. Cases like the lake murders made it most difficult.

For even the most experienced officer there is the ever-present danger of stepping too far beyond that fine emotional line. Simons had heard it time and time again: Flip that imaginary switch. Pretend it isn't real. Do your job and keep your distance. Allow yourself to really care about some poor kids you didn't even know whose futures have been brutally taken away from them, and you are through. At best, it affects your good judgment; at worst, it will drive you crazy and out of the business.

Simons had seen it happen. Marriages ruined; cops who suddenly went past the invisible barrier and put a gun to their mouth to blow life and memories away in one berserk flash. Some men, strong men, simply reached a point where they could no longer deal with the never-ending crises that waited out there on the streets. And even if they were able to deal with them, they never let them go. Not really. Not completely. Not even if they gave up and left the force.

It's something nobody but another cop understands. You go home and your wife meets you at the door with her version of a crisis. The washing machine went out, the kid got sent home from school, Sears called again to say your bill is overdue. She doesn't even know what a real crisis is. But a cop does. He's spent part of the day trying to comfort a heartbroken parent whose infant has been killed in an automobile accident, and the remainder of the day trying to understand how a mother could have murdered her own child. He goes home to get away from it, to hide until his next shift. But there's no place to hide, no sleep deep enough to erase the scenes of horror that are burned inside his eyelids.

On the other hand, some protect themselves so vigorously they become hopelessly jaded. They work at achieving an emotional vacuum, refusing to let even the most disastrous occurrence have any effect on them. Expect the worst and you will never be surprised. Or disappointed. The world is rotten, filled to overflowing with psychos and junkies and whores ready to do things for a buck that would turn most people's stomachs. Doesn't matter a shit whether it's New York City or Waco, Texas. It's the same everywhere. The bad guys outnumber the good guys. Always have, always will. It's not a fair fight. Once you accept that, it becomes just another business. You can go on automatic pilot and maybe, if you're lucky, come away with your sanity and a paycheck. You stick your finger in the dam for eight hours, then turn the no-win battle over to somebody else until it's time for you to go back out there and fight again.

But the bottom line is, you aren't supposed to give a damn. You've got to remember that. It's the only ticket to survival.

Throughout his career Simons had worked hard at avoiding either of the extremes he had seen others driven to. There was no way, he had long since decided, to divorce himself completely from the emotional aspects of his job. The fact that he wore a badge didn't excuse him from the human race. The hurt felt by a mother who has just learned that her son has been arrested for drug dealing still touched him. The hopelessness in the eyes of the whores in east Waco disturbed him and he could not help but feel pity for their plight. Not everyone on the wrong side of the law was totally without redeeming qualities. Hell, they were people, too. Maybe, if their lives had been different; if they had been helped at the right time . . .

Had he tried to verbalize such thoughts to many of his fellow officers, Simons would immediately have been branded a bleeding heart. For that reason, he kept his feelings private.

In the minds of most in the Waco Police Department, Truman Simons was as hard-nosed a cop as you were ever going to find. Maybe even a little too hard-nosed. For years there had been suggestions that once Simons got on a case he would do whatever was necessary to solve it. A little pressure on some ex-con to fabricate testimony, maybe even a little planted evidence if there wasn't enough to satisfy the district attorney. Hell, yes, Sergeant Simons knew how to play hardball with the low-life bastards who needed to be locked up. That's why he made so many cases. Maybe he wasn't popular with his peers, but there were a lot of fellow officers who had to say he was a damn good police officer. He made his cases and they stuck. He tended his business. He had found his own way to survive.

There were times, however, when he wondered; times when reality got blurred and distorted and almost unreachable.

There was that night, long ago, when he had taken a shooting victim to the emergency ward. She was suffering from a severe gunshot wound to the chest and the smell of death was all about her even before she was wheeled into the operating room. Simons stood by as the doctors furiously worked over her opened chest cavity, draining blood from her lungs while, at the same time, trying vainly to repair the damaged organs the bullet had struck. Finally they gave up. The woman was dead.

Her body was placed on a stretcher and the coroner was called. As he had done so many times before, Simons sat alone in the room with the nameless body, waiting, smoking a cigarette. The victim's purse lay on a table near him and he opened it. Nothing much: makeup, an address book, less than a dollar in change, a stick of gum, and a package of menthol cigarettes.

He thought back to his service days and recalled those warnings always posted in the infirmary: *If you smoke menthol cigarettes, we can't help you.* Menthol smokers, he understood, were the most likely to develop lung cancer. He had heard the horror stories of what happened to the lungs. And now he began to wonder.

With no one around to see him, he went over to the body of the victim, her chest still open, and shined his flashlight into the cavity. Putting his hand into the opening he began gently moving the lifeless organs to one side so that he might get a better view of the lungs. For reasons he would never be able to explain he wanted to see what, if any, damage the menthol cigarettes might have done. It was nothing more than idle, emotionless curiosity—until after a couple of minutes it occurred to him what he was doing. What if someone had walked in and seen him? Surely they would have thought him sick. Probably crazy. And maybe, just maybe, for that short space of time he had been. There was no rhyme, no explainable reason for his actions.

For several days afterward, he wondered about himself. Had he become so detached from the real world? Had a dead body become nothing more than an item of curiosity? The frightening questions weighed on him for some time, and he seriously considered turning in his badge, saving himself before it was too late.

This time, however, his reasons were far different. The game playing and the politics of police work had been gnawing at him for too long. The half-truths and botched cases and cops who worked by the time clock frustrated and disappointed him. He had heard the rumors of how he supposedly bent the rules to make cases. They were untrue, of course, but, hell yes, it hurt to know that some people believed them. The department had changed drastically since he was an idealistic rookie patrolman, making him feel much older than his forty years.

The resistance he had met in his investigation of the lake murders was simply the final straw. It had given him the push he needed.

In a few weeks, after the formalities of an interview and filling out applications with the sheriff's department, and turning in his resignation to Chief Scott, he would take a couple of weeks off and spend some time with Judy and their son, Jason. Then he would join the sheriff's department.

There, somehow, he was going to solve the murders of the three teenagers. His determination to do so bordered on obsession, and he knew it. He had allowed himself to become more emotionally involved in this case than any other he had ever worked. Yet he felt no discomfort in that knowledge. On that July night which now seemed so long ago, he had made a promise. And he fully intended to keep it.

# 17

Before he left for work on Monday morning, Truman Simons had made up his mind to spend as little time as possible in the office that day. After hearing the results of Deeb's polygraph test, Dennis Baier had told Truman he had some vacation time coming and was going to the Gulf Coast for some fishing. He had suggested to his partner that it might be a good idea if he also took a few days off. And Truman had considered it. But the events of the previous Saturday nagged at him, and he wanted to ask Johnny Sherrill, one of the department's most experienced and respected polygraph operators, to look at the chart which had been run on Deeb.

Sherrill pulled the folder and reviewed it for several minutes before saying anything. Shortly, Simons' patience ran out. "Well, what do you see?" he asked.

"The only way to get a really accurate reading," Sherrill said, "is to have personally administered the test, so what I'm going to tell you is very unofficial, only an opinion."

"That's all I'm asking for," Truman said.

"Okay, as far as I can see, your Mr. Deeb did show deception on the question posed to him about whether he knew who committed the offense. And on several other relevant questions."

Simons shook his head. "Where were you when I needed you?" he asked jokingly.

Sherrill grinned. "I worked a lot of years to reach the point where my phone wouldn't ring on weekends," he said. "And I like it that way. Sorry."

Simons spent much of the remainder of the day alone, reviewing files on the case, hoping to find a new starting place. Thumbing through some of the notes taken by Detective Salinas early in the investigation he came across an entry dated 8/10/82. Simons squinted as he tried to decipher the detective's scratchy handwriting, fascinated by what he was reading. Ramon had apparently talked either with a psychic or with someone who had been an eyewitness to the crimes. As soon as he finished, he called Salinas.

"You must be looking at the notes I took when that crazy gal called," the detective said.

"Glenda Thomas," Simons replied, reading the name from the legal pad.

"That's her. She really had my attention for a while. I was taking notes like crazy. Then she told me all of it had come to her in some kind of vision or something. That's when I lost interest real quick."

"You ever hear from her again?" Simons asked.

"Not a word."

After hanging up Simons read through the notes again. One of the men Glenda Thomas said was at the scene of the crime was "left-handed and had a tattoo of an eagle on his left forearm."

The autopsy reports, he remembered, had indicated the strong possibility that the majority of the stab wounds had been made by someone who was left-handed. Simons went to Records and pulled the file on David Wayne Spence. Under his physical description was a notation that he had a tattoo of Harley-Davidson wings on his left arm. The wings, Truman thought, did look similar to those of an eagle. Whoever Glenda Thomas was, he wanted to talk with her.

Glenda Thomas was pleasant when Simons spoke with her on the telephone. Yes, she said, she would be happy to talk with him. He could come right over if he liked. She was staying with her parents, she said, then gave him the address.

He had been there only a few minutes, explaining that he had happened on Salinas's notes and wanted to discuss them with her, when her father entered the living room where they were seated. He was immediately hostile.

"What are you doing here?" he asked.

"I'm investigating the Lake Waco murders," Truman said, extending his hand.

Mr. Thomas made no move to shake hands with the officer. "What you should be doing, sir," he said, "is out investigating instead of bothering sick people. My daughter has not been well. She has just returned from the hospital, the psychiatric ward at Providence, and she's still under a doctor's care. I'll have to ask you to leave." His voice grew firmer with each sentence. "We know nothing about any of this and I would appreciate your leaving our family out of it."

Simons nodded, keeping a tight rein on his temper. "Mr. Thomas," he said, "I'll leave your family out of it. But there are some other families, good people you don't even know, who wish they could be left out of it too. But they didn't have a choice."

"If you're trying to make me feel bad," the father said, "you're wasting your time."

"I guess I am," Simons shot back.

Glenda Thomas followed him into the front yard, apologizing for her father's behavior. "I'd still like to talk to you," she whispered. "I want to, very much."

"What's your doctor's name?" Truman asked. "If he thinks it's okay, maybe he can set up an appointment for us." He looked back toward the front door where the woman's father stood, glaring through the screen door. "Away from here."

Glenda Thomas nodded and gave him the name of her doctor.

The following afternoon, Simons was sitting in the office talking to Dennis Baier, who had returned from his brief fishing trip, when a secretary stuck her head in the office to say someone was there to see them.

"Who is it?" Simons asked.

"I think it's the man some detective in Oklahoma called about yesterday while you were out," the secretary said. "Evidently he wants to talk with someone about the lake murders."

Simons went out front and saw a clean-cut, Hispanic-looking young man smiling at him as he approached.

"Can I do something for you?"

"My name is Albert Everett Mendoza," he said politely, "and this is Kenneth Franks' shirt." He handed the officer a white tennis shirt. "The one that is missing," he added.

Simons led the way toward one of the interrogation rooms. "What makes you think this is Kenneth Franks' shirt?" he asked. He was remembering only too vividly the bloodstained orange shirt Kenneth had been wearing, and he did not recall anything about another shirt being missing.

"The people who abducted me and took me to Oklahoma told me so," the young man replied.

Mendoza, who told the officers he had once served as a counselor at the Methodist Home, said he had been abducted two days earlier, placed in the trunk of a car, and driven to Oklahoma where the two men, whom he didn't know, had finally released him. The men had told him about the murders at the lake, he said, and then had threatened to kill him because he knew too much. The two men had killed Kenneth Franks and cut his heart out. And they had cut off Kenneth's penis and put it in his mouth. He didn't know what the two men looked like because he had been blindfolded.

"Okay," Simons said finally, "let me get this straight. You're saying these guys drove you all the way to Oklahoma to kill you because you knew too much. Then for some reason they decided to just let you go and gave you Kenneth's missing shirt. And all this time you never saw them . . ."

"They blindfolded me," Mendoza said.

"Albert," Simons said, "you're full of shit. What the hell are you up to?"

The young man didn't answer. Instead he stared at the floor. He was perspiring and his entire body had begun to shake. Simons called his name again. "Albert, dammit, I'm talking to you. What's this all about?"

Suddenly Mendoza jumped from his chair and Simons, startled, recoiled. For a moment he thought the young man was about to attack him. Mendoza began waving his arms, his eyes flashing with anger. He was staring at the empty chair where, just seconds before, he had been sitting.

"You sonuvabitch," he yelled, "it's all your fault. You did this to me, goddamn you." His voice had changed dramatically.

"Albert, what the hell is going on?" Simons asked, regaining his composure.

The young man cut his eyes in the direction of the officer, then returned his angry stare to the empty chair. "I'm not Albert," he said. "My name's Everett. That sonuvabitch is Albert." He was pointing at the chair. "He's always trying to get me in trouble. I told him not to come. I told him, man, don't fuck with the police or you'll get your ass in deep trouble. But no, he had to get involved in this thing. The bastard's just trying to get me in trouble again."

He turned back to the chair again. "I hope you're happy now," he said.

Lord help us, Truman thought, had this guy really been a youth counselor? He turned to his partner, who looked as if he'd seen a ghost. "What do we do now?" Truman asked.

Baier shrugged, then took a step toward the young man who was still glaring at the empty chair. "Everett," he said, "sit down. Let's talk."

"Naw, I don't want to sit down. I'd rather stand." Unlike Albert, Everett made direct eye contact with the officer.

"Okay, fine," Baier said. "Just tell us why you're here."

"Don't ask me, ask that motherfucker," Everett replied, pointing again to the chair.

For the next half hour Everett responded to the officers' questions, continuing to berate Albert for getting him into this. It was all Albert's fault; Albert never listened to him. And Albert was gay, a fucking queer. "But he's ashamed of it," Everett said. Yes, he had known Kenneth Franks. Kenneth had been Albert's lover. Everett had caught them together one time, Albert going down on Kenneth right there in the car. No, he didn't kill Kenneth Franks. No, he didn't know who did.

"Then why in the hell did you come down here?" Simons asked.

"I told you, goddammit, you'll have to ask him," Mendoza said, once more indicating the chair.

Feeling quite foolish, Simons turned his attention to the imaginary person. "Albert," he said, "can you tell me why you came down here?"

Everett, hands on his hips, stood as if awaiting an answer. Finally he sighed and looked at Simons. "See, he's not going to talk anymore. That's the way he does. He gets us in a lot of trouble and then he leaves me holding the bag."

"What's all this business about Albert being kidnapped?" Simons asked.

Everett laughed, "Shit, he wasn't kidnapped. He just went to Dallas for a couple of days and laid up with a bunch of his queer friends. It made me sick to see the things they were doing. He wasn't abducted or kidnapped or any of that shit. He doesn't know anything about those killings, either. He's just trying to get me in trouble."

Stunned by the bizarre experience, the officers persuaded Everett to sit down and relax and got him a soft drink.

"I don't know whether to laugh or run like hell," Baier said out in the hall.

Later that day, Albert Everett Mendoza was admitted to Providence Hospital's psychiatric wing. Whether or not Simons and Baier had actually interviewed their first-ever split personality, they never knew for sure. The only thing they *were* sure of was that neither Albert nor Everett could help them with their investigation. It was just another crazy, time-wasting, frustrating dead end.

Three months later, Truman saw Albert Everett Mendoza again, standing at the checkout counter of a department store. Albert/Everett smiled and waved. Truman turned quickly and left, choosing to do his shopping elsewhere.

## 18

Glenda Thomas was a small woman, almost frail, with sparkling blue eyes and long sandy hair worn straight. Neatly dressed and wearing only the slightest trace of makeup, she did not seem at all uneasy about the meeting with Truman Simons which had been arranged by her doctor. Divorced and in her mid-twenties, she was studying to become a nurse.

Simons had met earlier with her physician and told him about the resistance he had encountered from Glenda's father. When Truman explained his purpose in wanting to talk with her, the doctor firmly stated his disbelief in psychic phenomena but, after hearing what Simons had to say, suggested it might benefit his patient to talk to someone about her unusual experience. He went on to assure the police officer that his patient was not suffering from any form of mental disorder. He had admitted her to the hospital, he explained, because she was suffering from severe fatigue, brought on, no doubt, by a demanding schedule of work, classes, and late-night studies.

"I know I'm not crazy," Glenda said, smiling at Simons. "What I'm going to tell you may *sound* crazy, but let me assure you I've never had anything like it happen to me before. I don't understand it, but I know it happened. And I've wanted to talk to someone about it for quite some time. In fact, the night it happened, I did call the police. But when someone answered I hung up. I was afraid they would think I was a real wacko."

Simons, glancing at the notes Ramon Salinas had taken when she finally called again almost a month after the murders, assured her he was genuinely interested in her story. "The truth is," he said, "I'm fascinated by this sort of thing. I've read some about it and, frankly, I believe there are people who have the ability to utilize their brain in unexplained ways. I approach an investigation willing to listen to anybody who might be able to help. So if it makes you feel any better, rest assured you have a sympathetic ear."

"I appreciate that," Glenda said. She was still smiling, perfectly at ease.

"I have the notes made by the detective who took your call," Simons explained, "and there are some specific questions I would like to ask you. But first I would rather you just tell me everything you can remember about what happened."

Glenda shifted in her chair as if to make herself comfortable. "Okay," she said.

Shortly after nine o'clock on the night of July 13, 1982, Glenda had been in bed in the small garage apartment where she and her young son lived, studying for an upcoming exam. Exhausted from several nights of staying up late, reading in preparation for a test, she suddenly felt dizzy. Putting her book aside, she lay back and briefly closed her eyes. After a few minutes she felt better and returned to her reading. Shortly the dizziness returned and she again put down her book.

As she lay there, looking toward the ceiling, fuzzy images began to appear. It was as if she were looking at a home movie being shown at high speed. The images came in jerky flashes, moving quickly from one scene to another, as though gaps had been erased from what she was watching.

Slowly at first, a young man and two girls whom she did not recognize came into focus. One of the girls was blonde, the other a brunette. The girls, Glenda somehow knew, had left the man earlier and gone to a Mexican restaurant—El Chico, she felt—to have enchiladas, but had returned after only twenty or thirty minutes.

They seemed to be at a park near the lake, sitting on a bench, talking, enjoying each other's company. Shortly after the girls' return, though, a small man with long, straight black hair and a beard approached. She could not determine whether he was Indian or Hispanic. He was wearing an Army green fatigue shirt and combat boots with the legs of his jeans stuffed down into them. Glenda guessed he was approximately thirty years old.

Accompanying him was a bushy-haired white male wearing a sleeveless blue jean jacket. There was a tattoo of an eagle on his left forearm. He was dark complexioned, looked to be in his late twenties or early thirties, had a black beard, and wore a cap she would later say "looked like a baseball cap but it wasn't." The two men had arrived in a red van which had a bed or foam mattress in the back. On the left windshield was a flower-shaped sticker of some sort. The Indian/Hispanic-looking man approached the girls, telling them they had a flat tire on their car and offering to help fix it.

What she was watching made no sense to Glenda Thomas. Never before had anything like this happened to her. She knew none of the people whose images she was seeing on her ceiling. She began to feel a sense of danger but didn't understand why.

Suddenly she was aware of the van moving, being driven from the park, past a small store. The driver was talking angrily to the brunette, attempting to fondle her as he drove. The girl was obviously angry, demanding that she and her friends be let out of the van. The driver laughed and said he would take them back to their car later.

The scene then jumped to the interior of the van where the smaller man was playing with the blonde's hair with one hand while holding a bronze, dagger-shaped knife in the other. "I can cut you with this," he said, stroking the frightened girl's hair. There was a cruel, menacing sound to his voice.

Glenda, her dizziness gone, lay mesmerized by what she was seeing. As the man threatened the girl, she heard the voice of the young boy urging the blonde to play along with the advances. If she did so, the boy was thinking, she would not be harmed. The man laughed at the boy's suggestion and said he was going to cut off some of her hair.

Then, however, her attention returned to the back of the van. The Indian/Hispanic was telling the girls to remove their clothes. The blonde was obviously frightened. And for good reason. Her assailant, continuing his cruel game, threatened to cut her genitals. "Just lie back and try to go to sleep," he was saying. "That way you won't feel anything." Then, sensing the girl was about to scream, he placed his hand over her mouth and stopped her.

Glenda's viewpoint then seemed to change. Once focused so strongly on the blonde, she was suddenly watching the scene from some high, distant vantage point. She saw the brunette and the young boy running toward a road. The boy, she felt, carried a knife but was too terrified to try using it for his own protection.

They never reached the road. Before her vision ended, Glenda saw the man in the cap stab the brunette. The knife was in his left hand.

And then it was over.

\*     \*     \*

Truman sat silently for a minute after hearing the woman's story. She seemed relieved to have finished telling it and sipped from her soft drink.

"I didn't sleep at all that night," she said. "I was scared to death. Before that night was over, even I was wondering if maybe I was a little crazy. I turned on the television set and flipped from channel to channel looking for news about any murders at the lake. Then I turned on the radio, thinking I might hear something there. But there was nothing.

"Finally, I got up the nerve to call the police. I thought maybe what I had seen was something that hadn't happened yet. I thought I would try to warn them. But when they answered, I froze. As I thought about telling someone what I had experienced, I realized how farfetched it was going to sound. They would think I was stark raving nuts. So I hung up without saying anything.

"When I did finally get up the nerve to make the call several weeks ago, I just told the officer I felt I had some information on the lake murders that might be helpful. He listened for a while and then asked me where I had gotten the details I was giving him. When I told him they had come to me in a vision his interest dropped off pretty quickly. I'm sure he had a good laugh after he hung up. I never expected to hear from anyone about it again."

Simons thought back to his conversation with Salinas about the notes but said nothing.

The young woman went on to explain that she had still been awake the following morning when the paper was delivered and had searched through it to see if there was any mention of the killings.

"I spent all the next day listening to the news," she said. "I kept the radio and the television on constantly and didn't even leave the house. But there was nothing. Finally, about eight that night I went to bed, exhausted."

Had she stayed awake for the ten o'clock news on the evening of July 14, Simons thought to himself, she would have heard the report she was waiting for.

Again looking over the notes written by Salinas, the sergeant saw that her story closely paralleled what she had related a month earlier. "Are you certain about the date when you had the vision?" he asked.

"It was a Tuesday," she said without hesitation. "The first I heard about what had actually happened at the lake was the following Thursday. As I recall, they found the bodies of the girls and the boy sometime Wednesday night." Her vision, then, had closely coincided with the time frame in which the crimes had occurred.

Simons went through the notes, asking about minor points she had not mentioned this time. She had indicated to Salinas, for instance, that she felt the Indian/Hispanic was out of work, was married to someone whose name was possibly Joan, and had eaten at a Sambo's Restaurant shortly before arriving at the lake.

Thinking about how she had described the two attackers, it occurred to Simons that she was actually talking about three people. At one point in her re-creation of her vision she had unthinkingly referred to the Indian/Hispanic man as "the guy with the brown beard," after earlier saying he was clean-shaven. She had also seen flashes of cowboy boots and a wide belt. And one of the men wore a necklace and bracelet. He asked her about the possibility of a third party.

"It's funny you should ask that," she said. "When I thought back on what I saw, there were times when I had a faint awareness of a third person, somewhere off in the background. But I never saw him. It was as if he was there but never stepped into the picture. I don't know. The only ones I really saw were the man with the cap and the short one who looked like an Indian."

After repeated trips to Koehne Park, where the abductions had apparently taken place, and the wooded area of Speegleville, where the bodies were found, Simons was not convinced the actual killings had taken place at either location. With no real evidence to go on, he felt there was a strong possibility the teenagers had been taken to Speegleville, killed there, and their bodies then moved to where they had been found. There was no store near the entrance to Speegleville Park, however, like the one Glenda had described.

"It was an older, country store," she explained. "I distinctly remember them driving past it shortly after they put the kids into the van."

There was a store, Simons knew, less than a mile from the

entrance to Koehne Park, a wood-framed drive-in that sold beer and fishing tackle.

"Okay," Simons continued, "Detective Salinas has something written here about 'proof being in the house . . . the bra is in the living room.' What's that all about?"

Glenda seemed embarrassed. "I told him that," she said, "but I was wrong. I got it straightened out."

Simons looked puzzled. "What do you mean?"

"Well," she said, "after the stories about the murders came out in the paper I started playing detective. One newspaper article mentioned that some of the girls' clothing had not been found. I was driving home one afternoon, thinking about that, and when I passed this particular house on South Twenty-Ninth, I got a real strange feeling. For some reason that I can't explain I decided there was something inside that was connected to the murders. I drove by several times and always got the same feeling. I made up my mind that some of the missing clothing—a bra and maybe even the girls' purses—were in there. The whole thing was silly. There was nothing in the house."

"How do you know?"

"Raylene told me," Glenda replied.

Simons straightened in his chair. "Raylene told you?"

"Yes," Glenda said, "the pretty blonde."

"Maybe you had better explain that to me," the officer said.

Several months earlier, Glenda said, a friend had mentioned an interesting book she was reading about automatic writing. Automatic writing, according to those who claim expertise in the field, is a phenomenon performed without using the conscious mind, instead utilizing unconscious muscular energies in the hand and arm. A pencil is held in an ordinary way over a piece of paper. If proper concentration is achieved, involuntary movements of the pencil will occur. By abstracting oneself from consciously directing the movement of the pencil, the writer supposedly is able to receive written answers to questions asked by his conscious mind.

"I became fascinated with the subject," she said, "and after that experience I had, I felt very involved in the whole thing. In fact, I guess that's why I started to play detective. Anyway, one night I sat down and concentrated on the three kids who had been killed and asked them, 'If you can, try to help me.'

After a while my hand began writing an answer: 'I don't know them.' " Glenda appeared poised and dignified as she told her strange story.

"I asked who I was talking with," she continued, "and the answer came back, 'Raylene.' The only thing I could figure out was that since I had been so intently focused on her during my vision that night, she was the one most likely to answer me.

"I figured, though, if she didn't know the people who had killed them, she wouldn't be much help. So I asked to talk with Jill Montgomery. But Jill wouldn't answer. Then I tried Kenneth Franks. All he told me was, 'I can't believe I let them sucker me into this.'

"So, I went back to Raylene. I asked her why Jill wouldn't talk to me. She said 'Because Jill won't accept the fact she is dead. Until she does, she will not answer.' "

For a moment Simons was speechless, conscious that his attempt to conceal his skepticism was not working. "Did you ever try Jill again?" he asked.

"A few times," Glenda said. "She finally responded a little. Once I got something about a ring, and another time something about her left arm, but it didn't make much sense. One night, I got back in touch with Raylene. That was after I'd driven by that house several times and had such a strong feeling that something in there was connected with the crime. So I asked her if the bra was in the house. Her answer to me was 'Don't look for the bra. It's tied around my leg.' "

Without saying anything, Simons got to his feet and paced the length of the room. Glenda followed his movements curiously. "Does that mean something?" she asked.

The police officer didn't hear the question. He was thinking back to the crime scene and the first time he had seen Raylene Rice. He was remembering the bloodstained cloth gag that covered her mouth, and the bindings around her wrists. And her painted toenails. And the piece of a bra which was tied to her right leg.

According to Raylene's sister, she had not worn a bra on her trip to Waco that fatal July afternoon. The bra on her leg had belonged to Jill Montgomery.

Returning to his chair, Simons studied Glenda Thomas intently. He liked the way she looked him squarely in the eye when she spoke. She seemed honest. And she had insisted she had never had such an experience before. He was reasonably sure she was not seeking publicity or trying to make a name for herself as a practicing psychic. But he was not at all sure what to make of her story. The mention of the bra had completely unnerved him.

Glenda sensed his confusion. "I know this all sounds very unbelievable," she said. "And I won't even try to explain how it happened. Or why it happened to me. But I do know that I am not crazy."

"No," Simons said, "I don't think so, either. Have you tried to get in touch with Raylene again?"

"Not in some time. After a while the whole thing began to frighten me. I decided to leave it alone."

Simons asked if she would be willing to try to contact the dead girl again.

"If it will help," she said.

"It might," Truman said. "At this point I can use all the help I can get."

For the next few weeks she tried on several occasions to communicate with the dead youngsters but with no success. Whatever tie she might have had was gone. The sergeant never heard from her again.

The evening after his interview with Glenda Thomas, Truman waited until his son was asleep and he and his wife were sitting quietly in the den. "I've got to talk to someone about this," he said.

Judy studied her husband's face as he told her about his meeting with Glenda Thomas. He was careful to stress how she had impressed him with her straightforwardness and matter-of-fact manner. If she was a mental case, she concealed it better than anyone he had ever been around. "I saw a lot of strange people when I worked security at the Providence mental ward," he said, "and I think I can spot them. Glenda Thomas isn't one."

That afternoon he had contacted Christy Juhl to see if she might have a picture of David Spence and she had told him there were some she had left at K-Mart to be developed but had not bothered to pick up. He was welcome to them. As Truman told Judy about Glenda's description of the man wearing "a cap that looked like a baseball cap but wasn't," he showed her a photo of Spence. In it he was looking over his shoulder at the

camera, wearing a sleeveless blue jean jacket and a billed cap
like those favored by bikers.

When he told her about the automatic writing and Raylene's
explanation that Jill Montgomery refused to accept the fact she
was dead, Judy Simons began to cry.

In Waxahachie, word of Muneer Deeb's release had sent
Jill's father, Rod Montgomery, into a renewed state of depression. The arrest of a suspect after so long had briefly given him
hope that the murder of his daughter and her friends might be
solved.

Rod was having lunch at Esparza's Cafe, a Mexican restaurant favored by many who worked downtown, when he noticed
Ennis police detective Ronnie Roark sitting at a nearby table.
He knew Roark had earned considerable attention in 1980 when,
with the aid of Dallas psychic John Catchings, he located the
body of a Navarro County teenager who had been missing for
four months. Clutching the senior ring of the missing youngster
in his hand, Catchings had led Roark to a shallow grave where
the boy had been buried. The gravesite was less than a quarter
of a mile from the home of the man eventually convicted of the
murder. The Catchings-Roark team had been featured in newspapers across the country and on such television shows as
"That's Incredible" and "PM Magazine." People called from as
far away as Germany, seeking their services in finding everything from lost loved ones to family heirlooms.

Aware that Roark had shown an interest in the Waco murders, Montgomery approached the detective. "Mind if I sit
down?" he asked. He went straight to the point, telling Roark
of his frustration with the lack of progress made by the Waco
police. Rod explained how he and other family members had
heard little news about what, if any, new leads were being pursued and then asked the officer how he would approach the case.

"If I was working the case from here," Roark said, "you
would be my main suspect—at least until I could make certain
you had nothing to do with it."

Rod had heard rumors that he had once been considered a
suspect but no one had ever confronted him. "Tell me why," he
said.

"Rod, I don't have any real reason to believe you were involved, but there are things that might raise questions. You and
your wife are divorced. Maybe it got pretty nasty; maybe there

was a big custody battle going on. Hey, family members kill each other all the time—over things that don't amount to a hill of beans. What I'm telling you is, if I had nothing to go on and was starting from scratch, I'd want to know a lot more about you."

"Do *you* think I had something to do with it?" Rod asked.

Roark smiled and shook his head. "No, I don't," he said. He didn't tell his old classmate he was the one who had suggested to Waco authorities two months earlier that they should consider Rod a suspect. "And from what little I've heard about the investigation, neither do the people working on the case."

Montgomery then asked the question that had been on his mind since he'd seen Roark sitting there. "Do you think John Catchings might be interested in this case?"

"I've wondered the same thing," Roark replied.

"Would you ask him if he might look into it?"

"Sure," Roark said, "but even if he is interested, the Waco police would have to agree to it. He won't get involved without their okay." Roark promised to contact Catchings and, if he was agreeable, then he would get in touch with the Waco authorities.

Standing, he shook Rod Montgomery's hand. "I hope you didn't take offense to what I said earlier."

"No," Rod said.

"I was just shooting straight with you."

Rod smiled faintly. "I wish more police officers would do the same."

Ronnie Roark left the cafe, never mentioning to Rod Montgomery his conversation with Karen Hufstetler.


John Catchings came by his profession naturally. His mother, Bertie Catchings, was making a name for herself as a psychic when he was a teenager. Though she never gained the popular stature or recognition of Jeanne Dixon, she earned a comfortable living giving "readings" to a long list of clients including a number of bored housewives and some show business celebrities. Occasionally her name appears in Dallas newspapers or the supermarket tabloids along with predictions or opinions on highly publicized crimes.

On the Fourth of July in 1969, 22-year-old John Catchings was leaning against his car, watching some steaks he was barbecuing, when a bolt of lightning from a single dark cloud suddenly struck near where he was standing. The story of what happened thereafter has been written by numerous magazine and newspaper reporters:

"I had an experience that psychics talk about—an out-of-body experience," Catchings remembers. "I could see myself, I could see the car, I could see a blue glow around me, and I could see a friend approaching me. I remember thinking, 'If he touches me we both will die.' About three hours later my feet began to swell and turned black and blue. They looked like someone had been beating me with a baseball bat. After that I did a lot of thinking about what had happened, a lot of soul-searching about 'Who am I? Where am I going? What am I supposed to be doing with my life?' I had an experience like a minister would have—a calling to become a psychic. So I quit my job, sold my house, moved to Dallas, and spent the next eight or nine months following my mother around, trying to determine whether it was something I really could do." He soon found that he could.

When Ronnie Roark telephoned him about the Lake Waco murders, relating his conversation with Rod Montgomery, Catchings was eager to see if he could help. In Waco, Sergeant Dennis Baier was skeptical at first when Detective Roark phoned to say Catchings would like to come to Waco, but after talking with Chief Scott and Simons, he called Roark back. "What the hell," he said, "it can't hurt."

Sitting in one of the interview rooms at the Waco Police Department, the bearded psychic huddled over several crime scene photographs Baier and Simons had provided. His squinted eyes roamed from the photographs to the autopsy reports for several minutes, then he listened as the two officers briefed him on the investigation. He had said little since he, Detective Roark, and Rod Montgomery had arrived that Saturday morning, except to qualify his abilities.

"I'm sure," he told the officers, "that you're quite skeptical about psychics. I have no problem with that; I've dealt with it for years. All I ask is that you understand that I've been right approximately sixty percent of the time in investigations like this. My only request is that you listen to whatever I might say and then decide if it justifies any follow-up. You should also know that in cases like this, I've never gotten everything one hundred percent right. No psychic ever does. We deal in bits and pieces of information that are sometimes very confusing. It is your job to determine where the parts fit—if they do. I would like to add that while I've never been completely accurate, I've always been right on something of significance." He then asked that they take him to Koehne Park and Speegleville.

Rod Montgomery, who had been waiting in front of Ronnie Roark's house in Waxahachie earlier that morning, uninvited but determined to make the trip to Waco with Roark and Catchings, was told without explanation that he would have to remain at the police station. Angry at being excluded, he waited for an hour, then walked to the bus station and purchased a ticket to Waxahachie.

While Simons, Baier, and Roark kept their distance, Catchings roamed the wooded area of Speegleville Park where the bodies had been found. He walked through the underbrush to the lake and stood for some time, staring across in the direction of Koehne Park. For nearly an hour he wandered about aimlessly, stopping at times to pick up a twig or a stone, holding it briefly, then dropping it. Leaning against the car, Simons watched with fascination. He had expected more of a show, some kind of ritualistic mumbo jumbo.

Finally, the psychic returned to the waiting officers. "I think a boat was used; some sort of flat-bottomed boat," he said. "It's possible the victims were killed on it, then their bodies brought over here. There were three persons involved: the man who did the killings and two other people who were with him. I think you are going to find that a dark-haired woman, in her twenties, knows something about the crime. She could be the crucial link to your solving the crime. You may already suspect her.

"The feelings I have are not that strong, but I believe the young people were killed by one man, and two others—perhaps a man and the woman I'm talking about—were with him. And I keep seeing the color yellow, but I can't attach it to anything."

As Catchings spoke, his statements triggered a variety of suggestions to Simons. He strongly felt that David Spence's girlfriend, Christy Juhl, dark-haired and nearing twenty, knew more about the crime than she had admitted. Could she be the "crucial link" to whom Catchings was referring? Glenda Thomas had described two men to him and thought there might have been a third party. Now Catchings was also suggesting that there were three people involved.

"Do you think," he asked, "that the yellow you've picked up on might be the color of a car?"

"I really can't say," Catchings answered. "Why?"

"Muneer Deeb's car is yellow," Simons said.

All in all, however, Catchings' visit was a disappointment. He provided nothing specific, only a few impressions which he admitted reservations about. Several days later, as the investigators sat drinking coffee and reviewing the case, Baier looked over the notes he had made on the psychic's visit. "I don't think we fell into his sixty percent success rate," he said to his partner.

"I wish to hell we had," Simons replied.

Simons was becoming more than a little weary of lunatic confessions and stories of psychic visions and automatic writing. The case was beginning to grate on him. Never in his entire career with the Waco Police Department had he been given a case which he hadn't solved. Now he was leaving the department in a matter of days with everything in limbo.

Despite the unexplainable resistance he had encountered, Simons knew he had made progress. Yet he felt as if he were searching for a needle in a haystack. And for the first time he began to wonder if he would ever find it in the spare time his new duties as a jailer would afford him.

Suddenly he closed the file he was reading and slapped it down on the desk. "Let's go visit the jail," he said. "I want to see what the hell this guy David Spence looks like," he said.

Dressed in jail whites, Spence appeared glad to have company. For almost an hour Simons and Baier questioned him about his relationship with Muneer Deeb and Christy Juhl. Neither suggested to him that he might be a suspect, saying only that his name had come up in conversations several times during their investigation.

"I'm not surprised," Spence said. "My old lady worked at Deeb's store. And I spent a lot of time there." Friendly and smiling, he asked if they thought Deeb had killed the teenagers. Before they could answer he offered an observation: "If he did those murders, you're going to have a hard time finding out anything about it from his people. Those damn Arabs stick together." He said he felt strongly that anyone who committed such a crime needed to be jailed. He would like to help, he said, and offered to have Christy ask around to see what she might find out.

"We'd appreciate it," Simons said. "I'm leaving the police department in a few days, but if you come up with anything, just give Sergeant Baier a call."

That night Truman Simons slept fitfully, awakened several times by a recurring nightmare in which he saw David Spence cutting Jill Montgomery's throat.

# PART THREE

"I feel things are getting hopeless. I have to try to keep my sanity and am trying to think of other things because no matter what Waco tells us, I have a feeling that things are not going well. My thoughts are leaning toward thinking that nothing will ever be resolved about the case. If they had a good case something would have been done by now. Too much time has elapsed since they told us they 'could go to court now and get the death penalty.' If this is true, why are they waiting so long? Is it a political game they are playing while all of us are gradually losing our sanity?"

—entry in the diary of Jan Thompson,
Jill Montgomery's aunt, September 1, 1983

*The jailer had read the psychological profile many times, always wondering how anyone could come up with such a collection of information after having seen only autopsy reports and photos of a crime scene. The profile had been prepared by the FBI at the request of the Waco Police Department. There were agents, the jailer knew, who were specially trained to prepare such profiles from only sparse facts about a crime. It amused him to think of spending a career writing descriptions of criminals with neither names nor faces. Even if the agents were right, he thought, they would rarely, if ever, have the satisfaction of being involved in the apprehension of the person whom they had profiled. The jailer wondered how many investigators ever bothered to contact the FBI agent who had prepared the profile to tell him if he had been helpful in solving a crime. Or how accurate his profile had proved to be.*

*And did the agent really care? The jailer read no hint of passion in the report, no sense that the person who wrote it really cared—only sterile paragraphs filled with assumptions and probabilities. Why should the author care, really? He had only read a few typewritten pages and seen one-dimensional photographs. A murder in Waco, Texas, no matter how senseless or brutal, was hardly the kind of case on which the image-conscious Bureau could polish its reputation.*

*Yet the jailer repeatedly searched the report in the slow-passing hours of his graveyard shift. When he tired of reading a paperback or talking with inmates suffering from insomnia, he would pull it from his briefcase and review it. It contained some things that fascinated him:*

*The following is a summary of an offender profile that was discussed with investigators of the Waco P.D. It is based on research and probabilities. Any suspect developed by you may or may not fit in each and every category.*

*This crime in all probability was committed by an offender who knew either one or all of the victims. He will be a white male between the ages of 30–36 years of age. He is muscular and/or heavy set in body build. He considers himself as macho or masculine; however, he has difficulty maintaining personal relationships with either males or females. He basically is inadequate; however, he handles this personal deficiency by aggressing against others. He is basically a coward and prefers to associate and bully those younger than himself by intimidating them.*

*He is sloppy in appearance and does not maintain personal property (i.e., auto). His choice of vehicle, if he could purchase one, would be a van either black or red in color.*

*He is a beer drinker and in all probability smokes marijuana; however, is not in all probability a heavy user of drugs.*

*He comes from a broken home, where he was raised by either an aunt, grandmother or mother. He despises women and personally feels women are here on Earth to be used by men.*

*When employed he will seek masculine types of employment (i.e., truck driver, heavy equipment operator, etc.).*

*This offender demonstrates he felt comfortable at the point of abduction and point of execution. For him to develop this degree of comfortability he either frequents those areas because he socializes at these sites or because he had or is employed in some capacity that takes him to these locations.*

*This offender does not or will not demonstrate guilt or remorse relative to these homicides. In his way of thinking the victims deserved to be killed. He will probably not grant an interview if or when he realizes he is a suspect. His only concern would be whether the police investigation has any concrete evidence that could link him to the homicides.*

*This profiler feels that the point where the victims were found is also the point of execution or killing. Inasmuch as all three victims were bound in the same fashion we feel that he acted alone. Although the male victim received multiple stab wounds in the chest we feel his primary motivation or aim was to assault the female victims once the male victim was killed by him.*

*Generally crimes of this type are not perpetrated by parents. Based upon certain elements in this crime scene analysis we would not expect to find a father responsible for same unless he himself has demonstrated severe psychopathy in the past.*

There were at least some elements of the profile, the jailer felt, which fit. For instance, he was convinced the man who had *become his primary suspect did know at least two of the victims. And he did have a muscular build and presented a macho attitude. Word on the street was that he was a bully who enjoyed intimidating those younger or weaker than he was. The jailer also felt that his suspect was basically a coward. He was a beer drinker and came from a broken home. That fit. And evidence pointed to the fact that he frequented the park from which the victims had been abducted.*

*On the other hand, there were just as many elements in the report which caused the jailer problems. The offender in the profile was older than his suspect. The jailer was certain the crimes had not been committed in the location where the bodies had been found. And it seemed highly improbable that the murders could have been carried out by a lone assailant. Maybe one man did do all the killing, but it seemed likely he would have needed the help of an accomplice to restrain three people.*

*The part about the choice of vehicle fascinated him. In the young nursing student's vision the assailants had arrived at the park that night in a red van. And in their lengthy late-night conversations, the inmate who had become his primary suspect had repeatedly told him of his desire to own a van. A red one.*

*Sometimes, after rereading the profile and putting it away in his briefcase, the jailer would catch himself staring at the cell which housed the man he suspected of committing the lake murders. If his suspicions materialized—if he did solve the case—he would write a letter to the FBI agent.*

# 19

One afternoon in the late spring of 1979, Dorothy Miles was sitting on the front porch of her little house on North Fifteenth Street, enjoying the early evening breeze, strumming her guitar while her freshly washed auburn hair glistened in the final rays of sunlight. Now in her mid-fifties, there had been a time, in her younger days, when she played with a country music band which toured the beery dance halls of central Texas. God, how she had loved the music and the excitement. But the money a single mother needed to raise. two children just wasn't there. Begrudgingly she put her music career aside and went in search of a better-paying job. With no high school diploma to show prospective employers, Dorothy searched long and hard before she found work as a security guard. For a while she drove a truck. Having been raised in a family which included nine brothers, Dorothy Miles was not uncomfortable making her way in a man's world. To supplement her income, she occasionally rented out her back bedroom to boarders.

But it was music which provided food for her soul: Merle Haggard, Hank Williams, Bob Wills and his Texas Playboys, western swing, and bluegrass. Seldom did an evening pass when she did not bring out her guitar and play, her soprano voice still crisp and clear as she softly sang the plaintive ballads of lost love and honky-tonk heaven.

Dorothy's music was a magnet, constantly drawing neighborhood youngsters to her home. In spite of her tough-talk demeanor and her obey-the-rules attitude toward her visitors, Dorothy Miles was a favorite of the young people who lived on her north Waco street. The youngsters knew they were always welcome to come and visit with her daughters in the front yard. They also quickly discovered that she was an excellent cook. Rarely did the Mileses' dinner table not include extra place settings for guests.

As she played that evening a handsome young man walked

into her yard and stood listening. His deep blue eyes seemed to dance to her music. Only after she had finished did he speak.

"Hi," he said.

Dorothy smiled and nodded.

"Think you could teach me to play?" her visitor asked.

"Maybe," Dorothy said. "What's your name?"

"David Spence. I live down on the corner."

Sitting on her porch steps, he told her of his ambition to be a rock singer someday and asked if she might like to see some songs he had written. When she said yes, he hurried to his house and was back in a matter of minutes with a spiral notebook containing lyrics he had composed.

Dorothy read them and shook her head. "Son, I'm afraid this isn't my kind of music," she said.

"I didn't really figure it was," the young man said.

Their musical differences, however, did not prevent a fast friendship from developing. Polite and well-mannered, David soon became a regular at the Miles household, spending more time there than at his own home. He quickly became friends with Dorothy's daughters, Linda and Ojeda, but it was their mother's company he most enjoyed. He liked to sit and talk with her, sometimes late into the night. In time he asked if he might call her "Mom."

Dorothy immediately recognized a sadness in David which troubled her. She found him very immature for a young man twenty years old, and he seemed starved for attention and affection. Soon he was coming to her with the problems he was having at home, often telling her how angry it made him that his younger brother seemed to get all of his mother's attention. Dorothy would always stop him when he became critical of Juanita White. "David," she would say, "regardless of what she's done and how she conducts her life, she's your mother. She deserves your respect for that."

Sometimes David would argue briefly. "Aw, Mom, you don't understand . . ."

"It isn't my business," Dorothy would snap, cutting him short. "All I need to understand is that she's your mother. And I don't want to hear you talking badly about her."

Thus David did not tell her of the violent arguments he and his mother had constantly. He never mentioned the time when both were drunk and he had chased her into the front yard, two-by-four in hand, threatening her life; or how it infuriated him when she staggered home late at night with men he didn't know and would never see again after they left the following morning. It would, in fact, be some time before Dorothy Miles was introduced to the violent side of David Spence.

Late one afternoon David and a friend were in her front yard, horse-playing with sawed-off broomsticks. As they carried out their mock sword battle, a couple new to the neighborhood walked past and stopped briefly to watch. Dorothy happened to be standing at her front door when she saw David turn toward the man, his broomstick held over his head in a threatening manner, and yell, "You crazy motherfucker, what are you looking at?"

Stunned, Dorothy immediately ran into the yard and scolded David furiously as the couple hurried on down the street. "Young man," she said, "I think you had better go home. And don't bother coming back until you can act right."

Later that evening, two Waco police officers appeared at her door, asking for a young man who fit David Spence's description. The man who had walked past her house had filed an assault complaint, saying the same person who yelled at him from her yard had followed him to his car and hit him over the head with a broomstick.

The event left Dorothy puzzled and distressed. She had never before seen that side of David, and it frightened her to think that his temper was so short-fused.

It was a week before he meekly returned to her house, apologizing and asking if it would be okay for him to come in. Dorothy firmly stated that she would never again tolerate such behavior or language, then smiled at him. Actually, she was glad to see him. In the short time she had known him, she had developed a fondness for him that approached the feelings she had for her own children. His infectious, childlike enthusiasm for life amused her. Yet the sadness that seemed always present, hidden behind his smile and outgoing manner, tugged at her heart. She knew David badly needed a friend and she had made up her mind to fill that need.

Except to admit his regret that he had quit school in the eighth grade, David never talked about his past and Dorothy, who considered her own life a private matter, never pried. She was satisfied to allow their relationship to develop naturally from that spring-day beginning when he had first walked into her yard.

But even after Dorothy had become his most trusted confidant, there were secrets he never shared with her. He never mentioned that at age sixteen he had married a fifteen-year-old girl named June Ewing, who had been a student at the Methodist Home. Or that they had had two sons before his wife, frustrated by his constant abuse and excessive drinking, left him and took the children to Louisiana.

It was after the breakup of his stormy marriage that he began mixing drugs—marijuana, speed, hash, and occasionally LSD—with his alcoholic binges. He had joined the Army but was given a medical discharge after only four months. Distraught upon notification that his divorce was final in 1978, he had checked into an Austin drug treatment center for two months. While physicians there warned him of the dangers of any sort of chemical dependency, they emphasized that his greatest problem was alcohol. He displayed all the symptoms, they told him, of a full-fledged alcoholic.

Though Dorothy knew David sometimes drank beer to excess and suspected that, like most of the young people she knew, he smoked pot, she had no indication of the degree of his dependency problems.

And when David told her in June that he was moving to Fort Worth, where his father had found him work, Dorothy Miles was saddened to see him leave. Although she had known him only a few months, she had begun to look on him as one of her own.

Dorothy heard from David again toward the end of July when he wrote to her from Fort Worth to say that he was in trouble. He had been charged with armed robbery, he wrote, and went on to explain that he was also facing charges of attempted murder of a police officer with whom he had been involved in a shoot-out following the robbery.

Disheartened by the news, Dorothy had no way of knowing that most of what David had written was highly fictionalized. The shootout and the attempted murder charges were nothing more than the inventions of a man who was too embarrassed to give an honest description of the twenty-five-dollar robbery that had actually taken place.

The remainder of his letter, however, was chatty, mostly

questions about Dorothy's daughters and happenings in the neighborhood. "Well," he wrote in closing, "I guess I'll be going away for awhile. I miss you all, especially you, Mom."

Dorothy thought often about answering, but was uncertain what to say. By the time she made up her mind to write, to tell David she loved him and still wanted to be his friend despite his troubles, she had lost the envelope with his return address.

Sentenced to four years in the Texas Department of Corrections (TDC), David split his time between the Coffield and Beto units from April of 1980 until July of 1981. Upon his release he requested to be paroled to Waco and soon thereafter moved back in with his mother on North Fifteenth Street. He was greatly disappointed to learn that while he was away, Dorothy Miles had moved from the neighborhood.

Those who had known him before he spent fifteen months in prison immediately noticed a change. David began dressing like a biker; he was drinking even more heavily than before, and proudly displayed the tattoos he had acquired in prison. There were two hearts on his right hand and a set of dice on his shoulder. The tattoo of the Harley wings on his left forearm was his favorite.

When drunk he would talk almost nostalgically about penitentiary life. He had been one of the respected leaders at the Beto Unit, he assured anyone who would listen. According to David, other inmates had quickly learned to fear him, particularly after he had stabbed a fellow prisoner in the eye.

Most people who heard his tales took him at his word, never thinking that anyone would invent such stories. The truth was that David Spence had quietly served his time as a virtual outcast in prison society. He had fit in no better there than he had in the free world.

Things did not go well after his return to Waco. Though Gene Deal, his parole officer, helped him find work, the jobs neither interested him nor lasted any length of time. He had worked a month and a half for a construction company before giving notice to take a job with a plastics firm. He had been on the job just three weeks before he was fired when, during a fit of anger, he threw a hatchet across the room. The foreman insisted it had been thrown at him; David argued that was not the

case and tried to apologize. Whatever the truth, he was again
out of work.

Just before the end of 1981, a friend helped him land a job
as a stable boy on a local horse farm. But he was dismissed
after just two months when the owner, hosting a party at his
ranch, saw Spence for the first time and immediately disliked
his unkempt beard and long hair. He instructed his foreman to
get rid of him.

In June of 1982, David's younger brother, Steve, helped him
get a job as a part-time instructor at the YMCA where he spent
most of his time playing pickup basketball with young businessmen trying to keep their waistlines in check.

For the young man who had aspired to celebrity status as a
rock singer, the world was looking like one giant dead end.
David was barely earning enough to buy beer and pot. To make
ends meet, he began selling drugs whenever he could get someone to front a deal for him.

And he was drunk or high more often than not. Even David
himself knew by then that he was an alcoholic. Yet he made
certain he was sober on those days he was to see his parole
officer, and he always had a reasonable excuse for having just
lost another job. Things were getting better, he continually assured Deal.

Things might not be going as well as he would have liked
on the outside, but he had no intention of returning to prison.
Though involved in several activities that would justify revoking
his parole and sending him back to TDC, he was careful not to
do his drinking in bars. That would be grounds for Deal's
quickly recommending him back to prison to serve the remaining time on his sentence. On the other hand, dope-dealing, assault, rape, and keeping company with felons—all far more
serious violations of his parole agreement which he had been
involved in since his release—seemed not to concern him. In
essence, David followed only those rules which he felt had some
merit and adopted a cavalier attitude toward those he found
inconvenient or unreasonable.

Day by day that attitude boiled into frustrated anger. He was
getting nowhere. The basketball-playing businessmen he met at
the YMCA treated him like a second-class citizen despite his
unabashed attempts to impress them and gain their favor. Bosses
had fired him from futureless jobs simply because they didn't

like his looks. He was forced to drive an unreliable clunker rather than the new-model sports car or van his heart desired. His fictional stories of tough prison life impressed only the Waco street punks still too young to shave or buy beer legally. During bouts of drunken depression, David Spence would tally his scorecard and realize he was miserably short of his own unrealistic yardstick of success. He was a nobody going no-where.

The only thing he had judged positive since his return to Waco was his meeting a slim, brown-eyed brunette named Christine Juhl. Nearing her eighteenth birthday, she was working at the Taco Torch, one of the numerous fast-food restaurants on Valley Mills Drive, when David first saw her in October of 1981. He immediately asked her out. Soon they were living together in David's mother's home.

The little corner house on North Fifteenth had become some-thing of a gathering place for David's new acquaintances. As his mother spent less and less time there, and then moved out to live with a man she had been dating, David made the house available not only to his new girlfriend but to several others with no permanent residence of their own. Among those who began living there were Tony Melendez, with whom David had gone to junior high school, and his older brother, Gilbert.

Christy soon learned that David was a different person in the company of his friends. When they were alone he generally treated her well. But with an audience, he seemed seized with the need to prove something she did not understand. She was his "old lady," his "bitch," he would say, taking on the affec-tations of a biker, and would do whatever he demanded. One evening as she stood in the kitchen, preparing dinner, David and Gilbert entered and David, picking up one of the carving knives from the counter, suddenly ordered her to stand against the door so he could show Gilbert his "knife act."

Christy thought he was kidding and continued her cooking. With a crazed look on his face, David issued a cursing demand which made it clear that he was not joking. Frozen with fear, Christy stood there while David took aim and feinted throws in her direction several times, laughing as Christy grimaced and closed her eyes. Gilbert was uncomfortable with the dangerous game and tried to reason with his friend. They were going to catch hell from David's mother if he put holes in the door, he said. "Fuck it," David replied, again taking aim. "You don't think I'll really do it, do you? Well, I damn sure will—and she'll stand right where she is." Shaking, Christy could not summon the strength to move away from the door.

And then David threw the knife, laughing as the blade buried into the wood, the handle vibrating dangerously close to Christy's shoulder. "I can get closer," David said ominously, the laughter gone from his voice. Christy ran from the house, crying, before he could take aim again.

But for reasons Christy cannot fully explain, she always returned when a sobered David would apologize and assure her his behavior would improve. It would, however, only get worse.

One evening after a case of beer had been consumed, David sent Christy to the bedroom, then turned to Tony. "You like my old lady, don't you?" he said. Tony only shrugged. "Wait here a minute," Spence said, "I'm gonna fix you up." Wobbly, he rose and went in the bedroom, carrying a small hatchet he kept in the house. "Tony's coming in here," David told Christy, "and I want you to fuck him."

But after Tony was in the bed with Christy, David stormed into the room in a rage. "You goddamn whore," he screamed at Christy, "I ought to cut your fucking head off." Waving the hatchet wildly as he yelled his obscenities, he then turned his anger to Tony. "The bitch is my old lady," he said. "And you're supposed to be my bro, my fucking friend."

It is entirely possible that Gilbert's intervention, hurrying his younger brother from the house and helping Christy escape through the bedroom window, prevented David from killing them both.

David was still in a cursing rage. Turning up the stereo to an earsplitting level, he raced outside, the hatchet in his hand, and began maniacally hacking away at the windshield of his pickup. Before he calmed down he had broken all the windows and badly damaged the hood and fenders.

Then it was over. The alcohol-induced rage seemed suddenly to drain from him and he slumped to the ground and began to cry. He loved Christy, he said, but he treated her like shit. And he didn't know why. He had to find her and apologize.

The following morning he located her at a friend's apartment and told her how sorry he was about what had happened. She agreed to accompany him into the parking lot where he had parked. But once there his gentle mood disappeared. He tied her up and forced her to follow at the end of a rope as he drove slowly back to his house.

In the spring of 1982, Christy was offered a job as cashier at the Rainbow Drive Inn. Muneer Deeb, whom she had also met at the Taco Torch, suggested that she move into a little apartment that was vacant just behind the store. She would be able to afford the fifty-five-dollar monthly rent, he said, on the salary he would pay her. Within a week David had moved into the apartment with her. When he wasn't working himself— which was becoming more and more frequent—he spent his time in the Rainbow, playing video games and talking with Deeb. Extremely jealous, David also took advantage of the opportunity to keep an eye on Christy.

One day in March of 1982, Dorothy Miles' washing machine was broken and she stood folding clothes at a laundromat in her new neighborhood. Just as she was preparing to leave, a local prostitute entered, followed by David Spence. He had grown a beard and his hair was longer than she remembered, but Dorothy recognized him immediately and called his name.

"Mom," he responded, rushing to hug her, the prostitute forgotten. "I've been looking all over for you since I got home. How have you been?"

For the next half hour they sat and talked. David told her about his job at the YMCA and the girl named Christy with whom he was in love. Things were going great, he assured her. He helped Dorothy load the laundry into her car and asked if she would mind him stopping by to visit and say hello to Ojeda and Linda.

"David," she said, "you're welcome anytime. As long as you behave."

He began to laugh. "Mom, I promise not to take a broomstick to any of your neighbors."

"In that case," she said, "you come by, real soon."

She had been glad to see him. But Dorothy was disturbed that his eyes no longer seemed to have that same sparkle she had once seen. Now they were cold and dull, encircled by dark rings. She sensed, much as a mother might, that he was not nearly as happy with his life as he had tried to make her believe.

David did stop by soon after that, and the visit provided more indication that he was not the same person the Miles family had known before he left for Fort Worth two years earlier. Slightly drunk when he arrived, David was there only a short while before a car driven by a man Dorothy had never seen before pulled into the driveway. "That's a friend of mine," David said. "His name's Gilbert Melendez. I'm going with him for a few minutes, but I'll be right back."

It was almost midnight when David returned, bragging loudly about a fight in which he and his friend had been involved. "This dude came at me with a knife," David said. "But he wound up getting it used on him instead."

For the next several weeks David was a frequent visitor, usually going to the Miles house whenever he and Christy had a fight. On those occasions he would appear at Dorothy's front door with a cooler of beer under his arm and ask if he could stay the night. Generally morose and showing little inclination to talk, he would sit in the living room watching television until he had finished the beer. Then he would go to sleep on the floor, covered by the blanket Dorothy had left for him.

By the summer of 1982 David was spending as many as three nights a week at the Miles house. Dorothy felt there were demons gnawing at him, things he wanted to talk about. But the decision to do so, she thought, would have to be David's.

There were several occasions when he came close. One evening in June he appeared at her home, nervous and drinking, talking about a "score he had to settle" with someone. Though he would not elaborate, he grew increasingly nervous as he sat in Dorothy's living room. Finally, he said, "Mom, I need to talk. I think I'm in trouble."

"What is it you've done?" Dorothy asked.

David, looking frightened, opened himself a beer. "I don't know," he said. "Just forget it."

Dorothy had the strange feeling that he really didn't remember what, if anything, he might have done.

She knew by then that David's problems had grown well beyond difficulties with Christy and disappointments with his jobs. Dorothy was reasonably certain David was using and selling drugs. One evening he stopped by with a young man and woman she had never met before. They sat in the living room, visiting for a few minutes, and then David motioned his com-

Jill Montgomery, left, and Raylene Rice.
ROD MONTGOMERY

Kenneth Franks.
MCLENNAN COUNTY
DISTRICT ATTORNEY'S
OFFICE

Waco Police Sergeant Truman Simons, right, helps carry one of the bodies from the wooded area of Speegleville Park. *WACO TRIBUNE-HERALD* PHOTO BY ROD AYDELOTTE

Truman Simons.
PAT STOWERS

David Spence. MCLENNAN COUNTY
SHERIFF'S DEPARTMENT

Tony Melendez. MCLENNAN
COUNTY SHERIFF'S DEPART-
MENT

Gilbert Melendez. MCLENNAN COUNTY SHERIFF'S DEPARTMENT

Assistant District
Attorney Ned Butler.
JOHN BEN SUTTER

The Rainbow
Drive Inn,
Muneer
Deeb's
grocery store.
PAT STOWERS

Richard Franks at
the funeral of his
son, Kenneth.
*WACO TRIBUNE-
HERALD* PHOTO BY
ROD AYDELOTTE

Nancy Wiser. JOHN BEN SUTTER

Sandra Sadler, mother of Kenneth Franks. PAT STOWERS

Rod Montgomery, father of Jill Montgomery. *WACO TRIBUNE-HERALD* PHOTO BY ROD AYDELOTTE

Jan Thompson, Jill Montgomery's aunt.
PAT STOWERS

Karen Hufstetler, Waxahachie secretary who had a psychic vision of the crime.
PAT STOWERS

Court appointed attorney Russ Hunt, left, talks with client David Spence during a break in the trial. *WACO TRIBUNE-HERALD* PHOTO BY ROD AYDELOTTE

David Spence poses for photo to be sent to bite mark experts. MCLENNAN COUNTY SHERIFF'S DEPARTMENT

Muneer Deeb being escorted to court by McLennan County Deputy
Sheriff Coy Jones. *WACO TRIBUNE-HERALD* PHOTO BY ROD AYDELOTTE

Gilbert Melendez prepares to testify at Muneer Deeb's trial in
Cleburne. *WACO TRIBUNE-HERALD* PHOTO BY ROD AYDELOTTE

Gayle Kelley enters the Johnson County courthouse to testify in the trial of Muneer Deeb. PHOTO BY JIM WEST, *CLEBURNE TIMES-REVIEW*

Walter (Skip) Reaves, Spence's attorney during the aggravated sexual abuse trial in Waco and capital murder trial in Bryan. PAT STOWERS

panions toward a back bedroom, explaining to Dorothy that he needed to talk privately with them about something. When they had been in the bedroom longer than Dorothy felt reasonable, she opened the door to find David heating a spoon and the man holding a needle. Dorothy angrily ordered them from her house and told David that he was never again to bring drugs to her home.

She would later talk with him about the people he had started bringing to her house. Dorothy particularly disliked Gilbert Melendez. She felt he was evil and told David he was not welcome in her house. Nor was his girlfriend Christy, after she burst into the living room one night, cursing Dorothy's daughters and accusing them of trying to steal David from her.

Dorothy Miles was beginning to consider the possibility of telling David he would have to stay away until he got his life in order.

In July of 1982, Dorothy decided she would no longer wait for David to initiate a conversation about the things that were bothering him. His moody behavior, his drinking, and his association with drugs convinced her that he needed professional help. She had decided to bring up the subject one mid-week evening when he came by.

For a long time Dorothy sat in her living room watching David as he drank beer and stared at the television set with a haunted expression on his face. "David," she finally said, "what's wrong? Honey, there's something eating you up inside. I can see it. And, if I can, I'd like to help you."

David did not turn his attention from the TV screen as he said, "I've done something real bad, Mom."

"What now?"

"I think I've killed somebody."

Dorothy felt a shudder run through her body and was suddenly so weak that leaning forward in her chair was difficult. "My God, David, what do you mean, you *think* you killed somebody? Don't you *know?*"

He fixed his attention on the floor, refusing to look at her. "Just forget it. Let's drop it."

She finally brought up the subject that had been on her mind for some time. "David," she said, "you need some help. You've got feelings inside you that need to come out. I can see it. You need to talk to somebody about your problems."

"I don't need a shrink," he replied, his voice sharper than she had ever heard it.

The two sat in silence for several minutes before Dorothy stood. "If you don't want to talk anymore," she said, "I'm going to bed."

"Good night," David said, the tone of finality in his voice strongly suggesting there would be no more discussion of the matter.

That night Dorothy Miles tossed fitfully, wondering if David really was in serious trouble. Several times he had told her about fights where knives had been involved. He had admitted cutting people. It had made her nervous when he sat in her living room, constantly flipping the ivory-handled buck knife he carried in a leather scabbard on his belt. Still, she could not bring herself to imagine David killing someone.

Yet she had seen him become almost like two people. Sober, he was polite and charming, still displaying the childlike qualities which had first attracted her to him. When he was drinking, however, there was a meanness about him that had begun to frighten her.

When she woke the following morning, he was already gone, his empty beer cans carefully collected into a paper sack and placed in the kitchen trash can.

The following Saturday, Dorothy was relieved to see that David was sober when he arrived at her front door late in the afternoon. She immediately noticed that he did not have his knife on his belt. Though he appeared nervous, constantly jumping up to look out the window whenever a car passed, he seemed in better spirits than she had seen him in some time. That evening he was more like the David of old than he had been for some time.

He spent the night and the next morning was up early, asking Dorothy if she would cook him a "birthday breakfast" if he went to the store and purchased the ingredients. Dorothy had forgotten that Sunday, July 18, was his birthday. She would be happy to cook for him, she said.

He returned with potatoes, eggs, bread, milk, and sausage and Dorothy cooked as he sat at the kitchen table, talking. For the first time in a long while there was even some laughter mixed with the conversation. "You know," he said, "this is like old times."

The Sunday paper, with its story on the funerals of the three teenagers who had been murdered on the previous Tuesday evening, lay on the front porch, unopened.

## 20

The fourth floor of the McLennan County jail is populated primarily by prisoners being held for parole violations, awaiting trial, or those already sentenced and biding time while their lawyers complete required appellate paperwork before they can be transferred to the Diagnostic Center at the Texas Department of Corrections. Many have reached the end of the line; they are second- and third-time offenders aware their return to the free world won't come anytime soon. It is generally an older, more mature group of inmates than one finds on the other floors of the jail. With few exceptions, those incarcerated on the fourth floor have learned how to do time. They talk little, pick their friends carefully, play cards, watch mindless game shows and soap operas on television, read jail-provided paperbacks (mostly westerns), and sleep a great deal. It is a slow-motion kind of existence in which patience is a premier virtue.

It was there that David Wayne Spence was being held, awaiting his trial for the aggravated sexual abuse. Because he was a parolee, he was being detained on a "blue warrant," making him ineligible for bond. The fourth floor was the part of the jail where Truman Simons urgently wanted to begin his new career as a jailer.

When Simons reported to the sheriff's department in mid-October of 1982, he spent the first couple of weeks in a training program, moving throughout the jail, learning the routine from booking desk procedure to meal distribution. Occasionally while making the rounds with another jailer, Simons would see Spence and, if they made eye contact, David always nodded or waved.

One afternoon, while Spence was still being held on the second floor, they spoke briefly. David indicated he had tried unsuccessfully to get in touch with Sergeant Baier on several occasions, hoping to learn how the investigation of the lake case was progressing and to tell him that Christy was hard at work, asking questions in an attempt to help. Simons displayed little interest, suggesting only that Spence keep trying to contact Baier at the police department.

As soon as Spence was moved to the fourth floor, however, Simons began seeking a way to have himself assigned there. Just before Thanksgiving, a day-shift position opened on the second floor and Simons persuaded the jailer who had been working nights on four to take it. Simons was then given the fourth-floor assignment.

The jailer watches over those housed on the fourth floor from a narrow, glassed-in area called the picket, furnished only by a desk, the large lighted control panel from which cell doors can be locked and unlocked, and a telephone with a long extension cord. The picket runs the length of the floor and looks out onto the semicircular dayroom which is ringed by the cells. The dayroom contains several tables where inmates eat their meals, play cards, and sit and talk. Mounted high on one wall is a single television set. Inmates determine what shows are viewed by vote. At the end of the picket nearest the elevator is the chute, a small security area enclosed on three sides by barred doors—one leading into the picket, one into the dayroom, the other into the small hallway that leads to the elevator.

It did not take long for Truman Simons' presence to arouse the curiosity of the inmates over whom he would watch from midnight to eight each morning. Several were there because Simons had put them there, and they were the ones who quickly began spreading the word throughout the jail population that there was something strange about a veteran police sergeant suddenly taking on the duties of a lowly jailer. But it was David Spence who first proposed the suggestion that Simons was actually there working undercover in an attempt to gather information on the Lake Waco murders.

Others, however, assumed him to be there in hopes of strengthening the case against a twenty-eight-year-old man named David Drakeford who would soon go on trial for the murder of a gift shop cashier in a downtown Waco hotel. Regularly, inmates stopped by the glassed-in picket where Simons' desk was located, playing guessing games with the new jailer. He would neither confirm nor deny his purpose in being there.

"Well," said one black inmate who had been busted by Simons several months earlier on a narcotics charge, "just tell me this: Why would a guy who's been a cop all his life suddenly leave the police department to become a jailer?"

Simons gave an innocent shrug and smiled. "Just seemed liked the thing to do," he said.

There is actually precious little to be done by the jailer keeping the midnight vigil. He sees that trusties carry out the various cleanup duties upon his arrival, makes certain the prisoners are locked down, and turns on the intercom in all cells so that he might hear any requests for trips to the infirmary. At 5:00 A.M. the lights are turned on and all prisoners are awakened for breakfast. Beyond that, the job provides one an excellent opportunity to catch up on his reading.

It was usually after the morning meal that the inmates approached Simons to talk, trying to persuade him to allow them phone calls to family and sweethearts, offering up complaints about the food, or seeing if he would help them get messages to attorneys who were ignoring their plights.

In short order David Spence was approaching the glassed-in area more regularly than most. Rarely during their brief conversations did he fail to ask about progress on the lake murder investigation.

On a morning in early December, Spence and an eighteen-year-old inmate named Kyle Moore, who would soon be serving a five-year sentence for burglary, approached Simons. David tapped on the glass window to get Simons' attention, then introduced him to Moore.

Spence explained to his companion that Simons had previously worked for the Waco Police Department and had been the man who arrested Muneer Deeb. "Hell, he even came over and questioned me once, thinking maybe I was a suspect," he said.

Then turning his attention to Simons, David said, "This dude here might be able to help you on the case."

"How's that?" Simons asked.

"Well, he was down in Aransas Pass before he came here and ran into this guy who said he had seen a letter some girl from Waco had written. The guy—somebody named Toad—said the girl mentioned the names of the people who killed those kids. I told you I'd try to help you on this thing, remember? I just thought it might be something worth checking out."

Moore said he couldn't remember the girl's name but gave

a vague description of the area in Aransas Pass where Toad might be found.

The conversation then turned to a general discussion of the case. "You really think it will ever be solved?" David asked.

"Oh, yeah," Simons replied. "It's pretty complicated and it'll probably take a long time, but it'll be solved."

"Well, it sounds to me like whoever did it did a pretty good job."

"No, they didn't," Simons quickly replied. "In fact, they fucked up pretty bad."

Spence nodded knowingly. "Yeah, I guess they did. They fucked up by killing the wrong Gayle."

Straining to maintain his composure, Simons said nothing for several seconds, then leaned forward and looked Spence straight in the eye. "How did you know that, David?" he asked.

A strained expression tightened across Spence's face. Without answering, he turned and left.

"What does all that mean?" Kyle Moore asked, puzzled.

Truman smiled. "It doesn't mean anything—except to me and David."

With the help of the police in Aransas Pass, a small town on the Texas Gulf coast, Simons eventually located the letter Moore had mentioned to Spence. Written by the stepdaughter of a police officer from the Waco suburb of Northcrest, it included names of a number of possible suspects which she had obviously overheard her stepfather discussing. The letter meant nothing. But the fact that David had evidently developed a friendship with someone might, Simons thought. From his vantage point in the glassed-in picket, he began to watch Spence and Moore carefully.

A few days later, Truman put aside the book he had been reading to focus his attention on the inmates as they ate breakfast. Spence was seated across from Moore, his back to the jailer. They were obviously engaged in conversation. Suddenly he saw David raise his clenched left hand and make several quick up and down motions. Moore's eyes widened as he first stared at David, then shot a quick glance in the direction of Simons. The jailer sensed a sudden, cold fear in the eyes of Spence's breakfast companion.

Leaning back in his chair, Simons smiled to himself. *Pa-*

*tience*, he thought. *Just be patient. Sooner or later someone's going to start talking.*

It was sooner than he expected. Just a week before Christmas a black inmate approached Simons. "You're working on the lake murders, right?" he said, his voice and face completely devoid of emotion. Simons didn't reply.

"If you're looking at David Spence," the inmate continued, "you're looking at the right man. But you've got a problem."

"What's that?"

"This dude Kyle Moore is real protective of David. Won't let him talk to nobody. You ain't gonna learn shit until you get Kyle's ass off this floor." Then he turned and walked away.

Later that day Kyle Moore was moved to another floor.

The departure of Kyle Moore obviously troubled Spence. He spent his days alternately pacing and staring from the window. One evening as Simons reported for work a fellow jailer greeted him near the booking desk. "Your boy's having a pretty rough time. He's been acting really hinky all day. He tried to call his girlfriend several times and can't get her. He's been bawling his head off."

Simons went to the fourth floor and pushed the button that unlocked Spence's cell door. Spence stuck his head out, looking in Truman's direction. Simons waved him over. "I hear you've been having some problems," he said.

"I can't find Christy," David replied. His eyes were red and irritated from crying. "Everything's falling apart on me. I'm afraid she's going to leave me." He again began to cry.

"Come on around here in the chute," Simons said. "I'll let you call her." Dialing the numbers David gave him, Simons put the receiver through the small opening in the glass. A half-dozen calls failed to locate the elusive girlfriend. Finally David called his mother and talked to her for several minutes.

Resigned that he would not be able to talk to Christy, Spence sat on the floor with his knees gathered to his chest and talked with Simons. It was not long before he asked about the lake case. "You still working on it?"

"Yeah, some," Simons said.

"Got any suspects?"

"Yeah."

"Who?"

It was time, Simons decided, to level. "Well, David," he said, "you're one of them."

Spence looked up at the jailer, expressing surprise, shaking his head. "Aw, man, you haven't got off that shit yet?"

"Nope."

"Damn, I don't see how you could think I would do something like that. I've been trying to help you."

"You haven't helped me," Simons said.

"Well, I've been trying to help Sergeant Baier, but he won't call me. You tell me how I can do it, and I'll help you anyway I can."

"About the only way I know you can help me," Simons replied, "is to tell me who was with you."

A pleading whine crept into Spence's voice. "I'm telling you, I didn't have anything to do with it."

"If that's the case," Truman said, "then you don't have anything to worry about."

"But you think I had something to do with it. Why?"

Simons ignored the question. "David," he said, "do you know what the word hypothetical means?"

"Yeah."

"Well, let me explain how it applies to the law. Let's say we talked about some things, even if they were true. As long as we were talking hypothetically, anything you told me couldn't be used in a court of law or anything like that. It wouldn't be any kind of admission on your part; nothing binding."

"I take it you have some questions you want to ask me," David said.

"Yes, I do."

Spence shrugged. "Okay, ask them and we'll see what happens."

"Let's try this," Simons said. "Let's say you did do that business out at the lake. Who would have helped you, the Arab or Gilbert?"

A smile came over Spence's face as he looked directly at the jailer. "You understand I didn't do it," he said, "but I wouldn't trust that camel jockey to help me. I'd have my bro Gilbert. That answer your question?"

The streets of downtown Waco were still decorated for the Christmas season when Simons received word from the second-floor jailer that an inmate wanted to talk to him. His name, the jailer said, was Carl Casey. And he wanted to talk about the lake murders.

When his shift was over, Simons had Casey called down to one of the interrogation rooms. Not yet twenty-one, Casey had already accumulated an impressive record of trouble with the law. Looking over his rap sheet, Simons saw a series of arrests for assault, burglary, car theft, DWI, and the forgery charge for which he had been recently indicted. Simons had never seen him before, either as a police officer or during his brief tenure as a jailer.

"What can I do for you?" he asked.

Nervous and hesitant to make eye contact, Casey said, "I was told you're working on the Lake Waco murder case."

Simons nodded. "You have something to do with it?"

"No, but I think I can help you. I know who did it."

"I'm listening," Simons said.

"It was David Spence.

"How do you know?"

"He told me."

Certain Casey had spent no time on the fourth floor since David had been moved there, Simons was immediately suspicious. "Where did you talk with David?"

"When we were on the second floor together."

He began to tell his story, hurrying his sentences as though there was some urgency to complete his task. One day in November, he and several other inmates had been talking about the lake murders when Spence walked up. He didn't join into the conversation, just listened as the others talked about the crime. After a while the conversation changed to other subjects—cars and women. Then Spence finally spoke. "You guys really want to know what happened out at the lake?" he asked. Casey said he asked David how he knew. Spence smiled, offered him a cigarette, and said, "Hell, I was there. I did it." Then he turned and walked off.

The following day, Casey said, he and Spence were sitting in the dayroom following the noon meal and the subject came up again. At that time David went into detail about how he had cut the girls' throats and stabbed the kids repeatedly.

Simons stopped him in mid-sentence. "Here's what I want you to do," he said. "Go back to your cell and write it all down.

Everything you can remember; everything David said. Think about it and be sure you get it straight. I'm going to go home and get some rest, then I'll come back this evening and we'll talk some more."

For Simons, trying to sleep that day was useless. Although his shift didn't start until midnight, he was back at the jail at eight that evening, anxious to see Casey again.

The statement Casey had written was more detailed than Simons had dared hope. It told of Spence's reactions and gestures as he described the two girls, a pretty blonde and a brunette with large breasts. He had carefully phrased Spence's exact words as he detailed the number of times he stabbed the victims, and he described Spence standing with a crazed look in his eyes, swinging his arm in a stabbing motion as he told his gruesome tale. The brunette, Spence had said, would not die quickly. That's why he had stabbed her fourteen, maybe fifteen times. He said he had tried to have sex with "the girl with the big tits" but had decided not to because of all the blood. It had been worth it, though, Spence had said. He got six thousand dollars and some crank out of the deal.

The statement was too good, too pat. Almost as if it had been rehearsed. One part of Simons wanted to run to the D.A.'s office, proudly waving the statement as proof that his theory was coming together. Another, however, signaled caution. Something was not right. After months of dead ends and runarounds, it was too easy to have someone he didn't even know provide the first real break. That night as he sat monitoring the fourth floor, he read Casey's statement over and over. It sounded good, and he wanted badly to believe it. But something was wrong.

The following morning after his shift ended Simons began going through the jail records to see when and where Casey and Spence might have been together. He felt a rush of disappointment and anger when he found that David had been moved from the second floor to the fourth the day before Casey was jailed. There was no way they could have spent time with each other.

He immediately had Casey returned to the interrogation room and, making no attempt to suppress his irritation, began quizzing him about where the conversation had taken place.

"When we were on the second floor," Casey insisted.

"Bullshit," Simons spat back. "You've never been on the second floor with David Spence."

"Okay," Casey said, "maybe it was in the gym."

Simons glared. "You've been here long enough to know that the second floor and fourth floor don't go to the gym at the same time. I don't know what the hell is going on here, or why you're lying to me, but you're about to get yourself in deep shit."

"Hell, I don't know for sure," Casey said. "It could have been when we were down at the booking desk or something. But he told me, I swear."

"I don't believe you. Somebody told you all this, but it wasn't David. Why don't you just tell me the truth?"

"I'm telling the truth."

"Like hell," Simons said, pitching the statement on the table and walking out the door.

Disappointed and puzzled, Truman searched through the daily roster sheets kept for each floor, hoping he might find the name of someone who could have provided Casey with his information. The statement had been too detailed, too thorough to have been nothing more than the product of his imagination. After several minutes of searching he found the name he was looking for: Kyle Moore.

Simons wasted no time getting to the point with the young man who sat across from him in the interrogation room. "Kyle," he said, "Carl Casey came to me with a pretty interesting story about the lake murders, one there's no way he could have made up. But it doesn't work. He didn't get his information from David. Somebody else gave it to him—and I think that somebody is you."

He didn't allow Moore time to reply before continuing. "When you were up on the fourth floor, I think maybe David told you a lot of things about the lake case. And I know you were trying to keep him from talking to anybody else, me included. Hell, Kyle, that's why you aren't up there anymore. I'm the one who had you transferred to the second floor. And that's where you told Casey the things David had been telling you. Then you sent him to me. Right?"

Kyle did not answer.

"Look, I don't know what you're trying to do," Simons continued, careful not to raise his voice. "It looks like you're trying to help on this thing, but you're going about it all wrong. There's no doubt in my mind that Carl would have climbed up on the witness stand and sworn to that shit he was telling me. But we aren't going to play the game that way. We're not going to have any perjured testimony in this case. If David Spence did the lake murders we're going to get him fair and square. And we don't need anyone's lies to do it.

"If David told you what happened out there and you don't want to talk about it, that's fine. That's something you've got to decide whether you can live with. What I'm saying to you is, if you can't help us, then for God's sake don't hurt us. Just stay the hell out of it."

Kyle Moore began to cry. "I put Casey up to it," he finally said. "David told me all that stuff."

"Will you help us?" Simons asked.

"I like David," the youngster said. "And I feel sorry for him. But you can't ever turn him loose. He'll just kill somebody else if you ever let him back on the streets." He was quiet for a minute, as if wrestling with a decision. Then he said, "Yeah, okay, I'll help you. I'll give you a statement or testify or whatever you want me to do. You've just got to make sure David never gets out of here."

Before leaving to write out his statement, Kyle mentioned the names of several other inmates with whom Spence had spoken about the murders. "I just couldn't make him keep his mouth shut," Moore said. "It was like he just had to brag about it." He was still crying when the jailer delivered him back to the second floor.

Moore's statement closely paralleled that which Casey had written. There were detailed descriptions of the girls and references to Spence becoming almost glassy-eyed, pale, and shaking as he told of the stabbings. Moore said that he and David had talked about the murders on three occasions, beginning in early December. David had told him that the brunette he was most attracted to and "really wanted to fuck" had struggled, even pulling a knife on him. It was the first indication Simons had that Jill Montgomery had carried a knife.

Other things in Kyle's statement lent a ring of truth to what he was saying. Spence had told him about taking the victims' money and giving it to someone who had been with him that night. When mentioning the money, Spence would nod in the direction of Gilbert Melendez who was on the south wing of the floor, separated from them only by a wall of glass. Kyle had, in fact, noticed that Gilbert always seemed to watch them closely whenever he and David talked. He said David had mentioned that the victims had been tied with their own shoestrings and one of the girls' bra—another fact not generally known. And he talked about "some foreigner" who he said should be paying for his attorney.

When Kyle Moore gave his statement to Simons, six months had passed since the murders had occurred. Though encouraged, Truman knew he was still a long way from having the kind of information that would command the interest of the district attorney's office or a grand jury. Both, he knew from years of experience, lent little weight to the testimony of convicts.

# 21

Jail society is something of a spoiled cornucopia from the American mainstream. Lives which would never have touched under other circumstances are joined together by the strict, grinding demands of incarceration. There is little in the way of democratic structure separating the good from the bad, the unrepentant criminal from the good father and provider who made one senseless mistake, the educated from the uneducated, the young from the old. By the legal system's design, there is a collective sameness that most eventually come to accept. The McLennan County jail, like most, is a modern-day Babel, its tower four stories high.

Inmates, their spirits driven to the limits by the tiresome waiting and the mindless routine of each new day, fight a never-ending battle with boredom. Though few have anything to sell or with which to barter, their confined world is something of a thieves' market wherein cigarettes are traded for phone calls, commissary privileges exchanged for a guarded copy of yesterday's newspaper. Valued items such as stamps are hidden like expensive jewelry, only to be found and ripped off by those whose experience has taught them all the hiding places. Denied drugs, prisoners make deals to collect the rations of medication passed out to others by jail attendants. Eventually one can accumulate enough aspirin and antibiotics to dull the ache of the waiting for a few hours. Prisoners quickly learn who is receiving money from friends or relatives on the outside and, depending on the individual, become friendly or threatening until the wealth is shared.

Some satisfy their sexual needs by trading stories, often greatly exaggerated, of past conquests; others content themselves with masturbation fantasies conjured while looking at pictures of the provocatively dressed, heavy-breasted young girls featured in biker magazines like *Easy Rider*. A few who find masturbation unfulfilling "catch a shower" with some other willing inmate. Jails and prisons make bisexuals of many who have previously lived straight, heterosexual lifestyles. The admitted homosexuals, though looked down on by most in jail society, find themselves serving a perverted usefulness.

And there are soul-baring conversations between those who normally would not even bother to become acquainted in the free world. Seeking comfort for their private agonies, prisoners talk with great candor to fellow inmates of unfaithful wives and girlfriends, their search for God's mercy, legal loopholes overlooked by careless lawyers, and the hope of a better life once society's debt has been paid. There is always talk of fast cars and big money. And some, feeling a need to prove their importance and knowing no other way, boast about the crimes which have brought them there.

David Spence was looked upon by his fellow inmates as one of the most nervous residents on the fourth floor. While others lay quietly in their bunks, read, or played cards, he paced constantly, walking the perimeter of the dayroom much like a caged animal hoping that perhaps one more round would reveal some previously overlooked avenue of escape. When Spence tired of walking, he stood by the window that looked out onto a park where youngsters practiced soccer and Little League baseball. By straining to get just the right vantage point, he could also see the parking lot at the end of the alley which ran alongside the jail. Better than anyone else confined to the fourth floor, David Spence knew the comings and goings of jail visitors.

He was also a "talker." When newly arrived inmates would ask what he was being held for, David rarely mentioned the aggravated sexual abuse charge. He was, he said, a suspect in the lake murders—which, of course, he had nothing to do with, he would add.

Spence was talking about the murders to a number of his fellow prisoners, but the details, if he gave any, constantly changed. At times he would interrupt a conversation about the crime to boast that he knew more than anyone, then walk away after throwing out his teasing remark. Many of the inmates ignored his broad hints, thinking he was only trying to call attention to himself, to somehow prove he was something more than a run-of-the-mill jailbird.

Other inmates, however, felt a growing discomfort in the

knowledge that David, in all likelihood, did have something to do with the killings of the three teenagers.

If nothing else, David Spence was one of the strangest people they had ever met. He talked of a "Satan's temple" in north Waco where he and others would meet to meditate and lay complicated plans for violent crimes. The publicity received by convicted murderer Gary Gilmore, who became the subject of a Norman Mailer book and made-for-television movie, fascinated him, and he referred often to the Utah convict who was actively seeking the death penalty as "a great man." Spence boasted to some that he, too, would one day be immortalized in print. A letter reached the editorial desk of *Texas Monthly* magazine, offering his life story for a price. It would be the story of one victimized by the system, however, not of a multiple murderer. He never received a reply.

Though he frequently veiled his own involvement, Spence spoke often of the murders of Jill Montgomery, Raylene Rice, and Kenneth Franks. To some he confided that he and his girlfriend had been at the park the night of the crime, witnesses to the torture and the killings. He insisted he knew where the knife the killer used was hidden and would lead authorities to the weapon—but only if they would first agree to drop the sexual abuse charges against him. The murdered teenagers, he told one inmate, had seen something they were not supposed to see. He also said he knew there was a payoff for the murders, including six thousand dollars in cash and a new Bronco for the person who committed them. The job, he insisted to several, was as good as any done by a professional hit man.

While Spence confided to some that he was nothing more than an accidental witness to the crime, going so far as to include his girlfriend in the scenario, others heard a story which more strongly suggested that David himself had committed the murders. Some heard details of the rapes which occurred, of how the victims were bound, and that someone named Lucky was the orchestrator of the event, the "money man."

When a suspect in the murder of a young woman named Gail Beth Bramlett in nearby Axtell was taken into custody, the new inmate told anyone who asked that he was being questioned not only about the Bramlett case but the lake murders as well. Spence, learning of the man's claim, angrily approached him and announced, "You haven't got anything to do with those killings out at the lake. *I'm* the only one in here who knows anything about that business." He sounded much like a jealous child, protective of those things which were his and his alone.

There were many who spent time with David, first on the second floor and then the fourth, who remained unconvinced that he was responsible for the crime with which he seemed obsessed. His constant references to the lake murders, they suspected, were to draw attention away from the sex crime for which he awaited trial. Few, however, doubted him capable of murder.

Some felt he was mentally unbalanced. Members of the black inmate population, whom David had made clearly aware of his racial bias, feared him. Though he was no more physically imposing than many of the others in the jail, Spence's behavior caused the blacks to shy from him. What made them most uncomfortable was the chanting he would occasionally do late at night in his cell. It was nothing more than a rambling stream of monosyllables, spoken in a low, gravelly voice, yet several of the blacks were convinced it was part of David's "devil worshipping."

And there were his piercing blue eyes that seemed to scream a warning of evil and hatred. "You look in that man's eyes," one inmate said, "and you see the Devil himself."

Many found it strange that Spence, who generally showed very little interest in watching television with others in the dayroom, was adamant in his demand that the channel not be changed from the afternoon reruns of a show called "Three's Company," a situation comedy whose stars were two girls—one a blonde, the other a brunette—and a young man. Spence would stand directly in front of the television throughout the show, his hands shoved deeply into the pockets of his jail whites. Some described the expression that would come over his face as trance-like while he watched the program. His concealed hands appeared to be moving in the area of his genitals.

For those who had kept up with the details of the lake murders in the local papers and on television, the resemblance between the three actors on the show and the three teenagers who had been killed was not lost. Immediately after each segment of the show ended, David would quickly retreat to his cell, speaking to no one, and stay there for the next half hour.

And when he spoke of Christy Juhl to fellow inmates, he

described her as a five-foot-four brunette with fashion-model good looks and an eye-catching figure. Much interest was generated in anticipation of her first appearance at the jail. When those who saw her in the visiting room reported back that she was nothing like David's description—Christy was tall and skinny and hardly model material—it was duly noted that the girl he had described bore a far greater resemblance to the murdered Jill Montgomery than to Christy Juhl.

During his thirty years, Daryl Beckham had spent time inside jails and prisons in Florida, Kentucky, Texas, and New Mexico. And now, as 1983 was beginning, he once again faced imprisonment in the Texas Department of Corrections. A series of low-paying jobs, none of which seemed to last long after his employer learned of his criminal history, had driven him back to old vices. With his wife expecting her fourth child, Beckham had unsuccessfully tried forgery to make ends meet.

Waiting in the McLennan County jail for his transfer to the state prison, he mixed with few other inmates, choosing to remain to himself, reading his Bible and writing long letters to his wife, assuring her that once he was free again he would never get into any more trouble with the law, even if it meant working two jobs.

One morning as Beckham was reading scriptures, Spence approached him and told him he too had begun to seek comfort in the Bible. Not only that, but he had stopped using profanity and was even trying to quit smoking. He had stopped talking about being a member of a Satanic cult. At night in his cell he no longer engaged in his demonic chants, instead praying that God would forgive his sins. If he interpreted the scriptures right, forgiveness would result in freedom. And it was freedom that Spence wanted more than anything.

In addition to everything else, Spence confided to his new-found friend Daryl Beckham, he felt he was losing Christy. More and more often Christy was not at home when he called. Her visits, once regular, had become sporadic and short. After failing to show on visiting day, she would explain that she had been unable to find a ride, or that when she had finally managed to get there, it was too late for the jailer to allow her to see him. David's reaction would range from rage to unashamed tears as he spoke with her on the phone. They had planned to be married

just as soon as he got out, he told Beckham, but now she seemed
to have cooled on the idea. He failed to mention to Beckham
that Christy had already married Mahir Tumimi. He did say that
he suspected she was running around on him, dating others
while he was unable to do anything about it.

Aware that the other inmates seemed to want little to do with
Spence, Beckham felt sorry for him. Daryl, too, had known the
unique pain that accompanies concern over a wife or a girlfriend
on the outside, thus he listened to David as he poured out his
feelings of hopelessness and depression. Hoping to offer some
comfort, Daryl suggested they read the Bible and pray together.
It was hard for him, too, he assured David, but he had found
strength in his faith. Unable to control things any longer, he had
placed his problems in the hands of the Lord. Maybe if David
did the same, things might look better.

Beckham was amazed at how quickly Spence picked up on
the Bible study he had suggested. He read scriptures tirelessly
and was soon quoting them to Daryl. And David gradually began to feel that Beckham was someone he could trust with the
private pains he was enduring. Sensing in him loneliness much
like his own, David felt no need to impress Beckham. He was
his friend, someone in whom he could confide his fears without
concern they would be viewed as a sign of weakness.

Daryl, meanwhile, had begun to feel uncomfortable in David's presence. His sudden shifts of emotion, his love-hate attitude toward this girl named Christy, and his sudden, fanatical
interest in the Bible convinced Beckham that Spence was on the
verge of a mental breakdown—if he hadn't already had one. He
began to send notes to the head jailer, suggesting that David
needed the help of a psychiatrist.

Beckham had been working in Oklahoma at the time of the Lake
Waco murders and therefore was one of the few inmates in the
McLennan County jail with no knowledge of the crimes. Because he chose to isolate himself from the other prisoners, he
had heard none of the whispered discussions of David's bragging remarks. After they had known each other for several days,
Spence was the one who first made Daryl aware of the killings.

It was one of those evenings when David, again unable to
get in touch with Christy, sat in front of his cell crying while
Beckham tried in vain to offer comfort. For a while he read

aloud from the Bible, hoping the sound of his voice and the scripture he was reading would turn Spence's thoughts to something else.

With no provocation, David began telling Beckham about the sexual abuse charges. "But that's not what I'm worried about," he said.

Daryl didn't understand.

Talking in a whisper, his voice controlled, Spence said, "Have you heard about those kids who were found murdered out at Speegleville Park?"

"No," Daryl said, unsure where the conversation was leading.

"See, if I hadn't cut that boy, they would have never even thought about me as a suspect in those murders."

"I don't know what murders you're talking about," Daryl said, confused.

Then David began to tell him the story:

There was this foreigner named Lucky who owned a grocery store called the Rainbow, and he had this girl—her name was Gayle—who was messing around on him. He had rented her an apartment but she kept seeing another guy named Kenneth. The foreigner had explained how, back in his country, it was dishonorable for one man to fuck around with another guy's woman. If something like that happened, it was a tradition—a matter of honor—to get even.

Thus, Lucky had told David he wanted him to kill both Gayle and Kenneth. If necessary, he could get someone to help him. But he was to tell anyone else involved that the killings were over some kind of dope deal. Lucky wanted to make sure there was no way he could be tied to the crime. David had agreed and told Lucky that he had a friend named Gilbert who would help him.

Beckham said nothing as he listened to the bizarre confession. It seemed impossible that this man with whom he had been reading the Bible, this man he had felt such sympathy for, could have been involved in murder.

Now David was on his feet, pacing as he spoke. Anger crept into his voice. "Lucky was going to pay," he said. "He was going to let me and my old lady move into the apartment he had rented for Gayle. We were going to just tell anybody who asked about her that she moved away. And Lucky was going to open up a game room and let me manage it. Then later he was going to buy out his partner there at the Rainbow and take me in as his partner. Man, I was going to be set for life."

"David," Beckham said, "I don't think I want to hear this."

"Naw," David said, "I guess you don't." Picking up his Bible, he walked into his cell and lay down on his bunk.

It would not be the last Daryl Beckham would hear of the lake murders, however. Now more convinced than ever that David was suffering from mental problems, he continued to try, without success, to persuade officials to get psychiatric help for David. And though he tried to avoid Spence it was impossible. Growing increasingly depressed, David sought him out. And continued to unburden himself. A few weeks after their initial conversation David again brought up the subject of the murders.

"It was me who killed them," David said. "Gilbert was there and he helped me tie them up. He raped the girls, too, but I was the one who did all the killing. It was like something came over me, like I was possessed. I couldn't stop myself after I started. The girls kept screaming and squirming. I was afraid someone was going to hear us. So I kept stabbing them. Stabbing and stabbing . . . but they wouldn't shut up."

As Spence spoke he appeared glassy-eyed, as if in a trance. His hands shook and he began to cry.

"We made the boy watch while we fucked the girls. I had this stick—my 'love stick'—and I stuck it up in the girls while he watched. Then, after we were through with them, I killed him. I had to kill them all."

Several times during his brief, horrifying description of the murders, he made quick stabbing motions with his left hand.

"It all happened in Koehne Park but Lucky told us he wanted the bodies left at Speegleville because none of us ever went there. That way, see, there was no way they could tie us to the killings. So we loaded them into the car and drove over there. My old lady followed us in another car."

As though exhausted by the revelation, David suddenly fell silent and slumped to a sitting position on the concrete floor. Though tears slid down his face he seemed calm.

"There are only four people other than you who know anything about this," he said, fixing a threatening stare on Beckham. "If it gets out, I'll know who talked."

Beckham nodded. He understood what David was saying.

"You think God will forgive me?" David asked.

"I don't know," Daryl said, shaking his head. "I just don't know."

In early February Truman Simons reported to work to find that Spence had been placed in a medical cell earlier in the day. For no apparent reason he had begun yelling incoherently and beating his fists against the wall. He threw things and tried to pick fights, running back and forth from his cell to the dayroom, raging at other inmates and the day jailer on duty. Fearful that he might hurt himself or someone else, the jailer had summoned help and had David taken downstairs where he was given a shot of Thorazine to calm him.

Having come in early, Simons decided to look in on David before reporting to the fourth floor. He found Spence pacing back and forth in the cramped isolation cell, his fists clenched, his eyes red from crying. The effects of the Thorazine had apparently worn off.

"I hear you had a pretty rough day," Simons said. "Want to talk about it?"

David was standing with his back stiffly arched against the far wall of the cell. "It's all falling apart on me, Mr. Simons," he said as he began sobbing. "Everything's going bad. I don't know what I'm going to do."

"You feel like going back up on the fourth floor?"

"I gotta get out of here," David said, angrily waving his arm at the small, windowless isolation cell in which he was being held.

"I'll get you moved back up," Simons said. "If you feel like it, we can talk some later."

Prior to that evening, Simons had purposely kept his relationship with Spence low-keyed. He had been friendly but distant. He had allowed David to come into the chute and make late-night phone calls to Christy or his mother and had listened on occasion when David wanted to stay and talk. But Simons had rarely spoken of the lake murders, and then only when David brought up the subject, asking about the progress of the investigation.

Simons had made it clear to David that he was a suspect, but had pressed the issue no further. Spence had no idea that the jailer had been quietly building a case against him, gathering statements from several inmates who had told him of David's references to the murders. Nor did he know of the times during the day when Simons, unable to sleep, had returned to the jail to sit in the TV monitoring room, watching Spence's every move for hours at a time.

Never in his law enforcement career had Truman Simons so carefully studied a suspect. He had become familiar with David's mannerisms, his speech patterns, even the way he walked. He knew to whom he wrote letters and who wrote to him. He had talked with numerous people who he knew could provide no insight into the lake murders, just to learn more about David's personality. Simons had come to know David Spence far better than the troubled inmate could have imagined.

That night after the other inmates were asleep, Simons pushed the button which unlocked Spence's cell and waved him to the chute. For the remainder of the night he listened as David wallowed in self-pity.

"This whole mess is a pretty sad situation," David said. He was seated on the floor, his back against the bars, his knees drawn up under his chin.

"What do you mean?"

"Well, think about it," David replied. "Everybody's turned against me. Nobody cares about what happens to me. I got that blue warrant on me, so I can't bond out. I'm just stuck here, getting nowhere. Everything's just closing in on me. What's really funny is that the only person in the world who acts like he cares a thing about me is you. And you're the guy who's trying to get me killed over those murders at the lake."

Simons did not answer for several minutes. In a manner of speaking, what Spence was saying was true. There had been occasions during their series of late-night conversations when the jailer found himself enjoying Spence's company. When not morose or overwhelmed with self-pity, David was pleasant, even personable. More than once Truman had found himself pulling the handwritten statements given to him by several inmates from his briefcase to reread them after having sent Spence back to his cell. There were times when he had to remind himself of who David was. He had to force himself to remember what he was sure David had done.

"Look, David," Simons finally said. "I'm not going to lie to you. I know you're going through some hard times and I wish there was something I could do to help you . . ."

David smiled faintly. "Like send me to death row?"

Simons did not return the smile. "If you killed those kids at the lake—and I think you did—then you've got to pay. It's nothing personal, David, just business. I want you to know that."

Spence studied Simons' expression but said nothing for several seconds. "I wasn't crazy," he finally said. "They didn't have to take me down there and give me a shot. I just wanted somebody to talk to me."

"I'll tell you what," Simons said. "The next time you start having problems like you did today, call me at home. We'll talk on the phone or I'll come down here—whatever you want. I'd like to help you if I can. I'll let the other jailers know it's okay for you to get in touch with me anytime."

"You serious?"

"David, I told you—I'm not going to lie to you."

"I appreciate that, Mr. Simons."

Truman nodded. "Now, go get some sleep."

In the days to come, Judy Simons would come to dread the times she would answer the telephone and hear the frantic voice of David Spence, telling her that he urgently needed to speak with her husband.

# 22

When Vic Feazell, age thirty-one, announced that he would be a Democratic candidate for the office of McLennan County District Attorney, few in Waco political circles paid him much attention. Felipe Reyna had held the office for six years and confidently told friends that the youthful attorney, just four years out of Baylor law school, would be nothing more than a political nuisance during the primary.

Reyna did not anticipate the vigorous campaign Feazell would wage, directing his speeches and advertising at the city's common man rather than the influential upper echelon of Waco's society and power structure. With a strong backing from the middle class and the blue-collar worker, Feazell upset the incumbent in the primary and went on to win a bitter battle with the Republican candidate in the November general election.

Promising to "get the district attorney back in the courtroom," the handsome, smooth-talking Feazell pulled no punches. As the campaign heated he made enemies. But as the polls would show, he had gained the favor of the majority of the voters.

As soon as the new district attorney had been sworn in, he instituted a new policy of security which abruptly ended the Reyna tradition of an open-door policy for defense attorneys who wanted to drop by to review files, discuss cases, or just drink coffee. To see the D.A. or a member of his staff, attorneys were forced to sit in a small outer lobby, waiting their turn to be allowed through locked doors into the offices of Feazell and his assistants. Disgruntled lawyers began calling the third floor of the courthouse annex "Fort Feazell."

To assure his detractors that he had no intentions of changing the new security policy he had instigated, Feazell had bumper stickers printed which read "I Visited Fort Feazell" and saw to it that the receptionist distributed them to all who called on his office. It was immediately clear to the legal community that the new district attorney, though inexperienced and sometimes brash, was not going to be easily intimidated.

The son of a "hellfire and brimstone" Baptist preacher, Feazell grew up in parsonages in out-of-the-way towns in Louisiana, Texas, and New Mexico where his father fought sin with one hand and an endless financial battle with the other. Destined to minister to small congregations in small churches for wages which imposed a constant economic strain, the Reverend Fred Feazell nonetheless held high hopes that his son would one day follow his footsteps and preach God's word. Vic was just thirteen when he entered the pulpit to deliver his first sermon during a youth worship service.

However, by the time he had entered high school in tiny Leander, Texas, near Austin, Feazell's interest focused more on such teenage pleasures as dating, cars, coon hunting, and occasional experiments with liquor and drugs when not working after school on a chicken farm. Graduating from high school shortly before his seventeenth birthday, Vic enrolled in the cadet training program sponsored by the nearby Austin Police Department. He had made up his mind to pursue a career in law enforcement.

After a year with the Austin Police Department, however, Feazell took the advice of a friendly sergeant and turned his attention to the pursuit of a college degree. With the help of his father, Feazell enrolled at the predominantly female Mary Hardin-Baylor College in Belton where he would serve as one of the dozen "campus boys" at the school, young men who performed various landscaping and maintenance chores on the campus in exchange for the privilege of attending classes. To help fund his education, he took a part-time job as a counselor in the Bell County Juvenile Probation Department and, after being ordained, served as pastor of a small Baptist church in the nearby community of Dyess Grove.

It was not until his senior year at Mary Hardin-Baylor that Feazell decided to seek a law degree at Baylor University. To pay his way through law school he continued preaching and working in juvenile probation, eventually landing a full-time job as a social worker with the Mental Health and Retardation Center in Waco. By the time he graduated he was director of the MHMR Drug Abuse Treatment Program.

Just out of law school, Feazell served as co-counsel in a highly controversial lawsuit filed against a prominent Waco bank in which his client received the largest settlement awarded by a jury in McLennan County judicial history. It was the role of prosecutor, however, which most intrigued him.

Shortly after he took office in January of 1983, public concern about the progress of the Lake Waco murders investigation came to the attention of the new D.A. Knowing little more about the case than what he had seen on television and read in newspaper accounts, Feazell spoke with several Waco police officers who had been involved in the early stages of the previous summer's investigation. There was still a considerable amount of suspicion, he learned, directed toward the father of Kenneth Franks. The possibility that the crime had been drug-related was also still being pursued. Feazell was assured that the police were making progress. There was no mention of Truman Simons.

Feeling his office should stay abreast of developments in the case, Feazell instructed assistant Dennis Green to check occasionally on the progress of the investigation. Already, Feazell was thinking, far too much time had passed since the crime. If the public was to have respect for local law enforcement, such highly publicized cases had to be solved and prosecuted. If the police made no headway in the near future, Vic decided, he would involve his office in the investigation.

Meanwhile, he had a great deal of organizational work to accomplish before settling into the daily routine of his new office. Too, he had to begin soon to think about fulfilling his campaign promise of serving as prosecuting district attorney. Feazell's first court appearance would be the trial of an aggravated sexual abuse case. According to the file which was already on his desk, the defendant was a twenty-four-year-old Waco man named David Wayne Spence.

Since their conversation after David's trip to the jail's medical cell, Truman Simons had dramatically altered the approach he had first taken in his investigation. He no longer played the passive role, always allowing Spence to think he was in control of the situation. In a subtle way, Truman had become the aggressor.

David Spence had begun to fascinate Truman. It was almost as if he were two people. In the controlled environment of jail he was pleasant, almost charming—even enjoyable to talk with. Generally able to conform to the standards of incarceration, David was a near-perfect inmate. Yet on the streets he was an entirely different person: a robber and rapist, a man fascinated with knives, a murderer. Perhaps, Simons had begun to think, David, the handsome charmer, was fighting some dark battle with an alter ego named Chili.

There were some dramatic parallels, Simons felt, between the personalities of David Spence and the much-publicized Ted Bundy, the man who had finally been apprehended in Florida after being suspected of killing as many as thirty-five young women throughout the United States. Bundy had been charming and good-looking. But there had been the dark side which few ever saw and lived to tell about.

Such a personality disorder was the badge of a stone-cold psychopath, a tag, Simons felt, that fit David like a glove. And he wondered to himself if it were possible Spence might have a split personality.

It was no secret among the jailers that Simons was talking to Spence about the lake murders. The sheriff had advised the other deputies of the fact, ordering them not to interfere and to allow Spence phone calls to Truman's home any time he requested them. Seldom did an evening go by when Truman reported for duty that someone didn't ask if he was making any progress in his talks with David.

One morning as a young relief jailer arrived on the fourth floor he saw David seated on the floor of the chute, crying as he talked quietly to Simons. Truman, sitting in a chair on the opposite side of the bars, gave the jailer a signal to go on down to the other end of the hall until their conversation was over. Unknown to the newly arrived jailer, David had spent another upsetting night trying to get in touch with Christy. Feeling she had deserted him, he was feeling sorry for himself, pouring out his problems to Simons.

The daytime jailer, who for weeks had been pressing Simons for details of the conversations he had been having with Spence, assumed the emotional display was something more. Perhaps David had decided to confess, or if not, was on the verge. Shortly after Simons left, the new guard called David back to the chute and began to make conversation, noting that he apparently had been having a rough time earlier. Spence made no comment on the matter, then asked if he could make a phone call.

The jailer said he would allow him to use the phone only if he would tell him whether or not he had committed the lake murders. Suddenly defensive, David told the jailer that he had no intention of confessing to murder just to be allowed a phone call. The jailer then informed the prisoner that he would never again allow him to make a call until he told him whether he was involved in the crime.

The next evening David told Simons about the exchange. Though he masked his anger, Truman went directly to the sheriff after getting off duty and related what had happened. "The idiot could have fucked up everything," he said. "Hell, David just might have confessed, just to get to use the phone. Then we're all wrapped up in coercion and all kinds of shit. I'd appreciate it if you would keep that guy off the fourth floor." Sheriff Harwell went Simons one better: he fired the young jailer that day.

On February 15 Truman Simons anticipated a long day. Immediately after leaving the fourth floor, he went downstairs and began making arrangements for Daryl Beckham to see a hypnotist, in hopes that he might be able to recall additional details about his conversations with Spence. And Jerry Jackson, one of the inmates who had heard David talking about the murders, had agreed to give a statement. In fact, Jackson's girlfriend had admitted to him that she had once been sexually abused by David, and he had convinced her to come to the sheriff's office and give her statement also.

It was late afternoon before all the details had been worked out. Beckham had been pulled off the fourth floor to await his hypnotic session and Jackson sat in one of the interview rooms with Simons, awaiting the arrival of his girlfriend. They had just begun to discuss the procedures involved in giving a statement when a deputy knocked on the door and asked Simons to step outside.

"We just had to bring your boy Spence down," the deputy said. "He went ape shit up there a while ago and we can't do anything with him. He's back there in one of the medical cells, screaming and hollering for you. He won't let us give him a shot. He's fighting everybody. He says he wants you to come over there."

"What happened?"

"I don't have a clue. He's just acting crazy. I don't know what the hell to do with him."

Simons shook his head. "I'm in the middle of taking something pretty important right now," he said. "Just put him in one of the rooms across from booking and get somebody to go talk to him until I can get there."

"I'll see what I can do."

Simons had just begun taking the young woman's statement when he got a call from one of the sergeants in the jail. "Can you come over right away?"

Disturbed by the second interruption, Truman said, "I'm pretty tied up right now."

"Well, we need your help. Spence is really flipping out."

"Let me see if I can get somebody to finish taking these statements," Truman said. After finding a deputy to take over, Simons explained to Jackson and his girlfriend that an emergency needed his immediate attention. "I'll be back to talk with you in a little while," he said, then hurried down the hall in the direction of the jail.

He could hear David's screams long before he arrived at the cell where David was being held. He entered to see two jailers standing near the door and David, crying and wild-eyed, backed into a corner. When he saw Simons, Spence let himself slide down the wall to a sitting position, his legs folded beneath his chin.

Simons looked down at David for several seconds. He seemed almost frail, and more frightened than Truman had ever seen him. Pulling a chair over near where Spence sat, Simons looked back at the puzzled jailers. Both were stunned at the calm which had suddenly come over the prisoner as soon as Truman entered the room. "You guys can go now," Simons said. "I'll take care of this." They left, closing the door behind them.

"David, what's the matter?" Truman asked.

For several minutes Spence refused to speak, his crying becoming more intense.

"David," Simons repeated, "what's the matter? What's got you so upset?"

"Christy," Spence finally said in an almost childlike voice. "She's nothing but a whore."

"You can't get her on the phone?" Truman asked.

"She's been lying to me," David replied. "All that business about not being able to get down here to see me, stuff like that. She's just been lying. I saw her today. I was sitting up there in the window and saw her get out of a car and run into the jail. I was about to jump down and get ready to go visit, but she ran right back out to the car and got in with this dude who drove her down here. She moved over by him and kissed him."

"Who was the guy?"

"I don't know; some fat guy driving a white Pontiac. I just can't stand it anymore. I can't handle it."

"Well, David," Truman said, "you've got to understand—she's a young girl, full of piss and vinegar. She's got her own life to live. And you're here in jail. You've got to figure she's going to go out with other people. That's just something you're going to have to accept."

Simons' suggestion angered David. "No," he said. "That's not how it's supposed to be. She's supposed to wait for me. If I was out there and she was in here, I'd wait."

"All I can tell you is that you're going to have to handle it as best you can. You can't let things like that get you down."

"I want to talk to her."

"Okay, I'll tell you what. As soon as I come on duty tonight I'll let you call her."

"No, I want to talk to her now."

"There's no way you can talk to her now, David. There aren't any phones in here. Besides, we probably wouldn't even be able to find her right now."

With that Simons rose from his chair. "Look, I've got some work I need to finish up over at the office. You just relax, settle down, and I'll come back in a little while and get you. Maybe we can get her on the phone then, okay?"

Spence looked up at Simons and again began crying. "I don't want you to leave," he said.

"David, I can't sit up here all evening with you. We can talk tonight. Right now I've got some things I need to do."

A trace of a smile spread across Spence's face for the first time since Simons had entered the room. "I know," he said, "but I think you *want* to talk to me."

Simons sat down.

"Look," David said. "I want to talk to Christy, then I'm going to do something that will make this whole city happy."

Truman's body momentarily tensed. David, he had learned, was most vulnerable in times of depression. He had long ago decided that it was only in such a state that Spence might finally talk of his role in the lake murders.

"What do you have in mind?" Simons asked.

"You know what I'm going to do," David snapped.

*I hope I do*, Simons thought, but he pled ignorance. "I can't read your mind," he said.

"Well," David said, "you've been working hard, spending a lot of hours down there at the jail. I hear things. I know you've been working night and day. You need to be home with your family. I'm going to do something that will help you finally get some rest."

"What's that?"

"I want to talk to Christy first. I'm going to tell her what I'm going to do, then I'll be ready."

"Give me some idea of what you're planning to do."

"Like I told you, I'm going to do something that will make everybody happy—you, the police, the sheriff, everybody."

"How do you want to do it?"

For a moment the question seemed to puzzle David. "If somebody wants to talk about something he did," he asked, "how does he go about it?"

Simons was fast growing tired of the game-playing. "Well," he said, "if someone wants to confess to a crime he's done, there are several different ways. He can write it out on paper, or he can have it tape-recorded, or he can be videotaped. It depends on what it is and what you want to do." Simons stressed the word "you."

"You guys have videotape machines?"

"Yes."

"I'd like to do it on videotape."

"About how much tape do you think we're going to need?" Simons asked.

"Not much. I've just got a few words to say."

Truman shook his head. "David, I can't imagine anything you have to say that would take only a few words. A few words won't make anybody in this town happy."

Now Spence was relaxed, smiling. He felt he was again in control of the situation; he was enjoying the cat-and-mouse game.

"Okay, David," Simons said. "Let's quit playing around. I think I know what you've got in mind. You and I have talked about the law enough for you to know that anything you say to me can't be used against you." The jailer again explained to him the fact that any statement made orally and not recorded—and which does not lead to the finding of some evidence or facts previously unknown to the state—is not admissible under Texas law. "This room isn't bugged. Why don't you just go ahead and tell me what you're planning to do and I'll tell you what you have to do to get it taken care of."

Spence continued his game. "You know what I've got in mind."

"I think I do, but the way you've been acting lately, I'm not sure."

David stiffened. "I'm not crazy, if that's what you mean. I know I'm not crazy."

"But, dammit, you're playing word games," Simons argued. "That's not getting us anywhere. I think you want to make a statement."

"That's right," David answered, "but not until I talk to Christy."

"You're going to tell Christy that you're going to make a statement?"

"That's right. Everybody thinks I did it, right? People up in the jail been telling you I did it. Everybody's got me guilty. So I might as well tell you. My world's falling apart anyway."

"If you do decide to make a statement," Simons warned, "you had better be prepared to tell everything; start at the beginning and run the whole business down. If you're going to convince me you did it, you'll have to tell everything you know about it."

"Hey, I thought you were already convinced."

"I am," Simons admitted, "but you've got to convince me beyond any doubt. And the only way you're going to do that is by going through the whole thing, start, middle, and end."

"I don't want to do that. I just want to make a statement about me, nobody else."

"David, if what you're talking about is making a statement

that you were one of the people who did the lake murders and ending it at that, there's no use wasting the videotape. I won't take it that way. Some people might, but I don't work that way."

"What's wrong with me just saying I did it?"

"That's not enough for me. If you want to play it that way, talk to somebody else."

"If I'm going to do this, the only person I'm talking to is you. But I'm not getting off into it until I talk to Christy."

Simons took David to the booking counter and waited as he made several calls in an attempt to locate Christy. No one seemed to know where she could be found.

It was well after midnight as Simons sat at his station on the fourth floor. His muscles ached and his eyes burned, yet despite his lack of sleep he was alert, keyed up over the prospect of Spence's admitting his guilt. David placed call after call in an attempt to locate Christy but had no success.

Feeling it would be fruitless to discuss David's promised statement, Simons said nothing more about it. Instead he listened as Spence rambled on about how badly Christy had treated him since he had been in jail and about the fact that he had begun reading the Bible with several other inmates.

As they sat talking, Simons was keenly aware that David was attempting to read him. He was obviously surprised that Simons had made no further mention of their earlier discussion. But if the game was to begin again, Simons thought, David was going to have to start it.

"If I wanted to talk to you about something," David finally said, "but I didn't want to say I'm the person I'm talking about, what do you call it? You know, like it isn't for real?"

"You mean hypothetical?"

"Yeah, that's it," David said. "Can we maybe talk like that? Like we did that time before?" He glanced up at the speaker overhead in the chute where he was sitting.

Simons went over to the desk and turned up the radio. "Bugs won't pick up anything but a radio if there's one playing," he said.

For several seconds David sat with his face buried in his hands, as if contemplating what he was about to say. "It's like a dream," he began. "In this dream this guy sees himself killing somebody."

Simons could tell that Spence was having trouble adjusting what he was trying to say into a hypothetical situation. He had decided to mask it as a dream.

"This guy," Spence continued, "has this girl down on the ground and he's over the top of her and he's stabbing her. I mean, he just loses it. He's not himself any more. It's like he's standing over here watching and the guy over there is actually doing the killing. But even though he's over here, he likes it. It's crazy."

Interrupting his hypothetical narration, David asked, "Would that be crazy? If someone felt something like that, would he be insane?"

"I'd say there's definitely something wrong with someone who kills a person like that," Simons answered.

Spence returned to his story. "You know," he said, "when I had that brunette down and I was stabbing her and cutting her, it was like it wasn't really me. It was like I was standing somewhere else, watching. But I was enjoying it." Simons felt a shiver run through his body as he realized David had slipped from the hypothetical into the first person.

At precisely that moment the nearby elevator bell rang and two jail guards stepped off, making their nightly rounds. As they approached, David stood up and stretched. "I've got to go take a leak," he said.

As soon as Spence had left the chute to go to his cell, Simons asked the guards not to make any more stops on the fourth floor that night. "Just tell the people downstairs that I've got some pretty heavy duty shit going with David up here," he said. As the guards returned to the elevator Simons cursed under his breath.

A few minutes later David walked back across the deserted day-room. He was smiling. Reentering the chute, he said, "Did I ever tell you about my stick?"

"Not that I can remember," Simons said. The games were beginning again.

"I've got a name for it."

"What's that?"

"I can't tell you that."

"Aw, come on."

"No, I better not tell you."

"What do you do with it?"

"Oh, I just carry it around to hit niggers on the head with," David said. "And sometimes I use it for other things."

"What kind of things?"

David just smiled and ignored the question. "Okay if I try to call Christy again?" he asked.

Dispirited, Truman handed him the telephone. Whatever else Spence might have told him about the murders at the lake had been lost the moment the elevator door had rung. But he had gotten close. It was now only a matter of time, he felt.

By five in the morning David still had not reached Christy. Now growing tired, his spirits took a downward swing and he again began crying and talking about how badly she was treating him.

When five-thirty arrived, Simons summoned a relief guard to turn on the lights and wake the inmates for breakfast. Then he took David back downstairs to one of the interview rooms on the first floor and let him call several times more.

By nine Simons was completely exhausted. "Look, David," he said. "I'm out of gas. I've got to go home and get some rest. You need some sleep, too. I'll come back down this afternoon and we'll try to get Christy."

"Don't go yet," David pled. "Stay a little while longer. I'm going to do it. I'll do it just as soon as I talk to her."

"Shit, David, I'm beat," Simons said. His voice was almost as pleading as that of Spence.

While Simons was at home sleeping, David, his adrenalin pumping, was walking around on the fourth floor, spreading the news among the inmates that he planned to confess to the lake murders just as soon as he spoke with Christy Juhl. "I'm going to give it up," he said repeatedly, his voice full of excitement. "I'm going to tell 'em about it and get it over with." He also insisted he was going to implicate Christy. If she wasn't going to be faithful, he said, he was going to take her down with him.

Instead of returning to the jail that afternoon, the exhausted Simons telephoned to tell the jailer on duty to allow Spence to continue calling for Christy. If David was successful in locating her, Truman said, he wanted to be called immediately. He heard nothing before reporting to work that night.

It was almost midnight when Spence, his lack of sleep beginning to show, finally managed to reach his girlfriend. Simons waited anxiously as the phone conversation stretched for over an hour.

When David finally returned the telephone to the slot in the glass window which separated the jailer's office from the day-room, Simons tried to appear nonchalant. "Well," he said, "did you two get your business straightened out?"

David nodded without expression. He was obviously exhausted. As badly as Simons wanted to press the issue, feeling certain Spence was finally near the breaking point, he knew he would have to wait. If he did get a confession, he didn't want it to be clouded with the kind of doubt that defense attorneys like to attack. Everyone in the jail was aware that David had not slept for forty-eight hours and was under considerable emotional strain. A statement taken under such stressful conditions, Simons knew, wouldn't be worth the paper it was written on. Truman had been too careful for too long to let the burning impatience he was beginning to feel disrupt his judgment.

"You look like hell, man," Simons said. "You've got to get some sleep. We can talk later. Why don't you go hit the sack for a while?"

"Yeah, I'm exhausted," David said. "I think maybe I can sleep now."

The following day when Simons asked Spence about his plans to make a statement, David laughed it off. "Aw, I was just depressed," he said. "I was just going to do it to punish my old lady. See, that's why I wanted to just give a short statement and not get into any details."

"I'm not sure I follow you," Truman answered.

Spence shrugged. "I don't *know* any details," he said, turning to go to his cell.

Truman knew any chances of David confessing were lost, at least for the time being. But they had come close. Perhaps they could get there again.

In the days to come, however, Simons would deal more cautiously with David. He knew that virtually everyone in the jail was aware of the all-night conversations he and Spence had been having. Soon, he felt, there would be rumblings about him keeping David awake against his will. For his own protection, then, Truman explained to Spence that he would be glad to continue talking to him, but only if David first filled out a written request.

\*       \*       \*

As they talked one evening, Spence mentioned that his mother had told him about finding a ring that she could not identify. "She says she found it when she was cleaning house and doesn't know where it came from," David said. "It might be something Christy left there. I'd appreciate it if you would go by and take a look at it sometime."

Simons, who had spoken with Mrs. White on the telephone, had not met her personally. "Maybe I will," he said to David. "That would give me a good excuse to meet her." He was certain David was again playing some kind of game.

The set had been lost from the small, inexpensive ring which Juanita White showed Simons. It appeared to be the type he'd seen many young girls wearing on their little fingers. As he looked at the ring, Juanita spoke: "You know David called me and told me he was going to confess to those murders at the lake," she told the deputy. "He said he would rather face the death penalty than go back down to TDC. I tried to talk him out of it."

"He didn't confess to anything," Truman said.

"I'm not saying David isn't capable of killing somebody," Juanita said. "When he gets drunk, he gets crazy. But from what I've read and heard, that thing out at the lake was an organized, well-planned kind of murder. I just don't think he would be involved in something like that."

Simons was surprised at her candid manner. "Were you aware of David's relationship with Muneer Deeb?" he asked.

"Oh, yes," she said. "He once told me about a plan they had to wreck Deeb's car for the insurance money. I told him that was a stupid thing to even consider.

"Being David's mother, I probably shouldn't be telling you these things, but he called me one night—it was three or four in the morning—all upset, yelling into the phone about Deeb. He said that Lucky and them had killed Gayle out at Axtell and that he was afraid they were going to be coming after him next. He was really scared. So was I. I told him to come on home. But he didn't.

"Then, a few days later he showed up and I got on him real good about scaring me like that. He just brushed it off and said it had turned out to be another Gayle.

"You know, after that sexual abuse thing he had a lot of trouble sleeping. He would wake up in the middle of the night, screaming. And he got sick at his stomach a lot. I think if he had been involved in killing those kids he would have had the same reaction."

Simons listened quietly, not bothering to remind Juanita White that her son had not been living at her house after the sexual abuse incident. There would have been no way for her to know if he had been bothered by nausea and nightmares. On the other hand, David had slept at her house on several occasions following the lake murders.

"You think he did it, don't you?" Juanita said.

"Yes, ma'am, I do," Truman answered.

She rose from the couch and walked toward the bedroom. "Before you go," she said, "I want to show you something else. I also found a watch the other day and I don't know where it came from."

It was a woman's small 21 jewel watch with a black dial and a black plastic band. Simons walked out onto the front porch and examined it in the sunlight. Imbedded between the band and the dial was what appeared to be dried blood.

"Do you mind if I take this?"

"No, that's fine," Mrs. White said.

Simons took the watch directly to the lab and asked that tests be run to determine if, in fact, it was dried blood that he had found. A technician carefully scraped the tiny particles from the band. Two hours later he called Simons to report that the chemicals used in the testing had been bad. There would be no results to report.

The following morning, Simons and Baier went to the Waco Housing Authority where Star Clompton, Jill's former roommate at the Methodist Home, worked. "We have some jewelry that we'd like you to look at," Baier told the young woman after explaining they were investigating the lake murders.

Star said she didn't recognize the ring, but she began to cry when shown the watch. "That's Jill's watch," she said.

"It's important that you be absolutely sure," Baier said. "Are you certain?"

Regaining her composure, the young woman looked at the watch again. "I can't be sure," she said, "but Jill had one that looked like that."

Though Jan Thompson recalled ordering a watch for her niece from JCPenney's which was similar in design to the one

Simons showed her, she was unable to positively identify it as
Jill's. Neither could anyone in the family remember Jill having
a ring like the one Juanita White had given him. Disappointed,
Truman accepted the fact that the items would never qualify as
evidence.

When David first began showing an interest in the Bible, Truman was not surprised. Many prisoners grasped at religion as a
final lifeline when battling overwhelming feelings of guilt or
facing a lengthy jail sentence. Spence, he assumed, was doing
the same. The difference, however, was that David displayed a
knowledge of scripture that the jailer had not expected. During
a brief period when David and Christy had attended church, he
had read the Bible with a passion, memorizing scripture and
asking his minister for interpretations of what he had read.

As he sat talking with Simons one evening, David opened
the Bible he had brought with him and began to talk about the
Ten Commandments. "I want to be a Christian," he said, "but
it's too late for me. I've broken every one of the commandments, so there's no chance for any kind of salvation."

"You know, David," Truman said, "everybody's got different
interpretations of what's in here. You could get a half dozen
preachers in here right now and ask them about one chapter, or
even a verse, and you would probably wind up with a different
viewpoint from each one. And mine would probably be different
from what they had to say."

"How did you decide what it all means?" Spence asked.

"The way my mother raised me, I guess. She's been reading
the Bible every day for as long as I can remember. Most of
what I know, she taught me. And I think as I grew up and
understood things a little better, I began to make some interpretations of my own.

"See, what you have to remember is that the Ten Commandments are in the Old Testament. They were set down for
the Jews—the chosen people—to live by. We're Gentiles; we
aren't expected to be perfect. We're expected to be sinners.
That's why Jesus came and died for us, so we might have salvation, too.

"Now I'm not saying that we've got a free ticket to run
around robbing and raping and killing, you understand. But the
way I read it, we're just supposed to do the best we can do, and

believe in Jesus Christ and that he came to earth and died for our sins."

Spence sat listening intently as Simons continued. "See, David, I think that God can forgive even the worst sinner and provide him peace of mind. If you live long enough to turn your life around and accept Jesus Christ and accept the things you've done as being wrong, I think maybe you could be forgiven. I don't know. That's just the way I interpret the scripture. The only way you'll know for sure is to try it. And if, at some point, you have peace of mind, then you'll know. That's the true test."

Spence handed Simons his Bible. "Show me where I can find all this. I want to read it myself."

"Let me bring my Bible tomorrow," Simons said. "I'm not enough of a Bible scholar to find the things we're talking about. But I've got some scriptures marked in the one I have at home."

When Truman got off duty that morning he immediately called his mother. Without explanation, he told Maude Simons that he needed everything she could find in the Bible on the subject of salvation. Before returning to the jail the next evening, Simons had marked verses from the books of II Timothy ("And that from a child thou has known the holy scriptures, which are able to make thee wise unto salvation through faith which is in Christ Jesus"); Matthew ("But he answered and said, it is written, Man shall not live by bread alone, but by every word that proceedeth out of the mouth of God"); Luke ("But he said, Yea rather blessed are they that hear the word of God, and keep it"); and John ("Sanctify them through thy truth; thy word is truth"), as well as a dozen others his mother had called to his attention.

Simons had also marked additional verses in his Living Bible. "I think," he told David, "that Romans 5:20 explains what I was trying to tell you about the Ten Commandments." As Spence found the verse in his own Bible, Truman began reading: "The Ten Commandments were given so that all could see the extent of their failure to obey God's laws. But the more we see God's abounding grace forgiving us . . . before, sin ruled over all men and brought them to death but now God's kindness rules instead."

Then he told David to turn to Romans 10:8-13 and continued to read aloud: ". . . salvation that comes from trusting Christ is already within easy reach of each of us; in fact, it is as near as our own hearts and mouths. For if you tell others with your own mouth that Jesus Christ is your Lord, and believe in your heart that God has raised him from the dead, you will be saved. For it is by believing in his heart that a man becomes right with God; and with his mouth he tells others of his faith, confirming his salvation. For the Scriptures tell us that no one who believes in Christ will ever be disappointed . . . anyone who calls upon the name of the Lord will be saved."

Still, David was not completely reassured. His life, he said, had been one big mess after another. He told Simons of the time when, in a fit of jealous rage, he had tried to kill his younger brother. "See, I really love my brother," David said. "He's one of the best people I know. But all my life I've resented the fact that he was the favorite. One time, back when we were both just kids, I had taken all of it I could and I held him down and put a pillow over his face. I wanted to kill him. He finally passed out and I got scared and stopped, thank goodness. But I could have killed him. He never snitched me off, though. He never told anyone."

He had sinned too much, too often, David felt. "Do you really think there's a chance that God would forgive me?"

"I can't answer that question for you," Simons replied. "But it's something you'll know if it ever happens."

"Well, it's hard for me to believe I'll ever be forgiven."

"David, I think I know what you're talking about and I'd like to think that our God is a forgiving God. I think if you get your heart right He will forgive you. But that's between you and Him, nobody else."

"Yeah, but you don't understand."

"Well, I think I do."

Spence looked squarely into Simons' eyes. "No you don't," he said. "See, you're thinking three. I'm talking five."

Simons was speechless for a moment. Was Spence telling him that he had killed two others in addition to the three youngsters at the lake? "You're right, David," he finally said. "I don't understand."

Spence, the game-player, quickly changed the subject, offering no further explanation.

Soon David was not only quoting scripture to Simons nightly but had begun conducting Bible study among the inmates during the day. He no longer cursed and had stopped smoking.

One evening as soon as Simons came on duty, David signaled him to open his cell door. He approached the jailer, Bible in hand, a wide grin on his face. "I've really, truly found the Lord," he announced.

"That's good, David; I'm glad to hear it."

"I've been praying for a sign, and He gave it to me today. My Bible just fell open to a scripture. He's going to set me free, Mr. Simons. I'm going to go to trial and they're going to find me not guilty. Then God's going to swing the doors of this jail open and I'm gonna walk out of here."

David had found his answer not in Simons' New Testament, but in a verse from the Old Testament. He immediately read the skepticism in Simons' face. "What's the matter?" he asked.

"Well, I don't want to mess up your religion, but I think you're reading too much into whatever the message is you've gotten."

"It's right here," David said, opening his Bible and showing Simons the page from Isaiah 55. " 'Seek ye the Lord while he may be found, call ye upon Him while He is near,' " Spence quoted rapidly. " 'Let the wicked forsake his way, and the unrighteous man his thoughts; and let him return to the Lord . . . and he will have mercy upon him; and to our God, for he will abundantly pardon . . .' What do you think about that?" David asked.

"I think you're setting yourself up for a real disappointment," Truman said. "See, what I've been trying to tell you is that even if God does forgive you for your sins, you've got a responsibility to man. It's the judgment of man that determines whether or not you pay for your crimes. What I'm trying to say is, it isn't very likely you're going to just walk out of here, David. I'd hate for you to get your hopes built up. If you base your faith on that kind of belief, you're going to wind up throwing your Bible in the trash before too long."

On March 23, 1983, David did just that. The jury deliberated only eighteen minutes before finding him guilty on the charge of aggravated sexual abuse. He was given a sentence of ninety years.

His co-defendant, Gilbert Melendez, had earlier pled guilty in exchange for a seven-year sentence.

Simons, who had not seen David during the course of the

trial, went to the courthouse to sit in on the punishment phase. David's mother came up to him and told him she had just had words with Richard Franks, who had been present through the entire trial, glaring at David. Franks had confronted her, saying he knew her son was a strong suspect in the lake murders, and had appealed to her to convince him to confess and get it over with. "I'd appreciate it if you would tell him to leave me alone," she said. Truman sought Franks out and talked with him briefly, urging him to stay away from Juanita White.

After the trial ended, Simons stopped Juanita and David's father, who had come down from Fort Worth. He told them that he was going over to see David shortly and, if they were going to be at home soon, he would allow their son to call. Edwon Spence said he would go to Juanita's and wait for David's call before returning to Fort Worth. "I understand he's a suspect in a murder case," the tired-looking father said.

"Yes sir, that's right," Truman said.

"You think he did it?"

"Yes, I do."

"Well, do I need to see about getting him a lawyer?"

"At this point," Simons explained, "he hasn't been charged or indicted. If that comes about, the courts will provide him a good lawyer. He'll get as good a representation as you could buy. I don't know anything about your financial situation and it's none of my business, but a capital murder trial can bankrupt a wealthy man."

"I appreciate your advice," Edwon Spence said. "All I'm concerned about is, if David did it, I want him to have a good lawyer."

Back at the jail Simons found David far more composed than he had expected. Sitting in one of the downstairs interview rooms, Spence talked calmly about the trial, criticizing witnesses for lying, the jury for not taking his testimony into consideration, and district attorney Vic Feazell for his theatrics throughout the proceedings.

Once again Simons had guessed wrong on David's behavior. He had expected tears or rage. The sentence seemed to have had less effect on him than the failure of his girlfriend to show up on visiting day. Instead of being despondent over the prospect of facing years behind bars, it seemed Spence was still enjoying the fact that he had been the focal point of a great deal of public attention in recent days. Truman, lighting a cigarette, was beginning to wonder if he would ever figure the guy out.

"Want to give me one of those?" David asked, nodding in the direction of the package of Carlton 100's lying on the table.

"I thought you gave up smoking."

David laughed. "Yeah, I quit smoking. I quit cussing. I tried to turn my life around. But it didn't work, did it?"

Truman shook his head. "David, if I thought smoking and cussing kept a person out of heaven, I'd be in big trouble. I'm not proud of the fact I do things like that, but I don't think I'm going to burn in hell for it. It goes back to what we were talking about; how you interpret the Bible. Besides, I figure I've got a little something special working for me."

"What's that?"

"It's over in the Book of Matthew," Truman said. " 'Blessed are the peacemakers, for they shall be called the sons of God.' Look it up sometime."

"Man," David replied after taking a deep drag on his first cigarette in a month. "I could use some help like that."

They both laughed. It would be the last time they spoke of religion for some time.

"Your dad ought to be at your mother's house by now," Simons said after they had talked several more minutes. "Maybe you better give him a call before he has to get on the road."

Simons sat across the table, trying not to appear too interested as David talked with his father. They had talked only a few minutes when Spence abruptly ended the conversation and hung up the phone. "Hey, Mr. Simons," he said excitedly, "could you run me up to the fourth floor real quick?"

Truman shrugged. "Sure. What's happening?"

"My dad said they're about to show something about me on television."

## 23

Though Dennis Baier and Ramon Salinas remained assigned to the lake murders case, instructed to check whatever new leads might develop, there was little police department activity on the investigation until late in February of 1983 when a new suspect surfaced.

In the oceanside community of Imperial Beach, California, a former Waco resident named James Russell Bishop was arrested and charged with the sexual assault and attempted murder of two high school girls. Bishop, a former grounds-keeper at McLennan County College, had abducted the two teenagers near the high school which they attended and forced them into his camper. After tying them up and blindfolding them, he drove around for several hours before taking them to a beach area near a naval amphibious base where he raped both girls, then forced them into the surf and shot them. One, a seventeen-year-old Japanese exchange student, was paralyzed from the waist down by a bullet which had severed her spinal cord. The other girl, fifteen years old, had been wounded in the back, chest, arm and hand.

A call from the Coronado, California authorities, requesting additional information on the twenty-seven-year-old Bishop, created a new wave of interest in the lake case.

The similarities of the California crime—teenage girls abducted, sexually assaulted, tied up—to the events of Lake Waco in 1982 made Bishop an immediate suspect. When it was learned that he had left Waco suddenly just two weeks after the three teenagers had been killed, Baier, Salinas, and Lieutenant Marvin Horton began making plans to fly to San Diego, where Bishop was being held, to interview him.

Upon their arrival, Bishop's attorney refused to allow them to talk with his client, but the three Waco officers discussed the California case at length with local investigators, reviewed evidence, and requested that samples of Bishop's hair be sent to the Waco Police Department. While their hoped-for interview would have to wait, they returned home encouraged that a break had finally come in the Lake Waco murders.

Within a matter of days they had gathered a wealth of background information on Bishop. Twice divorced, he had been honorably discharged from the Army in 1981. Friends who were interviewed said his behavior was "erratic at times" and described his fascination for guns. A girlfriend told investigators that Bishop owned several rifles and always carried a .38 in his boot. However, a check revealed that his only brushes with the law prior to his arrest in California had been a couple of DWI charges. Still, there was enough to generate renewed enthusiasm within the ranks of the Waco Police Department.

Meanwhile, the local media, which had reported little on the lake murders for months, immediately began referring to Bishop as a "suspect" in the Waco case.

In the McLennan County jail, Truman Simons gave the newspaper reports little attention. If the police wanted to spend their money and man-hours investigating James Bishop, a man he had never heard of, it was fine with him. He had already reconciled himself to the fact that the police had no interest in the information he had been gathering for months.

On several occasions, Simons had called Baier and asked that he stop by the jail so he might show him the statements he had taken from inmates who had pointed the finger of guilt directly at David Spence. Eventually Baier did visit his former partner to discuss the case, but Truman was disappointed in the lack of enthusiasm shown by the sergeant. Simons sensed an uneasiness on Baier's part as they talked; it was clear to him that Dennis no longer felt comfortable in his presence.

It was, in fact, shortly after one of Baier's visits to the jail that Robert Fortune called a sergeant at the sheriff's department to complain about Simons' work on the lake case. It's a police department case, Fortune argued, and then insisted that any information Simons might have gathered should be turned over to his investigators. The sergeant, who had worked for the Waco police before going to work in the sheriff's office, told Fortune that what went on in the jail was "none of your fucking business" and hung up the phone. A few days later Marvin Horton telephoned Sheriff Harwell with the same complaint. Horton showed little interest in who Simons had been talking to; he simply wanted Truman to leave the case alone. Choosing his words a bit more diplomatically than had the sergeant who had talked with Fortune, Sheriff Harwell said only that Simons was conducting his investigation with his full blessings.

Beyond the boundaries of the sheriff's office, Truman was getting little help—even from the few he sought out. Following the elections he had approached assistant district attorney Dennis Green with the statements he had gathered from inmates in the jail, only to be told they were legally insufficient and would not be admissible in court. Certain the prosecutor was wrong, Simons had taken his case to Claude Giles, a Waco attorney who was also a long-time friend. For several days Giles researched case law before calling Simons to express his opinion that inmate testimony was admissible so long as it was given of the person's own accord and the inmate had not been acting as an agent of the state. Green, however, refused to research the case numbers which Simons took to him.

After his second meeting with Green, Simons decided it was time to talk with the new district attorney. Standing in Vic Feazell's office, Truman briefly explained that he had been working on the lake case. He generally outlined the information he had been gathering in recent months, then told of the problems he had encountered with Feazell's assistant.

"I can't work with that sonuvabitch," Simons said. "He won't listen. Is there somebody else up here I can deal with?"

Feazell was not impressed with the hostile approach of the man standing in his office. The D.A. immediately adopted a guarded opinion of Truman.

"I'll look into it," Vic said.

"I'd appreciate it," Truman said as he turned to leave.

His conversation with Simons troubled Feazell. Already he had talked with Police Chief Larry Scott about the possibility of forming a coalition, based in the D.A.'s office, to intensify the investigation of the lake murders. Scott had agreed to assign Baier and Salinas to his office with the understanding that all information gathered would be shared equally between his department and Feazell's office. When he outlined the plan, Vic had been unaware that anyone in the sheriff's office was investigating the case. Now there was another political element to consider. If a unified effort was to be made, it would have to include both law enforcement agencies. Simons would have to join forces with Baier and Salinas.

Unaware of the tension that had built as a result of Truman's involvement in the case, Feazell saw no reason it wouldn't work. After all, he assumed, the main objective was to finally solve the case which had hung over the city like a dark cloud for over a year.

The first week in March, 1983, as Feazell was preparing for the aggravated sexual abuse trial of David Spence, the District Attorney's office officially took charge of the case. It was agreed that Baier and Salinas would operate out of the D.A.'s office while Simons continued to work in the jail. The arrangement would work, Feazell felt, although he had begun to wonder, after talking with several police officers, if he could trust Simons. Feeling that the lake murders coalition had been properly set in motion, Feazell returned his attention to preparations for his first trial and the daily responsibilities of his new office.

At the same time, Walter (Skip) Reaves, an attorney from nearby West, was preparing to defend Spence. Appointed by the court, one of the first things he had done was to travel to the Ramsey Unit of the Texas Department of Corrections to talk with his client's codefendant, Gilbert Melendez. During the course of their conversation, Reaves discussed the possibility of Gilbert's testifying. Though Melendez emphatically insisted he had no interest in taking the stand, the attorney said he was planning to have him bench warranted back to the McLennan County jail nonetheless.

"And there's something you ought to know," Reaves said as he prepared to leave. "I heard that David Spence is doing a lot of talking about the lake murders to people there in the jail. Evidently your name's come up quite a bit. When you get back, one of the first people you're probably going to see is a guy named Truman Simons."

"Who's he?" Gilbert asked.

"You'll find out soon enough," Reaves said.

## 24

Gilbert Melendez was sixteen when he ran away from home for the first time. Adolescent pressures had steadily mounted during his first year of high school as he and his stepfather argued endlessly about everything from the length of his hair to his frequent habit of skipping school to drink beer, sniff paint, and shoot pool with a group of older dropouts.

He bore the extra burden of being a unique social misfit in a community where Hispanics generally banded tightly together. Gilbert had been preparing to enter the fourth grade when the family moved to Germany where his Air Force stepfather was stationed. There he spent three years in a military base school where he and his kindergarten-aged brother, Tony, were the only Hispanics. By the time their stepfather's tour of duty was completed and the family returned to Waco, the boys spoke very little Spanish. Neither had even a trace of an accent. Consequently there was no segment of their youthful society into which they really fit. They may have looked Hispanic, but they sounded Anglo. There were times when Gilbert cursed the day his mother had decided to marry a white man. But the truth was, her husband had been good to the Melendez children and, for that reason, he could never understand the rebellion of his older stepson. Neither did he understand that both boys felt trapped in a social no-man's-land.

Careful to remove anything from his billfold that might identify him, Gilbert persuaded a friend to give him a ride to the edge of town one evening and began a hitchhiking journey that would last for a year and a half. During that time he told anyone who asked that his name was either Gilbert Fajardo or Gilbert Tovar, depending on his whim at the time, and that he was eighteen years old.

He traveled from Waco to Dallas, then into Oklahoma, stopping wherever he could find a few days' work, then moved on. Ever fearful the police would pick him up and return him to his parents, he felt it was important to stay on the move. Gradually, however, he ceased to worry that he was being sought as a runaway and began laying plans to work his way to California.

In Salt Lake City he got a ride with a couple from Mound, Minnesota, who operated a small carpet cleaning business. Although they doubted his story that he was eighteen and originally from a small town in Kansas, they liked him, and after hearing his false claim that he had experience as a carpenter, offered to let him travel back to Minnesota with them. They were building a small house on some country property, they said, but the demands of their business provided little time for the project. They offered lodging, food, and a small salary in exchange for his working on the house.

Thus Gilbert's journey turned eastward, his fantasies of walking the California beaches postponed. For the next six months he lived in a trailer house parked near the house on which he worked when not helping with the carpet cleaning business.

An elderly couple who lived nearby had also befriended Gilbert, and when the house-building job was completed he moved in with them. They began talking of adoption and, without his knowledge, contacted a local social worker about the necessary procedure. During a routine investigation of his background it was determined his name was not Fajardo, as he had told them, but Melendez; and that his parents resided in Waco, Texas.

Surprised and disappointed—because they had enjoyed again having a youngster in the house—they convinced him to call home and assure his parents that he was alive and well. The sound of his mother's voice made Gilbert unexpectedly homesick, and he surprised himself at how readily he accepted her offer to send him a bus ticket. Soon he was back home, enrolled in school, and working the evening shift at a fast-food Mexican restaurant.

But not for long. Soon bored again with school, Gilbert joined a group of friends on a spur-of-the-moment trip to Florida. Their purpose, designed in a drunken rush, was to travel to Miami Beach and attend some now-forgotten rock concert. The group made it as far as Orlando before car troubles and financial difficulties dulled the excitement. All but Gilbert turned back. On juvenile probation for his previous runaway, he feared he would be placed in reform school if he returned to Waco. So, panhandling and working at odd jobs, he made his way to Miami, then to the Florida Keys. He was occasionally picked up for vagrancy, spending a night in jail, but he was pleased to learn that whenever the police ran a check on Gilbert Fajardo there would be no warrants or criminal history. He decided to stick with the name.

After several months and dozens of odd jobs in Florida he began to think once more of going west. Along the way he met another hitchhiker en route to Washington, D.C. He encouraged Gilbert to accompany him on his trip to see his aunt and uncle. The visit lasted for a month before the heavy snows and cold weather began to wear. Given the loan of an Army overcoat, Gilbert again set out for California.

The onset of winter made travel difficult, and finding jobs as a construction laborer all but impossible. Occasionally he would seek the shelter of the Salvation Army where, in exchange for attending a brief prayer meeting, he could get a meal, a shower, and a bed for the night.

Eight months after having left Waco for a Florida concert, Gilbert arrived in Mason, Ohio, cold, road-weary, hungry, and broke. He walked several miles to the farmhouse where his stepfather's parents lived. There he was urged to contact his parents. Assured there was no danger of being sent to reform school, he again took a bus back to Waco.

Though just seventeen, Gilbert Melendez had seen more of the country than many do in a lifetime. A year later, however, his wandering would give way to the confinement of the Texas Department of Corrections.

All thoughts of a high school diploma dismissed, Gilbert had taken a job with a construction company which was building the Northwood Apartments near the McLennan County College campus. The $2.75-an-hour wages weren't much better than his catch-as-catch-can jobs on the road had earned him, but it was steady. And Tommy Myers, a friend who also worked for the company, had offered to let him live with him and his wife.

The youngest member of the crew, Gilbert was nonetheless accepted and regularly joined the others for beers after work. On days when weather prevented their working, the entire crew would gather at a local beer joint to drink and swap tales all day.

On one such rainy day Gilbert and Tommy spent the early

part of the afternoon drinking beer, before it was mentioned that dove season had officially opened the day before. They returned home for Tommy's shotgun, loaded a case of beer into the backseat, and spent the rest of the afternoon hunting on the outskirts of Waco. The trip was generally unsuccessful. They managed to kill only a few birds, and then they didn't bother to retrieve their prey, choosing instead to stay near the car, drinking beer.

Rather than return home once darkness halted their hunting, they made the rounds of several north Waco beer joints until the midnight closing time. Since neither had eaten all day, they decided to stop at a newly opened Sambo's Restaurant before calling it a night.

As they walked across the parking lot they saw two men arguing loudly and stopped to watch, anticipating that a fight would soon break out. The men, however, halted their conversation and looked in the direction of the two spectators.

"What the shit do you guys want?" the larger man, dressed in a three-piece suit, asked. "Why don't you just get the fuck out of here?"

"Why don't you kiss my ass?" Gilbert yelled back, his voice slurred by the beer he had been drinking all day. "And then mine," his companion added with a giggle.

Suddenly the smaller of the two men who had been arguing raced over to them, pulled a pistol, cocked it, and pressed the barrel to Gilbert's temple. "Didn't we say to get the fuck out of here?" he growled.

"Okay, man, we're splitting," a quickly sobered Gilbert answered.

Once in the car, Gilbert's fear turned to rage. "That sonuvabitch could have killed me," he yelled, pounding his fist against the dashboard.

Tommy motioned to the shotgun in the backseat. "Let's shoot the motherfucker."

Gilbert reached over the seat for the gun as Tommy quickly circled the parking lot. As they approached the two men still standing near a row of parked cars, Gilbert stuck the barrel of the .12 gauge out the window, aimed it at the man who had put the pistol to his head, and pulled the trigger.

Though the man he had shot was not seriously injured—he was taken to the hospital, had eleven buckshot removed from his chest, and was immediately released—Gilbert Melendez was charged with assault with intent to murder. In April of 1974 he began serving a three-year prison sentence. After sixteen months he was paroled.

For the next seven years Gilbert engaged in a variety of unlawful acts, yet managed to avoid spending any more time in jail. A friend whom he had met in prison moved to Waco upon his release and Gilbert joined him in a three-month spree of burglarizing homes. He also sold marijuana and Quaaludes and crank for $100 a gram and was fined $500 for possessing a .22 pistol which he had taken as partial payment for a loan he had made to a friend.

Once when police stopped him while driving a stolen car, he managed to elude them on foot, hiding in a group of shrubs near a house. As the officers searched through the residential area, a woman walked out onto her porch to see what was going on and looked straight down at the frightened fugitive. She said nothing as her husband returned from talking with the officers and told her they were searching for a man who had stolen a car. They turned and went into the house. Gilbert held his ground for the next several hours, certain the woman would tell her husband and the police would soon return. When darkness fell, he crawled from his hiding place. It was time, he knew, to hit the road again.

In San Antonio he was briefly reunited with his brother Tony, who had also fled the restrictions of home and the drudgery of school, and both worked painting rooms in one of the city's fashionable hotels. When that job was completed the crew, based in Nashville, moved to Memphis. Gilbert traveled with them.

For six months he worked there, managed to purchase a Harley Davidson, and rode with a motorcycle gang known as the Iron Horsemen. But when the group began to urge him to seek full membership he begged off. He did not want to be tied to any one place.

His next stop was Austin where, with the help of Tony, he got a job working for a company laying cable. Then, when Gilbert and Tony learned that their parents had moved from Waco to Corpus Christi and that their stepfather promised to help them find work, they decided to rejoin their family.

After a while, however, Gilbert began to feel uncomfortable

living at home. He was too old to burden his parents, he explained to his mother, and felt he should be on his own. He asked her to give him a ride to the edge of town, and when she asked where he was going, he told her he didn't know. He was telling the truth.

For the next two years Gilbert lived in San Antonio, working for a carnival operator who took his rides and game booths to small towns on weekends. For the first time in his life, he was doing something he enjoyed. He was put in charge of running the games, earning a percentage of each night's profits. He drove one of the trucks to such dot-on-the-map destinations as Boerne, Eagle Pass, and Sweetwater.

It was while working for the carnival that Gilbert met Donna, who at sixteen was already divorced and had a small child. Kicked out by her parents, she had gone to work for the carnival, running the shooting gallery. Gilbert was immediately attracted to her and she to him. They were soon living together and her son began to call him Daddy. Gilbert contacted Tony and urged him to join them.

Before long, however, things began to sour. Donna reached a point where she could no longer tolerate Gilbert's drinking, and she also began to suspect he was seeing other women. Finally she decided to leave the carnival and try to reconcile with her parents.

Saddened at having lost her, Gilbert continued to carry her photograph in his billfold. He knew he had ruined the best thing that had ever happened to him. She was the first woman he had ever felt real love for. When he telephoned her several months later, Donna told him she had met someone and was planning to remarry.

Shortly after his breakup with Donna, Gilbert received word that his natural father had died. Though his parents had separated when Gilbert was only eight, he had seen his dad, who had remained in Waco following the divorce, a few times. As he had grown older, he and his father had occasionally met for a beer. Returning to Waco for the funeral, Gilbert learned that his father had been hit by a car while attempting to cross a busy intersection on Lake Waco Drive. He had been drunk at the time. The patrolman who had worked the accident was a young man named Truman Simons.

Thereafter the carnival life turned to drudgery for Gilbert.

He quit and moved back to Austin where he stayed for eight months, working sporadically, and living in a fog of booze and drugs. He was twenty-eight years old and going nowhere. He began thinking of returning home—to Waco—where he had friends and at least some good memories. And his brother was there, having tired of carnival life after a brief stint. Gilbert considered the danger of the auto theft charge that he knew was probably still hanging over his head. And there was the matter of failure to pay the $500 fine assessed him for possession of the .22. But if he returned as Gilbert Fajardo and kept his nose clean, he decided, things might work out.

By the summer of 1981 Gilbert had managed to save enough money to purchase a used Plymouth Duster and was working alongside Tony as a painter. He was planning to contact an attorney as soon as he got enough money together and see if he could have the fine taken care of. His life, he felt, was beginning to straighten out.

One afternoon as they got off work, Gilbert and Tony walked past a man sitting in a pickup, waiting to pick up another of the painters.

"Hey, Tony," the man yelled, climbing from his truck and walking in their direction.

"Gilbert," Tony said, motioning toward the man with whom he had once attended junior high school classes. "I want you to meet a friend of mine. This is David Spence."

## 25

By late in 1981, the home of David Spence had become the nightly gathering place for the Melendez brothers, Spence, his girlfriend Christy Juhl, and an in-and-out assortment of friends and acquaintances looking for a place to drink beer, get high, and listen to music.

With his mother working nights as a bartender, David had the house to himself and took full advantage of the opportunity to serve as host. Then when Juanita White announced she was planning to move out and take up residence with a man she had been dating, the situation became ideal. Her son agreed to pay her rent while he remained at home, then quickly invited Gilbert and Tony to contribute to the rent and make the North Fifteenth Street house their home. Christy also moved her things in.

Gilbert, who had been living with friends and relatives since his return to Waco, was far less enthusiastic about living with Spence than was his brother. Though generally friendly and always ready for fun and excitement, Spence had displayed a temper, particularly when he was drunk, that gave Gilbert cause for concern. Often it fell to him to prevent late-night fights between David and Tony, sometimes finding himself forced to offer to fight one or the other himself to settle their disputes.

And while he and Spence quickly became friends, Gilbert had reservations about David. He talked too much and bragged incessantly. And he could not be trusted. Gilbert quickly learned that he was given to lying even about things that were meaningless. For instance, David talked often about a Harley-Davidson he had in Fort Worth, but when Gilbert would ask why he didn't go and get it, David would explain that it was being repaired. Eventually Gilbert even offered to go to Fort Worth with him to get the bike, then to help him repair it. When Spence turned down the offer, Gilbert realized that no such bike existed except in his friend's active imagination.

And the presence of Christy both puzzled and concerned Gilbert. She neither drank nor joined in when pot was being passed around. Nor did she seem to mind when David brought other girls to the house. Still, she and Spence argued constantly, their screaming battles often evolving into physical fights. Yet she seemed devoted to David, eager to please him in any way she could.

One evening as the three of them were driving around the lake, David had become so enraged at Christy that he began cursing madly, threatened to kill her, and purposely drove his pickup into a tree. Once the truck had come to a stop David jumped out, climbed onto the hood and sat, legs folded, silently glaring at his girlfriend through the window. Shaken by the insane show of temper, Gilbert got out, checked the radiator for damage, then demanded that David let him drive home.

Then there was David's habit of using a dog collar to chain Christy to a chair on nights when they sat in the living room drinking beer and watching television or listening to the stereo. Sometimes he would keep her there for hours. If she said she needed to go to the bathroom, David would force her to beg, then lead her by the leash and stand watching as she relieved herself. The knife-throwing incident, David's offer to allow Tony to have sex with Christy, and his insane attack on his pickup with the axe had further convinced Gilbert that he was courting unwanted trouble by remaining there.

When David's mother returned and announced she was moving back into her house, Gilbert was relieved. She had given him the out he had been looking for. Packing his few belongings, he returned to his nomadic lifestyle, living with friends and relatives or occasionally spending a few nights in cheap motels, before eventually moving into a small apartment owned by his boss.

Though he still saw David occasionally, Gilbert had little to do with him after moving out. He knew David had moved into a small apartment behind the Rainbow Drive Inn with Christy, then later to the Northwood Apartments, but he had visited neither residence.

Then one afternoon in the first week of July he was in a liquor store buying beer and saw David. Spence urged him to ride around and talk for a while. For the next half hour Gilbert listened as David bemoaned the fact that he and Christy had split up again.

Finally, Gilbert had had enough. "Look, man," he said. "I can't help you with your problems with your old lady. That's between you and her. I don't want to hear about the shit, okay? Why don't we go to some club and have a few drinks, have some fun?"

David gave his companion a surprised look. "You know I can't do that," he said. "Man, I'm on parole."

Then, in a classic example of his ironic double standard concerning parole violations, David began to tell Gilbert about a friend of his who had been ripped off on a drug deal. "The dude's willing to pay good money—I mean good money—if someone will take care of the situation for him. I'm thinking about doing it," he said. "You want in on it?"

Gilbert laughed and shook his head. "Sounds like you're begging for a shit-load of trouble, if you ask me. Anybody who has balls enough to rip somebody off on a drug deal isn't going to be easy to scare. No thanks, man. I'm not interested in getting mixed up in that kind of business."

"It was just a thought," David said. He didn't mention it again.

A few days later, however, he sought Gilbert out. "Let's go get some beer," he said. "I'm buying." Instead of driving to the liquor store where they normally made their purchases, they went to the Rainbow Drive Inn on Herring Avenue. Inside, David introduced Gilbert to the owner. "This is Lucky," he said, "the guy I was telling you about who got ripped off."

Muneer Deeb clenched his jaw muscles as he glared at Spence, obviously upset, but David only smiled and draped an arm over Deeb's shoulder. "Hey, it's cool," he said, lowering his voice, "Gilbert's my bro. Hell, he might even help me."

"No fucking chance," Gilbert said.

A week later, as Gilbert was walking home from work one afternoon, he saw David again. Tony, who had been in Bryan, Texas, on an apartment-painting job, was with him, and both had obviously been drinking for some time. They picked Gilbert up and asked why he was walking.

He explained that the pickup he had recently purchased for three hundred dollars had not been running right, so he had left it with a man out in Bosqueville who was going to adjust the timing for him.

"Well, then," David said, "you might as well come with us. We're going to get some more beer and see if there's any pussy hanging around out at the lake."

It was July 13, 1982.

From that date on, Gilbert Melendez was inescapably tied to David Spence. He thought of taking to the road again, resuming the wandering lifestyle of Gilbert Fajardo. But he knew David was too much of a talker, too much of a braggart.

Already, in fact, he had been talking too much. One Sunday afternoon, less than two weeks after the murders, Gilbert and David had been with a group of people at the lake when David had accidentally backed his car into a tree. Several people began laughing and Spence, his temper flaring, had tried to start a fight. "You motherfuckers had better shut up," he said. "Me and some of my biker friends are the ones who took care of those people out at the lake, you know."

Gilbert knew he would have to watch him closely, at least until he could develop a plan of action. Spence had mentioned some money that was coming to him. Gilbert decided to wait until David was paid and then suggest they both leave Waco for good.

Three weeks after the lake murders, Gilbert was returning home from work when he saw David drive by in a station wagon. It appeared to be loaded with personal belongings and, for a moment, it occurred to Gilbert that David might be leaving town.

"I've got to move out of the apartment," David told him. "Me and Christy split up again and I don't have the money to pay rent over there. You think maybe you could let me bunk in with you for a few days?"

Gilbert did not cherish the idea of Spence's constant company again but saw such a living arrangement as a way to keep an eye on David. He helped unload the station wagon, then went back to the Northwood Apartments with him to pick up another load. Neither spoke of what had happened at the lake.

One evening shortly after David had begun sharing Gilbert's small apartment they decided to drive out to Lake Waco. This time, however, they carefully avoided Koehne, choosing instead to visit Airport Park. There they encountered a group of girls whose car had stalled. Among them was a girl named Kathy whom Gilbert recognized as the "old lady" of a Waco biker named Jerry Jackson.

David, Gilbert, and the girl left to find jumper cables but never returned. Instead, they stopped while Kathy telephoned a friend and asked him to pick up her stranded girlfriend at the lake. She then accompanied David and Gilbert to the Northwood Apartments where David's lease still had a few days to run. When she told them her boyfriend was in jail, they decided to "party." Well into the night the two men alternately visited the girl in the bedroom of the apartment.

Gilbert was in the living room, drinking beer, when he heard loud yells from the bedroom. Concerned that things might be getting out of hand, he entered to find Kathy, still naked, sitting up in bed, staring at David as he stood near the dresser. It was obvious the girl was frightened.

"You want to go home?" Gilbert asked her.

"Fuck, no, she's not going anywhere," David said drunkenly. "We're just starting to have fun. Besides, you've been hogging her all night. Just get the hell out of here."

Gilbert ignored him and again directed his question to Kathy: "Do you want to go?"

Spence became enraged and smashed a mirror mounted on the dresser.

"Look, asshole," Gilbert said, "if you want to get rough with somebody, it's going to have to be me. I've had about all your shit I want." His experience in apartment construction made him aware of the manner in which the walls were built. Careful to find a spot where he knew there was nothing but a thin layer of sheetrock beneath the wallpaper, Gilbert slammed his fist into the wall. David looked at the hole, then at Gilbert, and decided he was serious. The "party" was over.

A couple of days later Jerry Jackson was released from jail and ran into Spence at a service station. "You Chili?" he asked.

David nodded.

"My old lady says you and some Mexican dude raped her the other night."

"I don't know what the fuck you're talking about," Spence said.

"You know a girl named Kathy?"

Only then did David realize Jackson was the jailed boyfriend the girl had told him and Gilbert about. "Look," he said, "I didn't know she was your old lady. But we damn sure didn't rape her. We had a little party, but she wanted to. Hell, man, it was her idea."

Jackson was silent for a minute. "Aw, fuck it," he finally said. "That bitch has been lying and running around on me a lot lately. Just be sure you stay away from her from now on."

David assured him that he would. As Jackson left, Spence breathed a sigh of relief. He was pleased with himself; he had managed, for once, to talk himself out of a potentially bad situation.

But not for long. Before the weekend was over, he and Gilbert had paid their visit to the house of Danny Powers' grandmother.

Gilbert was pleased to find that David was not there when he returned home from work. He turned on the air conditioner, drank a beer, then decided to walk down the alley to the nearby Piggly-Wiggly supermarket for something to eat. As soon as he walked out of the door, however, he was met by Detective Ramon Salinas and two other Waco police officers.

"Are you Gilbert Fajardo?" Salinas asked.

"Yes. What's going on?"

"You're under arrest," Salinas said as he snapped handcuffs in place and began reading Gilbert his rights. "Anybody else here?"

"I live here by myself," Melendez said.

Salinas then suggested that they go inside the apartment so that he might turn off the radio and air conditioner before leaving. Gilbert felt certain they wanted to search the apartment and was hesitant. "Do you have a search warrant?" he asked.

"We're not interested in searching your place," one of the other officers said.

"Okay," Gilbert said. "I'll go in if you just let me turn things off. But I don't want you guys tearing through my shit in there. There's nothing there anyway."

Melendez says that as soon as they entered his apartment, Salinas began rummaging through drawers. "One of the other officers said something to him about not searching the place,"

Gilbert recalls, "and Salinas just said, 'Hey, I'm not searching.' He lifted up the mattress from my bed and picked up a small bag of marijuana. When he found that he looked over at me and smiled.

"Then one of the other officers—this woman named Melissa Sims—saw a little pocketknife on top of the dresser. They all talked for several minutes about whether they should take it or not. After a while, they decided to take the marijuana and the knife.

"Salinas asked me if David was still living with his mother and I told him I didn't know. When we left my place, we drove by David's mom's house over on North Fifteenth, but no one was there.

"After they had booked me and put me in a cell, Salinas came and got me and took me back up front to the booking desk. We went in this little room and he handed me the bag of marijuana that he'd picked up at my house. He pointed to the toilet and told me to flush it.

"I sorta laughed and said, 'Fucked up when you searched my place, didn't you?' He didn't answer me."

In days to come, Truman Simons would express an interest in the pocketknife which Gilbert told him David had given to him shortly after the lake murders. The description, Simons thought, closely matched that of the one Jill had been carrying in her purse the night she was killed. The pocketknife, however, had disappeared.

# 26

Truman Simons made it a point to keep track of Gilbert after he left the McLennan County jail to begin serving his sentence on the aggravated sexual abuse charge. He knew when Melendez reported to the Texas Department of Corrections Diagnostic Center, when he was moved to the Goree Unit, then when he was transferred to the Ramsey Unit.

Truman telephoned the warden at Ramsey to explain that Gilbert was a suspect in the lake murders case and requested that someone make note of any inmates Gilbert spent time with. Maybe, Truman hoped, Gilbert would confide his role in the crime to someone. And if he did, Simons wanted to know whom to talk with about anything he might have said.

The warden called back a few days later to tell Truman that an inmate he trusted had been made aware of the situation and was keeping an eye on Melendez. The inmate, however, proved far less trustworthy than the warden had thought. Rather than monitoring Gilbert's activities and associates for the warden, he went straight to Melendez and warned him to "watch his back." The word going around the prison, the inmate told him, was that he had been involved in a triple murder in Waco with someone named David Spence.

By the time Gilbert was bench warranted to Waco, he had made up his mind that David had implicated him in the murders. He had been back in the McLennan County jail only a day when Simons paid him a morning visit.

"I was wondering if maybe you and I could talk a little," Truman said.

"Yeah, why not?" Gilbert replied. "I've been expecting you. An attorney came down and told me David's been talking to you a lot, running his head about that shit out there at the lake."

"That's what I'd like to talk to you about," Simons said.

"That's what I figured." Gilbert's hands were shaking as he lifted the cup of coffee the jailer had brought to him.

"I'm not here to play any games," Truman began. "There's no point in us sitting here bullshitting each other. I wanted to talk to you because I think you know something about that business out at the lake. You either know about it through your association with David, hearing him talk about it, or because you were out there with him that night."

Gilbert stared down into his coffee cup, avoiding looking directly at Simons. *If Spence is already talking about it, bringing my name up*, Gilbert thought, *I don't owe him anything.* "Yeah," he said, "I know about it."

"Okay," Simons warned, "if we go on talking the shit's going to get pretty heavy. You know you don't have to talk to me. But if you do, if you want to help get this business over with, I'm ready to hear what you've got to say."

Gilbert nodded. "I'll talk to you about it."

"In that case," Simons continued, "let's get something straight before we go any farther. Are you going to tell me what you know because it's something David told you? Or because you were there?"

"David told me about it," Gilbert said. "He told me about these biker dudes and how . . ."

Simons could tell Melendez was already lying. "Gilbert," he interrupted, "I don't want to hear a lot of bullshit. Don't waste my time or yours. If we're going to talk, all I want to hear from you is the truth. Understand?"

"Yeah, I understand."

"You want some time to think this over?" Truman asked.

"Yeah," Gilbert said. "Let me think about it."

Simons left to go home and catch a few hours' sleep. He wanted to be alert when he returned later in the afternoon to continue the conversation. As he drove home he felt confident that Gilbert was ready to confess his role in the killings.

It was mid-afternoon when Simons returned to the jail and went into Dan Weyenberg's office to tell him what was going on with Gilbert. "Is there a chance he's going to give it up?" the captain asked.

Simons smiled. "Don't run off," he said. "I might need you."

Gilbert was pacing in his cell when Truman arrived. "Want to go downstairs and drink some coffee?" Simons asked.

Both sat silently for several minutes before the jailer asked

Gilbert if he had thought about what they had discussed earlier in the day. Gilbert nodded.

"You want to talk about it now?"

"Yeah."

Again Simons explained the ground rules. If they were to talk, he wanted nothing but the truth. "First of all," he said, "when I ask a question I want a 'yes' or 'no' answer; I'm not going to ask you for any details right now."

Gilbert nodded to show he understood.

"Okay, Gilbert, are you going to tell me what you know because you heard about it from David, or because you were there and know firsthand?"

For the first time, Melendez looked squarely at Simons. "You know I was out there."

"Yeah, I do," Simons admitted. He then tossed out an observation he'd been wanting to test since his conversation with Glenda Thomas, the young nursing student who had so vividly described what she had seen in her vision the night of the murders. "I can probably even tell you how you were dressed. You had the legs of your jeans stuffed down into the top of your boots, and . . ."

"Shit," Gilbert said, "I told David somebody had seen us."

"The question now," Simons, his curiosity satisfied, continued, "is, are you going to talk to me about it? If so, there are several ways we can do this. First thing, I've got to get a judge over here to warn you because we're talking about a capital murder. Then, if you're ready to give a statement, we can write it out as we talk about it, or we can bring in a tape recorder and turn it on while we're talking. It'll be you, me, and some other officer, probably Captain Weyenberg."

"What's going to happen to me if I tell you what you want to know?" Gilbert asked.

Simons explained that he had no authority to make promises but said he felt chances would be good that he would be able to avoid the death penalty if he did confess and then agreed to testify against David.

"I'll testify," Gilbert said.

"Okay, then, we'd better talk to the D.A. first and see how he feels about cutting some kind of deal. We need to get him over here so you can tell him that you want to do some negotiating. He's the man who holds those cards. I'll get you another cup of coffee and you can wait right here."

Gilbert looked at the key Simons was holding as he prepared to lock the door behind him. "I ain't going nowhere," Melendez said.

As soon as he turned the lock, Simons took off running down the hall to Weyenberg's office. Grinning broadly, he stuck his head in the door and said, "Find us a tape recorder and a bunch of cassettes."

"What's going on?" Weyenberg asked.

"Gilbert's going to give it up."

The captain jumped from his chair, smiling broadly. "Hallelujah!" he said.

A driving rainstorm pounded against the windows as Simons and Weyenberg took Melendez's statement. Though obviously nervous, Gilbert spoke in a steady, matter-of-fact voice. Vic Feazell, who was listening to the statement in an adjacent room, had assured him some kind of plea bargain arrangement would be worked out if what he had to say proved to be of value and was true, and if he would agree to testify.

Melendez smoked one cigarette after another as he gave his statement. Rarely did he lift his eyes from the gaze he had fixed on the surface of the desk where the tape recorder sat.

It was early in July of 1982, he said, when Spence had first mentioned something about people having ripped a friend off on a dope deal. Then on the night of July 13, David had come by and picked him up. They rode around for a while, drinking beer before going out to Koehne Park. When they arrived at the park they saw three people—two girls and a boy—seated on one of the three benches. David said he knew them—that they were the ones who had ripped his friend off.

"David called them over," Gilbert said, "and they started talking to him. He asked them if they wanted to get high and drink some beer. We still had some beer and David told them there was still time to go to the store and get some more. That's when they got in the car. The brunette got in the front seat between me and David and the other girl and the boy got in the back seat."

He told how Spence almost immediately began to fondle the brunette's breasts and how she had pushed his hand away and tried to slap him. "David put the car in park and started trying to put his arms around her. She was pushing him away and cussing. I opened the door and got out. The boy in the back seat asked something like, 'What's going on?' and I told him to just shut up.

"David was still hassling the girl in the front seat, telling her to take her clothes off, saying he was going to fuck her."

Pausing only to light another cigarette or take a sip of coffee, Gilbert detailed the struggle between Spence and Jill Montgomery. "All of a sudden David had a knife," he said, "and he was acting like he was going to cut her."

For the next hour he related his horror story, detailing how the girls had been raped while Kenneth Franks was forced to watch; how he had handed David a bra and a blouse to use to tie them up; and, finally, how Spence had stabbed and killed each of the teenagers.

At one point, Melendez said, he left and walked down toward the water's edge. "I told David I was splitting," he said, "but he said, 'Don't leave; you gotta help me get these people in the car. We gotta take 'em somewhere. I can't do it myself. We can take 'em to Speegleville. I know a place where we can drop them.' "

Gilbert said David was already loading the limp body of the dead boy when he walked back to the car. "We got them all loaded in the back seat and I told David something like, 'Let's go; we've got to get the hell out of here before somebody sees us.' "

It was after midnight, he said, before they left Koehne and drove to Speegleville where they would dump the bodies. He described in detail how the bodies had been unloaded. He also had some recollection of Spence throwing something from the car as they crossed the twin bridges, returning to town. "When we headed back to the highway I turned on the radio and got us a beer. I told David that we were in big trouble and that I was getting out of town. He said, 'Don't worry, nobody's going to know. The only ones that know are me and you. I know you won't say nothing and you know I won't. And, hey, they're gone; they're dead. They can't say nothing.' "

Gilbert leaned back in his chair and looked at Simons.

"There's a lot I can't remember," he said. "My mind wasn't clear that night. We'd been drinking quite a bit."

\*     \*     \*

Feazell and Weyenberg waited while Simons took Melendez to his cell. "Did you notice," the D.A. said, "how the storm stopped almost the minute we turned off the tape recorder?"

"Kind of eerie, wasn't it?" the captain said.

After Simons returned they sat talking about the statement Gilbert had just made. Each agreed that the details he had given were strong indication that he had been involved in the murders. None, however, believed that he had not had a greater hand in the killing than he was admitting. Or, for that matter, that he was telling everything he knew.

"In the morning," Truman said to the D.A., "we'll take him out to the lake and see if he can drive us through it."

As Feazell and Weyenberg were preparing to leave, Dennis Baier telephoned to ask how things had gone. Simons suggested that Dennis give Ramon Salinas a call and then come down and listen to the tape. "Gilbert's given us a pretty good story," Truman said. "I'd like both of you to hear it."

Only Baier came to the jail. After hearing the tape, he agreed that the statement seemed strong. "Did Gilbert ever say anything about what car it was they were in?" Dennis asked.

"No," Simons said, "he just referred to it as David's car. We'll get off into a lot more detail before we're finished."

In his excitement over wanting Baier to hear the tape, Truman had forgotten that he had promised to take Gilbert a package of cigarettes. "Hell, let's just run up there and ask him right now," he said. A few minutes later, standing with Baier outside Melendez's cell, Simons made his biggest mistake since he had begun investigating the lake murders.

"Gilbert," he asked, "when you were talking about David's car, which one was it?"

Without hesitating even a second, Gilbert replied, "It was that white station wagon of his."

Baier waited to say anything until he and Simons were back downstairs. "He's lying," he said. "David didn't even buy that white station wagon until a couple of weeks after the murders took place."

"I'm not saying I don't have some problems with some of what he said," Simons replied. "But, I sure as hell think he and David were out there that night. Dan and I are going to drive him out there tomorrow and see how he walks us through it. You and Ramon want to go?"

"Tomorrow's Saturday," Dennis said. It was the day he would be quarterbacking in the police department's annual charity football game.

Upstairs Gilbert lay on his bunk cursing himself, already regretting the statement he had given. He had mistakenly assumed the authorities had known far more than they did. Not only did they not know what car had been involved, but he had overheard someone remark that they hadn't even known the murders had taken place in Koehne Park.

And since no one had asked, he assumed they still did not know there had been a third person with him and Spence that night. If they had no more than it now appeared, he decided, they were going to have a difficult time making a solid case.

The next day, accompanying Simons and Weyenberg to the lake, Gilbert tracked his statement carefully, showing where they had first seen the three teenagers, where the cars had been parked, and where the altercation between David and Jill had begun.

However, the location to which he directed them, pointing to it as the spot where the murders had happened, was far removed from where the killings actually had taken place.

Then, after showing them the route he and David had taken to Speegleville Park, Melendez demonstrated great difficulty in locating the actual area where the bodies had been left. Simons and Weyenberg exchanged weary looks as Gilbert walked along the rutted road, left muddy by the previous night's rain, past the stake which after all this time still marked the isolated spot where Kenneth Franks' body had been found.

"It was really dark out here that night," Gilbert said. "And I was pretty messed up."

Gilbert Melendez, Simons had already decided, could play games too.

Returning to the paved road where they had parked, they sat and scraped mud from their shoes. When Captain Weyenberg finished, he handed the pocketknife he had been using to Melendez. Simons looked on silently, then called the captain over to the car where he stood.

"Captain," he said, barely suppressing a grin, "do you realize what you just did?"

Weyenberg looked puzzled. "What?"

"Hell, man, we're out here with a guy who just finished telling us he was involved in the stabbing murders of three people . . . and you hand him your pocketknife."

Weyenberg blushed and turned to look at Gilbert who sat on a rock, one leg crossed over the other, scraping away the mud. "Truman," Dan said, "if you ever tell anybody about this I'll kill you myself."

Returning to the office, Truman reviewed the transcription of Gilbert's statement which had been typed by one of the office secretaries, replayed the tapes, and found several words had been omitted. Knowing how important it was that everything be right, down to the last "and" and "the," Truman called Captain Weyenberg at home and suggested they meet at the office Sunday afternoon. "I think the best thing to do," he said, "is to pull Gilbert out and let him go over the typed version page-by-page. If there are things he wants to add or correct, we'll let him do it. As he does it, we'll get it typed up."

"Who are we going to get to come in and type on Sunday?" Weyenberg asked.

"Best typist and shortstop in town," Simons said. "I talked to Judy and she said she would do it for us if we could promise her we'd be finished in time for her to get to her softball game."

Late the next afternoon, Judy Simons, already dressed in her uniform, sat at the receptionist's typewriter while Melendez, sitting at the desk in Sheriff Harwell's office, read each page of his statement carefully, occasionally making some minor changes. As he finished each page, Weyenberg took it to Judy.

She worked silently and swiftly, careful to make no mistakes, but trying also not to dwell on what she was typing or to look through the open door in the direction of the man whose terrifying words she was recording. Knowing the chore he had asked her to do was unpleasant, Truman rose from his nearby chair. "Want me to get you a Coke?" he asked.

Judy nodded as she continued typing. After completing another page, she looked up to see that her husband had not returned from the soft drink machine located in another part of the building. She also noticed that Captain Weyenberg was no longer seated in the sheriff's office with Gilbert. Unaware that Truman had left to get Judy a soft drink, the captain had gone down the hall to the rest room.

When Truman returned, he was immediately aware of her discomfort. She was nervous and much of the color had drained from her cheeks. "We're almost through," he said, assuming the subject matter she was typing was getting to her.

"We're not going to get through if you leave me here all by myself with that guy again," Judy said, nodding in the direction of Melendez. For a second, Truman didn't understand her anger. Then he saw that Weyenberg was not with Gilbert.

"Oh, shit," he said. "I'm sorry. I thought the captain . . ."

Judy didn't even allow him to finish his apology. "I'm sitting here, typing all this stuff about people getting raped and stabbed, and the guy who did it is right over there. Right over there. And you're running around getting Cokes like it's a party or something. Just stay here with me until I finish this, okay?"

Captain Weyenberg returned to overhear enough of what Judy was saying to realize the mistake that had been made. He, too, tried to apologize but was cut short. "Let's just get this over with," Judy said.

When the chore was completed, Judy left quickly for her softball game, saying nothing more.

"I think," Weyenberg said to Truman, "you'd better take her out for a nice dinner pretty soon."

"I think you're right," Simons agreed. He then took Gilbert back to his cell while Weyenberg left to return home.

Truman was rereading the statement when Ramon Salinas and Dennis Baier came to the office later that evening to read it and listen to the tapes. There was little conversation until both had heard what Gilbert had to say and had read his lengthy account of the murders.

It was Salinas who finally spoke. "You know," he said, looking at Truman, "it's too bad that you had to quit the police department to solve this case. You've done a helluva job. It's just a damn shame things had to work out this way."

Aware of the tension which had steadily built during the course of the investigation, Truman was surprised at Ramon's remark.

Then Baier joined in the congratulations. "Ramon's right," he said. "I wish you were still with the P.D., too. I understand why you felt you had to leave, but I wish it hadn't been necessary.

"Even though a lot of shit has happened," Dennis continued, "I know you still have a lot of loyalty to the police department. And the fact of the matter is, this is a P.D. case. I think it's time you turned it back over to the Waco Police Department."

Suddenly, the purpose of the praise was clear to Simons. He had taken the investigation this far; now they wanted him to step aside and give the case away as he had done so many times while working with other officers in the police department.

Shaking his head as he looked directly at Baier, Truman said, "Dennis, if I had been loyal to the Waco Police Department, I would never have left. The truth of the matter is, I don't feel comfortable turning this case over to the police. No fucking way. Now, you guys can help me or I'll help you on it from this point on. But I'm not going to dump it. Not this time."

With that he gathered the tapes and the statement, put them in his briefcase, and walked toward the door. Behind him, Baier and Salinas sat in silence.

By the following Monday a copy of Gilbert's taped statement had circulated through the office of the Waco Police Department where it was greeted with a general attitude of skepticism. Before the day was over Feazell was beginning to have his doubts as well. The discrepancy about the automobile used to transport the bodies troubled him. So did Gilbert's denial of having anything to do with the actual murders.

Simons, too, was becoming increasingly convinced that Melendez had mixed too many lies into his admission. But why? Over the weekend he had gone over the statement, memorizing Gilbert's voice inflections, visualizing him as he spoke the words on the tapes. Something was wrong. He was hiding something, trying to protect someone. Simons thought he knew who it was.

In a statement taken months before, a young man named Clint Olson had said that he and several friends had visited David Spence's apartment in the early-morning hours the night of the lake murders. During the course of their conversation Olson had asked David what he had been doing that night. He remembered Spence offhandedly replying that he had been out at the lake with some guy he worked with named Tony. David had mentioned someone else who was with them, Olson had stated, but he could not remember a name.

The "Tony" David had referred to, Simons was sure, was Tony Melendez, Gilbert's younger brother. Simons decided to have another talk with Gilbert.

"I'm not going to sit here and call you a liar," Truman told the prisoner, "but I've got some problems with your statement. There are some things I'm not comfortable with." Melendez, again acting nervous, asked why.

"Somebody's missing. You're covering for somebody."

Gilbert shook his head in an emphatic denial as Simons continued talking. "I know this is hard for you. I know it was hard for you to admit you were there. And since you and David were tight, it was hard for you to give him up. And it would probably be even harder to give up someone who means even more to you than he does. In fact, I can't think of but one other person who would mean that much to you."

"You think I'm covering up for somebody?"

"Yeah, I do. Tony."

Gilbert again began shaking his head.

"Now wait a minute," Simons said. "Just listen to me. I know I'm wrong a helluva lot. I may be wrong here. But if Tony did have something to do with this thing, I need for you to tell me. Let's find him and get him down here and see if we can work something out."

"Tony wasn't there," Gilbert said. As he spoke, his right leg was shaking. He made no mention of the fact that he had already sent word to his brother through family members to get out of town as quickly as possible.

As Simons rose to leave, Gilbert asked about David. "How's he acting?"

"He's doing okay," Truman said. "Still playing games."

"How would you feel about putting me and David together so I could tell him what I'm doing? Maybe he'll come around and we can get this shit over with."

"I'll have to think about it," Simons said.

In a meeting held in Vic Feazell's office it was decided that Gilbert should be given a polygraph test. Of the series of questions he would be asked, there would be five which would indicate whether he was telling the truth or lying about his involvement in the murders:

Do you intend to answer each question truthfully about the three people at Koehne Park?

Did you see David Spence stab the brunette female in the front seat of his car on July 13, 1982?

Did you point your knife toward the face of the white male standing outside David Spence's car?

Did you help David Spence carry the brunette female from the back seat of his car into the weeds on July 13th or 14th of 1982?

Did you get any blood on you or your clothes while you helped David Spence carry the two females into the weeds on the night of July 13, 1982?

Answering "yes" to all five questions, Gilbert passed the test. The examiner who administered the test reported that Melendez had shown a degree of what he termed "confusion" in his answers to the relevant questions. "It appears," he said, "that there are a lot of things which Gilbert is not sure of."

Now even more uncertain that Melendez was dealing squarely, Feazell, Baier, and Salinas listened as Simons told them of Gilbert's request to be allowed to speak with David. It was finally agreed that Spence and Melendez would be taken before Justice of the Peace John Cabaniss, who would officially advise them they were under investigation for a capital murder and explain their legal rights.

At 4:10 on the afternoon on March 31, 1983, Simons, Baier, and Salinas escorted the inmates to the courthouse where they went before the justice of the peace. Spence and Melendez listened as he explained that no charges had been filed, that they were under no obligation to give statements to any law enforcement official, and that they had the right to request attorneys. When the brief session was ended, Gilbert asked if he might talk briefly with Spence before they returned to their cells.

After Cabaniss agreed, Simons indicated they could talk in a far corner of the room, out of earshot, but that he would have to remain to watch over them. While Baier and Salinas prepared to listen in on the conversation in an adjacent room, Gilbert looked at David, then cut his eyes toward a spot near the ceiling where he assumed the listening device had been placed. Silently, he mouthed the word "bug" before telling David that officials had been talking with him about the lake murders. "They told me some shit that you told them—that I was with you," he whispered.

"They said that I said you were with me?" David asked.

"There's a lot of shit happening, man," Gilbert said. "I don't know what the fuck it is. You know something they want to know."

"I don't know what the deal is," David replied.

"I ain't going to fucking death row for this shit," Gilbert said. "I ain't interested in rottin' down there . . ."

"Let me ask you something," David interrupted. "Did you do it?" Before Gilbert could speak, David answered the question for him. "No. And did I? Of course not. So what the hell can they do? What kind of evidence could they have?"

"They've got something. They're telling me they know what the fuck went on, that me and you was out there, kids got killed, everything, man. They could take us to a grand jury, get us for capital murder and put us on death row."

"How?" David asked.

Gilbert ignored the question and began to explain how he felt they could beat the death penalty. "They said, you know, if we start talking they'll work something out. If you talk to them, they'll work something out with you. We don't have to fucking die. Man, this is serious shit. They're gonna nail us for this and I don't feel like dying.

"I know you've been talking to Simons," Gilbert continued. "I've talked to him; he's all right. You help him and he'll work something out with you to where you don't have to go to death row."

"Where are they getting all this bullshit?" David asked. "I don't know what the fuck they're telling you, but they're telling me they got enough to indict me."

From across the room Simons spoke up. "Gilbert, we've got to go pretty quick."

Melendez nodded in Truman's direction and continued talking. "I think we ought to tell them what the fuck went down and see what they can work out. I'm gonna tell them what happened."

Spence leaned back and began shaking his head. "Naw," he said, laughing nervously. "I don't believe this. I don't believe this, Gilbert."

Melendez did not return the laughter. "I don't want you saying that I snitched you off or that you snitched on me. We've been through a lot of shit together. But there ain't no sense in going and sitting on death row together. We can get out of this. You know what I'm talking about?"

"You say you're gonna tell them what happened?" David sounded puzzled, incredulous at what he was hearing.

"Yeah, I'm gonna tell 'em what happened."

Simons again interrupted. "Let's go, Gilbert," he called across the room.

While Truman was returning Gilbert to the jail, Baier and Salinas sat listening to David. "Something weird's going on here," he said, shaking his head. "Gilbert was sitting in there saying that he was going to go ahead and tell you what happened." For several minutes the police officers talked with him, urging him to do the same. "It's time to get your business straight," Baier said.

As Baier spoke, Salinas placed the crime scene photos of the three dead teenagers in front of David. "These are the people I'm supposed to have killed?" David asked. Neither his voice nor the expression on his face showed any emotion at all. "So, am I supposed to be indicted for this? Because if I am we've got one helluva problem."

"Well, explain it to me," Baier said.

"You're asking me to tell you what happened out there at that park when I can't tell you one fucking thing about it. That's the honest to God's truth because I don't know what the fuck happened out there. All these statements that people have got signed against me, saying I told 'em I did it, told 'em how it was done—I didn't tell 'em shit. Honest to God, man, that's square business. I don't know a fucking thing."

Feazell meanwhile tried to talk with Gilbert, hoping to persuade him to take another polygraph test. Sitting in the D.A.'s office, Melendez refused to discuss the case with Vic. He would not take another polygraph test, he said; nor would he say anything unless Truman Simons was present.

Feazell, angered over Melendez's attitude, could not understand Gilbert's apparent trust in the jailer. "You think Simons will go down to death row for you?" Vic asked.

"No, but he's the only guy I'm gonna talk to," Gilbert replied.

Feazell said nothing more and ordered Melendez returned to his cell.

Two days later Gilbert was sent back to the state prison. By the time he left, only Truman Simons remained fully convinced he had been a participant in the lake murders. Weary of chasing down blind alleys and discouraged by the growing resistance from his fellow law enforcement officers, Truman was beginning to have serious doubts that the case would ever be solved. No one in the police department had shown any inclination to help. And he was certain that Feazell didn't trust him.

For several days Simons battled a depression like nothing he had ever experienced before. At home he hardly talked at all to Judy and showed no inclination to play with his son. He spent a great deal of time alone in the garage, rearranging his tools or tinkering with the motor of his car. Sleep came grudgingly and then was fitful. He had little appetite.

And at night when he was on duty in the jail, he ignored Spence's signals to open his cell door so he might come into the chute and talk. Truman wanted to be alone. He tried to read a few paperback novels but could never seem to get past the first few chapters.

One night after all the inmates were sleeping, Simons rose from his desk and began to walk slowly back and forth in the small area of the watch room. "Lord," he said aloud. "I know You put the strongest tests on those with the strongest faith. But I'm not that strong. I'm afraid I can't handle this anymore. I've got to have some help. Help me pull this thing together or give me the strength to let it go."

# 27

Ned Butler is a bearish man who stands six feet five inches tall and battles constantly to keep his weight in the 230-pound range. Blond and bearded, he looks like a forty-four-year-old version of actor and folksinger Burl Ives. He talks with a rumbling, gravelly voice, yet people who know him are quick to note that the growl is much worse than his bite.

An outstanding athlete in high school, then at the University of Texas at El Paso, he developed an interest in pursuing a law degree only after several years of teaching and coaching high school football. Even today he punctuates his conversations with sports jargon, referring to his trial preparations as "getting my game face on" and the punishment phase as "the fourth quarter." The trying of a capital murder, he says, is "an attorney's answer to the Super Bowl."

After graduating from law school, Butler worked for two years as a prosecutor in the Harris County district attorney's office in Houston before moving to the small east Texas community of Gilmer where he advanced from an assistant's position to become D.A. He was a prosecutor in the Panhandle city of Amarillo when Vic Feazell, still in the process of reorganizing his office, called to ask if Butler would be interested in moving to Waco to concentrate his efforts on prosecuting capital cases.

An outdoorsman who loves to fish, Ned had wearied of the arid ranch lands of the Panhandle. Though he never mentioned it to Feazell, one of the primary reasons he accepted the job was the lure of fishing for sand bass on Lake Waco.

Reporting to work the first week in April of 1983, Butler was immediately assigned a long-delayed capital murder case involving a Waco man who had entered the gift shop of a local hotel and held a cashier hostage before eventually stomping her to death. Butler was in the midst of jury selection when Feazell came into his office late one afternoon with a problem. The district attorney explained the arrangement he and Police Chief Scott had made to have Dennis Baier and Ramon Salinas assigned to his office and investigate the Lake Waco murders. They were driving him crazy, Vic said. "They come into my office every afternoon and hang around, waiting for someone to tell them what to do."

Filling Ned in on what he knew of the case, Feazell said he would like for him to assume the responsibility of coordinating the investigation once he was finished with the Drakeford trial. "No need to wait," Butler said. "Turn them over to me now." With his family still in Amarillo, awaiting sale of their house and the end of the school term, he had nothing but work to occupy his time.

It was what Feazell had wanted to hear. The manner with which Butler had attacked the first case assigned him had impressed the district attorney. Feazell was pleased to find that his new assistant was a man who approached his work with a rare blend of enthusiasm and cautious attention to the most minor of details. His aggressive manner melded well with Feazell's philosophy.

Butler immediately met with Ramon Salinas and informed him that he would like to see the police reports on the case. Ramon said he could furnish him with everything but the crime scene photos. An interview with James Bishop had finally been arranged and Dennis Baier had left for California, taking the pictures with him.

The following evening, after a long day of jury selection, Butler sat alone in his office, reading the reports until two in the morning. The case immediately fascinated him. Though he had never personally investigated a case, it occurred to him that there was a lot of checking and interviewing yet to be done. Having been made aware of Truman Simons' theory and of the recent confession by Gilbert Melendez, Butler was surprised that the names of neither David Spence nor Melendez appeared in any of the reports given to him.

Though he had not yet met Simons, Butler had already heard rumors that he was obsessed with the case and would do anything, legal or not, to have his mistaken-identity, murder-for-hire theory proved out. Putting the file away in his desk, Ned decided he would not involve Simons in the investigation until he learned a great deal more about him.

The following Monday when Dennis Baier returned from California, convinced that Bishop had no knowledge of the lake murders, he met with Butler and turned over the crime scene photographs. Leaning back in his chair, his feet on his desk, Ned cradled the dozens of pictures on his chest and silently began to view the tale of horror they told. He pulled a magnifying glass from his desk drawer and examined several photographs of the slain girls more closely. Flipping from one to another, then going back to several he had set aside, looking at them again, he stroked his beard and smiled faintly. *Maybe*, he thought, *we've got something*.

During the two years he had worked in the D.A.'s office in Amarillo, Butler had helped fellow prosecutors do research in preparation for trials involving two brutal murders committed by a young meatpacking plant worker named Jay Kelly Pinkerton. In one case, a woman had been stabbed thirty times and her body mutilated. In the second murder, the woman had been raped and repeatedly stabbed with a bowie knife. In hopes of finding fingerprints in the blood on the bodies of the victims, the crime scene photographs were sent to Dr. Homer Campbell, a forensic odontologist in Albuquerque, New Mexico, and his partner James Ebert, a photo enhancement expert. They had no luck in finding fingerprints but did find numerous bite marks on the bodies of both victims. It was the bite marks which eventually led to Pinkerton's conviction and ultimate death by lethal injection.

After studying the photos Baier had brought to him for several more minutes, Butler rose and walked quickly down the hall to Feazell's office. In his excitement, he interrupted a conversation the D.A. was engaged in at the time. Spreading several photographs of Jill Montgomery and Raylene Rice over Feazell's desk, he handed Vic the magnifying glass. "I think we've got bite marks," he said.

Feazell looked carefully at the areas Butler pointed to but was unable to see the wounds. "Are you sure?" he asked.

"Not until I have a guy I know in Albuquerque look at the pictures," Butler said. "But I'll bet you a steak dinner right now that the guy who killed those kids bit them."

"Well, send the guy the pictures," Vic said.

"I'd rather take them," Butler said.

"It's your case now," Feazell said. "Do what you have to do."

Dr. Homer Campbell confirmed that the marks Butler had detected had been made by human teeth. He also found several additional bite marks which Ned had overlooked. "If this guy they've got in the jail had anything to do with those murders," Ned told Feazell in a midnight call from New Mexico, "we've got a way to prove it." As soon as he returned, Butler made arrangements to have impressions made of David Spence's teeth.

He also decided it was time he got acquainted with Truman Simons.

Simons had just come on duty when Butler, still dressed in the white three-piece suit he had worn in court earlier in the day, stepped off the fourth-floor elevator in the jail and signaled to him. "I want to talk to you about the lake case," Butler said without additional salutation.

Simons looked at the unsmiling figure standing before him. It crossed his mind that Butler, with his huge frame and white suit, resembled the television commercial's Mr. Clean with hair and a beard. He made little attempt to hide the excitement he was feeling over the fact that someone—even a stranger—was expressing an interest in the information he had gathered.

Truman opened his briefcase and showed the assistant D.A. the statements he had gathered from inmates. He explained his theory that Muneer Deeb had hired Spence to kill Gayle Kelley but that the wrong girl had been murdered. He gave Ned a copy of Gilbert's confession and elaborately answered every question Butler posed.

For over an hour Ned read over the reports and asked questions, his expression never changing. Then, handing the last statement he had read back to the jailer, Butler rose to leave. "I'll tell you in a couple of days whether Spence killed those kids or not," he said. His tone impressed Truman as condescending, even rude.

"Wait a minute," the stunned Simons said. "What the hell are you talking about? You come in here and I talk my head off and show you everything I've got, and now you're going to walk out with a statement like that? What kind of bullshit is this?" Truman was furious. "I don't know whether you're aware of it or not," he continued, "but I've spent a helluva lot of time on this, and I think it's pretty shitty for you to come big-assing in here and listen to everything I have to say and then just leave. I've got a lot invested in this case and I think I deserve to know what's going on."

Butler shrugged. "This case is no different from any other."

"You're full of shit," Simons said, his face reddening. "This case is a helluva lot different to me."

"I gotta go," Ned said, abruptly ending the conversation and turning toward the elevator.

As he left, Simons angrily stuffed the statements he'd shown Butler back into his briefcase. Then, looking toward the ceiling, he said, "You've got to be shittin' me. *This* is the help You sent?"

As soon as he got off duty, Truman went directly to Dan Weyenberg's office and related his late-night conversation with Butler. "What the hell's going on?" Simons asked.

The captain looked embarrassed. "I'm not supposed to tell you. The people over in the D.A.'s office don't trust you." As he studied the frustration in Truman's face, Weyenberg walked to the door and closed it. "Aw, hell, sit down," he said.

He explained how Butler had discovered bite marks in the photographs and told him about the plans to have dental impressions of Spence's teeth made for comparison. "They don't want anyone to know about it," Weyenberg said, "because they're afraid if word gets to David, he might try to knock his own teeth out."

"They think I might tell Spence all about this, so he can knock his teeth out?" Simons said.

"Something like that."

"That's pretty stupid reasoning, if you ask me," Truman replied. "When are they going to do these impressions?"

"In the next couple of days."

"Okay, I haven't been talking with David for the last few nights anyway. I won't talk to him again until they do whatever it is they're going to do. But hell, if they've got something I sure wouldn't do anything to mess it up."

"I know that," Weyenberg said.

The day after the aluwax impressions of Spence's teeth had been taken by a local dentist, Simons received a mid-afternoon call at home from Captain Weyenberg. "I just got a call from the D.A.'s office," he said, "and they're hot."

"What's the matter?"

"They had someone over here taking some pictures of Spence's mouth earlier today and while they were doing it, David asked if they were going to be sent to Albuquerque. They think you're the one who told him."

"Captain," Simons said, "you never told me where they were sending any of that stuff."

"I know," Weyenberg said, "but Ned Butler wants to see you."

"I'll go see him," Simons said, "but if he gets in my face I'm going to put him out that third-floor window."

On several occasions Dennis Baier had confided to Truman that the district attorney's office was quietly planning to remove him from any further involvement in the case. Feazell and Butler, the police officer had told him, didn't trust him. Simons assumed they were planning to use this latest incident to discredit him with Sheriff Harwell and Captain Weyenberg. If they wanted to play games, he thought, he would play, too. To see what their reaction would be, he made up his mind to tell them that he was the one who had inadvertently told David of the planned trip to Albuquerque. But if they were going to get him off the case, they would damn well have to work at it.

Ned was standing behind his desk when Simons walked in. "You want to see me?" Truman asked.

Butler immediately began asking how it was possible for Spence to have known the dental impressions and photographs would be sent to Albuquerque. Simons, in turn, admitted that he had spoken with David briefly the night after the impressions had been made but did not bother explaining that he had never been told where they were to be sent. "I guess if anybody told him, it had to be me," Truman said. "I confess; I'm guilty."

Butler calmed and sat down. "It's no big deal," he said. "Don't worry about it."

That night Simons called David into the chute. "I just got my ass chewed royally today," he said. "How in the hell did you know that dental stuff was going to be sent to Albuquerque?"

"When they had me down there, putting all that junk in my

mouth," David said, "I overheard Captain Weyenberg talking to somebody about it out in the hall."

"Well," Simons said, "if anybody asks, you tell them I told you about it."

"Why?"

"Just tell 'em." If someone was going to get in hot water over the matter, he would rather it be him than Captain Weyenberg.

Simons avoided the district attorney's office for the next several days, marking time until Butler made the trip to Albuquerque with the dental impressions and photographs of Spence's teeth. The next evening after Butler had left, Truman called Feazell at home. "What did Butler find out?"

Vic said he hadn't heard. Simons felt sure he was lying and called Weyenberg. "Dan," he said. "I can't stand it. Have you heard how they came out with the bite marks?"

Again Weyenberg was hesitant. "They matched," he said finally.

The next day Simons entered Butler's office. Mentioning nothing of his conversation with Weyenberg, he asked about the trip to Albuquerque. Ned was immediately evasive. This time Simons managed to conceal his anger as he calmly spoke his mind. "Look, I don't give a shit whether you tell me they matched or didn't. If it's some big top-secret deal, that's fine. But let me just tell you this: If there's anything to this forensic odontology business, and if that doctor you went to see is worth a shit, those bite marks matched David's teeth—because he's the one who killed those kids."

"Are you that sure?" Butler asked.

"I *know* he did it," Simons said. "And if your bite mark evidence is any good, you know it too. So why don't we quit all this tiptoeing around bullshit and go to work?"

For the first time since their initial meeting in the jail, Butler broke into a wide grin. "I think we can now prove what you've been trying to tell people for a helluva long time. David Spence's teeth impressions matched the bite marks." Though he was not yet aware of it, Simons had finally gained an ally.

Truman Simons had begun to fascinate Butler. Despite Feazell's admitted mistrust and the obvious animosity Salinas and Baier held for the jailer, Ned could find no legitimate reason to think

Truman was anything more than a hardworking law enforcement officer who had worked long hours toward solving a case which no one else had seemed to be able to get a handle on.

One of the first people Butler had contacted upon his arrival in Waco was attorney Claude Giles, an old high school classmate when both had lived in Abilene. They had spoken several times before Giles mentioned that he and Truman Simons were good friends and had known each other a long time. Butler immediately began to question the attorney, whose opinions he valued, about Truman. Butler confided his concern about whether Simons could be trusted, relating stories which had been passed on to him about Simons' planting evidence, falsifying statements, and stubbornly working to make cases fit his theories even when there was evidence to the contrary. Giles made no comment as Butler outlined his reasons for concern.

"Have you ever seen any proof of that sort of thing—ever caught him in a lie?" the attorney finally asked.

"No," Butler admitted, then recounted the confrontation between him and Simons over Spence's knowing that the teeth impressions were being sent to Albuquerque.

Giles smiled. Privately he thought it amusing that he was caught in the middle between two old friends. Unknown to Butler, Simons had been checking him out as well, and Giles had already heard the story of the meeting in Butler's office from Truman.

"You know how David Spence knew about where those teeth impressions were going?" Giles asked. "He overheard someone—whose name I'm not going to mention—talking about it out in the hall the night they had him downstairs in the jail taking the samples. It was just an innocent mistake on the part of the person Spence heard talking. But it damn sure wasn't Truman Simons who told him. I'll guarantee you that. Ned, I know the guy. And there's not a person in the world I trust more."

In the days to come Butler would begin to share the attorney's opinion, and he launched a quiet campaign to convince Feazell that if there was legitimate reason for skepticism, it might best be directed toward the efforts of the police officers assigned to the case.

\*      \*      \*

His spirits buoyed by the news from Albuquerque, Simons again began looking forward to his nightly jail visits with Spence. It also pleased him to know that Butler, whether he trusted Simons or not, had now accepted David as the prime suspect in the case. In fact, Ned had instructed Baier and Salinas to focus their efforts on building a case against Spence. One of his first suggestions was that they locate the car David had owned at the time of the murders and have it checked thoroughly for blood traces and hair samples.

The police officers managed to locate the automobile after tracing it through two owners. David was sitting in the fourth-floor window when he saw Dennis Baier park the gold Malibu on Columbus Street adjacent to the jail.

Spence was immediately upset and began ranting to several fellow inmates about the police having his old car. "They aren't gonna find shit in it," he said. "They're just wasting their time."

A young black inmate named J. D. Williams was amused by David's concern. Slapping his hand on the table where he was sitting to attract attention, Williams affected a deep, serious tone and began making an impromptu speech. "Ladies and gentlemen of the jury," he intoned, "we have here the car previously owned by the defendant, Mister David Spence. We have taken it to our special laboratory and checked it with a variety of scientific tests." He paused for dramatic effect, then continued, ". . . and we've done found bloodstains."

Even David was enjoying the campy theater of the young inmate.

"Now Mister Spence," Williams continued, "can you please tell the court whose bloodstains those are in the car?"

"I don't know, judge," David answered, entering into the spirit of the event.

Williams made a big production of frowning and stroking his chin as he continued. "We also found some hair in the car; hair that matched those kids. Mister Spence, can you tell us how that hair got there?"

David laughed. "I guess because the kids were in the car."

"All right, Mister Spence, would you now please tell the ladies and gentlemen of the jury where you were on the night in question when this alleged homicide occurred out at Lake Waco?"

"Your honor," David said. "I object. That question is leading and irrelevant."

"Overruled, Mister Spence. Answer the question."

"Aw, hell, judge, where do you think I was? Everybody knows I was out there."

The "jury" which had gathered quickly found David guilty.

Talk of the lake murders investigation by now dominated the almost nightly conversations of Spence and Simons. David repeatedly pressed the jailer for details of Gilbert's confession while, at the same time, insisting he could not understand why his friend had implicated him in the crime.

"I know it's hard for you to believe," Truman said, "but the way I see it, Gilbert just wants to save his own ass."

A reflective look crossed David's face. "You know," he said, "when Baier and Salinas were talking to me over there, there was something that really bothered me."

Simons, who had been in an adjacent room monitoring most of the interview the police officers had conducted, waited for David to explain.

"When we were talking, Salinas showed me a picture of one of those girls. Could I have done that kind of thing? And not remember it?"

"David, I don't know. That's something you and a psychiatrist would have to decide. Are you telling me you think it's possible that you could have done it?"

"Well, there was something in that picture that bothered me a lot."

"What was that?"

"The towel the girl was tied up with," David said. "That's my mother's towel."

Simons leaned forward in his chair, squarely facing Spence. "How do you think your mom's towel got out there?"

"I don't know. I'm beginning to wonder if I did it or not."

Truman studied David's face as he spoke. He continued patiently to quiz David about the towel he said he had seen in the crime scene photograph of Jill Montgomery.

"It was three or four different colors," David said. "The kind you get out of a box of soap."

"Where was the towel the last time you saw it?"

"In my car."

"Makes a helluva lot of sense, doesn't it?" the jailer observed.

David did not answer. Instead he asked Simons a question. "You know why I come down here and talk to you all night? Because if I go to sleep, I have this dream. I'm killing a girl, but she doesn't have a face. I can never see her face. I just can't stay in that cell at night. I'm afraid they're going to come see me."

"Those kids out at the lake?"

"Yeah."

As he listened, Simons was beginning to feel that David was trying to lay the groundwork for a plea of insanity. Nonetheless, he urged Spence to explain why he felt the kids might visit him in his cell.

"Because I don't know whether I killed them or not," David said. "I'm just afraid they're going to come see me in there. And, man, if they do I couldn't handle it."

Then he abruptly changed the direction of the conversation. "They played me part of Gilbert's confession, you know," he said.

"Was it true?"

"They didn't play much of it."

"What do you remember?"

"Well, Gilbert says me and him were riding around and went out to the lake. Then he said we saw those kids and I told him something about how they were the people who ripped me off. He said we stopped and talked a little while and hit them up about going with us to get some beer; that we still had time before the store closed.

"That part seemed strange. It sounded familiar; like I had said it before. He said he got in the car and I started talking to the girl with the big tits and reached over and grabbed one of them. Then he said she slapped me. Gilbert told them I stopped the car and me and the girl started fighting—that I pulled a knife and cut her."

Truman suppressed a smile. He had been sitting in the next room during the interview conducted by Baier and Salinas and had heard the portion of Melendez's confession that was played. The moment Gilbert said the kids got into the car, the recorder had been turned off. David had taken the narrative much farther than what he had heard on the tape.

"Does any of that do anything for your memory?" Simons asked.

"I don't know. It worries me. But the thing that really bugs me is that towel. I know that's my mother's towel. Do you think I killed those kids?"

"I sure do, David."

"Then why don't I know?"

Simons only shook his head.

"Well, if we go to trial and you all prove to me that I did it, I'm going to get on the stand and tell the jury to kill me. If I did kill those kids, I deserve to die."

"I don't think you'll have to beg too hard, David," Simons said. The jailer squared his chair so that he could look directly at the young man. "Let's go back to what you were talking about earlier. You knew there was a bug in that room when you were talking to Ramon and Dennis, didn't you?"

"I figured there probably was."

"Well, I was in another room listening. When you were telling me what Gilbert said on the tape, you went way past what you really heard. How'd you do that?"

David looked only mildly surprised. "It just seemed logical."

"Logical? Shit, David, are you saying that it would just seem logical that you would reach over and grab the girl and that you two would get into a big hassle and you would pull a knife . . ."

"Yeah."

"Okay," Truman said, "if that part sounds logical, why don't you tell me the rest of the story."

"I don't know the rest of the story."

"I mean how you think Gilbert would have run it down. You're always telling me how to investigate this case. You might make a damn good investigator yourself. You say you know Gilbert pretty well, how he thinks and all. Just tell me what you think Gilbert would have said happened. We're just talking hypothetically; it doesn't mean shit."

David leaned his head back against the bars as if composing his thoughts. "Okay," he began, "he would have said that I like big tits, so I probably would have reached over and grabbed one. This girl was just a young little chick so she probably would have slapped me. Now, there ain't no bitch in the world's gonna slap me, so I'd have done something to her."

"Would you have cut her?"

"Naw, I'd probably just slap the shit out of her."

"Then what?"

"With me and her fighting, I couldn't be driving, so I'd have to stop. If me and the girl and Gilbert are in the front seat and the other two kids are in the back, Gilbert's probably going to get out. He's probably going to pull a knife to make sure he can control the people in the back seat. If the chick in the front seat is still giving me trouble, I would probably holler for Gilbert to give me something to tie the bitch up with."

"What would he give you?" Simons interrupted.

"I've always got some towels or rags or some shit in the floorboard. He'd grab whatever's there and give it to me and I would tie her up."

He stopped for a moment, then continued, "I guess I would have gotten some off that broad in the front. She had those big tits and I was pissed off at her. I probably would have gotten some right there."

"What would have happened next?"

"Well, if those other two weren't out of the car yet, we'd have gotten them out. We'd probably tie that dude up so he couldn't get away from us. By then, Gilbert would probably want to get him some, so I'd let him get some off that other broad, the blond one. By the time he got through, me and this other chick had probably had a big fight and I'd cut her. See, we're both ex-convicts, so we can't stand a rape case, so we'd probably have to take care of them, do something to them. I guess that would be why we would kill them."

"What would you do after you killed them?" Simons asked.

"If you spend a lot of time in Koehne Park there's a good chance a lot of people will see you. No smart convict would probably decide to leave the bodies there. They'd probably take them somewhere they never hang out."

Then he smiled. "End of story."

The following day, Simons sought out Salinas and asked what picture David had seen when they were interviewing him. Ramon thumbed through the crime scene photographs and picked one out. In one corner of the picture, barely visible, was a white portion of the bloodstained towel which had been used to bind Jill Montgomery. There was nothing in the photo to indicate that the towel was multicolored.

"What's up?" Salinas asked.

"I think David's decided to start playing crazy on us," Simons said.

A few nights later David again brought up the subject of the lake murders as he sat in the chute, talking with Simons.

"If you had to go to trial today," he asked, "who would be your witnesses?"

"David," Truman answered, "like I told you, you're a pretty good investigator. Why don't you tell me?"

Spence thought for a minute before he replied. "Well," he finally said, "there's Gene Deal."

"Who's he?"

"My parole officer."

"Okay, who else?"

"Well, I'd probably talk with Ray Payne."

"Tell me about him," Simons said as he took mental notes of the names David was providing.

"He's a dude I worked with at the aluminum place. He heard me and Deeb get into an argument one time."

"Anybody else?"

David shrugged.

"Well, let me ask you this," Simons said. "If I was trying to find someone who would give you an alibi, somebody who would stand up for you in court, who would that be?"

"Probably Dorothy Miles," Spence said. Then, as if bored with the game, he abruptly changed the subject.

Simons was perplexed that David had so freely provided him a new list of people to talk with. He was not at all certain they would be of any help—until, several weeks later, he was able to contact Gene Deal by telephone in Copperas Cove, Texas, where he had moved.

After identifying himself and making the parole officer aware that he was investigating the lake murders, Simons could not understand the cool, almost hostile response from Deal.

"I think," Truman said, "that David was involved in killing those kids."

"That's interesting," Deal replied.

"I was hoping maybe you knew something that might help us."

There was a long silence before Deal made a statement that rendered Simons speechless. "I tried to give him to you people months ago," Deal said.

## 28

Dennis Baier and Ramon Salinas had promised to keep Jill Montgomery's family advised about whatever progress was being made on the case. Since teaming up on the investigation, they had made several trips to Waxahachie and had quickly realized that it was Jan Thompson, Jill's aunt, to whom others in the family looked for strength and guidance. They decided to maintain contact with the family through her. Even when no solid leads developed, the officers continued to telephone Jan on occasion. The conversations were generally casual, almost chatty. Their purpose was simply to assure the family they were still working on the case.

But as the weeks stretched into months, the calls became increasingly infrequent and a new form of depression fell over those who waited in Waxahachie. By the spring of 1983 Jan had all but lost touch with the Waco police and had begun to seriously doubt that Jill's killer would ever be found.

Jan also sensed a continued weakening of the morale within the family. She had watched Nancy become increasingly hostile, a hard, angry look fixed permanently on her face. Rod kept to himself, working long hours but showing no inclination to fashion a tombstone for Jill's grave, then disappearing into the nightlife of Dallas on weekends. And the guilt which Jill's brother, Brad, had initially felt at not having driven his sister to Waco that day in 1982 had not subsided. Several times his young wife, Gloria, had called in tears to express to Jan her growing concern over his constant state of depression. And Jan herself was finding it increasingly difficult to continue presenting the optimistic front she felt so necessary.

She had watched as the initial shock of the murders had worn away, dissolving into grief, then anger and frustration. Jan saw her family being ripped apart and she silently agonized over the fact that there seemed nothing she could do to halt the destruction. She was beginning to wonder how much longer her own sanity would hold out.

In early May, Jan received a telephone call from Bennie Shaw, Nancy's ex-husband. He had just had a strange conversation and wanted to see what she thought about it. Bennie said he had been in the Waxahachie courthouse earlier in the day when he was approached by a clerk named Karen Hufstetler who inquired about the progress of the investigation of Jill's death. She had asked if he knew why the Waco police had never contacted her. Then she had told him about the vision she had had nine months earlier and the notes she had given to Detective Ronnie Roark to pass on to those investigating the case.

"Where can I get in touch with her?" Jan asked.

Though Jan Thompson had serious reservations about those who claimed psychic powers, Karen Hufstetler would become her lifeline to sanity in the days to come.

Jan listened in mute silence as the high-pitched voice of the young woman she had telephoned told of her experience the night the teenagers had been killed. Though Karen was careful to avoid some of the more horrifying details, she talked for almost an hour, describing the area where she felt the crime had occurred and giving detailed descriptions of the nameless assailants as well as the victims.

Karen told her how she had continued to experience "flashes" about the murders in recent months and that she felt a strong need to go to Waco and visit the scene of the crime. She was certain there was evidence there that had been overlooked. She was only interested in going, however, if the Waco police embraced the idea.

Jan was almost in shock when the conversation finally ended. Though the woman she had spoken with had insisted to her there were details of her vision too gruesome to discuss, she still had told a story so incredibly horrifying that it had shaken Jan almost as badly as had that first indication the youngsters were missing those many months ago. Jan sat at her kitchen table long after replacing the receiver on the phone, trying to make sense of what she had heard. Was the person to whom she had been talking crazy? Or was she?

It seemed unbelievable that anyone could fabricate such a story. Yet how could someone who insisted she knew none of

the parties involved seem to know the things Karen had been
telling her? Jan could not shake the feeling that there were too
many details which fit into the sketchy scenario which the investigators had provided her.

Reflecting on the conversation and reading notes she had
written while listening to Karen, Jan felt a mixture of fright and
fascination. Was it possible, she wondered, that this woman held
the key to solving the murders? Or that she might even have
been somehow involved? That night Jan slept very little. By
dawn's first light she had made up her mind to phone Ramon
or Dennis and relay to them what Karen had told her.

She was surprised when Salinas, after hearing the bizarre
story, asked her to have Karen get in touch with him. She was
even more surprised a few days later when Dennis called to ask
if she and Karen could come to Waco and talk with them. They
had even agreed to drive to Italy, Texas, where Karen lived, to
pick them up.

The following Saturday morning, May 21, the officers listened
as Karen again told her story during the drive to Waco. As she
spoke, she held tightly a small necklace which she had asked
Jan to bring. It had once belonged to Jill.

The officers had heard psychics' stories before and were admittedly skeptical. Neither had ever seen information from such
a source result in the solution to a crime. It was Baier's curiosity
as much as anything that had prompted the decision to spend a
Saturday driving Karen Hufstetler around Waco. That, and the
off chance that she might somehow have been involved in the
crime. There was always the possibility, however remote, that
she had seen something firsthand rather than in a "vision."

The officers had explained to Karen that they would drive to
a number of locations but would give no indication whether or
not they were related to the investigation. If she had any "feelings" about a particular place she was to tell them. It sounded
much like the rules for a child's game of hide-and-seek.

For the next half hour, Salinas silently drove through the light
weekend traffic, taking Karen past the North Fifteenth Street
house where David Spence had lived, by the apartment where
Gilbert Melendez had been arrested, through the winding parking lots of the Northwood Apartments, and past the town house
of Richard Franks. Karen said nothing except that she was look-

ing for an older two-story house with a balcony which she had "seen" in one of her visions. Neither of the officers knew of such a house in Waco.

Karen showed no interest as they drove into the parking lot in front of the Rainbow Drive Inn but asked Salinas to stop as he approached the small two-story building behind the store. "There's something evil about that place," she said, pointing to the apartment where David and Christy had once lived. "There's something bad about it, but I don't know what."

Neither Ramon nor Dennis said anything as they pulled out of the gravel parking lot and drove toward Koehne Park. It was only when they approached the rest rooms located near the boat docking area that Karen first began to show excitement and asked that they stop. Getting out of the car, Karen hurried toward the concrete building. "They were here," she said, her voice more high-pitched than usual. "Jill went in that rest room after the people had picked them up." Again neither of the officers commented on her observation.

Driving back up the two-laned park road they turned into the area of the Circle where Raylene's deserted car had been found. It was vaguely familiar, Karen said, but not the place she was looking for. "This isn't it," she said.

Salinas cut his eyes at his partner as he turned to leave Koehne. The look spoke loudly. They were, it said, wasting a perfectly good Saturday.

As they approached the twin bridges, heading toward Speegleville, Salinas finally hinted at his skepticism. "Why don't you give me directions from here?" he said to Karen.

Leaning forward, she said she was looking for a road that led to the entrance of a park. "And I'm looking for a line of trees," she said. Hesitantly at first, she began instructing the driver, asking that he turn off the highway onto an access road. "This looks right," she said. "They came this way."

Sitting silently, Jan Thompson was beginning to share the same doubts she was certain the two men in the front seat were feeling. Through newspaper reports, it had been common knowledge that the bodies had been found in Speegleville Park. By directing the officers there, Karen was proving nothing.

Once past the main gate, Ramon continued to let Karen give directions. As he drove slowly toward a fork in the paved road,

Karen instructed him to turn right. Then, a few hundred yards later, she asked him to turn right again, onto a rutted dirt road near an open area where there were several picnic tables. They were close, she said. "Let's stop here and walk," Karen suggested.

The officers and the two women stepped into the midday heat which was muggy from the previous night's rainfall. Karen began walking quickly in the direction of a wooded area, Baier following closely. "I'm looking for a big tree," she said. Ramon and Jan followed at a distance. "If she does know anything," Salinas whispered, "we'll know pretty quickly." He looked down at the clods of mud which were already clinging to his polished boots and frowned.

Jan's eyes followed Karen's hurried movements until she and Baier disappeared down the small road into the nearby trees. After a few minutes she heard a scream. Breaking into a run, Jan hurried toward the sound of Karen's voice. She arrived to find the young woman kneeling at the base of a large tree, sobbing. "This is the tree I was looking for," Karen said. "This is where it happened." It was the tree where she had "seen" Jill Montgomery assaulted.

Once she had calmed, Karen rose and began walking along the road again. "He took her over here," Karen said, pointing, as she left the road and began frantically wading through the tall weeds. In a matter of minutes Karen was again crying hysterically, her body shaking, yelling for the officers. "This," she said, "is where Jill was. Oh, God, this is where they left her. I can see it all again." Jan quickly made her way through the weeds and placed her arms around the sobbing woman. "Come on," she said, "let's go."

Helping her back to the muddy road, Jan asked Dennis to take Karen back to the car. When they were out of earshot Jan turned to Ramon. "I'd like to know where Jill's body was found," she said. Salinas led her back into the heavy weeds to a spot just a few yards from where Karen had been standing. Saying nothing, he pointed in the direction of a thin wooden stake that had once marked the location of the body. It was no longer standing but was lying on the ground, almost buried in the underbrush.

"She was close," Jan said.

"Yeah, she was," Salinas said as they stepped back onto the road to follow Karen and Dennis to the car.

As they drove back toward town, questions filled Jan's mind as she comforted the still distressed woman who sat next to her. There was no way, she felt, that Karen could have seen the marker which Salinas had pointed out to her. From the road it had not been visible. And even when Salinas had pointed it out to her, Jan would never have recognized it as a stake marking any special location. It had looked too much like a number of other sticks she had seen strewn throughout the area.

Baier finally broke the silence, turning to Karen. "Do you feel like making one more stop?" he asked.

"I'm fine now," Karen said.

They drove in the direction of the police impound where the Malibu once owned by David Spence was being kept. Again telling Karen nothing about what she might find, they asked that she walk among the thirty-odd cars parked in the impound. For a half hour Karen roamed the fenced area, stopping occasionally to look inside various automobiles, sometimes placing her hand on a fender or a door. The officers and Jan waited and watched near the entrance.

Karen finally called to Salinas. When he reached her she pointed in the direction of a German shepherd chained in the far corner of the impound. She wanted to look at the cars in that area but was fearful that the dog might attack her. Ramon agreed to accompany her.

Once back in the area she again walked among the automobiles for several minutes. Salinas said nothing as she paced around Spence's Malibu for several minutes. Then she went to another car nearby and looked at it for some time. Her movements became more hurried as she walked back and forth between the two cars several times. Then a disappointed look crossed her face.

"I have bad feelings about both of these cars," she said. "But I'm not sure which is the one the kids were in." Pointing to a bumper sticker on the Malibu, she said, "The car I saw didn't have a bumper sticker."

At the time neither officer knew that the bumper sticker, an advertisement for a local radio station, had been placed on the car by the person who had bought the car from Spence two weeks after the murders. Out of curiosity they would later check and find that a violent crime had also taken place in the other car which Karen had pointed out.

By the time the officers returned the two women to Italy, they were as puzzled by Karen Hufstetler as was Jan. Intellectually, they felt there was an explanation for everything she had done. She had admitted that she had kept up with newspaper reports of the crime, so very likely she knew where Speegleville Park was, perhaps even the general location of the crime scene. Maybe she had even been there before and located the stakes which remained to mark positions of the bodies long after the crime scene investigation had been completed. It was also possible she could have just happened to see the remnant of the stake where Jill's body had been found. And since the interior of Spence's car was the only one in the impound that had been torn apart by investigators looking for hair and blood samples, she could simply have guessed right. And, too, before leaving Waco, they had stopped by the police station and showed her a buck knife which someone had recently found in Speegleville Park. Karen had held it for several seconds and assured them it was the knife used in the murders. The autopsy reports had indicated the stab wounds had been caused by a dagger-like blade. The officers were certain it was not the weapon which had been used.

However, Baier in particular found Karen intriguing. He told Jan to stay in touch with her and to let him know if she came up with any more information.

For the next several months, Jan talked with Karen almost daily, sometimes by phone, sometimes inviting Karen to stop by her house after work. Almost every time they spoke, Karen added some small detail that would further perplex Jan. Karen felt that the man who killed Jill had removed a small ring from her finger and had later sold it to a friend for thirty-five dollars. A third person Karen was beginning to feel might be involved drove some kind of small sports car. She was certain there was something in the killer's car overlooked by investigators—perhaps a piece of paper with a date on it that would prove the girls had been in the automobile. There was a Satanic cult, she felt, which held meetings in Speegleville Park near where the bodies were found. And if the police would search the rocks carefully near where the assailants had first encountered the teenagers, they would find something—probably car keys—the killer had tossed away.

Jan found the discussions troubling. How someone could envision such things baffled her, yet she found herself increasingly drawn to the bizarre exchange, wanting to believe what the young woman was telling her. Several times Jan telephoned Dennis Baier to share with him what Karen had said. And while the sergeant gave no indication of whether the observations meant anything, he began to give Jan questions to ask Karen. Without explanation of how they might fit into the puzzle, he gave Jan names and words to throw out. "Just ask if they mean anything to her," he said.

Karen was more than willing to play the game. Christy? No. Richard? No. Gayle? No. A purse? No. Lucky? No. The negative answers disappointed Jan but also further convinced her that Karen was not trying to impress her with psychic powers. She had seen something, Jan was convinced. But what? And did it really have anything to do with Jill's death?

If nothing else, the emergence of Karen Hufstetler had helped reestablish communication with the Waco investigators. Their interest in the young woman's story had given Jan new reason to hope the murders might be solved. She was delighted when Ned Butler called from the district attorney's office to invite the family to come to Waco and to bring Karen so he might listen firsthand to the story he had heard from Dennis and Ramon. The assistant D.A. then quickly added that he was highly suspicious of people claiming supernatural powers. "Even if she could tell us exactly what happened," he warned, "not a word of what she has to say could be used in court."

"I understand," Jan said.

A few days later Butler and Simons were sitting in Ned's office talking about the case. "I've never been out to Speegleville," Ned said. "Let's take a ride out there." Telling the receptionist only that they would be back in a couple of hours, they left and drove out to the area where the bodies had been found. As Simons slowly drove down the dirt road into the wooded area where Sidney Smith and Joseph Chambers had first seen the body of Kenneth Franks, Butler suddenly yelled for him to stop. He had seen a litter of kittens cross the road just ahead, trailing along behind their mother. Ned said he wanted to get one for his daughter.

As they chased the family of wild cats down the road, Ned stopped abruptly and called Truman's attention to something embedded in the weeds just a few feet off the road. Ned reached down to pick up what appeared to be a length of broom handle wrapped in black electrical tape. As he tried to untangle it from the weeds that had wrapped around it, the rotted stick broke into two pieces. Was it possible, they both wondered, that the kittens had led them to David's infamous "love stick?"

They had been back in the office only long enough to pour themselves a cup of coffee when Butler's phone rang. It was Karen Hufstetler, calling from Waxahachie. She had experienced a strong feeling, she told the stunned assistant D.A., that something important had been found at the lake. "I wish you could tell me what it is," she said.

"This call's for you," Butler said, rolling his eyes toward the ceiling as he handed the receiver to Truman.

Karen repeated her observation to Simons, and there was a trace of discomfort in his laughter as he asked if she had bugged their office.

It was after that episode that the Waco authorities began to refer to Karen Hufstetler as "The Spook." She was beginning to make them all nervous.

Though the involvement of Karen Hufstetler resulted in no solid leads, her "vision" remained a mystery to them. Much of what she professed to have seen appeared highly unlikely. For instance, the authorities were by then sure the murders had not taken place in Speegleville—certainly not in the location she claimed. Though Baier spent several hours in Koehne Park searching through the rocks where Karen felt something had been tossed away by the murderer, he found nothing. Disappointingly, lab tests on the stick Butler had found revealed nothing to indicate it might have been the one which David had bragged about. And while the car once owned by Spence was completely dismantled, no "piece of paper" was ever found.

But some of what she had talked about seemed to match the statement Gilbert Melendez had given. And whether it had been bitten off or cut away by a knife as Karen claimed, the nipple from Jill's breast had been severed.

There was speculation that Karen had, in fact, seen *something* but that perhaps her story had grown as Jan and the investigators continued to show an interest; that she was just a lonely young woman who, once drawn into the exciting climate of a murder investigation, simply enjoyed being a part of it.

On the other hand she was personable and engaging, never giving any indication that she wanted either publicity or remuneration. And she had freely admitted she did not understand what had drawn her into the story. She only wanted to help, if she could. And in a way that only Jan Thompson could explain, she did.


The involvement of Karen Hufstetler was no more strange than other things which had been happening. Nancy Shaw had begun to have a recurring dream about her dead daughter. In it, she would first see a pair of scissors floating lazily down from the sky. Nancy would walk to where they appeared to have fallen and find nothing. But as she turned, she would see Jill standing behind her, dressed in a white ankle-length skirt and peasant blouse. She would be wearing an Indian-style silver link belt. Smiling, Jill would tell her mother, "I'm fine and I'm happy. It's a lot of fun where I am, but we have a lot of work. I can't talk long. I just wanted you to know I'm happy." Then she would say that she had to go back and do her work. And suddenly she would be gone.

And, hundreds of miles removed from Waco, Christy Juhl would wake from a dream and immediately place a call to the McLennan County jail. Though she had not spoken to Spence since her brother took her away from Waco on his motorcycle, she dreamed that David appeared at the foot of her bed, telling her he had decided to take his own life. When her call came to the jail, it was transferred to Truman Simons on the fourth floor. He summoned David to the phone.

"David," Christy said, "I know what you're thinking about doing. Please don't. You've already put your mother and everybody else through too much. Don't do this to them."

David, who had been severely depressed since the impressions of his teeth had been taken, said nothing for a moment, then asked, "How did you know?"

On the evening of July 30, 1982, just fifteen days after the bodies of the murdered teenagers had been found in Speegleville Park, two Waco Police officers responded to a call from a south-side topless bar called Showtime. An Hispanic man, wearing cutoff jeans, Army boots, and a T-shirt, had slashed the tires of a pickup and two cars in the parking lot of the club. The manager explained to the investigating officers that the man had been asked to leave because he was drunk and abusive and had attempted to sell a small bag of marijuana to one of the dancers. Angered at having been thrown out of the club, the man had then gone into the parking lot and was randomly cutting tires with a buck knife when the manager stepped outside to make sure he had left the premises. At that point the man ran from the parking lot.

After talking with several witnesses, the officers located the suspect as he was walking down a nearby street and arrested him without resistance. He was taken to the police station, fingerprinted, and charges of reckless damage were filed.

The man told the arresting officers that his name was Tony Tovar. What he did not tell them was that he also occasionally used the names Tony Fajardo and Tony Salazar. Neither did they know there was a three-year-old warrant for his arrest on charges of robbery and rape in Corpus Christi, Texas.

The following day a relative paid his $192 fine and he was released. During his overnight stay in the city jail, the authorities never learned that the real name of the man in custody was Tony Melendez.

Shortly after Simons questioned Gilbert about the possibility that his brother had accompanied him and David Spence to Koehne Park on the night of the murders, Ramon Salinas and Dennis Baier went to the home of Tony's cousin in hopes of talking with him. When told he was not there, they left phone numbers where they could be reached. That same day, Tony left town without even picking up his paycheck.

Even as Baier and Salinas were attempting to locate the younger of the Melendez brothers, Simons was receiving information that Tony was being sought by the authorities in Corpus Christi. Additionally, Simons discovered that he was wanted in Waco for $133 in traffic citations.

The first week in August, 1983, Dennis Baier received a long-distance call from Tony, who said he was calling from somewhere in Tennessee to find out why the police wanted to talk to him. Baier briefly explained that Gilbert was a suspect in the Lake Waco murders and that he wished to talk with Tony about his association with his brother in the summer of 1982.

Tony insisted to Baier that he had seen Gilbert only twice in the last year, then hung up. Later that evening he again called to say that he had been working in Bryan, Texas, at the time of the murders. He told the officer that he had learned of the crime while watching television in a Bryan motel room that he shared with several other members of the painting crew he worked with. Tony sounded more nervous the second time he called.

Within a matter of days, Baier and Salinas had interviewed Melendez's employer and learned that he had received two collect telephone calls from Tony since he had left town. Each time Tony had inquired about pay owed him. At the urging of the officers, the employer agreed to sign a letter to the security director of Southwestern Bell Telephone, authorizing the release of information on the point of origin of the two calls he had received from Tony.

The employer also volunteered information to the officers that he and Tony had once discussed the lake murders. Tony had told him he had heard that a man named David Spence and the dead boy, Kenneth Franks, killed the girls. Then when Franks became nervous about the murders, Spence also killed him. Tony had said that he heard the story from his brother Gilbert.

With the help of Southwestern Bell, the investigators soon learned that the calls from Melendez had come, not from Tennessee, but Fort Worth, Texas. And on August 18, Baier and Texas Ranger Joe Wylie drove there, to the home of a friend of Tony's mother, took Tony into custody, and returned him to Waco.

In the McLennan County jail, Truman Simons was eagerly awaiting Tony's arrival. While he knew they could hold Melendez for only a few days before turning him over to the Nueces County Sheriff's Department which had issued the warrant on the Corpus Christi robbery charge, Truman hoped Tony might be weary of running and ready to add the final piece to the puzzle he had so long tried to put together.

Though Melendez talked openly with Simons about the robbery and rape in which he had been involved in Corpus Christi, he insisted he had nothing to do with the lake murders. He even agreed to take a polygraph test to prove he was telling the truth. Tony repeatedly insisted that he had been in Bryan the day the teenagers had been killed.

He was telling a different story, however, to those he met in the McLennan County jail. Tony had been there only three days when Simons and Baier received word that an inmate named James Blankenship wanted to talk with them.

Arrested in Dallas just days earlier on burglary and rape charges, Blankenship sat across the table from the two law officers and told his story. The previous Sunday morning, he said, Tony Melendez had offered to give his breakfast to him. Following the morning meal they had talked with several inmates in the dayroom for a few minutes before returning to their cells, their conversation turned to the reasons each was in jail.

Blankenship began to show his nervousness as he continued. "He told me that he had been picked up in Fort Worth on some kind of robbery charge out of Corpus Christi and that he was also being questioned about the murders of those kids out at Lake Waco about a year ago.

"I finally just came out and asked him about the killings at the lake and he told me he was with his brother and some white dude when the people were killed. He told me that he didn't kill anybody but that his brother had killed the boy and the white dude had killed the two chicks.

"He told me they were all drunk and were supposed to have some kind of orgy, but the dude with the chicks didn't want anybody messing with the girls. He said that's why his brother killed him."

Baier and Simons watched Blankenship intently as he recounted the brief conversation. "Did he ever tell you the names of the people who actually did the killings?" Simons asked.

Blankenship shook his head. "Never did," he said.

"Did you ask him?" Baier said.

"Shit, no. In fact, I figured out pretty quick that I didn't want to hear any more about what he was telling me. The guy scares me."

Disappointed that Blankenship had not included the names of Gilbert and David in his re-creation of the conversation, Simons was pleased nonetheless to hear that Tony was talking. If what he had told Blankenship was true, it meant that Tony was the missing person Gilbert had left out of his confession. Simons was now more convinced than ever that Tony Melendez was the fourth person he was looking for—and if Tony was talking about the murders, he was getting nervous.

On the same day he had talked privately with James Blankenship, Tony had expressed concern over his upcoming polygraph test to several others. He had approached Roy Willis, Lonnie Joe Wynn, and Ricky Young as they sat playing cards, and asked them if they knew how to beat the polygraph. Though none had ever been subjected to a lie detector test, each had suggestions to offer. Young gave Tony two sleeping pills he had hoarded from his medication ration and suggested he take them shortly before the exam. "The more relaxed you are," Young said, "the less likely your heart rate and blood pressure and all that shit's going to be jumping up and down on the chart." Roy Willis and Lonnie Joe Wynn advised him to concentrate hard on something other than the questions as the test was being administered.

When they asked what the subject of the test would be, Tony admitted to them the questions would be about his involvement in the lake murders. "A dude named David Spence has given some kind of statement that me and my brother were involved in the killings," Tony said. Then, shaking his head, he said, "I don't know why I ever got involved with that fucking psychopath."

Roy Willis, quickly glancing around the dayroom, said, "Man, you better shut up about that shit."

"They can't prove anything," Tony answered.

"They damn well might if you keep running your fucking head," Willis suggested.

The next morning Tony was surprised when he learned that

his polygraph test was postponed at the last minute. He had already taken the pills Ricky Young had given him.

The following day Tony failed the test. Though inadmissible in court, the charts indicated deception on every question asked about his involvement in the lake murders. When he was returned to his cell, Tony sat on the end of his bunk near the toilet, spitting blood into the bowl. In an attempt to focus his concentration on something other than the questions being asked, he had bitten deeply into the inner linings of his cheeks throughout the session.

By the end of the week Tony was on his way to Corpus Christi. Even before he had been booked in the Nueces County jail, Simons had telephoned Corpus Christi authorities with the information Tony had given him on the 1979 robbery/rape and asked that they keep track of who Melendez spent time with once settled into the jail there.

Simons then resigned himself to more waiting. His late-night conversations with David had become less frequent after Spence was allowed to talk with a psychiatrist. During the session, David had tested his split personality idea on Dr. James Jolliff, a prominent Waco psychiatrist, but knew he had done so with little success. He was resigned to the fact that an insanity defense wasn't likely. There was little point, then, of continuing to talk to Simons about dreams of murdering a faceless victim or fears that ghosts of the dead teenagers might appear in his cell at night. From that point, their infrequent discussions were generally marked by mutual disinterest.

One evening shortly before Spence was to be transferred to TDC, Butler went over to the jail and, in the company of Simons, spoke with David. "I just wanted to check in with you one more time before you left," the assistant D.A. said, "and let you know we're going to go for it. You can damn well figure on being back here pretty soon to stand trial for the lake murders."

Spence tried to ignore the grumbling voice of Butler, instead making idle talk directed at Simons.

"David," Butler said, "you're dead meat."

Spence continued talking to Simons.

"You hear me, David?" Butler said, raising his voice.

Spence glanced at him. "Yeah, I heard you."

"Look," Ned said, "you know anything you say here isn't admissible in court, so why don't you just go ahead and lay it out for us?"

David shrugged. "Why? Ya'll already got me."

"Not yet," Butler said, "but we're going to."

"Okay," David replied, by now seeming to warm to the confrontation. "I'll tell you what: If this thing does go to trial and you guys prove to me that I did it, then I'll tell you all about it. How's that?"

"We're going to prove it to you," Butler replied.

"So, where do we go from here?" David asked, turning back to Simons.

"The next step is the indictments," the deputy said.

"How many people you going to indict?"

"You and Gilbert and Tony," Simons said. "Looks like that Arab's going to make it. And that's a damn shame. Some day you're liable to look back on all this and be sorry he got away with his part of all this mess."

"What can I do?" David asked.

"You remember the times you told me about Deeb offering you the money?"

"Yeah, sure."

"Well, why don't you give me a statement to that effect?"

"What good would that do?"

"Maybe none," Simons said, "but you never know."

"How do you want me to do it?"

"Just write it out in your own words," Truman said.

In a brief, handwritten statement Spence recounted that he had heard Deeb making threats against Kenneth Franks and Gayle Kelley, saying he was going to get even with them. It was, he wrote, in June of 1982 that Deeb asked him if he would kill someone for $5,000. He had said yes and Christy, overhearing the conversation, got upset. He and Deeb both quickly assured her they were only kidding.

As he read the statement Simons smiled. On one hand, David still was not incriminating himself; but in previous conversations about his exchange with Deeb, David had never mentioned Kenneth Franks or Gayle Kelley by name.

Simons was relieved when Spence was finally transferred to the Texas Department of Corrections on August 30, 1983, to begin serving his ninety-year sentence for aggravated sexual abuse. Truman was confident David would be back—but not until Vic Feazell was ready to take the lake murders case to a grand jury. Before that happened, though, Truman wanted to have enough evidence gathered to convince the grand jury to bring indictments against everyone involved in the crime.

For the first time in almost a year, Truman tried to flush thoughts of the case from his mind for a few days. Three of his four suspects were in custody and Patty Pick had kept him informed on the whereabouts of Muneer Deeb. He would have to be patient just a while longer. In the meantime, he wanted to take his son Jason fishing for a few days.

Two weeks after Tony Melendez had been transferred to Corpus Christi, Simons and Ned Butler paid him a visit. Throughout a half-hour interview Tony continued to insist he knew nothing about the crime they were investigating. Even when Butler tossed several photographs taken at the crime scene onto the table where they were sitting and said, "Maybe this will refresh your memory," Tony expressed no interest, no emotion.

"I got nothing to do with that," he said, looking squarely at Butler. "Why don't you people just leave me alone?"

"We're not going to leave you alone," the assistant D.A. replied as he signaled to the guards that he and Simons were ready to leave. "You can bet your sweet ass on that. We'll see you back in Waco pretty soon. You're dead meat."

As the two guards escorted him to the door of the interview room, Tony turned and glared back at Butler. "Fuck you, man," he said as he left the room.

Simons grinned. "I don't think you made a very good impression on him."

"That sonuvabitch hasn't even *started* to hate me yet," Butler growled.

While at the Nueces County jail, Simons and Butler spoke with several inmates who had been spending time with Melendez. Among them was a young man named Julio Ortega who was being held on an attempted capital murder charge. Arrested two years earlier at age fifteen, Ortega and a partner had broken into a warehouse and were confronted by a security guard. Ortega's accomplice hit the guard in the back of the head as they made their getaway. The man lived but suffered severe brain damage. Once apprehended, Ortega was held as a juvenile, then finally certified as an adult and ordered by the courts to stand trial.

He was immediately hostile as Simons began questioning him about any conversations he might have had with Tony Melendez in which the Lake Waco murders were mentioned.

"He ain't never said shit about anything like that to me," Julio said, "except that you guys were trying to hang it on him."

Simons nodded, then began telling the young man some of the details of the crime. "This is what we're talking about," Butler added, pushing several of the crime scene photographs across the table. Ortega's face flushed as he looked at the pictures, then turned his head away to stare at the wall. Suddenly he was a seventeen-year-old kid again, nervous and crying. The photographs had upset him far more than the two law officers had anticipated. Ortega repeatedly shook his head as he rose to walk about the room, occasionally glancing back in the direction of the photographs still spread on the table.

Finally, he composed himself and said, "Those pictures don't tell the story he ran down to me. Okay, if you want Melendez, man, you got him."

At that moment Truman and Ned knew Tony Melendez had talked to Ortega about the crime. They also knew not to press him for details while he was in such an emotional state. "If you're willing to tell us the truth, you might be able to help us," Butler said. "But we're going to leave you alone for a while. We're going to go on back to Waco and let you think about it. We'll be back."

It was a weekend in late October when Simons returned to Corpus Christi in hopes of taking a statement from Ortega. He decided the trip would provide an opportunity for Judy and Jason to spend a couple of days at the beach before the final warmth of the extended summer was gone.

As they rode toward the Texas Gulf coast that Saturday morning there was nothing about the trip to indicate it was part of a murder investigation. Throughout their marriage, Truman had talked very little with his wife about his police work. There was a silent understanding that he left his work at the office. Only on rare occasions had that silence been broken. But this case was different, Judy knew. Aware of the maze of disappointments and frustrations her husband had faced during his investigation of the lake murders, she had tried with little success to encourage him to talk about it. A few times, when frustrations had become almost unbearable, he had tried to explain his feelings to her, hoping she would understand the obsessive motivation that was driving him. He had even introduced her to Nancy Shaw and Jan Thompson during one of their trips to Waco to visit the district attorney's office. It had pleased him that Judy immediately liked the two women and felt an empathy for their frustrations. And meeting them had helped her understand the long-distance calls to Waxahachie which had driven their telephone bill up to seventy and eighty dollars a month. Though there was no way she could share her husband's intense feelings about the case, Judy tried to understand, to help in any way she could.

As the miles passed by, they slipped into a conversation about the case. It was Judy who reminded her husband that there had, in fact, been humorous moments during the investigation.

"Remember when I had the ear infection?" she asked.

Truman smiled. It had been early in the investigation, shortly after he had arrested Deeb. Thinking at the time that perhaps others in the Arabic community might be involved, Truman had found himself overwhelmed with the list of Muslim names he had gathered: Muneer Mohammad, Karim Qasem, Mahir Tumimi.

He had been sitting in the den, the names rolling around in his mind like marbles, when Judy came in from the kitchen and said, "Would you look at my ear?"

All Truman had heard was "my ear." "Who the hell is he?" he had asked.

Arriving in Corpus Christi, they checked into a beachfront motel. Judy and Jason quickly changed into swimsuits and headed for the beach as Truman prepared for his visit to the jail. After they had left the room, he opened his briefcase and carefully organized the crime scene photographs he planned to show Julio Ortega again when he interviewed him. Laying them on the dresser top, he went into the bathroom to shave.

It was while he was still in the bathroom that Judy returned for her suntan lotion and noticed the gruesome photographs. Though Judy refuses even to watch violent programs on tele-

vision, she forced herself to look at several pictures of the lifeless, violated bodies.

She was sitting on the side of the bed, crying, as Truman
returned to the room. He sat next to her and gathered her into
his arms. "You've got to get the people who did that," she said.

"I will," he replied, then kissed her gently.

Ortega was far more subdued as he spoke with the McLennan
County deputy the second time. The crime scene photos remained on the corner of the interview room table as the young
inmate related what Tony had said to him.

"He told me that his brother and another dude picked those
kids up and were going to get some drugs. Some shit like that,"
Ortega said. "His brother got in this argument with the boy over
one of the girls and they started fighting. Tony said he went to
help his brother but before he could get there his brother had
stabbed the boy. He told me, 'Ortega, man, those were some
bad broads.' He said they had some bad snatches."

"Will you give a statement?" Truman asked.

"Yeah, I'll give a statement," Ortega said, his eyes still
avoiding the photographs lying on the table.

Judy and Jason, exhausted and sunburned from two days on the
beach, slept as Truman drove back toward Waco the following
evening. All the way home, he thought about Muneer Deeb.

After leaving Waco, Deeb had traveled briefly to Houston,
then to visit friends in New Mexico before settling in Dallas to
live with his cousin. There he enrolled at the DeVry Institute of
Technology, a computer programming trade school, and worked
part-time at a self-service gas station in an area of northwest
Dallas heavily populated by topless bars, liquor stores, and adult
movie houses. He illegally acquired both a chauffeur's and a
regular driver's license which identified him as Munin Dib.

On March 2, 1983, Deeb had also acquired a wife. On that
day he and Marcie Blackwood, a woman he had met in Dallas,
traveled to Waco in Deeb's Thunderbird. Upon their arrival they
went directly to the McLennan County courthouse where
County Judge Mike Gassaway performed the ceremony. The
new Mrs. Deeb then immediately walked to the nearby bus station and purchased a ticket back to Dallas while Muneer remained in Waco to visit friends.

The following month, Simons saw Deeb for the first time since he had arrested him in September of 1982. Kasey Rowe had phoned him to say that Muneer was in town and had been harassing her—following her to and from work, sitting in the parking lot outside her apartment at all hours of the night, and making threatening phone calls to her.

Kasey's call had come only days after Patty Pick had reported to Truman that Deeb had telephoned her late one evening, greatly depressed, and told her that he was "going to get Kasey." "She's the reason for the killings at the lake," Deeb had told Patty.

Simons had convinced Kasey to give a sworn statement so charges of terroristic threat and telephone harassment might be filed. Two patrolmen picked Deeb up later that night in the parking lot of the apartment complex where the young woman lived.

Fifteen minutes later, Deeb was seated in a chair near the booking desk when Simons approached him. Without salutation, Truman told Deeb he was aware of the threats he had been making. "If you want to make threats," he said, "I'm the one you need to be talking to. I'll meet your ass in the middle of Austin Avenue at sundown and we can settle all this shit in a big hurry. Do you understand what I'm saying?"

Deeb did not acknowledge the sudden tirade.

Putting up his car as collateral for the $4,500 bond which had been ordered by Judge John Cabaniss, Deeb was released after a week and made plans to go back to Dallas. He had decided never again to return to Waco. Seven months would pass before he would see Simons again.

After a meeting in his office in early November, Vic Feazell was satisfied that enough evidence had been gathered to seek grand jury indictments against David Spence and the Melendez brothers. At the same time, he was concerned that there was not sufficient proof that Muneer Deeb had been involved in a conspiracy to commit murder. As badly as he wanted to indict all four, he felt more evidence linking Deeb to the crime was necessary.

For the grand jury to return an indictment against the Jordanian, it would have to be convinced that Simons' murder-for-hire, mistaken identity theory was valid. Even then, there was only the fact that he had purchased the insurance policy and the statements of Gayle Kelley and Patti Deis that Muneer had admitted his role in the murders—an admission he had later assured them was only a "joke."

On the evening of November 10, just a few days before the grand jury was to meet, Simons suggested to Butler that they call Karim and Maria Qasem to the district attorney's office. Adamant in their belief in their former business partner's innocence after his initial arrest, they had never been asked to give statements. "There have been a lot of people who've told us things that didn't really seem important to them," Truman pointed out to the assistant D.A. "I think it's worth the time to see if maybe they might know something."

When the Qasems arrived, Simons asked that Dennis Baier interview Karim while he and Ned talked with Maria in Butler's office.

After less than an hour with Karim, Baier was standing in the doorway to Butler's office, shaking his head. "If you guys had come to me with this," he said, "I wouldn't have believed it."

"What do you mean?" Butler asked.

"He can hang Deeb; that's what I mean. He says he heard Deeb and Spence talking about Gayle and the insurance policy several times." Baier then began reading from the notes he had taken as Karim had talked: *"I remember Deeb talking to David many times about the insurance. Deeb would say something like 'Do you know anyone that would kill Gayle?' or 'Do you know somebody that would get rid of Gayle?' I remember David Spence saying, 'I can get somebody.' "*

Baier went on to explain how Karim had told him of David coming to the store after the murder of Gail Bramlett and arguing with Deeb. "He's got the whole damn story," Dennis said.

Butler quickly rose from his desk to accompany Baier back to the room where Karim waited. "Why haven't you told anyone about this before?" he asked.

"Nobody ever asked me about Gayle," Qasem said, his voice filled with innocence. "She's still alive. I never connected her to the murders at the lake."

That evening Maria also spoke of several occasions when Deeb had discussed the insurance policy he had taken out on Gayle, and of hearing Muneer remark after the lake murders that Gayle "should have been one of the ones killed."

"He said the boy who was killed was Gayle's boyfriend and he seemed pleased that it happened," Maria told Butler and Simons. "He also said if Gayle had been there he would have had a lot of money."

Deeb's former business partners, like so many others, had long held a piece to the puzzle, unaware that it fit. The frustratingly simple fact was that no one had ever bothered to ask them the right questions. Now, though, their statements would not only link Deeb to Spence, but would also lend additional credence to Simons' theory.

Butler called Feazell and excitedly told him about the statements Karim and Maria had just given.

"Then we go for indictments on all four," Feazell said. The final doubt had been erased.

With the help of Patty Pick and Dallas law enforcement officials, Simons had kept close tabs on Deeb's movements. He was delighted when he learned that investigators from the Dallas County D.A.'s special crimes unit were planning to arrest Muneer on charges of unauthorized use of a telephone credit card number. On the date of Deeb's scheduled appearance to answer the charges before a county judge, Simons, Dennis Baier, and Sheriff Jack Harwell drove to Dallas with a warrant for his arrest.

Though Deeb failed to appear for his court date, Dallas officials found him at the home of his cousin and took him into custody. He was being booked into the Dallas County jail when the Waco authorities arrived. As Simons approached him, a half-smile spread across Deeb's face. "Do you think this time you have enough to make it stick?" he asked in heavily accented English.

"This time I've got enough to stick it in your arm," Truman answered. Deeb's smile disappeared.

By the end of the week the McLennan County grand jury handed down twelve capital murder indictments: three each against David Spence, Tony Melendez, Gilbert Melendez, and Muneer Deeb. Eighteen months had passed since the Lake Waco murders had taken place.

A few days later David Spence and Tony Melendez were bench warranted back to Waco, arriving at the McLennan County jail within minutes of each other. Tony, upon seeing David, glared and shot him the finger. "Fuck you, Spence," he yelled as he was being escorted from the booking desk to the jail area.

After Spence had been processed, Simons and Butler visited with him briefly in one of the interview rooms.

"I just wanted to come by and say hello and let you know we probably won't be talking with you any more," Simons said.

"Why's that?"

"Well, they'll be appointing your lawyers pretty soon," Truman explained, "and they aren't going to want us talking to you. From this point on, the best thing you can do is shoot straight with the people representing you. We've got a damn good case, David, and if you don't tell them the truth they aren't going to be able to do a good job representing you."

Spence laughed. "Shit, if you think I'm going to tell a lawyer I killed those kids at Lake Waco, you're crazy. Give me two weeks and I'll have them convinced I didn't have anything to do with it."

## 30

Though he enjoyed a warm satisfaction when the indictments were handed down, Truman Simons continued to agonize over one remaining aspect of the case. Though certain the four men responsible for the deaths of Jill Montgomery, Raylene Rice, and Kenneth Franks would at last be legally dealt with, it troubled him that he still did not know the full truth of the events that had taken place at the lake that July night in 1982.

The fact that Gilbert Melendez had refused to implicate his brother in his original admission of guilt raised frustrating questions about the possibility of other omissions he might have made. Simons was convinced that Spence, even under the pressure of a life-or-death jury trial, would never admit his role in the murders. And there was doubt that Deeb actually knew any of the details of the murders. Simons was all but resigned to the fact that he might never know the complete story.

Only when the last juror for the Spence trial had been selected was Truman's hope rekindled. Tony Melendez, after consulting with his court-appointed attorneys, informed the D.A.'s office that he was interested in a plea bargain. He would admit his guilt in exchange for something less than the death penalty. Feazell, aware that another confession might well provide valuable information for the prosecution of Spence, agreed to allow Tony to plead guilty to the murders of Jill Montgomery and Kenneth Franks in exchange for two concurrent life sentences. Additionally, Tony would have to give a statement that would prove he was directly involved in the murders and direct investigators to the scene of the crime.

On June 14, 1983, Tony Melendez appeared before Judge George Allen to plead guilty to two counts of capital murder. And while his initial statement would provide only a sketchy re-creation of what had taken place, Simons felt it would eliminate any reason for Gilbert to remain silent about his brother's involvement.

In the months to come, Simons would hear far more detailed statements from both Gilbert and Tony. Though neither had talked with the other since their arrests and Truman never mentioned to one what the other had told him, their stories began to parallel once both realized there was nothing more to be gained by lying.

Only then was Simons finally able to piece together the horrible story he had to know . . .

Just before noon that day, Tony Melendez and his cousin, Perry Surita, weary of their job painting the Pecan Ridge Apartments in Bryan, Texas, had decided to quit work early. They had exhausted their supply of amphetamines and, having no drug connections there, they wanted to return to Waco and replenish their cache.

Drinking beer and enjoying the freedom from the boredom of apartment painting, they talked little during the ninety-minute drive except to agree to leave for the return trip to Bryan early the next morning. While Perry drove, Tony dozed as they passed through faceless communities with names like Hearne and Calvert and Groesbeck. He was asleep when they reached Waco and Perry pulled the van into his driveway. Tony woke and told his cousin he was going to walk the few blocks over to the Armadillo Club where he felt he might score the dope they had discussed.

Upon entering the darkened club, Melendez was disappointed to find it almost deserted. Still, the air conditioning was welcoming and he decided to have a few beers and play pool for a while, in hopes that some of his friends might stop by. It was good to be back in familiar, relaxed surroundings. Tony remained at the Armadillo for a couple of hours before finally deciding he was not going to be able to make a drug connection. If the drugs would not come to him, he would seek them out.

Feeling slightly light-headed from the beer he had been drinking since noon, Tony began to perspire heavily almost immediately as he stepped back into the late afternoon heat. He was walking down Fifteenth Street toward the house of a friend he knew dealt drugs when he saw David Spence standing in the front yard of his mother's house.

David, having seen little of Tony in recent weeks, expressed surprise that he was back in town. "I was gonna go check Gilbert out in a little while, soon as he gets off work," David said. "Why don't you come with me? We'll get some beer."

The proposition sounded far better than walking in the heat, Tony thought. And, too, he hadn't seen his brother in some time. They got into David's Malibu and drove directly to a nearby store and purchased two six-packs of Budweiser. Then, just minutes later, they saw Gilbert walking along the sidewalk toward his apartment. David waved and Gilbert, wearing a sleeveless Army fatigue shirt, jeans, and lace-up military boots, squinted through his wire-rimmed glasses to determine who was sitting in the passenger's seat. Recognizing Tony, he hurried toward the car. As Gilbert got into the back seat his brother smiled and handed him a beer.

"What the hell are you doing walking?" Tony asked.

"My truck's been running bad," Gilbert said. "I've got a guy doing a tune-up. What are you doing home in the middle of the week?"

"We came back to score some crank," Tony replied. "You know anybody who's selling?"

For the next half hour they sought out several local drug dealers but found no one at home. Resigned to waiting until later in the evening when activity at the Armadillo picked up, they continued to ride around, drinking beer and smoking marijuana. They drove through the parking lot of another club, Click's, on Valley Mills Drive, but saw no cars they recognized and didn't stop.

It was Spence who suggested they go out to the lake. Tony had assumed they would drive out to Airport Park, one of his frequent hangouts when in Waco. Instead, after stopping at the Hilltop Grocery for more beer, Spence drove the short distance to the entrance to Koehne Park and made a left turn. As they slowly drove down toward the boat ramp David stopped and pointed in the direction of a young black man who was sitting in his car, drinking beer. "What's a fucking nigger doing out here in our park?" David asked.

Gilbert and Tony ignored the question, sipping on their beers. Having seen no one they knew in that area of the park, they drove to the Circle where an orange Pinto was parked. At a nearby picnic table, two girls and a boy sat talking.

"I know those people," David said, suddenly excited. "Let's stop and check them out." Smiling as he looked back at Gilbert, he said, "Those are the ones I told you about that ripped that dude off."

Recalling their earlier conversation about Deeb's proposition to pay someone to recover drug money owed him, Gilbert immediately balked. "Fuck that shit," he said. "I ain't getting off into that kind of business." Tony, by now pleasantly drunk, had no idea what they were talking about.

Against Gilbert's protests David stopped the car and got out. Walking in the direction of the three teenagers, he was smiling as he asked, "What are ya'll up to?"

Kenneth Franks, sitting between the two girls, replied that they were just drinking a few beers. Gilbert heard David call the brunette by name and heard her reply that it wasn't her name. He wasn't sure what names were exchanged—only that they sounded similar.

After David had talked with the youngsters for several minutes, Tony left Gilbert in the car and approached the group, wobbling slightly as he walked. As he neared the park bench he heard David asking the boy if he still had his bike and the boy said it was in the shop. Foggily, Tony assumed the two men knew each other.

While Spence talked with Kenneth and Jill, Tony made conversation with Raylene. She was not from Waco, she told him. In fact, she had been to Waco only once before, she said, to visit a disc jockey who had previously dated her sister. Tony asked if Kenneth was her old man and she told him he was just a friend.

"Hey, we've got some pot in the car," David said. "Why don't you guys come smoke a joint with us while we run up to the store and get some more beer. Then we'll come back and party a little."

Jill Montgomery mentioned that they had to be leaving for home shortly. "We won't be gone but a few minutes," David insisted.

The youngsters agreed to accompany them back to the Hilltop Grocery, less than a mile away. As they walked to the car, David urged Raylene and Kenneth to get into the back seat with Gilbert. He wanted Jill to ride in front with him and Tony.

As David backed from the parking lot he caught Gilbert's eye in the rearview mirror. "Hey, bro," he said, motioning toward Jill. "This chick's really got big tits, huh?" In the back seat, Kenneth Franks laughed nervously.

Jill turned to Spence and said, "Don't be talking like that."

"Well, you do have big tits," he replied as he reached over and placed his right hand on her breast.

"What's the matter with you?" Jill yelled angrily, then slapped him. "Let me out."

Suddenly the smile was gone from David's face. He was glaring at the girl who had just slapped him. "I'll grab one if I goddamn want to," he said. Jerking at the steering wheel, he pulled the car onto the gravel shoulder of the road, stopped, and began struggling with the frightened girl, pulling at her terry cloth top. Trying to fight him off, she said, "What's the matter with you? Are you crazy? Leave me alone."

In the back seat, Kenneth Franks moved forward, fixing an angry glare on the driver. "Hey," he said, "what do you think you're doing? Cut it out; leave her alone." Gilbert reached across Raylene and grabbed Kenneth's arm. "Just shut up," he said in a threatening voice. Raylene sat speechless, her knotted fist pressed against her mouth.

As Jill continued her protest David slapped her hard across the face with the back of his hand. "Shut the fuck up, you bitch. No cunt's going to tell me what to do." In a rage he put the car in gear and drove off into a wooded cove immediately behind where they had earlier sat talking at the park bench. Once the car was hidden from view David stopped and turned off the motor. Though it was dusk, the thick foliage of the trees made the area much darker there than it had been out near the benches.

"Hey, what's going on?" Kenneth asked. "What the hell are you doing?"

"I told you to shut up," Gilbert said.

David opened the car door and ordered everybody out. Tony, still wrapped in the fog of beer and pot, gave David a puzzled look. "Man," he said, "you're crazy. What are we doing?"

"Just get your ass out and come around here on my side of the car," David said. "Make sure they don't try to run off."

Before leaving the car, Tony, sensing that things were beginning to get out of hand, reached into the floorboard, picked up a screwdriver, and put it into his back pocket. While he walked around the back of the car toward David, he heard Spence ordering Kenneth, Raylene, and Gilbert to get out.

David's face had become an insane mask as he commanded the frightening show. His breath seemed to come in quick, nervous gulps as he ordered the three teenagers toward the front of the car, positioning Tony and Gilbert on each side of the hostages. Then Spence focused his attention on Kenneth and Jill. "You should have known better than to burn my friend on that dope deal," he said.

"I don't know what you're talking about," Jill said, backing away. Tony grabbed her by the arm. "Just stay cool," he whispered, "nothing's going to happen." As he spoke he pulled the screwdriver from his pocket.

"Man, we haven't ripped anybody off for anything," Kenneth said.

"Like shit," David said. "You should have known better. Chili always gets even." It was then that he pulled a knife and ordered the girls to undress. If they didn't, he said, he would kill them.

"We've got some money," Jill said. "You can have it. Just leave us alone."

Spence ignored her plea. "Take your fucking clothes off." He then turned to Gilbert. "Get something we can tie this dude up with," he said nodding toward Kenneth Franks.

Gilbert quickly searched the inside of the car, finding a towel beneath the front seat. Returning to the front of the car, he saw that both girls were naked, trying pathetically to cover themselves with their arms and hands as Spence laughed. Gilbert handed the towel to David, but instead of tying Kenneth, he grabbed Jill by the arm and began pulling her in the direction of the small gully which bordered the wooded area. "I'm going over here with her," David said to Tony. "You watch him. Gilbert can go with the other chick."

Gilbert, unaware that Tony had already armed himself with the screwdriver, handed his brother a pocketknife, then told Raylene to get back in the car. Raylene was too frightened even to scream as Gilbert forced her naked body onto the front seat. "Please don't hurt me," she sobbed.

"I ain't going to hurt you," he said.

While raping the terrified girl, Gilbert heard David call to Tony from the dark corner of the area. "Bring the punk over here," he said. "I want him to watch while I fuck this cunt."

Tony shoved Kenneth in the direction of the silhouetted figures. Kenneth was forced to watch as Spence, on his knees over Jill, rubbed the blade of his knife over her breasts for several seconds, cursing the struggling young woman. David looked up into the horrified eyes of Kenneth. "I told you I get even," he said. Then he raped her.

Finished, David stood and motioned to Tony. "Go ahead," he said. As Tony knelt over the girl he was aware of David talking to Kenneth but could not hear what was being said. David, holding his knife to Kenneth's throat, then led him back in the direction of the car.

Though the sudden turn of events had sobered him, Tony was unable to get a full erection and quickly gave up. Getting to his feet, he told Jill to stay where she was, then walked back in the direction of the car.

As he neared where David and Gilbert stood, Tony noticed that Kenneth Franks was seated near a tree, his head down, his chin against his chest. What he had not witnessed was David shoving Kenneth against the car and yelling, "You've been fucking with Lucky's old lady." Even as Kenneth tried to speak David grabbed him by the throat. "You fucking punk," David said, then stabbed him several times in the chest. As Kenneth slumped to the ground, David knelt beside him, his face close enough to feel the last warm gasps for breath of the dying boy. David remained in that position, as if fascinated by the process of death, until there was no movement in Kenneth's body.

As Tony approached, David said, "The blond chick's in the car." Tony, wondering if the boy might already be dead, got into the car with Raylene and again attempted to have sex. Again the girl begged not to be hurt. "Don't worry," Tony said. "After this is all over you won't ever see me again."

Meanwhile David had accompanied Gilbert back to where Jill lay. Gilbert then raped her.

When he had finished, Gilbert walked back toward the car. He needed to talk to Tony. Things had gotten out of hand, he knew, and were likely to get even worse. Before he could say anything to his brother, however, David was again calling for Tony.

Walking back toward where Jill lay, Tony saw that David was sitting on top of her legs. "Now I'm going to get even with you," David was telling the horrified girl, poking at her chest with his knife. Placing his hand over her mouth to muffle her screams, he made several torturous cuts before raising his left hand and plunging the knife into her chest. Jill moaned and he stabbed her again. There was an evil smile on his face.

Turning to Tony, who was kneeling beside them, David handed him the knife. "We're in this shit together," he said. "You do it."

Tony shook his head. "Man, you didn't have to stab 'em."

"Goddammit, I had to show 'em," David spat, shoving the knife in Tony's direction. "Go ahead."

Tony took the knife and plunged it into Jill's chest. "Do it," David said again. "Do it." Tony stabbed the girl a second time but the blade failed to go in as deeply as it had before. It had hit a bone. The girl's body jerked.

"Shit, you're not doing it right," David screamed, shoving Tony away. "I'll show you how." David took the knife and stabbed her again, then bent his head down over her breast and bit Jill's nipple.

"You should have known better than to mess with Lucky," David said to the dying girl. It was the first Tony had heard the name. David, he assumed, was referring to him, providing him a false identity. At least he had sense enough not to tell the kids who they were.

For several minutes Tony watched as David stabbed the girl repeatedly, stopping after each thrust of the knife to look into her face. It was obvious he was enjoying the sadistic act, drawing it out, making the pain and suffering last as long as possible.

Tony rose and walked away, moving over to where he had seen Kenneth earlier. Kneeling down to look at the young man, Tony saw bloodstains on his shirt. Even in the darkness he knew he was dead. Suddenly wishing there was some way he could remove himself from the horror taking place, Tony walked toward the opening where David had pulled into the wooded area and checked to see if there were any cars nearby. Satisfied no one had heard or seen anything, he was walking back into the woods when he saw David and Gilbert standing by the car. David was telling Raylene to get out.

Terrified but unaware of what had happened to her friends, she stepped from the car and was immediately thrown to the ground. "Now you're going to get yours," David said as he began stabbing her repeatedly.

Gilbert walked quickly toward Tony, away from the sickening scene. "Man, I ain't done anything," Tony whispered to his brother. "This is too crazy. Let's split."

Gilbert tried to mask his own fright and calm Tony. "Everything's going to be okay. Just stay cool."

Tony returned to check for any traffic in the Circle while Gilbert went back to talk to David. In a few minutes Gilbert approached his brother. "We're going to get my truck," he said, "and move the bodies over to Speegleville Park. David says he knows a place. He's going to stay here until we get back."

Before the two brothers got into Spence's car, David approached the passenger side. He was sweating profusely and his entire body seemed to be shaking. "I gotta get something," he said. Reaching under the seat, he found a length of stick wrapped in electrical tape.

As Gilbert backed from the wooded area, Tony could faintly see David in the darkened distance, kneeling over Raylene. It appeared he had the stick between her legs.

As the brothers pulled onto Lake Shore Drive and turned left in the direction of the nearby suburb of Bosqueville where Gilbert had left his pickup to be tuned, it was Tony who broke the silence. "Fuck, man, let's just get the hell out of here. Let's just leave him out there. We're in big trouble."

Gilbert did not respond. They were too involved, he knew, not to see the thing through.

It took them fifteen minutes to reach their destination. Gilbert said he would drive the pickup and told Tony to take David's car to his mother's house. He would follow; then they would return to the lake.

In Koehne Park, David Spence was already getting anxious. Walking up toward the road which led into the Circle, he silently approached a parked pickup and looked in through the back window at a man and a woman who were embracing. The girl, Donna Cawthorn, screamed when she saw Spence's bearded face and he ran quickly back into the woods. Months later, the man she was with that night would urge her to relate the event to the authorities. Not wanting to get involved in the murder investigation, she gave the investigator who interviewed her a description that was just the opposite of what she had actually seen. The man she had seen, she insisted, was clean-shaven and wore his hair short. She did not tell the investigator that she was engaged to the vice-president of a successful Waco business but had been at Koehne Park that night with another man.

As Gilbert backed the truck into the woods, David appeared. He had found some money on the girls, he said, and had also taken a ring and a watch. David gave the money to Gilbert, who shoved it into his pocket without bothering to count it and walked into the darkness with David.

Tony, who had remained in the pickup, noticed that the arms of the girl they carried toward him were not dangling. Her hands, he discovered, had been bound. Her body also seemed to be far bloodier than he had remembered.

As Gilbert and David retreated for the second body, Tony got out of the pickup and went to Raylene's Pinto and found a small bag of marijuana. Reaching for the cellophane bag, his hand brushed across a pair of glasses on the console. Not wanting to leave any fingerprints, he put the glasses in his shirt pocket and rolled a joint. By the time Tony returned to the pickup, the loading of the bodies had been completed and Gilbert was covering them with a painter's drop cloth.

Gilbert drove with his brother seated in the middle and David next to the passenger's door, slowly pulling out of the park and up the hill toward town. Passing the small convenience store where they had earlier purchased beer, he turned onto a street which wound through one of the city's finest residential areas. It was the quickest route to Highway Six and Speegleville Park.

Passing by the main entrance to the park, David directed Gilbert onto an abandoned paved road, several hundred yards down the access road, that led into the park. After several turns which Spence indicated, they were on a dirt road deep in the trees which lined the lakeshore. "Here," David said, and Gilbert stopped the truck.

Tony climbed into the back of the pickup and lifted Kenneth's legs, moving them toward where David and Gilbert stood waiting. David grabbed the body under the arms with Gilbert carrying it by the legs. They disappeared into the darkness.

When they returned David was laughing. "Man, they're going to freak out when they find that dude sitting up under that tree with his sunglasses on."

Gilbert, who had not said a word during the trip to the park, told Tony to help with the girls' bodies. As Tony and David took them off into the waist-high weeds, Gilbert walked a few yards down the road in the opposite direction and vomited.

As they drove back toward town, across the Twin Bridges, Tony threw the screwdriver and Raylene's glasses out the window into the water. Gilbert was the first to say anything. "Man, I don't know what the fuck's going on. I'm gonna get my shit and get out of town."

"Hey, man," David replied, "ain't nobody knows what happened but us. They're dead—they can't say nothing. Dead people can't talk. Ain't nobody ever gonna know what happened to them. We're never gonna talk about this shit, right?"

Gilbert dropped Tony off near his cousin's house and, pulling bills from Jill Montgomery's last paycheck from his pocket, offered part of it to him. "I don't want it," Tony said. "You won't be seeing me for a while," he said, walking away.

Reaching his cousin's driveway, Tony got into the van and changed into his painter's overalls. He would sleep there, anxiously awaiting the early morning trip back to Bryan. As his adrenaline slowed, he suddenly realized he had never made the drug connection he had come to town for.

Gilbert drove David to his mother's house where his car was parked, then went to his grandmother's house where he kept some clothing in the garage. Changing in the darkness, he placed the clothes he had worn into a paper sack which was already half filled with trash. After getting some sleep, he planned to throw the sack into the dumpster behind a 7-Eleven that was on his way to work.

David had promised to pick Christy Juhl up at the Rainbow when she closed the store at 11:00 P.M., but when he had not shown up by 11:15 she asked Karim Qasem if he would give her a ride to the Northwood Apartments. She was already in bed when David entered the bedroom, wearing only a pair of jeans. When she asked why he had failed to pick her up as promised, he told her his car had broken down at the lake and that he had finally managed to get a ride home with someone he didn't know. Christy could tell he was drunk.

As they continued to argue about his failure to provide her a ride home, David climbed on the bed and slapped her with the back of his hand. "Shut up, bitch," he said. Then he had sex with her.

They were both asleep when a knock came at the door. As David went to answer it, Christy looked at her watch and saw it was just after 1:00 A.M. Getting out of bed she went to the bedroom door and looked into the living room to see David talking with some men she didn't know. She returned to bed.

Spence came back into the bedroom a few minutes later. "I've got to go somewhere," he told her.

"Who are those guys?" she asked.

"Just some people I know," David said. "Clint Olson and a couple of his buddies. They just came by to say hello."

Christy did not see David again until he returned to the apartment just before 7:00 A.M. and had sex with her again before she got up to dress for work.

David drove Christy to the Rainbow while the men who had visited the apartment earlier in the morning followed in a pickup. David followed her inside the store and got beer and cigarettes, marking the amount of his purchase down on Christy's time card.

It was David who suggested to his friends that they go out to Koehne Park. As they sat at the same concrete table where, just hours earlier, Jill Montgomery, Raylene Rice, and Kenneth Franks had been, David said little. No one mentioned the orange Pinto, parked nearby, which had evidently been left overnight.


At the Rainbow, Christy was surprised to see Muneer Deeb at the store so early. It wasn't yet nine o'clock when he entered and said, "They finally killed that sonuvabitch."

"Who are you talking about?" Christy asked.

"Kenneth Franks," Deeb said, "and I'm glad."

For the remainder of the day, Christy listened to the small radio on the shelf behind the counter. There was no mention of anyone named Kenneth Franks being killed.

# PART FOUR

"I'm no goody two-shoes. And I'm not saying that if I got in a fight, I wouldn't stab somebody. But I'm not going to go out there and butcher three kids like that for five thousand dollars, or twenty thousand, or a million. That's just not me.

"I didn't do it and I am not going to say something that is not true to clear the books for them. I would rather die for something I didn't do than say I did something that I didn't do. If I do die for it, I die with honor, because I know I didn't do it . . ."

—David Wayne Spence to Tommy Witherspoon
of the *Waco Tribune-Herald*, December 16, 1984

The dream visits the young woman's sleep regularly and is always the same. She and the man are running along the water's edge, hand-in-hand, laughing. It is wonderfully romantic, like those slow-motion commercials they show on television. She likes the first part of the dream.

Then, however, it changes. The man is holding her underwater, his hands around her throat, pushing against her. She can feel herself suffocating, drowning. From beneath the water level she is looking into the man's angry face and wondering what she has done to make him want to do this to her. She reaches up and touches his cheek gently, even as he is trying to kill her. "I love you, David," she says. And then she smiles.

She dreads the dream and wakes cursing it. Why, she wonders, is it always as if it is something she's dreaming for the first time? Why, after almost four years, hasn't she learned to anticipate its ending? Why doesn't she run away? Or fight back?

When she wakes she can smell him, feel his presence in her bedroom though he is hundreds of miles away, locked in a Texas prison cell. For a few puzzling seconds she is almost certain he is there.

And it is not always just in the half-sleep aftermath of the horrible dream. There are times when she is in a crowd that a chill will come over her. Her hands become sweaty and her face pales. Friends, aware of the sudden change, ask if anything is wrong and she always says she is fine. What the young woman doesn't tell them is that she is sure, for a fleeting second, that she has seen him out of the corner of her eye. He is there and suddenly gone. But, she knows, he will be back.

The man, once her lover, is now an unwelcome ghost she fears will haunt her forever.

## 31

Christy Juhl sat at the dining room table in her brother's apartment, staring at the subpoena and plane ticket which had arrived the day before. She had already packed and was dressed for the flight to Waco. Her hands shook as she tried to drink the glass of juice she had poured for herself. And then she began to cry, gently at first, then uncontrollably.

Despite the legal demands of the State of Texas and the insistence of the McLennan County District Attorney's office that she testify in the capital murder trial of David Spence, Christy did not see how she could possibly do it. She could not face David, even in the safety of a courtroom. The thought of looking into those eyes again terrified her.

As she sat there weeping, balanced on the ragged edge of a nervous breakdown, images she had blocked from memory came rushing back. The nightmare of the time she had spent with David—loving him, trying to change him, being abused by him—burned in her brain. If she was to survive, to put her life back together, Christy thought, she had to remain in hiding, leaving Waco far behind in memory's distance. It had been almost six months since she had climbed on the back of her brother's motorcycle with nothing but the clothes she was wearing and headed for a state she had never before even visited. There, her brother had promised, she would be safe. He would protect her, help her build a new life.

Now, though, the prospect of returning to Waco to testify had reopened the wounds. Painful memories revived old fears. She remembered, as if it were only yesterday, the last time she had seen David.

Christy had taken his brown corduroy suit, the one he planned to wear to a pretrial hearing related to the sexual abuse case, down to the jail that March morning in 1983. Afterward she had stopped by a department store, shopped for a while, then slipped a pair of shoes into her purse before leaving. A clerk saw her and called the store's security officer. She was arrested for shoplifting and taken to jail for the first time in her life.

As she stood near the booking desk that afternoon, hand-cuffed to three other women, Christy saw David walking down the hall, accompanied by two deputies. Dressed in the suit she had brought him, he was on his way to the courtroom. He was nearing the end of the hall when he turned and saw her. For a moment he only glared; then the anger she was all too familiar with exploded. He began yelling and pointed at her. "I'll kill you, you bitch," he said. "I'm going to fucking kill you."

At that moment Christy realized he would if the opportunity ever presented itself. It was the first time she can remember silently praying that he never be released from jail.

Only after leaving Waco had Christy begun to seriously consider the possibility that David might have been involved in the lake murders.

At David's request, she had had friends ask around to see if there was any street talk about the murders, any information that might remove David from suspicion. But no one ever came up with anything that anyone with the price of a *Waco Tribune-Herald* didn't already know.

Still, she could not bring herself to believe that David, whom she had loved deeply, could have done something so unspeakable. She had even hoped to bear David's child and had deliberately tried, throughout the time they were together, to become pregnant. And although Dennis Baier and Truman Simons and Ned Butler had made it clear while questioning her that they were certain Spence was the killer—even hinting that they felt she knew far more about the crime than she was admitting—she refused to accept what they were saying. Not until she was safely removed from David and the almost hypnotic influence he held over her did she find herself wondering—and then finally accepting the fact that he was indeed capable of murder.

David Spence—with his drunken rages, his obsession with blood and inflicting pain, and his morbid fascination with knives and Satanic rituals—was, she had finally accepted, insane.

As she sat in the apartment, her makeup ruined by tears, she reflected back on the agony and humiliation David had dealt her. She wondered why she had ever loved him. It was a question she could not answer because, though fearful of him and not wanting ever to see him again, part of her still held stubbornly to feelings she had wished a thousand times she could erase. He had abused her unmercifully, yet—why, she didn't know—there were still times when she missed him, ached for him, cried out for him.

There had been a time when Christy thought she could change him, could make him love her in the same devoted way she loved him. But she had been unsuccessful. Her failure, she had once felt, made her somehow responsible for the deaths of the three teenagers. If only she had been able to make him happy, to help him to stop drinking. Maybe if they had spent more time in church he would never have killed anyone.

Only after time and distance had removed her from all the people and places that triggered memories of David was she able to look back dispassionately on what had happened to her in the time she had known him.

How she had hated that dog collar! And the knife throwing, and the "love stick," and the drunken beatings that seemed always to precede their lovemaking. David, she finally realized, had been able to reach sexual climax only on those occasions when he had first physically abused her.

He had taken her out so seldom that she felt, in retrospect, that he was ashamed of her. In the time they were together there had been a few rare visits to a bar near his house and one trip to a nearby bowling alley. She could not remember their ever having seen a movie together.

There had been so few times when he had even called her by name. She was his "bitch" or his "seventeen-year-old slut." Still, she remembers that he was the first person ever to call her Christy, not Christine or Chris like everyone else. She had never liked the name but when David spoke it, it took on an endearing, lyrical quality which warmed her. Today she still uses it.

At first life with David was exciting. He didn't talk or dress like a biker then. The first time she saw him walk into the Taco Torch where she was working he was dressed nicely, wearing slacks and a silk shirt. He had no beard then, only a mustache, and his hair was neatly styled.

But he had changed so quickly. The drinking became a constant problem. He often said he could never get drunk enough.

And there was the crank and the coke and the marijuana. And the physical abuse.

During sex he bit her savagely, often drawing blood on her neck and shoulders and breast. On more than one occasion she feared he had bitten off one of her nipples. And he would hit her, sometimes with an open hand, sometimes with a fist. She hated him on those occasions and would run away. But he always found her and brought her back. Even when she moved out, into the small apartment near the Rainbow, he had followed. There was no escape. Like the battered wife, she was trapped, forced again to anticipate the next indignation.

One morning, she remembered, David woke her, grabbed her by the wrist, and pulled her into the living room where he ordered her to take off her nightshirt and panties and lie naked on the floor. Then, after awakening Gilbert and Tony, he had intercourse with her as they watched. And he often talked of his fantasy of breaking into the house late at night, wearing a mask, and raping her.

Her life became an exercise in fear and humiliation. If David had not returned home from his wanderings before midnight she knew his eventual arrival promised another beating.

And his sexual appetite seemed endless. They would make love as often as three times a day, yet Christy knew he was also sleeping with others. There was the Chinese girl named Kim and Jeannie, a woman in her mid-thirties. More than once he had brought them to the house while she was there. "If you won't give me enough," he would say, laughing, "I've got to go somewhere else."

His constant search for new sexual partners had, at times, been dangerous. She remembered the night he returned home with stab wounds in his neck. He had been in a bar, he said, with a woman he had slept with several times, and her husband had come up behind him with a knife. Frantic, Christy urged him to go to the hospital but he refused, insisting that such action might result in his parole officer finding out that he had been in a bar. It was not until the following day that he finally agreed to let her take him to an outpatient clinic for medical attention and pills for the pain.

While David enjoyed his own ambitious sexual adventures, he was paranoid in his jealousy of Christy, constantly accusing her of sleeping with other men. One evening as they walked out of the grocery store, a man in the parking lot whistled at her. David immediately dropped the bag of groceries he was carrying and rushed toward the man. Putting his knife to the man's neck, David threatened to cut his throat if he ever came near Christy.

Late one night, after returning home drunk, he again began accusing her of sleeping with others and, as he had done so many times before, began slapping her around. And for the first time Christy fought back, hitting and kicking, cursing him at the top of her voice. David ripped off her blouse before his brother Steve pulled him away and pinned him against the living room wall. As Steve restrained David he said to Christy, "Get a shirt on and get out of here before he kills you."

David's rage, usually triggered by drinking or drugs, was not always directed at her. She had seen him hit his mother several times and remembered a night when, during a frontyard fight, David had wrapped his belt around his fist and opened a deep cut across Gilbert's cheek with the buckle. David seemed fascinated at the sight of the blood running down his friend's face.

The sight of blood, she knew, stimulated him. It excited him when his bites during their lovemaking caused her to bleed, and he admitted a special interest in having sex with her during her menstrual period.

After his mother accidentally backed her car over his dog, he wrapped the dead animal in his denim jacket and held it close for several minutes before burying it in the backyard garden. Thereafter he refused to allow Christy to wash his jacket, saying he wanted the dog's bloodstains to remain.

Christy remembered, too, how he was constantly clipping stories of violent crimes—mostly murders—from the newspapers and reading them over and over.

As time went on David's behavior became even more bizarre. He developed a fear of being alone and began insisting she even accompany him to the bathroom while he bathed. She had to stay in the bedroom while he dressed and was not allowed to go to the kitchen to cook breakfast until he went with her. The fear of spiders which had haunted him as a child returned, and before bed every night he would inspect the room and the bed covers to make certain none were there. And there were the nights when he would wake and sit on top of her, shining a flashlight up into his face, laughing evilly and chanting. She never understood the words, if in fact they were words, but they were always the same.

The inexplainable love-hate she felt for him was turning to fear.

One afternoon, insane with dread of another beating and weary of the sexual abuses, Christy went to her stepfather's home and took his .38 pistol from its hiding place. She had made up her mind to go to where David was working and kill him. Before she reached her destination, however, she weakened. Instead she decided to resolve the problem by killing herself. That night she locked herself in the bathroom, took a razor blade from the medicine cabinet, and cut deeply into one of her wrists. Terrified at what she had done, she ran from the house screaming as blood streamed down the palm of her hand and into the web of her fingers.

David followed after her as she ran down the darkened street screaming hysterically for him to leave her alone. He finally caught her, forced her to return to the house, then drove her to her stepfather's house. Trained in first aid while in the service, her stepfather stitched and bandaged the wound and tried to calm her while David waited outside in the car, drinking from a can of Budweiser.

It was shortly after the suicide attempt that Christy called her sister in Fort Worth and begged her to come get her. She had to get away.

As Christy sat now, remembering, her thoughts returned to that day when she had finally summoned the courage to leave Waco, to leave David. She had been at the Rainbow working that final day when her sister arrived. David came to the store, begging her to stay. He loved her, he said. He was sorry for all the things he had done. Then he went over by the video games and sat down and cried.

As Christy was preparing to get into her sister's car, David had embraced her and kissed her, telling her again how much he loved her. As her sister pulled out of the parking lot onto Herring Avenue, Christy could see David running along behind them. "Christy, don't go," he was yelling. "Christy, I love you." His pleading voice echoed in her mind all the way to Fort Worth.

It seemed so far in the past, yet the images were still vivid in her mind. Why, she wondered, had it echoed the way it had?

Was there something she could have done that might have helped David, that might have turned him from the direction she had seen him headed?

She thought of that time so long ago when Steve Spence's father-in-law, a Nazarene minister, had visited her and David, urging them to begin attending church. They had gone for a while and she thought she had seen a change. For a time they had even read the Bible together and she was amazed at his interest and his ability to remember and quote the scriptures. She thought back to that night when David, crying so hard he could barely walk, had gone to the altar to be baptized. And one evening he had returned home after playing in a church-sponsored basketball game with a small ring he and Steve had found on the grounds. He had gently slipped it on her finger, telling her it was her promise ring.

But after only a few weeks David's interest in the church abruptly ended. Despite her urging, he refused to attend services. He stopped reading the Bible. The beatings and the drunken rages returned.

Why, dear God, did she still feel something for him?

For a time Christy felt that by hurting David she could rid herself of those feelings. Thus, she had returned to Waco after his arrest, even living briefly with his mother, motivated more by cruel intentions than concern. She made a point of not answering the phone at times when she knew he would be calling from the jail. And she wanted him to be aware that not only was she seeing other men, she had actually married Mahir Tumimi. By hurting him as he had hurt her, she felt, she could somehow free herself.

Yet as she sat alone at the dining room table, far removed from it all, she still wanted to believe David innocent of the murders. After all, he had never admitted to her that he had been involved in the crime. And for all his faults, he had never lied to her. But when she had asked him about it, he had refused to discuss the matter. The letter she had written, asking pointedly if he was guilty, had been answered but with no reply to the question.

She found herself thinking back to the strange behavior Muneer Deeb had displayed in the weeks following the murders. Once an immaculate dresser, he had begun showing up at the Rainbow in old jeans and shirts which had not been ironed. His hair was seldom combed, he was more nervous than she had ever seen him, and he had begun complaining of not being able to sleep.

A number of times he had asked her to take late-night rides with him after closing the store. Almost always they would go to the Taco Torch for something to eat. And while Deeb would always order something for himself, she came to know that he would soon have to hurry into the parking lot and throw up after eating. Several times Christy had suggested he see a doctor. One evening, not long after the lake murders, she recalled, Karim and Maria had taken Deeb to the hospital emergency room following a violent siege of vomiting.

At the time, Christy had assumed his problems stemmed from the financial disaster the Rainbow had become. Now, though, she wondered.

Despite the warmth of the day Christy felt a sudden chill and hugged her arms to her breast. Still crying, she closed her eyes and saw David's image. It was his eyes she was seeing, the eyes that at times seemed to be like bottomless pits, blank, completely devoid of feeling. When he was sober and pleasant they were the most beautiful shade of blue she had ever seen. But when he was angry they would change and become bright green, then almost gold. For some reason, it occurred to her that she had rarely ever seen him smile.

Christy's brother, worried about her fragile mental and physical condition, placed a long-distance phone call to Ned Butler in the district attorney's office. There was no way, he said, that he would allow his sister to return to Waco to testify at Spence's trial. He feared she was on the verge of a mental breakdown and would be unable to handle the pressures she was certain to face in the courtroom. He was adamant in his refusal. If necessary, he would hide her. He was prepared to go to jail himself. The trial, he said, would simply have to go on without her.

## 32

Assistant District Attorney Ned Butler, aware of the courtroom dangers of having such an unstable witness on the stand, finally agreed to excuse Christy Juhl from testifying. He didn't trust her anyway. And, too, Butler was confident that he had enough witnesses to present a strong case against David Spence without her.

In fact, as they prepared for the trial, the prosecutors were having difficulty reducing their list of possible witnesses. With only the complicated bite mark testimony to serve as physical evidence linking Spence to the crime, the state had decided to use an unusual amount of testimony from inmates with whom David had discussed the murders.

Butler and Feazell were both aware, however, that there was a fine balance necessary to gain a jury's acceptance of testimony from hardened criminals. They wanted to present testimony from enough prisoners to show the degree to which Spence had talked of the crime. On the other hand, they knew the hazards of building too much of the case on what defense attorneys were already referring to as "jailbird testimony."

One of the inmates they had decided to scratch from their list was Johnny Johnston. A Waco truck driver with a history of trouble with the law, Johnston was in the McLennan County jail for the attempted robbery of a local convenience store. The robbery had been doomed from the start. In an attempt to convince the store manager that he was armed, Johnston had entered holding a roman candle covered with a handkerchief. The manager had immediately realized that the disguised firework was no gun barrel and had pulled a pistol from beneath the counter, shooting Johnston in the chest. Thus, the would-be robber had spent several weeks in the hospital before arriving at the jail. He was one of the first inmates Spence had spoken with about the lake murders.

On several occasions David had talked to him about the

crime, first suggesting that he had been the killer, then changing his story to indicate that he and Christy had just happened to be at the lake and witnessed the murders. Over a period of time, though, it had become clear to Johnston that David really was the one who had killed the three teenagers. David mentioned money that was owed him, saying that had he been paid, he would have left the state and never returned. David also described to Johnston how the victims had been tortured before their deaths and said that he had murdered the wrong girls.

Truman Simons eventually took a statement from Johnston and indicated that he might be called on to testify should the case ever go to trial. Johnston had readily agreed. "That dude," he said, "is bad. He needs to die for what he did—and I'm going to help you kill him."

But when Butler began talking with Johnston prior to the trial, the inmate had great difficulty keeping the sequence of events in proper order. He had no problem remembering what David had told him and what he had overheard him telling others, but when he attempted to verbalize his story he became confused and rambled. Disappointed, Butler feared Johnston would be an all too vulnerable target on cross-examination and informed Feazell that he did not feel comfortable putting him on the stand.

Butler had Johnston brought to his office and explained that he appreciated his willingness to help but because of the large number of witnesses the state expected to put on the stand, they were forced to eliminate some. "You're off the hook," Ned said. "You won't have to testify."

Instead of being relieved as Butler had expected, Johnston was clearly disappointed. "Mr. Butler," he said, "I've done a lot of wrong things in my life. This would be a chance for me to do something right for a change. David Spence needs to be put away and I'd like the opportunity to help do it. You can't let him get away with what he did to those kids . . ."

". . . Johnny, we're not going to let him get away," Butler interrupted.

Johnston continued as if Ned had not even spoken. "If you can't use me, I understand. I know you've got to do what you think is best. But, by God, I just want you to know I'm ready if you need me."

Butler was not prepared for the urgency in Johnston's voice.

Regardless of the nature of the trial, most inmates who are called to testify are less than enthusiastic, fearful they will be branded as snitches by their peers. They are well aware of the danger of physical harm once they return to jail—and at best, a snitch can count on becoming an immediate outcast.

Thus, the willingness on the part of Johnston and several others to testify against Spence had, frankly, surprised the assistant district attorney. None of the inmates had even asked about the possibility of dropped charges or shortened sentences. To have done so would have been futile. Butler's reputation had preceded his move from Amarillo. There he had earned the nickname "No Case Ned" because of his insistence that any case he prosecuted be as strong as possible before he even went so far as to take it to a grand jury. Word was, if Butler sought an indictment, the subsequent trial would be little more than a formality. He was a prosecutor who rarely lost. And he never made deals in exchange for testimony.

For several days as he coordinated the preparation of the case which he and Feazell would present, Ned found himself thinking about Johnny Johnston. Finally, over coffee late one afternoon, he had a talk with Simons.

"I don't know what he might do on the stand," Truman said, "but what he has to say is pretty damn good. And the fact he was in intensive care with that gunshot wound at the time of the murders and didn't know anything about them until David started running his head sure as hell strengthens his story in my book."

Ned listened, rocked back in his chair, and nodded. "I'm afraid the guy will have real trouble once he gets on the stand," he said. "Some folks just can't handle it. The defense is liable to have him talking to himself before they get through turning him inside out. He could hurt us. But, dammit, he wants to do something right for once in his miserable life, something he can feel good about. Hell, tell him we're going to use him."

Simons grinned, "I like that."

On Monday, June 18, 1984, after three weeks of jury selection, the Spence trial finally got under way in Judge George Allen's 54th District Court. The prosecution had sworn in over fifty witnesses. None took the oath more seriously than inmate Johnny Johnston.

*    *    *

The picturesque McLennan County courthouse was built in 1901 but stood vacant for five years until two brothers purchased it for $10,000 to use as a headquarters for their steam laundry business. Eventually, however, it was retrieved to serve the judicial needs of the county. Today its ornate exterior, complete with stately columns, manicured lawns, and flowering magnolias, provides a dramatic contrast to the neighboring downtown architecture. With its sparkling white dome topped by the figure of justice, blindfolded and balancing her traditional scales, it is a throwback to another time in Texas history.

Inside there is the ever-present scent of polished wood rails and foyer benches, mixing with the inviting aroma of freshly brewed coffee served up by an elderly blind lady who runs the first floor snack shop. The path of anyone who enters can easily be traced by the clicking echoes of steps taken across the polished marble floors. Large photographs marking memorable events in the county's history share space with portraits of stern-faced judges who have presided over the courts housed in the four-story monument to the legal system.

On most days the atmosphere is almost church-like. People instinctively lower their voices as they enter. Those sitting in the halls outside courtrooms, nervously waiting to hear the judges' decisions or to be called to testify in less celebrated cases involving divorces, property disputes, and thefts of autos and television sets, quietly read newspapers or talk in low tones to unsmiling attorneys dressed in three-piece suits.

The atmosphere on the opening day of the Spence trial, however, was different. An electric excitement had spread throughout the building. In the city's modern history there had never been a case so highly publicized, so closely followed, as the lake murders. Television cameramen, though barred from the courtroom, arrived early to jockey for position, hoping to capture shots of lawyers and witnesses as they arrived. Reporters who generally gathered their information routinely and with little enthusiasm nursed cups of coffee, eager for the trial to get underway.

The third floor foyer was congested long before the 9:00 A.M. starting time which presiding Judge George Allen had announced. Elderly women, hair freshly blue-rinsed and carrying seat cushions, stood near the courtroom's massive oak doorway, eager to assure themselves good vantage points from which to view the proceedings. They whispered and sometimes pointed while trying to determine who among the crowd might be family members of the victims or of the man on trial.

Though there were several guesses, all were wrong. Over in the courthouse annex, Vic Feazell had invited the families of Jill Montgomery and Kenneth Franks to wait in his office until time to report to court. John Ben Sutter, his administrative assistant, had seen to it that seats would be reserved for them. The family of Raylene Rice did not attend the trial. The family of David Spence, extended no extra courtesies by the district attorney's office, was afforded the sanctuary of the judge's waiting room.

Bailiff Lex Hollis, a lean, affable man in his seventies who had been working in the courthouse for ten years, stood near the doorway of the courtroom, puffing steadily on his pipe as he viewed the waiting crowd. "This," he said, shaking his head, "is going to be a real circus."

During the first days of the trial the state carefully wove a dramatic story of murder-for-hire and mistaken identity. With Richard Franks as its first witness, the prosecution made the jury of eight women and four men aware of how Jill and Raylene had arrived at his town house on that evening almost two years before. In a voice which was sometimes almost inaudible, the weeping father of Kenneth Franks relived his frantic, unsuccessful search for his missing son. Wiping away tears as he testified, Richard often fixed a glare in the direction of David Spence who sat just a few feet away at the defense table, showing little emotion.

No one in the courtroom, however, looked in David's direction with more hatred than did Brad Montgomery, Jill's older brother. The family had expressed reservations about his attending the trial, fearful that his rage, which remained intense even after the passage of so much time, might erupt into violence. Truman Simons had worried for several days about Brad's frame of mind. He knew Brad had every right to be in the courtroom, to see that the man who had raped and killed his sister received the justice due him. But Simons also feared Brad was capable of trying to take that justice away from the judge and jury and making an attempt to see it done himself. Finally, he had decided to have a talk with Brad, warn him sternly that

any attempt at unsanctioned revenge would destroy what everyone had been working toward for two years.

"I'm not going to try to tell you that I know how you feel,"
Truman said, "but I can't let you go in there and screw things
up. It isn't going to be pretty. You're going to hear and see
some things that will make you want to kill David Spence with
your bare hands. But if you can't handle it, just go home. The
job we've got to do here is going to be hard enough without
having to worry about what you might do in the courtroom."

"I've thought about killing that sonuvabitch a thousand
times," Brad admitted. "Hell, yes, I'd like to do it. But I'm not
going to. I can handle it."

For two days he did. But after Brad heard his mother's agonized testimony and listened as the coroner graphically described the wounds inflicted upon the victims, he had had
enough. On the quiet drive home to Waxahachie that night with
his father, he said, "Dad, I can't go back tomorrow."

Rod Montgomery understood. He also felt a sense of relief.

The parents of Raylene Rice chose to deal with the traumatic
events in a different way. Raymond Rice had informed Vic Feazell that neither he nor anyone from his family would attend the
trial unless their testimony was ordered. The Rices, whose grief
was as real and lingering as that of the parents of the other two
dead youngsters, had decided the best way for them to get on
with their lives was to put the tragedy as far behind them as
possible.

They needed no trial to revive the agony that had lingered
since that July night in 1982. Raymond Rice, who had once
made numerous business trips to Waco, had begun finding ways
to avoid traveling to the city. And his youngest daughter, a
member of the Waxahachie High School band, had adamantly
refused to accompany her fellow musicians on a football trip to
Waco the year after Raylene's death. His oldest daughter had
become so upset over people's constant reminders of her sister's
death that she had moved to another city.

Vic Feazell had been aware of the family's desire to be isolated from the proceedings and had seen to it that they were
contacted only when some crucial development in the case occurred. Otherwise, they were left alone to tend their grief in
their own way. It troubled the D.A. that he and members of his
staff had never gotten to know the Rices as they had the mem-

bers of the other families. Raylene, the most innocent of the three victims, would, as the investigation continued and the trial began, become almost an afterthought.

For two days the jury listened attentively as the state called a series of witnesses who painstakingly established the sequence of events leading up to the disappearance of the three teenagers. Friends of Jill Montgomery and Kenneth Franks took the stand. Then came Sidney Smith and Joseph Chambers, the fishermen who had found Kenneth Franks' body at Speegleville Park. Several of the police officers who had been called to the crime scene gave detailed accounts of their investigation.

But it was only when Feazell showed a series of photographs taken of the bodies of the victims at Speegleville that members of the jury appeared to grasp the savage brutality of the crime of which they were sitting in judgment. Slowly they passed them among themselves as a hushed courtroom waited. Most were visibly shaken by the gruesome color pictures they were being forced to view. And for the first time several of the jurors solemnly stared at David Spence, studying his face.

In the crowd, Sandra Sadler, Kenneth's mother, gripped the hand of her sister Kay and looked down, fearful that she might accidentally catch a glimpse of the photographs of her blood-stained son. She had seen them once—Feazell and Butler had urged each of the family members to look at them in the privacy of Vic's office so they might be prepared for what was to come in the courtroom—but she never wanted to see them again.

Jan Thompson, seated next to Rod Montgomery, focused her attention on the note pad resting in her lap. The defense attorneys, after hearing her sister testify, had indicated to the judge that they might wish to recall her at some later time in the trial. By doing so, they had managed to bar Nancy Shaw from sitting in on the trial. Russ Hunt and Hayes Fuller, well aware of the emotional nature of the proceedings, did not want the jury exposed daily to the grief-stricken face of the mother whose seventeen-year-old daughter had been murdered. Angry and frustrated, Nancy sat on one of the wooden benches just outside the courtroom, waiting for recesses to hear detailed reports on the proceedings from her sister. As the trial continued, she came to despise Hunt and Fuller almost as much as the man they were defending.

\*    \*    \*

The adversarial tone of the trial had been established long before the state called its first witness. Even the most casual courtroom spectators were soon aware that the animosity displayed by prosecutors and defense attorneys for each other went well beyond the traditional trial theatrics.

Hunt, a former assistant district attorney, had been angered by the prosecution's refusal of informal discovery during trial preparations. Feazell had told him immediately after he had been appointed to represent Spence that no evidence would be provided without proper motions and orders from the court.

Early in the voir dire portion of the trial a discarded rough draft of a thirty-page letter which Hunt and Fuller had sent to federal authorities found its way to the district attorney's office. In one of those clandestine sequences of events which often occur during major trials, the document had apparently been found in the trash, retrieved, and anonymously forwarded to the opposition.

Ned Butler was the first to see it, then had given it to Feazell without comment. The district attorney sat alone in his office reading the defense's detailed synopsis of the crime and plea for a federal investigation into the matter. The letter pointed out that since the bodies had been found at Speegleville Park, which was the property of the Corps of Engineers, federal investigators legally shared jurisdiction with city officials.

The gist of the first few pages was that their client could not expect a fair trial if it was conducted in state court and prosecuted by officials of the McLennan County District Attorney's office. Strongly worded, the document not only asserted that David Spence was innocent of the murders, but that the manner in which Truman Simons, Ned Butler, and Feazell had built the state's case was filled with questionable ethics, intimidation of witnesses, and a tunnel-vision refusal to consider the possibility that the crime might have been committed by anyone other than those indicted.

It addressed the "obsession with the case" which Simons had displayed since the evening the bodies had been found and questioned his reasons for suddenly leaving the police department after seventeen years. According to the letter, three unnamed police officers had indicated Simons was "a liar and not to be trusted" and that he had "been accused of running blank search warrants and manufacturing evidence" in cases he had worked while with the department.

Stunned by the venomous, slanderous tone of the letter, Feazell continued reading. A mental health professional and a psychologist, also unnamed, had indicated privately that Feazell "displayed a paranoid and psychopathic personality." And at one point during his campaign for district attorney, the letter continued, it had been pointed out that "he had a poor reputation for honesty." The statements of Gilbert Melendez were questioned as was the expertise and honesty of the state's expert witness, Dr. Homer Campbell. The judge who would preside over the trial, the letter pointed out, was "extremely state's oriented" and "quite probably afraid of Feazell."

That was as far as he got. The photocopied pages still in his hand, Vic walked down the hall to Butler's office.

"They didn't leave out anybody, did they?" he said. There was no trace of humor in his voice.

"Did you read it all?" Butler asked.

"Enough," Feazell said. "I'm not going to waste my time with this kind of garbage."

"You might want to finish it," Butler suggested. "It gets even more interesting toward the end."

The district attorney sighed and slumped in a chair across from Ned's desk. In the final pages of the document, Hunt and Fuller had detailed their own theory of who the murderers were. Though the police had dismissed James Bishop as a possible suspect months before after interviewing him in California, the defense attorneys were convinced that he, along with Randy Baines—the husband of Joanne Baines, who had cashed Jill Montgomery's check at a local supermarket the day of the murders—were "potential suspects."

They wrote that the stepmother of Randy Baines had told friends her son had returned home in the early morning hours of July 14, intoxicated and covered with blood. He claimed to have been fishing most of the night at Lake Waco—and had lost his knife.

The letter stated that Bishop and Baines were closely associated and had been seen together on several occasions prior to the lake murders and Bishop's sudden move to California. Both men, it was noted, had access to a boat.

Feazell looked up in amazement. "*This* is going to be their defense?" he said, slapping the back of his hand against the pages. "They're going to try to convince a jury that James Bishop and Randy Baines killed the kids and then took the bodies over to Speegleville in a boat? They're going to stand up there and try to tell everyone that poor little David is being railroaded?"

"That's the way it looks," Butler said, then began to laugh.

Feazell studied his assistant. "What's so funny?"

"In the first place," Butler said, "they've laid out their whole damn game plan in that idiotic letter. And second, there is no connection between Bishop and Baines and the lake murders. Hell, even Dennis Baier, one of Russ Hunt's buddies, knows that."

Feazell wondered just how much of the letter's speculation and innuendo had been provided to Hunt by Baier. Was he one of the quoted police officers who had "requested strict anonymity?" How about Ramon Salinas? He wondered but said nothing.

"This sort of thing doesn't just show up in the mail one day," Feazell finally said, pitching the document over to Butler. "I find it a little hard to believe we have this kind of friend out there. We've had to fight the world every step of the way on this case and now, suddenly, we've got an outline of the defense's plan of attack. Do you think there's a possibility it could be a plant, something to throw us off track?"

Butler was still laughing. "Goddamn, Vic," he said, "maybe you *are* paranoid. But, to answer your question, no. Hell, they don't have that much sense. Just consider the source. Remember, Russ Hunt is the guy who said he would have no qualms whatsoever about having David babysit with his kids."

Feazell just shook his head. "This is too good to be true . . ."

As the first few days of the trial wore on, Russ Hunt and Hayes Fuller were able to do little to discredit the witnesses called by the state. When Dr. Mary Gilliland took the stand and described the wounds she had observed and recorded during the autopsies, the defense tried hard to make an issue of the fact that she had made no mention of bite marks on the bodies of the young women in her initial report. The medical examiner's explanation was simple and straightforward: She had overlooked them. But after subsequent reviews of the photographs she was convinced that the markings which Ned Butler had questioned her about were, indeed, human teeth marks.

During cross-examination, Fuller addressed her testimony that the wall of Jill Montgomery's vagina showed bruises and abrasions which appeared to have been made by some foreign object, then asked, "Isn't it possible the marks could have been made by a male penis?"

Dr. Gilliland, a picture of composure until the question was asked, looked at the questioning attorney for a moment, then glanced in the direction of Butler. A few brief snickers could be heard in the courtroom. Butler, shielding a slight grin, leaned toward Feazell and whispered: "You ever seen a *female penis?*" Dr. Gilliland appeared to have thought of the same absurdity, but she managed to maintain her dignified posture and answered the question. "It is possible," she said.

On the third day of proceedings the testimony shifted to David Spence. A young woman named Regina Rosenbaum nervously took the stand to tell of a visit she and three other friends had made to David's apartment in late July. As they sat drinking beer and talking, Spence began telling how he and some friends had flirted with two girls at the lake. The girls, he said, had become upset at their advances and they had tied them up and raped them.

"He said it was to teach them a lesson," the witness said.

"Isn't it possible," said Fuller, "that what you were hearing was nothing more than 'man talk,' that David Spence was just trying to impress you and the others?"

Pale and careful to avoid looking at the defendant, she said, "Sir, it isn't every day you hear someone talking about raping somebody. I think it would take a pretty wild imagination to make something like that up."

"Were you afraid?"

"Yes sir, I was. I told the people I was with that I wanted to leave."

Then came Cynthia Bernal and Ray Payne, a couple who had lived in the Northwood Apartments near David. Payne, who had worked with Spence at Burke's Aluminum at the time, described how Spence had frantically knocked on their door at 3:00 A.M. one morning in early August. Awakened, they answered to find him drunk and upset, yelling that "Lucky did it again; he killed Gayle, just like he killed those kids at the lake." Only after Ray was able to calm him did he find out that David, en route home, had heard only part of a radio report about the murder of a woman named Gail Beth Bramlett in nearby Axtell.

Payne went on to describe a heated argument between Spence and Deeb the following day at Burke's Aluminum. Spence, Payne said, accused Deeb of killing Gayle. Deeb, meanwhile, told Spence to "stay out of my business and keep your mouth shut" before storming out and walking across the nearby parking lot to the Rainbow Drive Inn.

The most devastating testimony, however, came from Dorothy Miles. In measured tones she answered Feazell's questions about her longtime relationship with David, how he had come to call her "Mom," and how his disposition had dramatically changed in the summer months of 1982. She told of the conversations in which David had told her that he had "cut somebody," then of his fear that he had possibly killed someone.

Hunt repeatedly pointed out during cross-examination that during that time frame his client had been despondent over his relationship with Christy Juhl, suggesting that David's depression and nervousness might well have been the result of domestic problems rather than worry over having committed some crime. And wasn't it possible that he was referring only to his and Gilbert Melendez's attack on Danny Powers when he had mentioned cutting and possibly killing someone?

She steadfastly held to her story that his first mention of trouble had come well before the sexual abuse incident.

"Mrs. Miles," Feazell asked, "why have you come here today to testify?"

Looking at Spence, her voice trembling, she replied, "Because I care about David very much—I love him—but I have to tell the truth."

During a break following her testimony, Richard McCall, Muneer Deeb's attorney who sat through much of the testimony, approached the court bailiff to say hello. As they stood together, leaning over the balcony, McCall said cheerfully, "Well, it sounded to me like the defense made some points in there."

Lex Hollis did not even look in McCall's direction. Striking a match and putting it to the well-worn bowl of his pipe, he replied dryly, "I guess I must have missed them."

Indeed, neither Hunt nor Fuller was feeling good about the direction the testimony had taken. Sitting in an office just outside the courtroom, they spoke quietly of Dorothy Miles' testimony.

"What do you think?" Fuller said.

"She gutted us," Russ Hunt replied, tossing an empty Styrofoam cup into a nearby trash basket.

By the time he returned to the courtroom, however, he was composed and smiling, sharing some private joke with his client. Several members of the jury, in fact, had begun to feel irritation at the constant smiles and handshakes shared by Russ Hunt and David Spence.

The casual camaraderie of the attorney and his client had not gone unnoticed by those in the gallery. "You reckon," whispered one spectator who watched as Hunt draped his arm across Spence's shoulder while waiting for the afternoon proceedings to get underway, "ol' Russ is gonna adopt the sonuvabitch if he gets him off?"

Nancy Shaw and Jan Thompson were already dressed for bed, waiting for the ten o'clock news, when Ramon Salinas knocked on the door of the small trailer at the Fort Fisher campground, where they were staying during the trial. Frightened at first, Nancy asked who it was before opening the door.

"It's Ramon. Sorry to come by so late, but I just got off work."

The detective entered, exchanged pleasantries, and stayed to watch the television coverage of the day's proceedings. As a reporter reviewed the testimony of Dorothy Miles, Salinas shook his head. "Just circumstantial," he said. "That's not going to help us."

Jan expressed surprise at his comment, saying that she felt the jury had been impressed by what the woman had to say.

Ramon shrugged and changed the subject. He was surprised, he said, that Tony Melendez had pled guilty. "I'd sure like to know what he confessed to," he said.

Nancy began to suspect the purpose of his visit was to see if they had any information which had not been provided him.

"We haven't read his confession or been told what it says," she replied.

"You don't know what kind of deal his lawyers worked out for him?"

"No," she said. "Maybe he was just getting scared he would

get the death penalty and decided that taking the life sentences was the next best thing."

"I don't think that was the case," Salinas said.

Nancy stiffened. "You don't think he necessarily had to be guilty to confess to murder?"

"No," Salinas answered.

"I can't believe that," Nancy said.

"What I hear is he didn't confess to murder."

"Yes, he did," Jan insisted.

"No, I hear he confessed only to being an accessory to murder. There's a big difference."

Jan was also beginning to feel uncomfortable about the officer's visit. She could not understand the negative attitude he seemed to be displaying.

Salinas went on to explain that a conviction on a capital murder charge was virtually impossible when the prosecution had nothing but circumstantial evidence. "The state has to provide one hundred percent proof of his guilt, and we can't provide that," he said.

"But what about the bite marks?" Nancy argued.

"Even if they are David's, they don't mean he killed the kids."

An angry tone began creeping into Nancy's voice. "Are you telling me that you think David could be capable of biting them like that, but wouldn't reach up and cut their throats?"

"Yes."

"If you don't think it was David who did the actual killings, who do you think it was?"

"Gilbert," he replied. "I've also got a feeling the defense is going to come up with a big surprise before this is all over. Have you heard anything about that?"

Both women shook their heads.

"One thing I hear," he continued, "is they're going to put some convicts on the stand to prove that Truman Simons harassed them, trying to get them to tell him things about the murders. I've got a feeling Truman is going to get ruined. Particularly if they put him up there. When he gets mad enough, he blows up. Frankly, I'm surprised they haven't already subpoenaed him."

After Salinas had left, Jan and Nancy sat in silence for several minutes. His visit both puzzled and disturbed them. "Do you think," Jan said, "that he was just trying to prepare us for a not guilty verdict?"

"I don't know," Nancy said, "but I'm going to talk with Ned Butler in the morning and find out what's going on." She found it strange that Salinas seemed to know more about what was going on with the defense than he knew about the prosecution.

When Butler heard the details of the detective's late-night visit he was furious. "The sonuvabitch was on a fishing trip," he said. "He doesn't know what's going on—and I'm damn sure going to make certain it stays that way." Throughout the remainder of the trial, Salinas avoided Nancy and Jan. Butler had given him strict instructions to do so.

Early on the morning of July 21, it was apparent that a standing-room-only crowd would be on hand. Rumor had spread throughout the city that among those taking the witness stand that day would be the young woman who, according to the prosecution, had been the target of the murder scheme. Judge Allen briefly considered instructing Lex Hollis to close the doors and not allow anyone else in once all seats had been taken. But the Judge knew that there were numerous attorneys and courtroom employees who had expressed interest in sitting in on the proceedings during coffee breaks and recesses of their own trials, so he had adopted a wait-and-see attitude.

Gayle Kelley, now married and eight months pregnant, had long dreaded the thought of returning to Waco and testifying. She had tried to put the deaths of Kenneth and Jill behind her, moving with her husband to a Houston suburb. Only after the indictments had Gayle learned that it was she whom Deeb had wanted killed. At first the knowledge had struck a resounding chord of fear; then she had experienced an overwhelming sense of guilt. Kenneth and Jill and Raylene had died because of her. What Gayle came to dread most about appearing at the trial was facing the parents of her dead friends. How they must hate her, she thought.

In the privacy of Ned Butler's office, Gayle's fears were quickly dispelled. While she waited for her turn to testify, Nancy Shaw and Sandra Sadler were almost tenderly attentive, helping her with her hair and makeup. As Nancy combed Gayle's hair, Sandra tried to make idle conversation which she hoped might have a calming effect. She asked about Gayle's husband, whether they were hoping for a boy or girl, how life in Houston had been since she left the Methodist Home. Privately Sandra wondered what thoughts must be running through Nancy's mind as she fussed over the hair of the girl who looked so much like her daughter.

Meanwhile, Feazell and Butler were in the courtroom preparing the jury for Gayle's appearance. Karim Qasem was testifying that he had been present when Deeb purchased the insurance policy for Gayle and had overheard his business partner ask David Spence if he knew somebody who would kill her in exchange for part of the insurance money.

When an assistant in the district attorney's office opened the door to advise the women that it was time to report to the courtroom, Nancy hugged Gayle. "You'll do just fine," she said. "And I want you to know how very much I appreciate what you're doing."

She turned back to the office to retrieve a comb and a tube of mascara left lying on Butler's desk. "Go on," she said as the others started down the hall. "I'll be along in a few minutes." She did not want Gayle to see her crying for the daughter she would never see grow to womanhood and for the grandchildren she could never anticipate.

From the moment Gayle took the stand she charmed the courtroom. Candidly she told about her relationship with Muneer Deeb and his habit of providing her with cigarettes, soft drinks, beer, and marijuana. "I heard he was giving away some good stuff," she said, "and I went over there to see if I could get my share. I don't know where he got his pot, but it was the best I ever had." Natural, unaffected, and smiling often in the direction of the jury, she was the perfect witness.

She admitted knowledge of the insurance policy Deeb had purchased for her, but said she had thought it was only a substitute for workman's compensation. "And I didn't know anything about that housewife thing he put on there," she told Feazell, referring to the fact that Deeb had listed her as his common-law wife.

Only when she spoke of her friendships with Kenneth Franks and Jill Montgomery did her voice waver.

When questioned about Spence, her tone hardened. Measuring her words carefully, she told of her encounter with him in front of the 7-Eleven when he had asked her how she would like to be "fucked by a real man."

"I've heard that word before," she said, "but I'm not accustomed to someone I don't even know talking to me like that."

Hunt spent several minutes cross-examining Gayle about her encounter with his client at the 7-Eleven store. When he addressed the issue of what David had said to her, he carefully substituted "F word" for the less-than-euphemistic four-letter expletive Gayle had spoken earlier.

Vic Feazell could not resist returning to the subject when the witness was returned to him for re-direct.

"Now," he said, "about your being appalled at what Spence said to you when he used what Mr. Hunt has called 'the F word.' You said you have heard that word used by people you know. But, now, there are different ways of using the word, aren't there?"

"Yes, sir."

"Have you ever heard it used just in profanity? I mean, just somebody getting mad and saying it?"

Gayle turned her attention away from the D.A. toward the defense table and looked straight at Russ Hunt. "What, just saying . . . fuck?" she replied.

"Yes ma'am," the amused Feazell said, "that's what I mean."

Even Judge Allen, stoic throughout the proceedings, laughed aloud.

## 33

Karen Cannon, the tenth juror selected, was already mentally and physically drained as the first week of the trial neared an end. One of the youngest members of the panel, the twenty-four-year-old kindergarten teacher was serving on a jury for the first time in her life and was already hoping it would soon be over.

David Spence scared her. When he would turn his attention to the jury box, measuring their response to testimony being heard from the witness stand, he seemed always to stare at her. And though his expression was generally dispassionate, his eyes bothered her. They were, Karen felt, evil.

Every afternoon she would return home where she lived with her mother and cry, letting the tension and pent-up emotion of the day's proceedings escape in the privacy of her bedroom. At night when she would close her eyes and beg sleep to come quickly, her mind would fill with images of the horrible pictures she and her fellow jurors had been forced to examine. At times she would see David's face, his piercing look focused on her. More than once she woke from nightmares, bathed in perspiration and screaming.

One evening she returned home and went directly to the bathroom and locked the door behind her. For over an hour she soaked in the tub, at times scrubbing her tense body frantically. When her mother became concerned over the length of time she had been in the tub, she knocked lightly on the door and asked Karen if she was all right.

Inside, her daughter was crying and shaking her head. "I can't get clean," she said. "I can't get clean."

On June 22 Ned Butler arrived at his office shortly after six in the morning, only to find that Truman Simons was already there, brewing coffee. Both were anxious about the list of witnesses the prosecution planned to call. Butler shuffled through papers on his desk, searching for the notes he had made before leaving late the previous night.

"You worried about Johnston?" Simons asked.

"Hell, yes, I'm worried," Butler growled. Several times he had questioned his decision to allow Johnny Johnston to testify. He still feared the inmate might fall apart under crossexamination. The defense, Butler knew, would do anything in its power to discredit the inmate testimony the jury would hear. Of all those he and Feazell would question, Johnston was the most likely to become confused and frightened by whatever questions Russ Hunt might ask.

"He'll do okay," Simons assured.

"I hope you're right," Butler said as he rocked back in his chair, his arms folded behind his head. "He's going to be first out of the box this morning. Dammit, you know he could lose the whole thing for us."

Then, for the first time that morning, he smiled. "But you know what? I don't give a shit. As bad as he wants to testify against that sonuvabitch, I've got to give him his chance."

A packed courtroom strained to hear the story Johnston had come to tell. Sitting stiffly upright and speaking slowly, he carefully detailed the conversations he and Spence had had in the jail. He told how David would become nervous and pace when he talked of the murders. "His eyes would get big and his voice would tremble and he would shake," the inmate said, directing his observations directly at the jury. When he became convinced that Spence really was the killer he claimed to be, Johnston began making notes about their conversations on a yellow legal pad.

It was the note-taking which the defense vigorously attacked on cross-examination. Had Truman Simons, the man he had first spoken with about David's discussions of the murders, urged him to keep such detailed notes? Wasn't he acting as an agent of the state during the time he was in jail with Spence? What kind of a deal had the prosecution offered in exchange for his testimony?

Johnston showed no signs of bending to the intimidating barrage of questions. He held firm to his story, insisting that no deal had been offered and that the note-taking had been his own idea. In truth, Johnston's talks with Spence had taken place before Simons had gone to work in the sheriff's department. Finally, Hunt fixed a disgusted look on Johnston for several seconds. "Pass the witness," he said.

Johnston was smiling as he left the courtroom. "How soon will they come in with a verdict?" he asked Simons as they walked down the hall. "It'll be a while," the officer said. "Hell, man, this trial's just getting started."

"Damn, I don't know what more they need to hear," Johnston said. Clearly, he was feeling good about his day in court. He had finally done something he was proud of.

Even as Johnston was leaving, the jury was hearing another inmate's recollections of conversations with Spence while in jail. Jerry Jackson, who was on parole after having been convicted for drug possession, told how David had confided in him in November of 1982 that he had cut the girls, raping one of them and sexually abusing them with what he called his "whoopee stick." Before he was transferred to the Texas Department of Corrections, Jackson had heard David talk about a payoff due him for the killings and say that a man he identified only as "Lucky" was the reason for the murders.

"One time when he was really down," Jackson said, "David told me that he might ought to give it up since he was guilty, thinking maybe they would go easier on him. After that, he talked a lot more freely about the murders."

The testimony of David Puryear was even more damaging as he told of being in a holding tank in the company of David Spence and Gilbert Melendez prior to their arraignment on the aggravated sexual abuse trial. He had heard Gilbert tell David, "This case was almost as much fun as what took place out at the lake." Angered by his friend's observation, Spence had told Gilbert to shut up.

"He looked like he wanted to rip Gilbert's head off for what he had said," Puryear testified.

After he was moved to the fourth floor of the jail, Puryear said, David began to talk to him occasionally about the trouble he was in. At first he insisted that he had nothing to do with the murders, then later said that he did them but didn't know why. Finally, Spence admitted to him that he had done the killings and had, in fact, enjoyed it.

"When he talked about it," Puryear testified, "he looked like the devil himself."

A few days before Spence's March trial on the aggravated sexual abuse charge, Puryear was sitting in his cell, drawing a picture of a girl on a T-shirt. Spence, he said, asked him to draw one for him. David requested that the picture include two girls: a blonde and a brunette.

On a pillow case, Puryear drew the two girls, a .44 magnum, the words "The Texas Outlaw," and an ice chest. "The Texas Outlaw," he explained, was the nickname given to Spence by other inmates.

"Why did you put the gun in the picture?" Feazell asked.

"No reason, really. I just had a good picture of a gun to draw from."

"And why did you include an ice chest in the picture?"

"I can't draw hands and feet very well," Puryear explained, "so I put the ice chest on there to cover where the hands and feet were supposed to be."

"And was there anything written on the ice chest?"

"Yes sir. I wrote Bud Lite on it."

"And what was David's reaction?"

"He got mad and told me I messed up the whole picture by doing that because he only drank Budweiser."

As they had with each of the inmate witnesses, Hunt and Fuller focused their cross-examination on the possibility that he had been offered some kind of deal by the prosecution in exchange for his testimony. Obviously, it was a question for which David Puryear had prepared himself. "I was not promised anything," he said. In fact, the prosecution had been so careful to avoid even the appearance of special favors that Puryear had actually spent an extra six months in jail beyond what would have been the normal time for his release on parole. "I have four reasons for testifying here today," he continued. "Jill Montgomery, Raylene Rice, Kenneth Franks, and my own seventeen-year-old sister."

The following Monday, the jury would learn that David's talks of the murders had not been restricted to conversations with inmates in the McLennan County jail. After the prosecution had Daryl Beckham recount his talks with Spence in the jail and his subsequent attempts to get psychiatric help for him, it called three inmates from TDC's Eastham Unit where Spence had been taken following his conviction of aggravated sexual abuse.

The testimony of Jessie Ivy would provide some of the trial's most dramatic moments. Short, stocky and bearing a long scar across his face, Ivy was almost a caricature of a convict. His voice was gravely, almost a growl. He had been in and out of prison since age seventeen and was then serving a thirty-five year sentence for aggravated robbery. From the moment he took the stand he glared at Spence.

He had never testified against anyone before but, when first questioned by Butler about what Spence had told him, he made it clear he wanted to tell his story to the jury. Throughout their interview he referred to Spence as a "baby-killing sonuvabitch." "Somebody," he said, "ought to tear his fucking head off and shit in his neck."

On the stand his language was less colorful but just as graphic. The jury heard him explain the unique standards set by some convicts. If a killing took place while a store was being robbed, Ivy explained, that was "just business." The murders which David had described to him, however, were "sick." Sick things like that, he said, made no sense.

Ivy testified that Spence had told him how he and Gilbert had held the girls down, taking turns raping them. David had detailed to him how he had killed each of the three youngsters, then bound them before taking their bodies to the other side of the lake. "Then he laughed and said he was guilty but that dead people couldn't talk," Ivy said.

David had also told him of biting one of the girls' breasts and cutting her throat. "He asked me if his teeth could get him convicted," Ivy continued, "and I told him they damn sure could, that teeth were just like fingerprints—everyone's are different."

Having taken notes throughout Ivy's testimony, Russ Hunt rose to question the witness. "Mr. Ivy, my name's Russ Hunt," he said. "One thing about your story bothers me," he said. "If I understood you correctly, you said that David told you that he killed the kids—and *then* tied them up. That seems a little strange to me. In fact, it makes no sense at all. If you were going to cut my throat, wouldn't you tie me up first, then do it?"

Ivy, his eyes hard and fixed on the defense attorney, leaned into the small microphone in front of the witness stand and pointed at the defense attorney. "Mr. Hunt," he said, "if I was going to cut your throat, I wouldn't *want* you to be tied up."

An audible gasp spread through the courtroom. Russ Hunt was visibly shaken by the ominous tone of Ivy's admission. At the prosecutor's table, Butler smiled at Feazell. He was reasonably certain that what the defense had been referring to as "bullshit jailbird testimony" had been even more effective than he had hoped.

During pretrial hearings the defense had unsuccessfully filed motions to prohibit the bite mark testimony of Dr. Homer Campbell. To allow him to testify, they argued, would be a "travesty of justice" since forensic odontology, a relatively new science, was not universally recognized within the medical community. Judge Allen had quickly ruled against their motion.

Campbell, a lanky westerner with prematurely gray hair and a pleasant manner, along with his Albuquerque associate, James Ebert, had been called in hundreds of cases where bite mark evidence had been introduced. Both had assisted Florida investigators in the highly publicized case against convicted mass murderer Ted Bundy.

Using plaster casts of Spence's teeth and life-size photographs of the nude torso of Jill Montgomery, Campbell explained the techniques used to match the marks on the photograph to the casts of the suspect's teeth. Ebert, telling the jury that his field, photogrammetry, was a "seventy-five-dollar word for a ten-cent idea," explained the procedure by which enlargement and computer enhancement of a photograph could provide a sharper, more detailed image for the comparison of forensic evidence.

Pointing to the bites on Jill's neck, shoulder, and breast, Dr. Campbell testified that, to a medical and dental certainty, the marks matched the teeth patterns of the cast taken from David Spence.

Jurors examined the cast and squinted attentively as the doctor pointed at the half-moon-shaped bite marks, explaining how they conformed to the curvature and wear patterns of David's teeth. Standing near the jury box, the defense attorneys took notes as Dr. Campbell continued with his lengthy, technical testimony. When Butler finally passed the witness, Hunt reviewed much of the testimony already presented, and raised questions about the reliability of such procedures.

While Butler had displayed no problem seeing the bite marks

which Dr. Campbell had described, Hunt was understandably more difficult to convince. During the lengthy cross-examination, however, he failed to discredit the odontologist's testimony. If that were to be done, it would have to be accomplished by the defense's own expert witness.

There was noticeable relief when the doctor stepped down from the witness stand. The jurors, confused by the technicalities and jargon of the testimony, had seen that the cast, when placed over the bite marks in the photograph, seemed to match. But the intricacies of the technique by which the presentation had been built escaped most of them.

Throughout the testimony, Jan Thompson had shielded her eyes from the terrifying photograph of her niece. Jill's father, seated at an angle which had prevented his having a clear view of the evidence being presented, waited until the judge had ended the day's proceedings, then walked to the rail near the jury box. There he stood alone in the courtroom for several minutes, his expression pensive, his eyes fixed on the picture of his daughter. Hard though he tried, he could not see the outlines of teeth marks which had been the topic of discussion much of the day. Privately, he hoped the jurors were more convinced than he was.

The state, most courtroom observers felt, had put on a strong case. Without eyewitnesses or any physical evidence but the bite marks to directly link David Spence to the crime, they had already won several members of the jury. Some were convinced of Spence's guilt after hearing the testimony of the inmates. One had felt the bite mark evidence was proof enough for a guilty verdict.

Most, however, reserved judgment, anxious to see how Hunt and Fuller might refute the prosecution's case. The defense had, after all, seemed almost too calm, too confident throughout the first stage of the trial. Even Butler and Feazell privately wondered what surprise Spence's attorneys might have up their sleeves.

Cordial and soft-spoken, Hayes Fuller stood before the jury to begin his opening statement. "Quite simply stated," he said, "David is not the person who did the crime. The prosecution has indicted the wrong individual in this case and they have not, shall not, and cannot prove that David is the person who killed Jill Montgomery."

The defense, he explained, would, in the days to come, show that hair samples found in the strips of terry cloth towel used to bind the victims did not match that of Spence or any of the other defendants in the case. The jury, it was promised, would hear expert testimony that would convince them the bite marks found on the body of the victim were too vague for analysis. Spence, Fuller said, had thought Deeb to be joking when he asked if he could find someone who would agree to kill Gayle Kelley and had, in fact, attempted to help the police in solving the case.

Rumors had already spread throughout the courthouse that testimony from witnesses the defense planned to call would not only provide reasonable doubt that Spence was involved in the murders, but would point the finger of guilt to others.

Ramon Salinas took the stand to explain that hair samples obtained from Spence's Malibu, which was purchased and dismantled by investigators in April of 1983—after having gone through two other owners—did not match that of any of the victims. They had found evidence of blood, he testified, but had been unable to determine its type or origin.

As Salinas spoke, neither he nor the defense attorneys knew that David's car had not been used to transport the bodies. They were also unaware that the bloodstains, in all likelihood, had been left by Christy Juhl when David had picked her up following her wrist-slashing suicide attempt.

The foreign hair samples retrieved from the crime scene, the prosecution would argue on cross-examination, had probably come from the blanket which the park ranger had placed over Raylene Rice's body the night the dead youngsters were found in Speegleville Park.

The defense, laying groundwork for its theory that the bodies had been delivered to Speegleville by boat, made the jury aware of the fact that the main gate to the park had been locked at the time the bodies were reportedly taken there.

Even as the park caretaker was testifying that there was no access to the park except through the main gate, an elderly man who sat through much of the trial was shaking his head. Borrowing a pencil from a woman seated next to him, he drew a map which showed the "shortcut" route he had taken into the park for years on fishing trips. "Hell," he whispered, "there's all kinds of ways to get into that park."

Hunt and Fuller knew their case would not be won or lost on the technicalities of such evidence. To create reasonable doubt in the minds of the jurors, it would be necessary to show that the crime could have been committed by someone other than their client. Two days later, Judge George Allen destroyed their defense.

Months earlier, Russ Hunt had heard from a fellow attorney that a Waco woman named Connie Baines had complained to him that her stepson had arrived at her home in the early morning hours of July 14, 1982, and had laundered bloodstained clothing in her washing machine. Drunk at the time, he had indicated to her only that he had been fishing at the lake all night. Before leaving that morning he asked to borrow her husband's knife, explaining that he had lost his while at the lake. The stepson to whom the woman referred was Randy Baines, the husband of Joanne Baines, the supermarket clerk who had cashed Jill Montgomery's paycheck the day she was murdered.

Hunt, then, had begun to investigate the possibility that there might be a tie-in to the crime. After all, it seemed strange to him that the clerk had asked for no identification before cashing such a sizable check. He began exploring the possibility that the clerk's husband, aware that both Jill and Raylene had a considerable amount of cash with them, might have followed them with robbery in mind. He was certain he was on to something.

He became even more enthusiastic when Sharon Hittle, another employee at the supermarket, told of being introduced to someone named "James" one evening as the cashier and her husband provided her a ride home. Hunt had felt that the circumstances surrounding the James Bishop case in California had not been properly investigated by the Waco police. Russ could not dismiss the fact that Bishop had left Waco shortly after the lake murders and the similar crime he had committed in Coronado, California.

Among those with whom Hunt shared his theory that James Bishop and Randy Baines might well be responsible for the lake murders was Dennis Baier. The police officer, acting on Hunt's suggestion, interviewed the young woman who had been introduced to "James." He spoke with Sharon Hittle for several hours, attempting to establish a link between the two men. It had been dark that night, she said, and the man to whom she was introduced was in the back seat of the car. When Baier showed her a photograph of James Bishop she said she had never seen him before.

Still, in the privacy of Judge Allen's chambers, the defense outlined the story they hoped to represent. The stepmother was called to recount the incident in her home that morning after the murders. When Butler began to question her about various aspects of her relationship with her stepson she became hostile and demanded to see an attorney. The judge agreed to allow her until the following morning to speak with an attorney and suggested she have him present when the questioning resumed.

The next day the woman returned to the judge's chambers and admitted that she had lied about the entire matter because she had been angry with her stepson. Butler and Feazell, pre-warned by the copy of Hunt's letter to federal authorities that the defense was likely to call the woman as a witness, were prepared. They offered to produce as many as fifteen witnesses who they said would prove that the story the stepmother had originally told was false. They were also prepared to show there was no evidence that her stepson had ever known James Bishop.

Feazell, while irritated over what he considered to be an absurd attempt on the part of the defense team to cast doubt on Spence's guilt, was even more upset at the fact County Court-at-Law Judge Mike Gassaway had issued evidentiary search warrants to Hunt and Fuller, allowing them to obtain bite and hair samples from Bishop and Baines. Feazell was certain Gassaway had exceeded his authority in issuing the warrants to people who were not certified peace officers and that he had breeched judicial ethics by involving himself in a felony case being tried in another judge's court. Feazell was already planning to ask the state attorney general's office to investigate the matter once the trial was completed.

Visibly angered by the time spent on the matter, Judge Allen wasted little time making his ruling. He had heard no connecting evidence, he told the defense attorneys, that would justify their present testimony involving Bishop or the stepson of the woman who had been summoned to his office. Because of its irrelevancy, he would not allow them to pursue any line of questioning that attempted to build a case against the two men.

Their plan of attack shattered, Hunt and Fuller could do nothing more than call Los Angeles odontologist, Dr. Gerald Vale. Often a courtroom adversary of Dr. Campbell, he testified that the photographs of the bite marks were of such poor quality that making a scientific match was impossible. Deeply tanned, with a shock of white hair, and far more formal than the state's expert witness had been, he detailed the formula by which bite marks were measured.

Before he was dismissed prior to the noon break he had testified that four of the wounds shown in the photographs were, in fact, bite marks. However, they were neither well-defined nor distinctive enough for him to determine that they had been made by the defendant. What had caught the jury's attention was the outline overlay of Spence's teeth impressions, which seemed to perfectly match the bite marks on the photograph.

"Dr. Vale," Butler finally asked as he closed his lengthy cross-examination, "from the evidence you have seen, can you exclude the defendant?"

"I can neither exclude nor include him," he answered.

That afternoon the defense rested. During the twelve-day trial the state had called thirty-nine witnesses to the stand. The defense had called only six.

34

On the morning of July 3, Vic Feazell had been up since first
light and was walking in the backyard, thinking of the closing
argument he would present to the jury later in the day. He and
Berni had stayed up late, writing, then rewriting notes and
phrases that he knew he would not refer to once on his feet in
the courtroom. Never had he been so emotionally drawn into a
case. And never had he felt so confident in the words he had
chosen to speak before the jury.

He sipped from the cup of coffee he carried with him as he
toured his wife's neatly manicured flower garden, admiring the
brilliant colors of the hibiscus and the daylilies. The early morning coolness, he knew, would soon turn into another hot July
day.

It would also, he felt, be a day when, after almost two years,
the first blow of justice in the lake murders would finally be
struck.

"Nervous?" Berni asked as he returned to the kitchen and
picked up their two-year-old son, Greg.

He smiled at her. "Yes," he said, "I am."

In the courtroom, however, it would not show. Dressed in a
black suit and talking with the families of the victims before the
proceedings got under way, Feazell appeared calm and poised.
Only when Hayes Fuller began to argue for the defense did
Feazell's expression become serious, determined. *Ned's right*,
he thought, *this is the Super Bowl.*

He listened attentively as Butler reviewed the indictment for
the jury, pointing out that the state had proven each of the
charges. Then Fuller and Hunt argued to the jury that there had
been nothing but circumstantial evidence presented against their
client; that the motives of the convicted felons who had taken
the witness stand with wild stories of Spence's jail rantings had
to be seriously questioned. Feazell listened patiently as the de-

fense tried once again to discredit the bite mark testimony of
Dr. Homer Campbell.

"David simply did not commit the crime," Hunt repeated.
Butler smiled. Hunt had so often used the phrase that the assis-
tant D.A. had begun privately referring to Spence as "David
Simply" during the final days of the trial.

It pleased Feazell to see that several members of the jury
were looking not at the defense attorneys addressing them but,
instead in the direction of Jill Montgomery's mother who had
finally been allowed to return to the courtroom. Nancy Shaw
had purposely chosen to position herself in the front row of the
section of seats directly across the room from the jury box.
There, she knew, they could see her. And, equally important,
she would finally have an unobstructed view of David Spence.

By the time the defense had concluded its arguments, Feazell
was aware of an almost welcome anger which had steadily
mounted as he heard Hunt and Fuller speak. Over the course of
the demanding trial he had experienced a growing dislike for
both attorneys seated at the defense table. Too many accusations, with neither purpose nor support of fact, had been made
by the court-appointed lawyers. First there had been the inflam-
matory letter to the federal authorities, filled with half-truths and
worse. Feazell was also aware of the rumors that had been
spread through the courthouse of unethical dealings on the part
of not only himself but Ned Butler and Truman Simons as well.

Right or wrong, the district attorney held to a philosophy that
required him to maintain a very real antagonism for any oppo-
nent he faced in the courtroom. He had never been able to understand how lawyers could face off all day, battling for the
high stakes of human life, and then meet for a drink when the
day's proceedings were completed. He could not work that way.
And the attitudes of Russ Hunt and Hayes Fuller, which he
viewed as arrogant, made it easier than usual to fan the fires of
his adversarial feelings.

"Folks," he said as he rose from his chair and approached
the jury, "in just a few more days it will have been two years
since the crime we've discussed here was committed; two years
since the parents were notified; since they felt the pain that only
a parent can understand. That pain is going to echo throughout
their bodies for the rest of their lives."

He set aside the small podium from which the defense attorneys had spoken and buried his hands into his pockets. As Hunt and Fuller had done, he thanked the members of the jury for their time and their personal sacrifices. But he stopped short of sharing the defense's apology for their having had to view the numerous crime scene photographs which he began placing along the rail of the jury box.

"I can't apologize to you for that," he said, "because that's why you are here—to look at these pictures and see what kind of crime we're dealing with."

Methodically he retraced the case he and Butler had presented, beginning with the activities of the young victims on the day they were killed and on to the frantic search Richard Franks had made for Kenneth.

"When Kenneth didn't come home by twelve o'clock, his daddy got worried. Somehow he knew something was wrong." Feazell looked into the crowd, making eye contact with Richard Franks. So did several jurors.

The district attorney was now sounding more like an evangelist than a prosecutor. His voice occasionally trembled with emotion as he spoke of Koehne Park. "Is there anything bad about Koehne Park?" he asked. "No; that's where the teenagers went. But they weren't expecting to run into something like that . . ." Feazell turned and pointed in the direction of David Spence. "They didn't expect to run into somebody with a motive to kill."

Pacing in front of the jury box, Vic reviewed the evidence. Unlike Butler, whose technique it was to speak softly, forcing the jurors to strain to hear him, Feazell was almost shouting. "People," he said, "there's more to these facts than just cold intellect . . . There's a humanness involved here, and don't ever lose sight of that. Because if we lose our humanness, we just might as well give up and quit and turn the world over to the anarchists."

As he continued, Feazell made no attempt to disguise his contempt for the defense attorneys. "There have been some insinuations, some allegations here, that the state, in effect, has tried to railroad Mr. Spence; that we planted inmate testimony; that we gave them all these great deals. Folks, did you hear anything about any kind of deals from anybody?

"I feel that my integrity has been insulted, right along with your intelligence. Ladies and gentlemen, there has been no attempt to railroad David Wayne Spence." Again the district attorney fixed a glare on the defendant.

"You heard testimony from a man named Clint Olson that he and others went to the apartment of David Spence early in the morning of July 14. The defense asked you to assume that David didn't do any kind of crime because when he answered the door he wasn't nervous; he wasn't covered with blood; wasn't saying 'Oh, my goodness, I just killed somebody.' Not nervous. You've had an opportunity to view him through two and a half weeks of trial. On trial for his life, and he doesn't appear nervous. He's not nervous about his own life; why should he be nervous about three strangers?

"But what did one of those visitors remember him saying? 'I have been with Tony.' And Clint remembered him saying, 'I've been out at the lake . . . with Gilbert.'

"And you heard the testimony of Dorothy Miles, the woman David calls 'Mom.' Do you think there is anything, anybody who could have twisted that woman's arm to get her to say something that wasn't so, or to get her to testify against her will about anything? No. What did she say about how she felt when David told her he thought he had killed somebody? She said she felt sick. I wrote it down. She said, 'I loved him, I hoped he was joking, but I knew better.'

"One of the things Jessie Ivy said on the stand in response to one of Mr. Hunt's questions made a lot of sense to me. When Hunt asked him, in reference to tying the children up after they were dead, 'Does that make sense?' And Jessie Ivy looked at him and said, 'Sick things don't make sense.' Remember that? 'Sick things don't make sense.' "

Feazell paused, letting the statement soak in as he picked up a glass of water and drank. Judge Allen advised him of how much time he had left.

His pace quickening, the district attorney reminded the jury of the testimony of Gayle Kelley and Muneer Deeb's business partner, and of those things the other inmates had heard Spence say. He recounted Daryl Beckham's testimony that David had said Kenneth Franks had been forced to watch the others die.

"You know what?" Feazell said. "One of those kids was lucky—lucky to be killed first and not have to watch the others die. Boy, that's sad, isn't it, thinking that one of those babies was lucky?"

Across from the jury box, Nancy Shaw sat weeping silently, making no attempt to wipe away the tears that streamed down her face.

Feazell then turned his attention to the bite mark testimony. "The defense told you there were conflicting opinions from the odontologists. Folks, I didn't hear any conflicting opinions. I heard Dr. Campbell say that to a dental certainty, a medical certainty, that David Spence's teeth made these marks. And I heard Gerald Vale say, from the evidence, that he couldn't tell. He didn't say Dr. Campbell couldn't tell; he said, 'From the evidence, I can't tell. I'm not going to exclude him or include him.' And then Mr. Butler asked him, 'Well, you said there are some similarities, and that the wear patterns line up,' and Dr. Vale said, 'Yes, there are similarities between these marks and Mr. Spence's teeth.' Then he said a lot of people have wear patterns like that.

"But remember what Mr. Butler asked next? He asked if the similar wear patterns didn't reduce the possibilities. And Dr. Vale said, 'Yes, the wear patterns bring it down to even fewer people.' Well, what about if somebody with those teeth lived in Waco? Well, that would bring it down some more. What if they could be placed at the park that night? That brings it down some more. What if they've admitted, I bit her nipple off? That brings it down some more.

"David Spence was wrong when he told Jessie Ivy that dead people can't talk. Thank God Homer Campbell can look at that and bring the evidence to you. Sometimes, dead people can talk."

The strain of the sustained emotion was beginning to show on the young district attorney as he concluded his impassioned argument. There were other things he had hoped to touch on, but his time was running out.

"Folks," he said, his voice suddenly soft, "it has been two years, and there are a lot of people who have been waiting for your decision. Two years. Two years."

Then he walked to the defense table and, standing just a few feet from the defendant, said, "You know, during this trial I found myself looking at David Spence and feeling what I confused at first to be pity. Then, I said, Vic, why are you feeling sorry for David Spence? Then I realized I wasn't sorry for him; I was sorry for our situation. It hurts. It hurts to deal with this

kind of thing. And I know it's going to hurt you, but I know
that you will do the right thing, based on the evidence. It's a
sad, sad situation."

For almost two hours the members of the victims' families sat
nervously waiting in the library of the district attorney's office.
Feazell and Butler retired to their respective offices, indicating
they had work which needed attending. In truth they only
wanted to endure the agonizing wait in private. Drained by the
long nights of preparation and the stressful days in the courtroom, both were nearing exhaustion.

When word came that the jury had asked to see the bite mark
evidence again, Feazell hurried down the hall to Butler's office.
"I can't believe this," he fumed. "If they've got questions about
that, we're in trouble."

Butler took a drink from his coffee cup and did not answer.
It was the third cup he had poured himself since leaving the
courtroom yet his mouth was still dry.

Thirty minutes later Truman Simons returned from the courthouse to say the jury was returning.

Judge Allen looked out into a courtroom filled to overflow. All
seats were taken and spectators stood silently along the walls.
Some sat in the aisles.

He then turned his attention to Glenn Wendell, the retired
Air Force officer who had been selected foreman of the jury.
"Has the jury reached a unanimous verdict?" the judge asked.

"Yes sir."

"If you will, deliver the verdict to the bailiff."

Lex Hollis took the folded piece of paper from the foreman
and handed it to the judge.

"I'm going to read the verdict of the jury," Judge Allen said
as he slowly put on his glasses. " 'We, the jury, find the defendant, David Wayne Spence, guilty of the offense of capital murder, as alleged in the indictment . . .' "

Even as individual members of the jury were polled, Feazell
and Butler shook hands, restraining smiles. Though his mother
broke into sobs as the verdict was being read, Spence showed
no emotion.

In the hall outside the courtroom, a battery of reporters
waited to talk with attorneys and family members. Hayes Fuller

would say only that he was displeased at the short time the jury had deliberated and that he was not really surprised at the verdict. "Because of all the pretrial publicity," he said, "David had already been tried before we walked into the courtroom."

At the same time Vic Feazell was talking with a television reporter. "We're pleased with the verdict," he said, "but the job is only half done."

The punishment phase of the trial would get under way the following day.

In weighing the punishment to be assessed in a capital murder case, the jury is technically relieved of the burden of assessing the penalty. Rather than voting on life imprisonment or death by lethal injection, they are asked instead to answer two questions. Before the judge could pronounce the death penalty which the prosecution was so determinedly seeking, the jury would first have to answer "yes" to two questions, called Special Issues, provided them by the court. A "no" answer to either question would automatically result in a life sentence for Spence. The questions were:

Special Issue No. 1: Do you find from the evidence beyond a reasonable doubt that the conduct of the defendant that caused the death of the deceased was committed deliberately and with reasonable expectation that the death of the deceased or another would result?

Special Issue No. 2: Do you find from the evidence beyond a reasonable doubt that there is a probability that the defendant would commit criminal acts of violence that would constitute a continuing threat to society?

To help them with their answer to the second question, they would be allowed to hear of past criminal acts of the defendant.

Linda Kelton, no longer a resident of the Methodist Home, had returned from Louisiana to testify that Spence had raped her on that long-ago evening when she had agreed to double date with her roommate Fran Peters. In an almost inaudible voice she told of David demanding, "You be nice to Chili and Chili will be nice to you," and of his biting and threatening her with a knife.

And Danny Powers, accompanied by his parents, was again forced to recount the night he had been sexually abused by Spence and his companion Gilbert Melendez. At one point during his testimony he stepped down from the witness stand to lift his pants leg and show jurors the scars left by Spence's knife.

Dr. Clay Griffith, a Dallas forensic psychiatrist, took the stand and listened as Feazell detailed a hypothetical profile of an individual with a five-year history of robbery, murder, rape, and sexual abuse. "Is it possible," the district attorney asked, "that a person of such background can improve his behavior?"

The psychiatrist directed his answer to the jury. "There is no chance at all of his behavior changing for the better," he said. "This severe type personality is limited to a very few people, fortunately. It has nothing at all to do with mental illness, but it is a personality disorder. The only change in his personality would be for the worse, though I don't see how it could get any worse.

"People like this act from an urge with no connection to property or persons. They will do anything to serve that urge and they are master manipulators and con artists. They never learn from experience or punishment.

"Sir," he concluded, returning his attention to Feazell, "this is one of the most severe hypotheticals I have ever seen. Without question this person, even locked up in TDC, would be a continuing threat to society."

Dr. James Jolliff, the psychiatrist who had examined Spence in April of 1983, testified that on a scale of one to ten—one being the best, ten being the worst—he would rate the defendant a ten.

The defense called no witnesses in Spence's behalf before Judge Allen instructed the attorneys to give their final arguments.

Russ Hunt made no attempt to hide his disappointment in the jury. They had been far too hasty, he felt, in determining his client's guilt. "Despite your quick guilty verdict," he said, "the state's case was based on extremely weak circumstantial evidence. The issue here shouldn't be 'let's feel terribly sorry for the kids and their parents and forget totally about David Wayne Spence.'

"Before you answer 'yes' to both of those questions, you sure better make sure that the way you're doing it is the reasonable way . . . that you have satisfied yourself that doubts don't exist. Because if you don't that's when the cancer of self-doubt is going to eat you up."

Hayes Fuller had already asked that the jury not "compound the crime by striking back at David with a death sentence." "Although David might be able to forgive you," he said to the jurors, "the question is will you ever be able to forgive your-selves?"

Feazell's final argument was even more dramatic than it had been in the guilt-innocence phase of the trial.

"Folks," he said, "it's time for this 'real man,' as he described himself to Gayle Kelley, to face the medicine. This 'real man' has finally been caught, something can be done about it, and it's time for him to really act like a real man instead of like a little bully.

"I take this personally. I feel it. I don't get up here and argue like this, just because, as Mr. Hunt says, I like to be dramatic. When something like this happens, it hurts all of us.

"When I looked at Nancy Shaw on that stand, and in my mind's eye could see the smile of Jill in the smile of that mama, or the smile of Kenneth in his mama, it hurt, just like it hurt you. When I would see Nancy sit on that stand and have to choke back the tears, it hurt. When I saw Richard Franks on that stand, choking back his tears, it hurt. And when I would see David Spence sit coldly and even smirk at times, it hurt."

Once more he called the jury's attention to the all-too-familiar crime scene photos. Holding one of Jill Montgomery, nude, her throat slashed, lying in Speegleville Park, he said, "Look at these pictures and study them carefully. And you re-member—this is the last picture of Jill Montgomery that her mama ever saw."

Worried over the tension which had built in his courtroom, Judge Allen ordered Sheriff Jack Harwell to have additional guards available when the jury returned. He also requested that everyone entering the courtroom be searched.

The jury took three hours to return with a unanimous vote of "yes" on both special issues.

Though Spence showed no emotion at the reading of the verdict, his mother broke into sobs and hurried from the court-room. Just outside the doorway she collapsed into the arms of friends and family members.

Truman Simons, who had stood near the back wall while the

judge read the verdict, glanced in the direction of David. His face revealed nothing of what he was feeling.

Meanwhile, Nancy Shaw, Jan Thompson, and Sandra Sadler, who had been seated together, embraced, their relieved smiles mixing with tears. Richard Franks shook the hands of Feazell and Butler. "I'll never be able to thank you enough for what you have done," he said.

After the spectators and members of the media had left, Butler and Feazell went to the jury room to speak one more time to the jurors. Patiently they answered questions about Spence and the murders which the law had forbidden them to raise during the course of the trial. Several of the women were still crying as they sought reassurance they had made the right decision. The prosecutors told them of evidence they had not put on and expanded on much of the testimony the jury had heard in recent days.

The jurors had heard the name of Truman Simons mentioned often throughout the trial and wanted to know more about his role in the case. "If it were not for Truman," Feazell said, "this case would never have been solved. He is the real hero in this story. In fact, I would like to have you meet him."

With that he asked Butler to go over to his office and bring Truman to the jury room. When he entered, Vic introduced him to the jurors. "Ladies and gentlemen," he said, "I thank God for men like Truman Simons. So should you."

Several thousand miles away, Christy Juhl was attending classes at the beauty college in which her brother had enrolled her. A woman whose hair she was working on was reading a newspaper. Looking over her shoulder, Christy's attention was drawn to the headline on a small Associated Press story near the bottom of the page. "Waco Man Sentenced to Die," it said.

She read the first paragraph of the story, then broke into tears and ran from the room.

# 35

Aside from false reports that the McLennan County jail had received several telephoned death threats directed at David Spence on the weekend after the completion of the trial, the matter of the lake murders, which had been the focus of public interest for two years, seemed to die an almost instant death. It was as if the jury's verdict and the judge's sentence had written the ending most Waco citizens needed. Though many were disappointed that Spence had not testified in his own behalf at the trial, the general attitude was that justice had been served. People were ready to turn their attention to other matters.

David disappeared from the headlines and public consciousness and awaited his transfer to Death Row. He spent three more months in the jail before notification came that he was going to the Texas Department of Corrections.

He was awakened on a Thursday morning in early October and taken downstairs to the booking desk where he was told he could only take his legal papers, a few letters, and some photographs with him. He was then escorted into a back room and allowed to change from his jail whites into the civilian clothing he would be allowed to wear on the trip.

It was just after 8:00 A.M. when Spence, wearing khaki pants and a plaid western-style shirt, returned to the booking counter and saw Truman Simons and Ned Butler standing near Captain Dan Weyenberg. Spence stared at the deputy and the assistant district attorney but did not speak as the captain began placing a waist chain through the belt loops of his pants and connecting it to the handcuffs David was wearing.

Spence again looked at Simons. "Is he going with us?"

"Yes, David, he is," Weyenberg said.

Spence stiffened. "I'm not going if he's going to be with us."

Weyenberg laughed. "David, you really don't have that choice. He's going, I'm going, and you're going. What's the matter? I thought you liked Truman."

"I don't trust him," Spence said, his voice hostile, "and my lawyers don't trust him. They think he might try to do something to me."

During the weeks prior to his transfer Juanita White had visited David several times, always warning him of Russ Hunt's fear that her son might be in danger on his trip to Huntsville. "If they stop somewhere along the road and tell you to get out of the car," she told David, "don't do it. They'll just say you were trying to get away and that they had to shoot you. If they stop, you just lay down in the floorboard and start yelling for help. Mr. Hunt says they're just looking for an opportunity to kill you."

Truman had heard rumors of the concern Spence's attorneys had for their client's life. One of the reasons he had told Captain Weyenberg he wanted to accompany David to TDC, in fact, was to prove that Russ Hunt's accusations against him were unfounded. And it seemed to him that he had earned the privilege of seeing David transferred to Death Row. It would, in a matter of speaking, close another chapter.

The three rode in silence as Weyenberg wound through the downtown area and pulled onto Interstate 35. Simons, riding in the front passenger seat, turned and looked at the sullen prisoner slumped in the back seat. "David," he said, "just what is it you think I'm going to do to you?"

"I don't know. I'd just rather not go down there with you."

Simons smiled and shook his head. "Do you really think I'm going to try to do something to you?"

"No. No, not really. I don't. But Russ Hunt doesn't trust you."

Truman was enjoying the game he was playing with David. "What does he think I'm going to do?"

"He thinks you're capable of doing anything."

"David, I don't know whether it will make you feel any better or not, but let me assure you I don't have any plan to hurt you. You don't have anything to fear from me, unless you try to get away or something stupid like that. The truth is, Russ Hunt has a lot more to worry about from me than you do. There are a lot of things he and I are going to sit down and talk about one of these days."

For the first time Spence relaxed and smiled. The fear he had shown when first seeing Simons earlier that morning disappeared. "I can believe that," he said. Soon he and the man who had been most responsible for the trip he was taking were engaged in conversation.

"Truman," he said, "do you realize that I'm not guilty?" It was the first time he had ever addressed the deputy as anything other than "Mr. Simons."

"No, David, I don't realize that. I think you're guilty. I have all along. You know that. There's just too much that points to you."

"I've turned my life over to the Lord again," Spence said, as if he had not even heard Simons' answer. "I've been praying a lot and I've been getting some good signs. I really feel He's going to turn this thing around for me."

Simons turned in his seat to look directly at David. "You know, a lot of people have prayed on this case. And there's some people who feel like their prayers have already been answered."

"Yeah, I know. But there are a lot of folks who pray to the wrong spirits."

Simons, reflecting on the stories of David's interest in Satanism, gave him an amused look.

"I know what you're thinking," David said, "but you've got me all wrong on that. I'm talking about praying to the Lord God Almighty. I've had people—like one of the ministers who came up to the jail a few Sundays ago—tell me they think the Lord has great plans for me. Several people have said that."

"You really believe that?"

"Yes, I do."

"I think it's very possible the Lord has plans for you," Simons agreed. "You know, there's a possibility He's going to use you as an example to a lot of people."

"I can't buy that," Spence said.

"I didn't figure you would," Truman replied.

As they traveled eastward, Spence spoke of his two sons and ex-wife June and how members of her church were praying for him. He no longer used profanity, he said, and repeatedly emphasized his certainty that his dilemma would eventually be resolved.

"Well, something's going to have to happen pretty soon," Simons said, "because, with the way things are going in the criminal justice system right now, I figure you've got about three years at best. And regardless of what Russ Hunt is telling you, I just don't see any reversible errors in the trial you had. You're going to have to pay for what you did."

"I know things looked bad at the trial," Spence answered, "but the whole thing was just a conspiracy."

For the first time during the trip Simons felt a twinge of anger but controlled it. "David," he said, "I don't think the whole world is conspiring against you. You know what the facts are, and we put them on the witness stand. Hell, you knew what was coming. You and I talked a lot up there in the jail. Truth is, I probably told you more than I should have about the investigation. But I don't think you can look me in the eye and tell me that I ever lied to you. You know I dealt straight with you from day one. I told you the second time I ever saw you that I felt you did that thing out at the lake and that if you did, I was going to get you. Remember?"

"Yeah, I remember. I don't know that you ever lied to me. I'm just telling you now that I didn't do it and one of these days I think you'll find that out."

"It may be too late by then."

"Well, I've got some things going for me. There are people who have some new information on this case and I don't think it will be too long before it's all cleared up."

Simons rested his chin against the backrest of the seat. "David, if you've got some information on this case that will prove somebody else did it, why don't you tell me about it?"

"Would you look off into it?"

"Sure, I would. I didn't set out to do anything to you personally. All I ever wanted was to see that the people who did those murders paid for it. If you can show me you didn't do it and that somebody else did, damn right, I'll look into it."

"Really?"

"I sure will. You come up with something that sounds reasonable and points a finger in another direction and I'll go look. If you didn't do it and can help us prove who did, I'll be the first to admit to the world that you're innocent. And I'll do everything I can to help you out of this mess."

"That's hard for me to believe."

For the first time Captain Weyenberg entered the conversation. "That's our job, David. If you didn't do it, we don't want you to go to jail. I'm like Truman—I think you did it. But if we had evidence that proved you didn't, I'd be the first one to stand up in front of everybody and say we made a mistake."

Spence turned his attention to the rearview mirror, looking at the reflection of the driver's face. "Yeah, but what are you going to do if they kill me and then, a couple of years later you find out that I didn't do it?"

"About all we could say," Simons said, "was that we fucked up."

"That's all?"

"I don't know what else I could say."

"You wouldn't have any feelings for me?"

"David," Simons said with a grin, "you would be gone."

Returning the conversation to the trial, Spence began attacking the testimony of the prosecution witnesses. "They were all lying," he said. "They were all part of the conspiracy."

"You keep talking about a damn conspiracy," Truman said. "Just who do you feel was conspiring against you?"

"Well," David said, "I don't really think it was Vic Feazell."

"He prosecuted your case, but he wasn't in on the conspiracy?" Simons asked.

"No, not really. He just got buffaloed. He didn't really know what was going on."

"Okay, then who are the conspirators?"

"I can't tell you. I'm not going to call any names."

"Well, let me guess, then. I guess I've got to be one of them, right?"

"I wasn't going to call any names."

"David, you aren't going to hurt my feelings. But why would I conspire against you? It doesn't make sense. I just believe you did it."

"Well, I didn't."

"Damn, David, what about all the evidence that came out in the trial?"

"It was all circumstantial. Like Jessie Ivy, He lied about all that stuff. He and those other guys down there at Eastham just didn't like me. He got up there and testified that I said something about 'dead people can't talk.' I never said those words. That isn't something I would say."

"That seems a little strange to me," Simons argued, "since one of the things Gilbert said about you on tape when he gave it up was your comment that 'dead people can't talk.' Hell, one of the first inmates I ever talked to said you told him all that stuff. It came up three or four different times, from different people. Sounds like your words to me."

"No," David said, "I never said that."

"Then you're saying everyone who got on the witness stand lied?"

"That's what I'm saying."

"What about Dorothy Miles?"

"Well, she wasn't lying, but they got her all confused about the dates. When I told her I thought I might have killed somebody, I wasn't talking about the Lake Waco murders. She just got it all screwed up in her mind."

Spence went on to criticize the testimony of Linda Kelton and Regina Rosenbaum. For reasons he couldn't explain, they had something against him and decided to lie.

"Yeah, David, everybody in the world was plotting against you," Simons said. "Who else lied?"

"Well, those black kids and that old man who said they were at Koehne Park. They didn't testify about hearing any screams or anything. If they had really been there when they said they were and had known anything, they would have testified about hearing the kids scream. They said they were right there close. But they didn't say anything about it, did they? They shouldn't have even been testifying."

Simons caught Captain Weyenberg's eye, then returned his attention to David. "There was never any evidence put on during the trial about where those kids were killed," he said.

"Yeah, there was." Suddenly David's eyes shifted. In his enthusiasm for the argument he had stepped out of bounds and had said something that he knew was incriminating. Indeed, from where the people said they had been sitting in Koehne Park, they should have been able to hear the noises that accompanied the murders taking place less than thirty yards away. Simons had thought even while they were testifying about being in Koehne Park and seeing an orange Pinto parked at the Circle that there was a good chance they had gotten the dates mixed up and had actually been there on the fourteenth, not the thirteenth.

Spence quickly changed the subject again.

*    *    *

Even before leaving Waco, Dan Weyenberg had told Simons he planned at some point in the trip to stop at a roadside park and suggest that they all get out and stretch their legs. "I want to see what David's reaction is," he said. "Let's see if he really does fall in the floorboard and start screaming for help."

"Want to get out and move around for a few minutes?" Weyenberg asked. He was disappointed at his passenger's quick acceptance of the offer.

A hitchhiker who had been seated at one of the concrete benches at the park eyed the handcuffs and chains on Spence and guns worn by the officers. He smiled weakly at Simons. "Morning," Truman said.

The man did not return his greeting. "Looks like this is someplace I don't need to be," he said, picking up a small bag and hurrying off in the direction of the highway.

After a few minutes Weyenberg was back at the wheel, urging Simons and David to get into the car. They rode in silence until they passed a sign which indicated they were but seven miles from Huntsville.

"Man, I didn't realize we were that close," David said. For the first time there was a hint of resignation in his voice.

"Time goes by fast when you're having fun," Simons joked.

"Yeah," David laughed, "good friends and all that kind of stuff."

"Just like in the beer commercials," Simons added.

Spence quickly became serious. "Truman," he said, "if I really came up with something on this case to show somebody else did it, would you really get off into it?"

"You've got my word on it," Simons said. "Look, David, I'm never going to get this case off my mind until I know every little detail and everything that happened out there that night. This thing is going to stay with me for a long time. I'm not going to just shut down and say I know everything, because I'm not comfortable that I do."

"Why don't you come down sometime and bring your notes on this case and read them to me. I can explain everything that everybody said."

"If that's the case," Simons replied, "why didn't you take the witness stand?"

"Well, my lawyers felt like I shouldn't."

"That really surprised me," Truman said, "because you

seemed to really enjoy testifying in your sexual abuse trial. I remember when you were even talking about defending yourself. Why didn't they want you to get up there?"

"Because I made that foolish statement one time—to you or Butler or Dennis Baier—that if you took me to court and found me guilty I would tell the whole story—tell about everything."

"Is that the only reason?" Simons asked.

"Yeah."

"Doesn't make much sense to me."

"We were sort of figuring you would get up there," David continued.

"David, I told you all along that I wouldn't be getting on the stand because I wouldn't be able to testify to what people told me. That's hearsay evidence, not admissible. And like I always told you, I would never be allowed to testify in court about the things you and I talked about because oral confessions are not admissible under Texas law. Hell, it was your side that subpoenaed me. Russ Hunt could have put me up there anytime he wanted to."

"He was afraid of what you might say."

"I would have damn sure told the truth."

"Well, I think they wanted to cross-examine you instead of putting you on as one of their witnesses."

"I can see where there might have been a problem for them. I imagine Butler or Feazell would have liked to cross-examine me, too. But you know, David, the only thing that really disappointed me about the trial was that I didn't feel like you had any defense at all. I felt like you could have had a better one. Russ Hunt and Hayes Fuller just got caught up in the whole thing and decided to make it a personal vendetta between them and Vic and just kind of overlooked your position in this thing. They didn't give you any defense at all. When the state puts on that much evidence, you've got to try to dispute it. I can't see how that jury would have held it against you if you had taken the stand and tried to explain away some of what they had heard. If you don't at least try, you're in trouble."

"We've got the answers for all that stuff," Spence said. "They're going to put it in the appeal and turn this thing around. And we've got some people looking into the whole thing."

"You referring to that letter your lawyers wrote to the feds?" Spence's eyes widened.

"Hell, David, I've read that thing. You and I both know it's a crock of shit. All that stuff Russ Hunt put in there was bullshit. The feds wouldn't touch it with a ten-foot pole because it was so ridiculous. Did you even read it?"

David nodded.

"Did you like what it said?"

"Well, there was a lot of it I didn't like."

"There was a lot of it I didn't like, either," Simons said. "Hunt alleging what a bad reputation I have and what a sorry bastard I am and saying I stole a bunch of electronic equipment from the Waco Police when I left. Those are just some of the things that got me pissed off at Russ Hunt—some of the things we're going to talk about one of these days."

"I want you to know I didn't have much to do with that. Russ just said he felt like if the federal authorities came in and looked around they might be able to come up with something that would help."

Simons knew time was running out and there were some other things he wanted to talk with Spence about before they arrived at the Diagnostic Center, where all incoming prisoners at the Texas Department of Corrections are processed.

"Let me ask you something else," he said. "You've been sitting back there, talking about how innocent you are and how you've been framed and all. Explain to me why everything that has come up has always pointed to you. When Gilbert confessed, he said, 'Me and David did it.' When Tony confessed, it was, 'Me, Gilbert, and David.' And all those inmates. David's always there . . ."

"Hey, Tony's just a wormy little kid and he was scared. He just said what he thought everybody wanted him to say."

"What about Gilbert?"

"He was told what to say before he ever gave his confession."

"No he wasn't, David. When we made that tape recording he was the only one doing the talking. Nobody fed him a bunch of leading questions. He sat there and rattled off the whole thing by himself. Hell, no, David, you haven't been framed. You're going down here because you're guilty."

"You're wrong," David said. "You'll find out one of these days."

Captain Weyenberg slowed and turned off the main highway

onto an access road leading to Huntsville. In just a couple of minutes they would be at the Diagnostic Center where Spence would be turned over to the TDC authorities.

The conversation died.

It was Simons who revived it. There was one more thing he needed to say. "David, there's one more thing we need to talk about," he said. "Frankly, it's been bothering me."

"What's that?"

"Remember back in the jail when we were up there talking every night. I told you then that I thought you were guilty but, still, we were pretty friendly for a while there. You brought that up several times—remember?—and I'd come back and say, 'Yeah, David, but you know you did that deal out at the lake and you're going to have to pay for it.' We went over that a lot of times, didn't we?"

"Yeah, we did."

"Back then I was telling you that it wasn't anything personal, just business. And I meant that. Or I felt like I did. But after I got away from all that and sat back and reevaluated the whole situation, I realized it wasn't true. David, it wasn't just business. It *was* personal."

Spence smiled weakly and nodded his head. "I can understand that." His reply was almost a whisper.

Inside the Diagnostic Center, Simons removed David's waist chains and handcuffs while Captain Weyenberg spoke with prison officials. Spence was then escorted to an area where a line of other incoming prisoners stood naked. Soon David too would have his clothing removed and his induction process would begin.

As Simons walked away he glanced back in Spence's direction. There was no smile on David's face, no look of anger in his eyes. His only expression was that of fear.

The warden had known Captain Weyenberg for a number of years and had come over to the Diagnostic Center reception area to invite him and Simons to lunch. As they sat in the prison guards' lunchroom, he questioned them at length on the lake murders case. His mother, he explained, lived in Hillsboro, near Waco, and had followed the case in the newspapers.

"When's your next trial coming up?" the warden asked.

"It looks like it will be the first of the year, maybe January,"

Simons said. "We're going to try Muneer Deeb."

"The Iranian or whatever the hell he is?"

"Yeah."

"Where's the trial going to be held?"

"It hasn't been definitely set yet, but there's some noises being raised about Cleburne. The judge up there has been talking like he would take it."

The warden smiled. "Cleburne's in Johnson County, right?"

Simons nodded.

"Well, if they do decide to try Mister Deeb up there, he just had a bad day."

Truman laughed. "What do you mean?"

"Folks out in Johnson County are pretty rednecked and conservative," the warden explained. "We got a lot of customers from that county and they always give out big time. If you've got a good case, they'll hang your boy out to dry."

As Simons and Weyenberg prepared to leave they returned to the reception area. Spence was standing near the wall, handcuffed and already dressed in his prison uniform. He had been given a haircut and the beard which he had grown again since the end of the trial had been shaved. He signaled for Truman to come over.

"You guys going back now?"

"Yeah," Simons said. "What are they fixing to do with you?"

David raised his arms to show the cuffs around his wrist. "I think they're going to take me over to the Ellis Unit."

"They don't fool around here, do they?"

"Sure don't," David said. He then paused for a second, stared at the concrete floor, then looked back at Simons. "You going to come see me?"

"You want me to?"

"Yeah, I'd like that."

"Well, drop me a line sometime. If I get an invitation, I might just surprise you," Truman said. "Good luck, David."

As he turned to go, Truman's attention was drawn to a small cut which the barber had evidently made while shaving Spence. A tiny stream of blood had run down the side of David's neck. For a second, it reminded Simons again of the night he had first seen Jill Montgomery. Saying no more, he turned and left.

Driving back toward Waco, Weyenberg was clearly relieved.

"That guy is something else," he said. "I've never been so glad to get rid of a prisoner. I don't know how you had the patience to talk to him like you did. It was kind of funny, though. I think when we got in the car this morning he was actually scared that something was going to happen to him. But it didn't take long for him to relax and start talking, did it?"

"I'm glad it worked out the way it did," Simons said. "I didn't want to leave things with David feeling a lot of animosity toward me. Maybe some day he'll decide he wants to talk about it and if he ever does, I want him to talk to me."

Back in Waco, Truman telephoned Russ Hunt but his secretary said he had left for the day. He then dialed the attorney's home number, only to hear a recording say Hunt was not in. He waited for the tone and left a message:

*"Russ, this is Truman Simons. I just thought I'd let you know I took David down to Diagnostic today and he said you were awfully concerned about his welfare if he had to ride down there with me. I just wanted to call and assure you he is safe and that I didn't do anything to him. When I left, they were getting ready to transfer him over to Ellis Unit. Probably by the time you hear this he'll be sitting on Death Row. He's comfortable and he's okay. I just thought you would like to know. Russ, I'll be seeing you . . . have a nice day."*

# 36

After watching the television reports of Spence's transfer to Huntsville earlier in the day, Gilbert Melendez had retreated to his cell, speaking to no one. The looming possibility of his being tried for capital murder and also winding up on Death Row had suddenly become a reality with which he was having great difficulty. He did not want to die.

Several times during David's trial Melendez had considered speaking with Truman Simons about the possibility of testifying, hoping perhaps that some kind of plea bargain with the district attorney's office could still be arranged. Since Tony had confessed—and even implicated him in the crime—there was no longer reason for Gilbert to continue trying to protect his brother. And he had begun to question the basis of his loyalty to David.

Now, though, he was concerned that he had blown his chance. By not telling the complete story in his initial statement, then recanting his second, he was not sure Vic Feazell would allow him another chance.

Gilbert finally decided to make an indirect approach to Simons through an inmate friend named Charles Blackshear. That evening while talking with his mother on the phone, Charles asked her to contact Simons and tell him that he needed to see him.

Simons had just returned home when he got the call. Immediately assuming that Blackshear might have something to tell him about Gilbert, Truman drove back to the jail and had the inmate called down.

"Gilbert wants to talk to you," Blackshear said as he sat drinking coffee with Simons in one of the small glass-enclosed interview rooms across from the booking desk. "I think he's ready to give it up, but he's worried that you guys won't talk to him anymore."

Truman laughed. "Hell, I'll talk to him."

"When?"

"I'll have him pulled right now."

Gilbert appeared nervous as he entered the interview room and shook hands with Simons. "How did David do on his trip down?" he asked.

Truman told him of Spence's fears that he might not make it to Huntsville alive. Gilbert laughed, then took a long drag on his cigarette. "You know," he said, "there were two or three times during the trial that I wrote out requests to see you."

"I never got any of them."

"I never sent them down. The more I thought about it, the more I was convinced that I couldn't get up on the witness stand and give him up."

In his years of dealing with criminals, Simons had learned to accept the code, the ground rules so many of them lived by. It was, in fact, a loyalty for which he held a begrudging admiration. "I can understand that," he said.

"But, hey, if I owed David anything," Gilbert continued, "I figure we're even now. Even though he was convicted, there's no way he can say I had anything to do with it. And I damn sure can't help him now. David's gone and Tony's made his deal, so I figure it's time for me to start thinking about Gilbert."

Simons nodded in agreement but said nothing.

"See, I'm not too crazy about the idea of going down there to Death Row. Seeing you guys taking David away on TV today sort of got to me."

"Gilbert," Simons interrupted, "what are we talking about here?"

Melendez's leg began to shake and his words ran together as he spoke. "I've been wondering if it's too late to make a deal."

"I'm not the one in a position to say," Truman responded, "but I would think there might still be some options open to you. But not if you're going to keep playing games. You're at a point where you've got to make up your mind whether you want to live or die. It's that simple.

"If you want to just go ahead and cop out, give it up, you're probably looking at three life sentences stacked. But that would mean you are probably going to die in the penitentiary. Doing twenty years for each sentence before ever coming up for parole would be tough. I don't think you can count on living sixty years down there."

"Not much of an option, is it?" Gilbert said.

"Not to my way of thinking," Simons said. "Look, I may be talking way out of school here, but Feazell is ready to get this whole lake murders business over with. I don't think he wants to make a career of trying this same case over and over. Butler feels the same way. It's gone on too long and hurt too many people. It could be that if you were willing to testify against Deeb, there might be something Vic could work out for you."

"What do you think the possibilities are?"

"I really can't say. I can tell you, though, that you would damn sure have to forget about playing any more games. It would have to be the one hundred percent truth—no bullshit— just straight down the line on what happened. Besides, I don't see where you owe that Arab anything."

Melendez leaned back in his chair and stared toward the ceiling for several seconds. "What do you think would happen if I testified?"

"I'm going to shoot straight with you," Simons said. "If we go to trial with what we've got on Deeb, I feel pretty comfortable that a jury will convict him. But I don't think the evidence we have is strong enough to get a death penalty. And that's not right, because none of this business with those kids would have ever happened if it hadn't been for Deeb.

"If you were to climb up on that witness stand and tell what happened that night, it would be a different ball game. I think the jury would hang him."

What Simons was saying encouraged Melendez. Truman's admission that the district attorney's office was far from confident that it could get the death penalty for Deeb's role in the murders meant that he might still have some bargaining power. Maybe he still had some say about whether he would live or die.

"You know," Gilbert said, "I wasn't sure you would come talk to me. I appreciate it. If you would, I'd like for you to talk to Feazell and see if there's still something we can work out."

Simons finished his coffee and looked at Gilbert. "You understand I can't make you any promises. I don't even want you to get your hopes up. But, yeah, I'll see what the district attorney has to say and get back to you."

Melendez had relaxed considerably during the half hour he and Simons had been talking. "There's something else I'd like to talk to you about before you go," he said.

"What's that?"

"I want to apologize to you for all the problems we had earlier. I know I caused you to take a lot of shit you didn't deserve."

"You didn't cause me any shit," Truman said. "It's part of my job."

"I just want you to understand that the reason I lied at first was because of my brother. See, I was ready to die for him if it came to it. But apparently he didn't feel the same way about me. Hell, he just rolled over me like a freight train. That really disappointed me. We might have had a chance if he hadn't given it up like he did."

"I really don't think your brother gave you up," Simons said. "You have to remember, Gilbert, we already knew you were involved. Your confession wasn't complete, but we knew you were out there that night. Tony didn't really tell us much we didn't already know. All he did was save his own ass, and I respect him for that. And you should, too. I really don't think you should hold anything against him.

"See, he's not ex-con like you and David. He didn't know the rules you guys have set up for yourselves. And when he first came in here I was pretty tough on him. He was scared to death and I played a lot of games with him. Sometimes I get lucky and win. But I don't think you should be critical of Tony for that."

"I don't know," Gilbert said. "I don't think I'll ever want to be around him again."

"Well," Truman said, "there's not much I can tell you about that. It's up to you. You've got to make your own decisions."

"Yeah, I know. Sometimes that isn't easy to do, is it?"

"I think maybe you made a pretty good one tonight."

Gilbert nodded and extended his hand. "Thanks for coming," he said.

Even before he approached Feazell, Simons knew the district attorney would be receptive to allowing Gilbert to testify against Deeb. The case had already begun to wear on everyone's nerves. If Gilbert would plead guilty, give a complete statement about what took place on the night of July 13, 1982, and then take the stand against Deeb he could help bring the whole thing to an end. The case had been a hardship on too many people for too long. It was time to begin thinking about finally putting the kids to rest.

Feazell agreed. Though he greatly disliked Gilbert, he was willing to let him plead guilty to two of the three murder counts against him in exchange for life sentences and his testimony.

"One of the things he's concerned about," Simons said, "is going back down to TDC after he testifies and getting killed by some of those folks who don't particularly care for snitches. I'd like for us to look into having him sent to a federal pen if he does testify."

"If he's willing to shoot straight and help us get this thing wrapped up," Feazell said, "I think we can do that."

"If I can tell him that," Simons replied, "I think we're in business."

"Then tell him."

Truman relayed Feazell's message to Melendez and, not wanting to appear too eager, suggested Gilbert think about it for a few days before making a final decision. There was little to do but wait; let him cool his heels for a while.

A few days later Simons was sitting in the D.A.'s office with Willie Tompkins, who had gone back into law enforcement and was now an investigator assigned to the district attorney's office. "Let's go for a ride," Truman suggested.

As he drove down Lake Shore Drive in the direction of the lake, Truman found himself wondering just how many times he had made the trip since the murders had occurred; how many times he had made that sharp left turn into Koehne Park in the last two years.

"You're pretty familiar with this place," Tompkins said.

"I don't even have to steer anymore," Truman replied. "If I don't head toward home when I leave the parking lot, my car just automatically heads in this direction."

"We looking for something?"

"Just looking," Truman said.

Parking by the dumpster near the entrance to the Circle, they got out and walked down the small incline to the wooded area where Tony Melendez had led officials after confessing. "This is where it happened," Simons said. His observation was not directed at Tompkins; rather, it was simply a statement of fact to himself.

Nothing more was said as the two officers walked through the shaded area. Because of the demands of Spence's trial, Truman had not been back to the park since the trip he had made with Tony. He stood, lost in his own thoughts, as Willie looked on silently.

For several minutes Simons and Tompkins walked the area, taking different routes, occasionally stopping to pick up some bit of discarded trash, look at it, then toss it away. As he approached a tree near the vine-covered gully which bordered the area, Simons was suddenly keenly aware of the feeling he had experienced so many times before while investigating a homicide. This was the area Tony had pointed to when showing them approximately where Jill had been killed. Truman could not explain it, but the residue of violence seemed to permeate the air.

Picking up a small tree limb, he began digging around in the heavy layer of leaves which covered the ground in front of him. He had cleared a space no larger than eighteen inches in diameter when his attention was drawn to a tiny gold serpentine bracelet. Picking it up, he rubbed the dirt from it and held it in the palm of his hand.

It had never been mentioned that Jill had worn a bracelet on that day she and Raylene had come to Waco, yet Simons felt a rush of excitement as he looked at the small piece of jewelry. If it was Jill's, he finally had physical evidence that put her in the wooded area where Tony said the murders took place.

Not far from where Truman found the bracelet, Willie Tompkins uncovered a tube of mascara and an eyeliner pencil. There was no way to prove whether they had been Jill's, but Simons felt sure that they marked the spot where Spence had gone through her purse after he had killed her.

Returning to the office, Simons placed a call to Jan Thompson and asked if she would find out if Jill had owned a bracelet like the one he had found.

Two days later Simons again returned to Koehne Park, this time accompanied by Gilbert Melendez. Gilbert had agreed to once again reconstruct the crime, this time including his brother in the events which took place. As they entered the park, Melendez was silent for a time before he spoke. "I know this is probably going to sound crazy," he said, "but I can still feel everything in the air—just like it was that night."

"I think I understand," Truman replied.

Gilbert showed how he, Tony, and David had entered the park, where they had met the teenagers, and the route Spence had taken as they started to leave. "After he and the brunette got into it," Gilbert said, "David pulled the car down into there."

He was, just as Tony had, pointing toward the same wooded area. Walking the same path Simons and Tompkins had taken earlier, Gilbert pointed out where the car had been parked. He pointed out the tree where Kenneth Franks had been placed. Then, walking in the direction of the gully, he stopped under a tree. "David brought the brunette over here," he said.

He was standing just a few inches from where Simons had found the bracelet.

In Waxahachie, Nancy Shaw had been looking through a photo album her daughter had kept and happened on a photograph she had forgotten about. Rod had taken it during a visit to Waco when Jill was still working at Fort Fisher. In it, her smiling daughter had her arm draped over a stone statue of a dog. On her left wrist was a small gold bracelet.

# 37

The Thompson house was bright and festive, the smell of the Christmas cedar mixing with the warm, spicy aromas from the kitchen. It was Christmas Eve, 1984, and, as was their tradition, there would be an elaborate dinner of turkey and dressing, cranberry sauce, and pecan pie; then there would be singing of carols; and, finally, the highlight of the evening: the exchange of gifts.

Jan Thompson loved the Christmas season, the cards from people she had not seen or heard from in ages, the shopping, the cooking, decorating the tree. And she liked having her family at home, gathered to share an evening away from all outside distractions. All that day friends and neighbors had dropped by to say hello and drink a glass of spiced tea and comment on how beautiful the tree which Robert had selected was.

Early in the evening Jan's son-in-law, Charlie, returned from a quick trip to the store to pick up some forgotten item needed to make the upcoming dinner perfect. The moment he walked into her kitchen, the holiday spirit erased from his face, she knew something was wrong.

In a halting whisper which he hoped would not attract the attention of those sitting in the living room, he said, "I've got to talk to you."

Jan Thompson checked the stove to make certain there was nothing that couldn't be left unattended for a few minutes. "Let's go into the back bedroom," she said.

At the store Charlie had been stopped by a friend who had appeared extremely upset. The friend told him that someone he knew was in danger and needed help getting a gun for protection. "The guy looking for the gun," Charlie told his mother-in-law, "might even know something about Jill's death."

Jan, feeling a sudden chill, tried hard to grasp the strange scenario her son-in-law was explaining, listening carefully to a list of names she had never before heard.

A young man named Roger Lowe had told Charlie's friend that some men who had previously lived in Waxahachie had returned and were now looking for him.

"This guy Lowe," Charlie continued, "says Jill and Raylene stopped by his house the day they left for Waco. They were wanting to buy some marijuana. Supposedly, he told them he didn't have any except a little for his own use and suggested they go see some guy named Lou Martinez. I don't know the guy.

"It's all pretty crazy, I know, but he says the girls supposedly went to see this Martinez guy, then went back to Lowe's place. The guy I was talking to says he figures maybe somebody went to Waco with them. And that he heard these other guys—the guys who are back in town—followed them. What do I do?" Charlie asked. "This guy wants me to meet with Lowe and hear what he has to say."

"Why you?"

"He knows I'm related to Jill's family."

Jan shook her head, still confused by the sudden unwelcome intrusion on her Christmas Eve preparations. "Charlie, do you know any of these people? Who are they? Why are they saying these things now?"

"I don't know. All I know is the guy is supposed to be pretty scared. He told this guy I talked to that he'd seen these men kill somebody back in 1979. Says he was actually there and saw it. They left town after that, he says, and lived somewhere down in the Valley. Rio Grande City, I think. Supposedly, they've just been in and out of Waxahachie since then."

"Why would they be after this man?"

"I don't know. Maybe they're afraid he's going to tell somebody about what he saw. I just don't know. But he wants me to help him get a gun."

Jan stood, her legs suddenly weak, straining to support her weight. "Wait here," she said.

In the living room she got her husband's attention and he followed her back to the bedroom where her son-in-law again told his story. "If this guy does know something about what happened to Jill," Charlie said, "I think maybe I ought to go meet him."

Robert Thompson stood silent for some time. Finally he spoke.

"No. No way," he said firmly. "It just doesn't make any sense."

"Maybe I ought to try to talk with him by phone," Charlie suggested.

"We're not going to spoil Christmas," Robert Thompson said, then turned and left the room. Too many holidays had already been ruined in the last couple of years.

Even as they talked, the man Charlie had talked with at the store was at his brother's house nearby, borrowing a pistol and fifteen rounds of ammunition to give to Roger Lowe.

Late that night, after all the presents had been opened and the guests had left, Jan and Robert talked about the curious story their son-in-law had told. Robert could tell that the episode had upset his wife, and he tried to convince her the story was nothing more than the invention of some crackpot. If there was anything to it, it would have come up before now. Surely all the investigating into the kids' deaths by the Waco Police, the D.A.'s office, and the Waxahachie Police would have turned up something like this. Somebody would have seen the girls going by people's houses that day. Besides, the people responsible for the murders were in custody. There had never been any link between the killers and anyone in Waxahachie.

"I know," Jan said. "The best thing to do is just forget about it."

Robert kissed her and smiled. "You're right. Merry Christmas," he said.

Neither slept well that night.

Two days later Jan placed a call to Waxahachie Police Chief Charles Sullins, her distant cousin, and asked if he could stop by the house.

After Jan told him the strange story, Sullins said he had picked up Roger Lowe just the night before. He had a bag of marijuana and a gun on him at the time of his arrest.

Lowe had told the police much the same story he had tried to relay to the Thompsons by way of their son-in-law. "The kid's definitely scared," Sullins told Jan, "but his brain is so burned up with drugs that it's hard to believe anything he's saying. He's paranoid, no doubt about that. But frankly, I don't believe his story."

Sullins had checked the police records and those at the Ellis

County sheriff's office for any unsolved murder which might have taken place in 1979 and had found none. "This guy may have some people after him," he said, "but I don't think it has anything to do with any murder he saw take place."

"Did you ask him if he knew the girls?"

Sullins hesitated for a moment, then said, "Yeah, he told me he knew Raylene. He even said the Rices had come by his house the day after the girls disappeared, asking if he'd seen them."

Two weeks later Roger Lowe walked into the Waxahachie Monument Company and asked to see Rod Montgomery. Without any preliminaries he asked in a rapid, breathless voice, "How satisfied are you that they've got the right people in your daughter's murder?" Not even waiting for an answer, he went on to explain that he knew things about Jill's death that could get him killed. He had tried to talk with others in the family and they wouldn't help. He'd even spoken with the police. He had to have help, a gun—a machine gun. Could Rod help him?

When Rod Montgomery refused, Lowe began to elaborate. The men who were after him had followed the girls to Waco, followed them back, then killed them in Waxahachie. Then they had taken the bodies back to Waco. He even knew where the car was that had been involved in the crime, he said. "That's where the girls' things, their purses, stuff like that, were. They burned it. I'll show you if you want me to."

Swept into the bizarre story being told by his strange visitor, Rod Montgomery said he would like to see the car.

"It's a Maverick," Lowe told him. "It's out at a junkyard."

At the junkyard on the outskirts of town, Lowe led Rod Montgomery to a Maverick which had obviously been burned from the rear forward. Inside the trunk were charred bits of clothing.

His hands shaking and his nostrils filled with the acrid smell of ashes, Rod Montgomery rummaged silently through the pieces of cloth for several minutes. Suddenly he felt a dizzy sickness. He could feel the rush of his own blood, pounding at his temples. What if he did find some of Jill's clothing? Maybe her purse?

There was nothing he recognized.

"Who the hell are you?" Rod asked, anger mounting as he turned away from the car and faced the young man who had driven him to the junkyard. The fright he sensed in the man was something almost tangible.

"I just want you to believe me," Lowe said. "Those guys are gonna get me." He now sounded like a small child, pleading to be believed lest he be punished for the real truth.

On New Year's Eve, Ned Butler received a call at home from Ramon Salinas. He was obviously excited. The Waxahachie police chief had called, he said, thinking he might be interested in hearing a strange story that had recently been related to him about the Lake Waco murders. Salinas quickly told the story to the assistant district attorney, then asked, "You want me to go down there and see what I can find out?"

Ned Butler took a deep breath, an exercise he does when trying to fight back anger. This time it didn't work. "Goddammit, Ramon," he said, "we've got the bastards who killed those kids. We've chased crazies all over the fucking state of Texas on this thing. But that's over. We've got the right people. I know it. You know it. And they know it."

Ramon Salinas did not bother to wish Ned Butler a happy new year before hanging up.

Still angry, Butler reflected for a moment on the irony of the fact that, following the indictments, City Manager Dave Smith had spoken at a local civic club gathering and praised the Waco Police for "solving the Lake Murders."

He cursed again and returned to the football game he was watching on television. He would be glad when the Deeb trial got under way. Then, finally, the world would get a detailed account of what really happened to Jill Montgomery, Raylene Rice, and Kenneth Franks that night so long ago.

# 38

The atmosphere surrounding the Deeb trial would be a drastic departure from that which had accompanied the David Spence proceedings. The curiosity of many Waco residents, it seemed, had been satisfied by the testimony, news reports, and conviction of the previous summer. And despite the difficulty of the task facing them, members of the district attorney's office had found it impossible to generate the same enthusiasm for their prosecution of Muneer Deeb. Their trial preparation had been self-enforced labor. The truth was, they were all becoming weary of the seemingly endless case.

Vic Feazell had seriously considered turning the task of prosecuting Deeb over to Ned Butler and first assistant Pat Murphy. A number of friends, concerned with his political career, had pointed out to the D.A. that his public popularity was at an all-time high after the successful prosecution of Spence. It was something Feazell should consider since his term in office was drawing to a close and a reelection campaign was on the horizon. The Deeb trial, it was suggested, offered Vic a no-win situation. He would be expected to get a conviction against Deeb; therefore he could not anticipate a victory to be applauded in the same manner as the Spence decision. On the other hand, should the jury find Deeb innocent, much of the public support gained during the first trial might be negated.

Feazell wrestled with the pros and cons. The trial would require a six-weeks absence from his office where a myriad of other matters demanded attention. Too, there was the awareness that gaining a death penalty decision in a complicated murder-for-hire case wherein the defendant was clearly not directly involved in the crime was judged by many to be one of the most difficult challenges a prosecutor could face. Yet anything less than the death penalty, Feazell knew, would be looked upon as a failure.

Sitting in the den of his fashionable home one early-January weekend, alternately watching as son Greg played at his feet and staring out the back window into the cold, damp day, Vic weighed the pluses and minuses. Berni, returning home from a trip to the supermarket, immediately recognized her husband's pensive mood and sat beside him on the couch, leaving the task of putting away the groceries for later. She held his hand but said nothing.

Vic placed his arm around her shoulder and gently pulled her closer. "I'm going to Cleburne," he said.

Berni, not surprised at the decision, smiled. "I knew that a long time ago."

"We promised the families we would see this thing through," he said. "And that's what we're going to do."

The first snow of winter hit Waco on a Sunday afternoon in early February as Feazell, Butler, and Simons met at the courthouse annex to load their cars for the sixty-five-mile trip to Cleburne. The enthusiasm each had privately hoped would develop as time to begin the jury selection phase of the trial neared was still absent as they quietly went about the task of placing boxes of files into the trunks along with a portable coffee maker and other items necessary for setting up an "office" away from home. Dread followed their steps as they contemplated being isolated from their families and familiar surroundings. Cleburne, with its 19,000 population, existed primarily as a shipping terminal for the Santa Fe railroad and as a shopping place for area dairy farmers. It was not the most idyllic place to spend six weeks.

A change of venue trial, particularly a lengthy one, presents something of a logistical nightmare for all involved. Attorneys, forced to anticipate every possible turn the proceedings might take, have to be certain they have gathered everything from their offices which pertains to the case. Then there is the complicated schedule of transporting witnesses. In this case many of them would be from Waco, but others would have to be flown into the Dallas-Fort Worth International airport, an hour's drive away. Simons' primary responsibility would be to taxi those who were to testify.

Late that Sunday evening, after having checked into the Gate One Motel on the outskirts of Cleburne, Feazell knocked on the door of the room where Butler and Simons were watching television. He burst into the room, a smile spilling across his face.

"I don't know why," he announced, "but I'm suddenly feeling good about this trial."

Ned and Truman, ironically, had just been talking about their own sudden rush of adrenalin since arriving.

Butler, stretched out on the bed, wearing a pair of cutoff jeans, grinned. Now, he felt confident; everyone had his game face on. "Old *Manure* Deeb's not going to enjoy his stay in Johnson County," he said. Throughout the next several weeks he would purposely mispronounce the defendant's name.

"It's *Mew-neer*," Simons laughed, drawing out the two syllables correctly.

"He's shit to me," Butler replied.

As voir dire got underway, the attorneys were not the only ones who noticed the different atmosphere surrounding the trial. Nancy Shaw and Jan Thompson had driven from Waxahachie on the first day of jury selection and had immediately found the dark gray marble interior of the Johnson County courthouse lacking in warmth or welcome. Their stay, the two women immediately recognized, would be considerably less comfortable in Cleburne. In Waco, they had been made welcome in the district attorney's office library during breaks in the proceedings. There they could have coffee and remove themselves from the frantic attention accompanying the trial. In Cleburne, Simons informed them, there would be only the hard wooden benches outside the courtroom or the small sitting room adjacent to the women's rest room on the first floor.

Having been subpoenaed as a witness, Nancy was unable to enter the courtroom during the questioning of prospective jurors. As she sat in the hallway outside, the elderly bailiff approached her and expressed concern that she was not allowed in the courtroom. "I know," he said, "that you would like to be in there, what with your son being on trial and all." Mistakenly, he had assumed she was the mother of Muneer Deeb.

"That's not my son," she angrily shot back. "He's the man who killed my daughter." The bailiff, his face suddenly flushed, profusely apologized. He would say nothing else to Nancy throughout the remainder of the trial.

"I'm not going to like this place," Nancy remarked to Vic later during lunch.

\* \* \*

Butler seemed to be enjoying the generally repetitious process of questioning potential jurors. The questions he and Feazell posed to those called were relatively brief and to the point, while defense attorney Richard McCall rambled, sometimes taking as much as an hour and a half questioning each panelist. His co-counsel, Jack Holcomb, did much the same. It was clear to Ned that McCall, who he knew would orchestrate the defense, was alienating jurors even before the trial began with his confusing and incomplete questions. More than once a prospective juror listened as one of McCall's questions turned into three, sometimes four, unrelated questions before an answer was sought. Then the attorney would display frustration when the person he had been questioning indicated a lack of understanding.

As the process continued, Ned Butler, an art major in college, would at times leave the prosecution table and position himself in the front row of the courtroom for a vantage point from which to draw quick pencil sketches of McCall as he questioned prospective jurors. Beneath one extremely accurate likeness, Ned wrote the question which McCall had asked each of those called to the courtroom: "Can you give my client Muneer here a fair trial just like you would a good ol' Johnson County boy?"

Several days into voir dire, Butler seized an opportunity to make it clear to McCall that the state had done its homework well. As the defense attorney was again explaining how Deeb, despite being a Jordanian, was a legal resident of the United States, Ned finally rose to object, pointing out to the judge that he was tired of hearing the claim. "Your honor," he said, "the fact of the matter is, the legality of Mister Deeb's citizenship is very much in question."

Though he smiled weakly, McCall was clearly taken aback as Butler explained to the court how the defendant had paid Marcie Blackwood $500 to marry him the previous May. "The only reason we have not reported this to the U.S. Immigration and Naturalization Service," the assistant D.A. said, "is because violation of immigration law is secondary to capital murder charges and would therefore be moot."

Deeb had not bothered to tell his lawyers of his marital status. The incident provided a hint of events to come. As the trial continued, it would become apparent that Deeb had not been truthful with his attorneys about a number of things.

\*     \*     \*

On the day the twelfth juror was selected in Cleburne, Patty Pick received a letter from Muneer Deeb. It was the first time she had heard from him since he had been moved to the Johnson County jail for his trial. Enclosed was a five-dollar bill and, unlike some of the chatty, rambling letters he had written her over the past year and a half, this one was brief, obviously written with a solitary purpose.

The money, he wrote, was for the purchase of a record which he asked that Patty buy and give to Kasey Rowe as quickly as possible.

The song, titled "Careless Whisper," was popular at the time and Patty was generally familiar with the lyrics. That Deeb would choose that particular song to send to Kasey seemed odd to her. After reading the letter several times, she decided to call Truman Simons.

"What's the song about?" he asked.

"I think you ought to get the record and just listen to it," Patty said.

Simons, a man who freely admits to a nostalgic craving for the popular music of the fifties and still owns most of the 45 rpm releases of Elvis Presley, knew little about modern rock music. The first disc jockey Truman called, in hopes of having him play the song, told him he'd never heard of it.

"It's supposed to be one of the most popular songs out right now," Simons argued. "It's by some group called Wham."

"Well, it ain't on the country charts, pal," the deejay replied.

Embarrassed, Simons hung up and began looking through the phone book for the call letters of a station whose musical format ran more to Wham and Prince than Tammy Wynette and Willie Nelson.

After waiting several minutes for another disc jockey to get off the air, Simons heard the song played for him over the phone. Making hurried notes of some of the lyrics as the song played, Truman began to smile. As soon as he hung up the phone, he left the office to pay his first visit to a record store in ten years.

Shortly thereafter Simons was playing the song on his own stereo. He listened to it several times, at first having difficulty hearing the words over the electrified instruments. Finally, after replaying the song a half dozen times, he began to carefully transcribe several of the lines:

> *"Time can never mend*
> *The careless whisper of a good friend*
> *To the heart and mind, ignorance is kind*
> *There's no comfort in the truth*
> *Pain is all you'll find . . ."*

and . . .

> *I'm never gonna dance again*
> *Guilty feet have got no rhythm . . ."*

and . . .

> *Should have known better than to cheat a friend . . .*
> *Is what I did so wrong, so wrong*
> *That you had to leave me alone?"*

For a long time Simons sat, staring at the legal pad on which he had written the lines. There was a message there. He was sure of it. This was no plaintive prisoner's love song. Hell no, Deeb, who knew Kasey had talked with Truman, was telling her something.

Truman's recollection of their first conversation so long ago still infuriated him. He could still hear her whining voice: "I'm real sorry about what happened to those kids," she had said, "but I needed things. I needed money for things . . ." In Truman's mind, she was as responsible for the murders as the man who was about to be tried. "The bitch," he said to himself.

Studying the lyrics he had copied down, Truman began to underline phrases: ". . . *careless whisper of a good friend . . . there's no comfort in the truth . . . guilty feet have got no rhythm . . . is what I did so wrong?*"

After a while he called Patty to thank her for telling him about the letter. "Sounds like he's trying to get a message to somebody," Simons said.

"That's kind of what I thought," Patty replied.

"Well, look, just forget it. Don't mention anything to Kasey."

"I wasn't going to. This whole business is getting to me." She sounded near tears.

"It's going to be over soon," Truman assured her. "You get

up on that stand and tell what you've got to tell, and it will be all over. Believe me."

"I hope so," she said.

Simons knew the ordeal had been trying for Patty. Since the time Deeb had been released after that first arrest back in 1982, she had helped Simons to keep up with the man he felt certain had been involved in the murders. She had reported telephone calls and letters she had received from Deeb while he was in Dallas and Houston and during his brief travels into New Mexico. Patty had not enjoyed keeping the lines of communication open with Muneer but had done it at the request of Simons and Willie Tompkins. She had never dealt dishonestly with anyone and it wasn't easy for her—not even with someone accused of murder. The only reason she had agreed to do it was her trust in Simons and Tompkins—and her own belief that Deeb was, in fact, guilty.

Though the state had trimmed its list of witnesses to thirty-five, it would present much the same case it had during the Spence trial. During his opening statement to the jury of seven men and five women, Feazell said the prosecution would prove that Deeb had purchased an insurance policy which included a $20,000 accidental death clause for Gayle Kelley, making himself the beneficiary and then asking David Spence if he knew anyone who would kill her.

For the first time the jurors seated in Judge John MacLean's 249th District Court heard how the bizarre scheme had been botched by Spence and his two accomplices. They also heard the promise of something which jurors in the Spence trial had hoped for but never realized: Feazell indicated that they would hear testimony from one of those actually involved in the commission of the unspeakable crime.

The first week of the trial followed a course much like that traveled months earlier in Waco. Again carefully weaving the story, Feazell and Butler called Richard Franks and Nancy Shaw to the stand to recount the agonizing hours prior to learning their children had been found dead. The men who had happened on the bodies at Speegleville repeated their stories as did Deeb's business partners, the insurance salesman, and Willie Tompkins.

Nancy was relieved when McCall and Holcomb agreed to allow her to sit in on the remainder of the trial after she had given her testimony. As she listened along with the others in the courtroom, the focus of the testimony quickly began to center on Muneer Deeb.

Nervous and refusing to look in Muneer's direction, Patty Pick took the stand to tell how women, particularly Kasey Rowe, had taken advantage of the defendant by encouraging him to give them expensive gifts and cash. Her testimony was the first to hint that there was a violent side to the well-dressed, composed young man sitting in the defendant's chair. She told how she had repeatedly tried to make him understand that he was being used. "Finally," Patty said, "there came a time when I think he realized what was going on. One night as we were talking he told me that he should have killed Kasey a long time ago; that she was the reason for everything that had happened to him—including the lake murders."

Patty recounted an earlier time in Skaggs when a drunken customer had entered and began making advances toward her as she was stocking shelves. "Muneer came over to us," she related, "acting really mad, and said he was going to do something to the man." Certain Deeb was no fighter, she had laughed off the matter, telling him to leave the man alone. Deeb had then explained to her, "I won't do it; I'll have somebody else do it. I know someone who does that sort of thing. If you have money, you can do anything."

Cynthia Bernal was again called to relate the story of Spence's arrival at the apartment she and Ray Payne had shared, screaming that he had heard a radio report about a "Gayle" being killed and thinking Deeb had murdered Gayle Kelley. After hearing her story, Feazell posed a question he had not asked the young woman in Waco. "Cynthia," he said, "just before you took the stand, you related an incident to me that took place earlier today."

"Yes sir."

"Would you please repeat it for the benefit of the jury?"

Looking in the direction of the jury box, Cynthia spoke softly. "A while ago," she said, "when I came into the courthouse, I saw Gayle Kelley. But in my mind, as I looked at her, I kept seeing Jill Montgomery's face. It was eerie. It scared me."

"You knew Gayle and Jill at the Methodist Home, didn't you?" Feazell asked.

"Yes I did."

\* \* \*

While Cynthia was testifying, Gayle Kelley and Patti Deis were waiting in Truman Simons' room at the Gate One Motel. Patti, who was now in the military service, had returned to the States from Germany on an extended leave after receiving her subpoena. Gayle had flown from Houston to Dallas earlier that morning. They were glad to see each other again, but both dreaded testifying. Gayle in particular was nervous and had brought a couple of joints with her. She was pacing in the room, trying to figure some place she could smoke one. "I don't think it would be too smart to smoke here in Truman's room," she laughed. "Be hell to get busted by the guy who has our plane tickets home." Instead, she picked up the phone and ordered a pizza.

On the stand the following morning, Gayle was determined to let Muneer Deeb know she was not intimidated by his presence. When she first took the stand he had smiled at her and even waved. Several times, as she once more told the story of his renting the apartment for her, his purchase of the insurance policy, and the anger he had displayed toward Kenneth Franks, she looked in the direction of Deeb and returned his smile.

When Judge MacLean called a recess shortly after noon, Feazell waited until he and Gayle were outside the courtroom; then, glaring at her, he motioned her into an empty office. Once inside with the door closed, he exploded.

"What are you trying to do up there?" he asked. "We're talking about a guy who wanted to have you killed, and . . . and *you're up there flirting with him*. What kind of show are you trying to put on?"

Feazell was pacing, waving his arms, continuing his tirade. "You did a good job in Waco. You handled yourself well and you just answered the questions. You were just yourself. Now you're acting like some kind of star. You're making a fool of yourself."

The tension which Gayle had managed to hide while on the witness stand broke through. Now angry and hurt, she started to cry and curse the district attorney. "Goddamn you," she said, "I'm doing the best I know how. What you see is what you get. I didn't ask for this shit. I'm sick and tired of you and these trials. You and everybody else can just go fuck off!"

Feazell stormed from the room.

A few minutes later Simons entered to find Gayle still crying. Puzzled, he asked what had happened. Sobbing, she spewed more curses at Feazell as she told Truman about her encounter with the D.A.

Her story bothered Simons. Though he had not been in the courtroom to hear her testimony, he felt Feazell had overreacted. "Vic's feeling a lot of pressure," he said. "This trial's pretty important to him. It isn't going to be easy to convince the jury that Deeb was involved in the murders. We're fighting an uphill battle here, and what you have to say is very important. That's what you've got to remember. I don't want you thinking about anything else. If you want to kick Vic's ass after this is all over, fine. Maybe I'll even help you. But for now you've got to get yourself together and do what you came here to do."

Gayle took the cigarette he offered and smiled faintly. "I'm doing the best I can," she said.

"That's all we're asking," Simons said. "Let's go get something to eat."

During the afternoon session, Gayle was more subdued as she answered the questions of Feazell, then McCall on cross-examination. She had not, however, been as good a witness as the prosecution had hoped.

"Our mistake," Butler said, "was praising her so highly in Waco. There she was natural. Hell, she had the jury eating out of her hand."

"But not this time," the worried Feazell said.

"Oh, I don't know," Ned said. "There are a half dozen people in that jury box who have kids about her age. I think they were able to cut through the bullshit and hear what she had to say."

"I hope you're right," Vic replied.

By the time the trial entered its second week, several members of the jury had already begun to form strong opinions about Deeb's guilt. They had seen the crime scene photos and heard the medical examiner discuss the torture the victims had endured before their deaths. And they had heard the convincing testimony of odontologist Dr. Homer Campbell. The mindless brutality of the crime had been vividly brought home to them. That a man's greed could have triggered such a horrible act was almost beyond comprehension. More and more, the jurors watched the actions of Deeb as he sat between his attorneys, alternately hunching forward to make notes on a legal pad and leaning back in his chair to smirk at the witnesses.

The jury was also becoming increasingly irritated with the manner in which McCall conducted his cross-examinations. He often ventured far from the subject before an objection from the state or an admonition of the judge redirected his questioning. And in the privacy of the jury room, several of the women discussed Holcomb's habit of constantly cleaning his fingernails while testimony was underway. In time a pot was started with each of the jurors offering a guess as to when Holcomb would wash his unkempt hair.

The air of electricity which had permeated the Spence trial finally visited Cleburne on the first Tuesday in March. Word that Gilbert Melendez would testify had spread and the courtroom was filled to capacity. Television crews and newspaper reporters from Dallas and Fort Worth joined members of the Waco media in the crowded courthouse rotunda.

Jack Holcomb stood smoking a cigarette near the entrance to Judge MacLean's chambers, telling McCall about an ironic bit of information he had just learned. "When I was a little kid we had a basketball goal on the garage in our driveway," he said, "and everyone in the neighborhood congregated there to play. Several times there was this short Mexican kid who came over and joined us. I don't think I ever knew his name. Well, I was talking to a friend of mine the other day and he told me who it was."

McCall rolled his eyes, already anticipating the punch line.

"That's right," Holcomb said. "It was Gilbert Melendez."

Among the new faces in the courtroom was that of David Spence's mother. As she stood alone in the hallway, Richard Franks positioned himself several feet away, focusing his camera on her, repeatedly snapping pictures. Tommy Witherspoon, a reporter for the *Waco Herald-Tribune*, watched the strange scene. "I wonder," he asked a fellow journalist, "what a psychiatrist would have to say about all that?"

Entering the courtroom, Juanita White took a seat beside a pleasant gray-haired woman seated on the third row. Pat Murphy, the assistant district attorney, had watched Mrs. White as she entered and, as soon as she was seated, jumped to his feet and quickly sought out the bailiff. "I'd appreciate it," he whispered, "if you would go over there and explain to the lady who just came in that the section where she's sitting is reserved for members of the victims' families."

The bailiff, who knew the section to which he was referring was not reserved, seemed hesitant as Murphy discreetly pointed out Mrs. White. Murphy, not wishing to explain further, became more firm. "Look, she's going to make a lot of people uncomfortable if she sits there during the testimony. Just ask her to move, okay?" The confused bailiff shrugged. He did not know that the woman seated next to Juanita White was Maude Simons, Truman's mother.

By the time Melendez was called to the stand, Mrs. White was seated at the back of the courtroom. Near the front, Nancy Shaw sat with Jan and Robert Thompson, tensely clutching a handkerchief. The night before, Simons had visited her at the motel to ask once again if she was sure she wanted to hear Gilbert Melendez's testimony. He knew how badly she felt the need to know what had happened to her daughter, yet he was concerned over how she would react listening to the grisly details. She assured Truman that she could handle whatever Gilbert had to say.

Clean-shaven, with his hair neatly trimmed, and wearing a three-piece suit which appeared a size too large for his small frame, Gilbert looked much younger than his twenty-nine years as he took the stand. He purposely had not worn his glasses so he would not be able to see clearly those in attendance in the courtroom. A hush fell over the crowd, and Feazell began the questioning.

Melendez told of meeting Spence and his brother, Tony, that afternoon of July 13 and of their eventual arrival at Koehne Park. He told of David's mention that Deeb had been "ripped off" on a drug deal. As Feazell posed his questions in a deliberate fashion, Gilbert explained how the three youngsters had been persuaded to get into the car, then told of the protest Jill Montgomery had made when Spence began to fondle her breasts.

Rod Montgomery, tears forming in his eyes, quietly left his seat and walked toward the courtroom exit.

As Melendez began to tell of David pulling a knife and ordering the girls to remove their clothing, threatening to kill them if they didn't obey him, a chill swept through Nancy Shaw's body. For a moment she felt as if she might faint, then she began to cry. At that moment she realized she would not be able to listen to what was to come. She, too, left the courtroom. Feazell turned and watched her leave before resuming his questioning.

As Gilbert described standing guard over Kenneth Franks while Tony Melendez sexually assaulted Raylene Rice, Richard Franks also rose and hurried toward the exit.

After Gilbert told of walking over to where Jill lay and seeing that she had knife wounds on her chest, Feazell asked, "How did you feel at that time?"

Gilbert, speaking clearly but obviously uncomfortable, said, "It's hard to talk about it. It bothers me because it isn't a good thing to talk about. I really can't describe how I was feeling. Everything just got messed up out there."

During a brief mid-afternoon recess, Judge MacLean made clear his concern about the intensity of the proceedings as he left the bench and walked quickly to the exit. Approaching Simons, who had been standing at the windowed doorway, MacLean said, "I want you to stand right here by this door. Things are getting pretty heavy in there. There's no telling what might happen."

Simons studied the strained face of the judge. "I understand," he said.

For the remainder of the day Melendez detailed the murders, then told of leaving to get his pickup and the eventual transporting of the bodies to Speegleville Park. When Judge MacLean finally recessed the proceedings for the day, the stunned spectators filed from the courtroom emotionally drained. Some exchanged silent glances but few spoke.

Though he had remained calm and composed while testifying, Melendez returned to the Johnson County jail later that night in a highly emotional state. Shaky and pacing, he was concerned that other inmates might learn his identity and that he was in Cleburne serving as a prosecution witness. When asked, he told a fellow prisoner that he was there only for the night, being transported to prison after conviction of an armed robbery charge. His name, he said, was Gilbert Fajardo.

The following morning when he returned to the stand it was obvious the ordeal was taking its toll on Gilbert. His voice was hoarse as he told of learning after the murders that Spence had made a financial arrangement with Deeb which had involved payoff from an insurance policy. He had thought of leaving town, he testified, but had been urged by David to wait until he was paid; then they would leave together.

"Gilbert," Feazell asked in closing, "why have you agreed to come here and testify against Muneer Deeb?"

"I'm testifying because I thought maybe this was one way I could make up for what was done—that maybe it would make it a little easier to live with. What happened out there was bad," he said, "and I wanted people to know what my part was and how I was brought into it.

"I decided to plead guilty and agree to testify to avoid the death sentence. I didn't think I deserved to die for the way it happened and for my part in it. I didn't think I would have a very good chance of being found not guilty if I had gone to trial."

For the first time during the trial, Muneer Deeb appeared visibly upset. As he listened to Gilbert's testimony, his jaws tightened and he focused a pained expression on the witness.

Later, after Coy Jones, a deputy from the McLennan County Sheriff's Department, had escorted Deeb to jail during the noon recess, he returned to tell Butler, "I think you people have finally got Deeb worried."

"How's that?" Butler asked.

"The minute we put him in his cell he got down on his knees and began praying to Allah."

In his cross-examination, Richard McCall immediately attacked the earlier false statements Melendez had given. The defense attorney reviewed the discrepancies in detail, noting there had previously been no mention of a pickup used to transport the bodies or any involvement of Tony Melendez.

"I played a lot of games," Gilbert said, "because I was doing everything I could to keep Tony out of all this. Until I heard that he had confessed, I wanted to try and protect him if I could."

"Why was that?"

"He's my brother. I love him."

The attorney, often smiling as he asked his questions, repeatedly commented on the remarkable detail of the testimony

Gilbert had given, suggesting the possibility that he had been well coached: that perhaps his memory of that July night had been freshened with details provided him by the prosecutors.

Gilbert leaned forward in the witness chair and looked directly at the defense attorney before replying. "The reason my memory of what happened that night is good," he said, "is because I was there."

Two hours later, the ordeal finally behind him, Gilbert sat in Feazell's room at the Gate One, awaiting his return to Waco. Sheriff Jack Harwell, who had traveled to Cleburne to hear his testimony, stood nearby as the district attorney entered. Without smiling, Feazell walked to where Melendez sat on the edge of one of the beds and extended his hand. "Gilbert," he said, "you've come a long way."

Melendez smiled and nodded in acknowledgement. "I feel pretty good about it."

"You should," Feazell said. "You've done something good for a lot of people."

It was almost dark as Simons, accompanied by assistant D.A. Pat Murphy, drove toward Waco, returning Gilbert to the McLennan County jail. Earlier in the trip they had talked briefly of the testimony and the course the trial was taking but, as the miles sped by, the men eventually fell silent.

It was Gilbert who interrupted the quiet. "You know," he said, "Richard McCall did me one favor today."

"What was that?" Simons asked, puzzled.

"When he asked me about Tony—why I hadn't told the truth in those first statements."

Simons, who had not been in the courtroom to hear the testimony, still did not understand.

"Well," Gilbert explained, "when he asked me why I had lied, I told him I was trying to protect Tony, because he was my brother and I loved him. I've never told my brother that I love him. McCall gave me the chance to finally do it."

A few miles later, Simons pulled into a roadside liquor store. While Murphy and Melendez remained in the car, Simons entered the store and returned with a single can of beer and handed it to his prisoner.

"I think you earned this," he said.

39

Richard McCall stood in front of the jury box, glancing down at his notes through horn-rimmed glasses which constantly slipped down the bridge of his nose. Stopping occasionally to push them back into place, he issued an opening statement which promised that he and Jack Holcomb would, in the days to come, not only prove their client had no involvement in the murder of Jill Montgomery but also provide reason for serious doubt that David Spence was guilty of the crime for which he had already received the death penalty.

The defense, he said, would show that money could not have been a motive in the crime and would present evidence that would prove that Muneer Deeb's Rainbow Drive Inn was financially solvent. "When he did get low on money," McCall said, "Deeb, like many of us, had family to rely on. And—I want you to think about this—had money been the motive for the killings, he would have taken out a $50,000 term life policy instead of the $20,000 policy he bought."

Before concluding his opening statement, McCall also stated that the murder of Jill Montgomery could not have been the result of mistaken identity. He intended, he said, to call witnesses to the stand who would testify that it was not difficult to tell Jill Montgomery and Gayle Kelley apart.

To Nancy Shaw's displeasure, it was the mistaken identity part of the crime scenario which McCall chose to attack first. Several times during cross-examination, he referred to Jill's bust size, asking witnesses to make comparisons to Gayle.

Calling a former Methodist Home resident named Dolores Perez to the stand, McCall posed the comparison again.

"You lived in the same home unit with Jill and Gayle?" McCall asked.

"Yes sir."

"Did you have any trouble telling them apart?"

"No, I didn't."

"Do you recall hearing Gayle Kelley say anything about Jill after she had been murdered?"

"Yes, I did."

"Would you tell the court what she said?"

"It was about two weeks after the killings and Gayle said she was glad Jill was dead because she thought she was a high society snob."

McCall then led the obviously nervous witness into a discussion of her relationship with the defendant. Dolores said that she had been a regular visitor to the Rainbow and had told Deeb just prior to the murders that Gayle was grounded and could not leave the grounds of the Home.

McCall turned to the jury to make his point. "Then it is reasonable to assume that Muneer Deeb knew that Gayle Kelley was grounded and therefore would not have been allowed to go to Koehne Park during that week in July of 1982 when the murders took place," he said.

Dolores Perez, unsure whether he was addressing a question to her or simply making a statement for the benefit of the jury, said nothing.

Butler, on cross-examination, made no effort at pleasantries as he approached the witness. He immediately began questioning her about the remark by Gayle Kelley that she had testified to having heard.

"Do you recall where this conversation took place?" he asked.

"We were either in the rest room at school or waiting for the bus one morning on the way to school," the witness replied.

"And this conversation took place shortly after the murders in July of 1982?"

"Yes."

"Are you saying that school was in session in July—in the summer—Miss Perez?"

A look of terror spread quickly across the young woman's face. Before she could answer, Butler was asking another question: "Did you attend summer school, Miss Perez? And, if so, do school buses generally run during the summer?" He knew the answer to each question was negative even before her reply.

Quickly, Butler turned his questioning to an incident in October of 1981 when the teenager had reported to the Waco police that she had been abducted and raped by two men.

"Miss Perez," the prosecutor said in a growling voice, "isn't it true that those charges were later dropped and that you told police that you had lied about being raped; that you had made up the story to avoid being punished for being late returning to the Methodist Home?"

The young woman began to cry and nodded. "I just wanted to forget about the whole thing," she said.

"I have no further questions for this witness," Butler said, making the jury aware of his disgust.

McCall waited for the witness to compose herself before he posed a final question on re-direct. "Dolores," he asked, "how would you describe your relationship with Muneer Deeb?"

"He was real nice to me," she said. "Respectful, I guess you would say. Everywhere I went, I defended him."

Butler looked up from where he had been making notes and frowned. Leaning to whisper to Feazell, he said, "I was too easy on her."

Feazell said nothing but smiled. He was thinking of a remark an attorney had once made to him about Butler's tactics when questioning a witness for whom he held no regard. Ned Butler, the man had said, sometimes likes to kill flies with a chain saw.

The following day the defense turned its attention to Deeb's financial records and provided opportunities for Feazell and Butler to get more damaging evidence into the record. After an official from the American Bank of Waco testified for the defense that Deeb's bank balance in January of 1981 had been $9,000, Feazell had a number of documents entered as exhibits and cross-examined the banker. "According to your records," the D.A. said, "a month later—in February of 1981—the defendant's balance had dropped to $130. Is that correct?"

"Yes, it is."

"And by June of 1982 Deeb's balance was $12.23."

"That is correct," the banker said.

"And shortly thereafter his account was overdrawn."

"Yes, it was."

Though McCall would weakly argue that his client had expected a sizable loan from his parents that summer, he was clearly having difficulty with the line of questioning he himself had instigated.

The manager of the Northwood Apartments testified that

Deeb had rented the apartment for Gayle Kelley in June of 1982. But during cross-examination she admitted to Feazell that the check the defendant had given her for the July rental payment had been returned, marked "insufficient funds." Deeb, she said, still owned the Northwood Apartments $369.

Seated on the front row in the courtroom, Sandra Sadler shook her head and turned to her sister next to her. "McCall," she observed, "is starting at the very bottom and building absolutely nothing." For several days, in fact, Sandra had been expressing concern that members of the jury might begin to feel sympathy for Deeb because of the futile effort his attorneys seemed to be making.

Indeed, the defense had done itself no good by bringing Deeb's financial status into the proceedings. Inadvertently, they had helped the state prove that the defendant was not only broke but deeply in debt at the time the murder-for-hire plot was first proposed.

The defense suffered an additional blow when David Spence's attorney, Russ Hunt, took the stand out of the presence of the jury and informed the court that he had spoken with David about McCall's request that he testify. Spence, he said, would take the fifth amendment to all questions if called.

Standing in the foyer of the courthouse after his brief appearance, Hunt was approached by Tommy Witherspoon of the *Waco Tribune-Herald.*

"How's David doing?" the reporter asked.

"He seemed in good spirits when I saw him."

"You still believe he's innocent?"

"I have no doubt."

Witherspoon shook his head. "Russ," he said, "do you really think this whole thing is some giant conspiracy—that those guys didn't have anything to do with the murders? The state has made a pretty strong case."

"It's all bullshit."

"I hear that you have a contract with David for a book about all this."

Hunt looked surprised, then smiled. "Where'd you hear that?"

"Somebody in the courthouse was talking about it."

"That's bullshit, too," the attorney said.

\*     \*     \*

The trial had entered its third week when Muneer Deeb took the stand and began his attempt to dispute the testimony of prosecution witnesses. Often smiling at members of the jury, he repeatedly insisted in hurried, broken English, that others had misinterpreted conversations they had overheard him having with David Spence and employees in the store. Many of the remarks he had made in the aftermath of the murders, he said, were not meant seriously. "I was only joking," he said.

As McCall questioned him, Deeb denied plotting the death of Gayle Kelley or ever telling his business partner he would have been rich had she been with the other teenagers at Koehne Park the night of the murders. His father, he said, sent him $10,000 a year for living expenses. Too, he had been "joking" when he told Alex Sanchez, the insurance salesman, to list him as the beneficiary on Gayle's policy. "Gayle had said to him," Deeb said, "that she knew no one to name and had no permanent address at the time."

His partner, Karim Qasem, had a limited English vocabulary, Deeb said, and in his attempt to translate their conversations from Arabic for the benefit of investigators and the jury, he had left the wrong impression.

"Mr. Deeb," McCall said, "have you ever been desperate enough for money to solicit the act of murder?"

"I have not," Deeb answered with a smile that had already begun to wear on members of the jury.

Feazell was on his feet quickly when McCall finally passed the witness. Clearly, he had been looking forward to questioning Deeb.

"Since this trial began," he said, "there have been a lot of statements from a lot of people. Now you tell us all these people—your friends, business partners, your banker, customers—were wrong; that you never said the things they have testified under oath that they heard you say. Do you have any idea how all these people could have been wrong?"

"Many things I never said," Deeb replied, "and many things I said, they told different. If they would have said it the way I said it and in the situation I said it in, it would have come out different. There is an explanation for it. Many times I was only joking."

One of the most damaging pieces of evidence the prosecution had, Feazell and Butler felt, was a document which showed that

Deeb had, despite his near-destitute state, paid a second premium on the policy he had taken out on Gayle Kelley. The payment had been made a week after the lake murders, indicating that he had still planned for her to be killed.

"Can you explain to the court why you made that second payment?" Feazell said.

"I do not remember making it," Deeb answered weakly.

"Do you remember telling Qasem, 'Just wait, Gayle will die just like the kids at the lake'?"

"No, I do not."

"You don't think maybe you were just . . . joking?" There was bitter sarcasm in the prosecutor's voice.

"No," Deeb replied.

On the afternoon of March 12, the defense rested its case. It had called twenty-two witnesses.

As the jurors left and the courtroom emptied, Deeb sat at the defense table, waiting to be taken back to the Johnson County jail. He watched intently as the woman court reporter gathered her tapes.

"Do you think I'm guilty?" Deeb asked.

Surprised that he was speaking to her, the court reporter hesitated before answering.

He repeated his question. "I just wondered if you think I'm guilty."

"That's not for me to decide," she said, then walked quickly in the direction of the judge's chambers.

Later that afternoon Deeb received word that his parents would not be able to make it to the States in time to attend any of his trial. For reasons they had not explained, they were having difficulty getting visas.

The following day the state called a number of rebuttal witnesses in an attempt to discredit Deeb's testimony. Willie Tompkins took the stand to again re-create his conversations with the defendant at Skaggs, and Dana Diamond repeated her story of Deeb's showing her the insurance policy and explaining how he would have been $20,000 richer had Gayle Kelley been at the lake the night of the murders.

Lending a new development to the proceedings was Doris Tucker, the young black woman Simons and Baier had rushed out to Lake Air Mall to question after she had called Crime

Stoppers. She lived near the Rainbow and had overheard an argument between Deeb and Christy Juhl. She had hidden behind the potato chip rack, she testified, listening to the heated conversation.

"The man sitting over there," she said, pointing to the defendant, "was behind the counter and Christine came in and told him she was there for David's money. Deeb was frowning and acting mad, like he didn't want her to say anything.

"Then Christine said, 'You said if he would do it, you would give him the money.' Deeb started cussing and threatened to call the police if she didn't leave. Then I heard her say, 'Go ahead and call 'em. After I tell the cops about what you've done, they'll lock you up for life and throw away the keys.' "

She stated that after Christy left, Deeb appeared frightened and angry. Doris said she left the store, went to the home of a relative, and called the Waco Police Department's Crime Stoppers program to report what she had heard.

That afternoon as he and Butler drove from the courthouse toward the motel, Feazell expressed for the first time his concern over the reaction of the jury. "I can't read them," he said. "I think we need more."

Since the beginning of the trial they had discussed the possibility of introducing some of the inmate testimony they had presented during the Spence trial. They had agreed, however, that the conservative Cleburne jurors were not likely to look on the convicted felons with favor. They had also felt that the testimony their witnesses had presented would serve to build a strong enough case for a conviction. But now, Feazell, an admitted worrier, had his doubts.

Butler knew what he was thinking. "Let's put Daryl Beckham on in the morning," he said, "and then shut it down." It was what Feazell wanted to hear.

As soon as he arrived at the motel Feazell began placing calls in an attempt to locate Beckham, who had been paroled several months earlier and was working for a trucking company headquartered near Waco. Beckham's supervisor, when finally reached early in the evening, was immediately uncooperative, insisting he had no way of getting in touch with Daryl. Feazell tried vainly to explain how important it was, yet got nowhere before the supervisor abruptly ended the conversation. Simons, meanwhile, had no luck reaching Beckham or his wife at their home in Waco.

Determined that he would have Beckham as a witness, Feazell again telephoned the supervisor. "Look," the now-hostile voice replied, "he's on the road. There's no way I can reach him for you."

"If you'll just tell me what area of the state he's in," Feazell said, "we'll have the highway patrol locate him. It's important that we get in touch with him right away. We've got to have him here in the morning."

"You don't seem to understand, fella," the supervisor said. "He's driving a $200,000 rig, hauling a $60,000 load. We can't just have him park it and come running to where you are."

Feazell was now furious. "Now you listen to me, *fella*," he yelled into the phone. "I don't think you're understanding me. If we don't find him, you're going to be sitting in our $6 million *jail* and Daryl might find himself back in the state's $200 million *prison* if he isn't here first thing in the morning." With that he slammed down the phone.

Less than an hour later Frank Smith, the owner of the trucking company, telephoned the motel room. "What the hell's going on?" he demanded. Again Vic explained the need to get in touch with Beckham.

"You the lawyer for the guy who killed those kids?" Smith asked.

Feazell rolled his eyes and sighed. "No, sir," he patiently explained. "I'm the prosecutor, the district attorney. We need Daryl Beckham's testimony to help put the guy away who was responsible for the killings."

There was a moment's silence before the owner spoke. "He just parked his rig up in Chicago and is waiting for your call. Let me give you the number," he said.

"Mr. Smith," Feazell said, "you don't know how much we appreciate your cooperation."

"Mr. Feazell," the caller asked, "is Daryl going to get in any trouble over this? I know he's in violation of his parole, going out-of-state, but he's a good kid. This trip was just a chance for him to pick up a good paycheck. I'd hate to see him get messed up over all this."

"Don't worry about it," Feazell said. "We'll work it out."

It was almost midnight when the arrangements were finally

completed to get Beckham to Cleburne. After talking with Feazell, the truck driver went directly to O'Hare Airport where a round trip ticket awaited him. He had not slept in over twenty-four hours when he took the stand the following morning.

There was a renewed hush in the courtroom as Beckham told jurors of his conversations with Spence while being held in the McLennan County jail, recalling how David had said that Deeb had wanted him to find someone to kill Gayle Kelley. He testified that David had said Deeb instructed him to leave the body in Speegleville Park since it was a place neither of them could be tied to.

The thirty-year-old truck driver, his pained face outlined by long sideburns, continued his story in an even voice. David had indicated to him, he said, that Deeb had promised to make him a partner in his business.

Having linked Deeb and Spence, Feazell then led Beckham through the retelling of Spence's description of the actual murders.

"He said it was like something came over him," the witness said, "like he was another person and once he started stabbing, he couldn't stop. While he was telling me this, it was like he was in a daze, and his eyes got real glassy."

As Beckham spoke, several members of the jury turned their attention from the witness stand to look at Muneer Deeb. For some, after sitting through almost three weeks of testimony, Daryl Beckham was the most believable witness they had heard.

By late that afternoon Daryl Beckham was on an airplane en route back to Chicago and Vic Feazell was delivering another impassioned closing argument.

"Just look at the man," the D.A. said as he pointed to Deeb. "One of the things that really bothers me about this case is the fact that he doesn't look like a killer. He doesn't look like Charles Manson. He doesn't even look like David Spence. But you don't have to look like a killer to have absolutely no regard for human life.

"Muneer Deeb is another Judas Iscariot, people. He was not at the scene of the crime that night, but he has dirty hands." Again displaying the crime scene photographs, Feazell continued. "He may not have held a gun or a knife, but this is his handiwork."

When McCall addressed the jurors he again insisted that his

client had no motive for wanting Gayle Kelley dead. "Gayle Kelley is alive," he said. "She's alive because there was never any agreement between Muneer Deeb and David Wayne Spence to have her killed."

Few spectators left the courthouse after Judge MacLean instructed the jury to begin its deliberation. Milling about in the foyer, several people were making bets as to how long it would be before a verdict was returned. Some guessed as little as twenty minutes, others as long as a couple of hours. No one seemed to have any doubt about what the decision would be.

Judge MacLean called the two alternate jurors into his chambers to inform them they were officially released and free to attend the remainder of the trial as spectators if they wished. Before they left, he asked what their verdict would have been had they been among the twelve with a vote. Both said they had no doubt that Deeb was guilty.

"What you've seen the prosecution do in these past weeks," the judge said, "is remarkable. The successful prosecution of a murder-for-hire case is nearly impossible."

It took the jury less than two hours to find Deeb guilty of the murder of Jill Montgomery.

As they left the courthouse, Simons stopped at the top of the marble steps to inhale the cold night air. "Funny how things work out, isn't it?" he said to Butler.

"What do you mean?"

"You know what today is?"

"Wednesday."

"No, the date."

"The thirteenth."

"Yeah, the thirteenth," Simons said. "Think about it. The kids were killed on the thirteenth. I arrested Deeb that first time on the thirteenth. And it was on the thirteenth when we arrested him again. Remember Spence's business about Gail Beth Bramlett, thinking it was Gayle Kelley? She was buried on the thirteenth."

"Want to hear something else?" Butler said.

"What?"

"We got a call from the office earlier today. The Texas Supreme Court upheld Spence's conviction on the aggravated sexual abuse case. You can add that to your list."

"Damn," Simons said, "we had a pretty good day."

"Sure did," Butler agreed.

Twenty-four hours later, their spirits would not be nearly so high.

Before the jury retired again to consider the same two questions as had those who sat in judgment of David Spence, the attorneys spoke one last time. Butler, again speaking in his low, controlled voice, repeatedly pointed in the direction of Deeb as he reviewed the testimony. "That man," he said, turning away from the jury to glare at the defendant, "sits before you as the man who hired David Wayne Spence to kill Gayle Kelley for money. And as a result, three kids died."

Jack Holcomb then took the floor and admonished the jurors for their guilty verdict, saying, "While I will not take issue with your verdict, neither will I stand here and presume to know how you arrived at it."

McCall, finishing the defense's closing argument, insisted to the jury that the death penalty in such a case would be "a miscarriage of justice."

Finally, Feazell spoke again. "I urge you," he pled with the members of the panel, "not to let this man's appearance convince you he is not capable of what he has done. Don't let his looks deceive you. You've all heard the story of the wolf in sheep's clothing. That's what we've got here. Mr. Deeb is in a trap; one he built himself."

It was shortly before 6:00 P.M. when the jurors, many of them looking pale and drawn, again left the courtroom to begin deliberations.

Outside, ominous thunderclouds were gathering. By the time the jury members took a dinner break just an hour after retiring to begin deliberations, a heavy rain began to fall.

Escorted to a restaurant by the bailiff, the members said little during the course of their meal. Two women members of the group ate nothing at all. One had admitted to several on the panel that she had begun wishing she was not on the jury long before the trial had ended. One of the youngest members of the panel, she had become increasingly certain the defendant would be found guilty as the trial had progressed. Long before deliberations were to begin, her thoughts had begun to focus on her feelings about the death penalty. Though she had assured the attorneys during voir dire that she believed it was justifiable in certain instances, she was now uncertain.

When the jury returned to the courthouse and cast its first vote, she was one of those who could not answer "yes" to both questions. On the second ballot, hers was the lone dissenting vote.

It was almost nine o'clock when Feazell sat down beside Butler. "It shouldn't be taking this long," he said.

The assistant D.A. agreed. He, too, was beginning to feel doubts that the jury would return with the answers that would force Judge MacLean to sentence Deeb to death. "Dammit," he said, shaking his head and rubbing his tired eyes. "I don't know what more we could have done."

Butler rose and approached one of the young television cameramen who was sitting on the floor, his back against the wall, idly looking at a discarded newspaper with a bored look on his face. "Don't you guys have one of those small TV sets out in your truck?" Butler asked.

"You mean the monitor?" the cameraman asked.

"Hell, I don't know what you call it. Just a little TV. Can't you just plug it in and use it like a regular set?"

"Sure."

"Well," Butler said. "How about bringing it up here to the sheriff's office so we can watch it?"

"Okay."

Ned sought out Truman, who was across the rotunda, talking with Rod Montgomery. "Come on," Butler said, " 'Hill Street Blues' is coming on in a few minutes. Let's go watch how the real cops do it."

As the storm raged outside, Nancy Shaw, Sandra Sadler, and Jan Thompson sat in the small room adjacent to the women's lounge, joined by Berni Feazell. Though there were occasional strained attempts at levity as they played cards, a tension built steadily as the night went on. It began to look as if the celebration Sandra had planned to host back at the motel would have to wait. She excused herself from the card game to call the manager of the motel and ask if he could put the cheeses and champagne she had asked to have placed in her room back in the refrigerator.

It was one o'clock in the morning when MacLean summoned the attorneys to his office and informed them of his decision to have the jury sequestered at a nearby motel for the night. Deliberation would resume at 10:00 A.M. the following day.

Outside the rain was still falling steadily as the attorneys, family members, and reporters left the darkened courthouse. For McCall and Holcomb, the delay presented the hope of salvaging some measure of victory for their client. For the prosecution team, it was not a good sign.

There was a clean freshness in the air the following morning as Vic and Berni sat in the restaurant next door to the Gate One, drinking coffee. "A brighter day," the district attorney said, smiling at his wife. She knew he had slept little, rising before the sun to dress and walk around in the parking lot of the motel. But there seemed to be a renewal of optimism as he continually checked his watch. It pleased her to see that he was eager to get back to the courthouse and resume the wait.

At 11:30 A.M. the bailiff announced that the jury had come to a decision and was returning to the courtroom. Watching each member of the panel as they made their way back to their familiar seats in the jury box, Feazell could see that several were crying. One young woman, in particular, appeared shaken. She had finally decided to answer "yes" to both of the questions, breaking the deadlock. Judge MacLean, aware of the emotional state of the jurors, excused them before passing sentence.

The trial completed, the hallway filled with members of the media anxious to get the reaction of Deeb. Limping noticeably, he squinted into the lights of TV cameras as he was escorted from the courtroom by two deputies.

"Do you feel you received a fair trial?" one reporter asked.

"No," Deeb said, then turned to the open elevator door.

Brad Montgomery stood across the hallway, watching as his mother was being interviewed. Only after she had answered the last of the questions directed at her did her son approach her. Smiling, he embraced her. "We did it," she said.

"We sure did," he said. Then after a pause he asked, "How do you think Jill's feeling now?"

"Son," Nancy said, tears again forming in the corner of her eyes, "I think she has to be very happy about what happened today."

"I think so, too," Brad said.

\* \* \*

At the Gate One, the delayed celebration finally took place. Sandra Sadler's room was crowded with people with whom she had become close friends in the years since her son had been murdered: Nancy Shaw and Rod Montgomery, Jan and Robert Thompson, Brad and Gloria Montgomery. And Vic Feazell, Ned Butler, Truman Simons, and Pat Murphy, men she had come to admire greatly. Her sister and mother, who had lent support throughout the trial, had remained to savor the victory. Richard Franks was there, talking with Berni Feazell and Ned's wife, Carla, who had arrived in time to hear the verdict. Curtis Franks, Kenneth's younger brother, sat with Ned and Carla's children, showing off the new labrador puppy he had received for his birthday.

There were no tears; just hugs and handshakes, and the relieved sound of laughter. For each person in the room, the family members of the victims as well as the men who had successfully prosecuted the case, the time had finally come to go on to other things.

After a while the conversation began to lag and Truman rose from his position in the far corner of the room and began shaking hands. It was time, he said, to get things packed and go home.

"Just a minute," Feazell said, blocking Truman's path to the door.

Raising his glass, the district attorney nodded in the direction of the soft-spoken man he had once mistrusted.

"To Truman Simons," he said.

As he drove back toward Waco, the question which Brad Montgomery had posed to his mother preyed on Truman's mind. What did Jill think of what had happened? And, he found himself wondering, were the kids at peace?

He stopped by the district attorney's office to drop off some of the files he had brought back from Cleburne, and it was late in the afternoon before he returned to the parking lot. A slow drizzle was threatening to turn to rain. Instead of going directly home, however, Simons drove toward Koehne Park one last time. There was one more thing he needed to do.

Pleased that the evening traffic of cruising teenagers had not begun, he found the Circle deserted. He parked and once again walked into the wooded area where the three teenagers had been murdered. For several minutes he stood in the quiet shadows, his thoughts interrupted only by the occasional droplets of water the wind shook from the canopy of post oaks and cedars above him.

Then he sat on the damp ground, pulling his knees to his chin, silently reflecting on the three years that had passed. He began to pray, giving thanks for the strength God had provided him; thanking Him that the case had finally been resolved; that the murder of Jill Montgomery, Raylene Rice, and Kenneth Franks had not remained just another unsolved murder.

"Lord," he whispered, "there's something I need to know. I need to know about the kids."

Truman suddenly felt uncomfortable with the pistol which was stuffed into the back of his jeans and with the badge that hung from his shirt pocket. He removed them and tossed them aside. And as he sat there, wrapped in the privacy of the moment, he felt a euphoric inner peace, unlike anything he had ever experienced, begin to sweep over him. It was a calm that made him want to stay forever, to languish in the feeling.

He had his answer.

# Afterword

In October of 1985, David Wayne Spence was tried for the murder of Kenneth Franks. The proceedings, moved to Bryan, Texas, on a change of venue, did not command the public or media attention of his first trial—a fact which clearly disappointed David. There were many of the same faces in the courtroom each day—families, members of the news media, and a few curious onlookers—but the large crowds which had battled for seats at his trial in Waco never materialized.

The prosecution, meanwhile, put on a much abbreviated case. This time it did not detail the mistaken identity theory. There was only casual mention of the insurance policy purchased by Deeb. Gayle Kelley was not called to testify; neither were many of the inmates who appeared at Spence's first trial. All Feazell and Butler wanted to prove was that Spence had stabbed Kenneth Franks to death. Tony Melendez had helped make a shortened trial possible when he agreed to testify. It was the only way, Tony confided to Simons, that he could tell his parents, who had continued to have difficulty believing he was involved in the crime, that he was, in fact, guilty.

The jury, then, heard both Gilbert and Tony detail from the witness stand the gruesome events of the night of July 13, 1982.

And, in addition to the bite mark testimony, the bracelet which Simons had found in Koehne Park was placed in evidence. Gloria Montgomery, Jill's sister-in-law, testified that the bracelet looked like one she had seen Jill wearing from time to time and had even borrowed on one occasion.

In his testimony at Bryan, Dr. Jolliff was even more emphatic than he had been in Waco about the danger David Spence represented to society. "I consider him dangerous, even to those of us here in this courtroom," he said. "If he had the means, he would kill each of us here. I have to admit I'm frightened at this very moment. The palms of my hands are sweating—and it isn't because I'm nervous about testifying. I've done this many times. It is because of the man sitting there." He nodded in the direction of Spence.

Unlike the first Spence trial, for which he had returned to Waco from Copperas Cove, Gene Deal did not have to travel far to testify against the man he had once served as parole officer. Having taken a job with the probation office in Bryan, he had only to walk across the street to the Brazos County courthouse where the proceedings were being held.

David's composure was not the same as it had been in Waco. When denied a visitor at the Brazos County jail where he was being held, he went into a rage and threatened to set fire to his cell. In court, he tried repeatedly to fire his attorneys throughout the trial. Though the attorneys volunteered to withdraw from the case, presiding Judge W. T. McDonald, Jr., denied Spence's motions that they be dismissed. "I do the hiring," he told the defendant, "and I'll do the firing." The amiable relationship he had enjoyed with Russ Hunt and Hayes Fuller was clearly absent with his new counsel. Though Bill Vance, one of Bryan's most respected criminal lawyers, and Skip Reaves, who had represented David in his aggravated sexual abuse trial, presented a thorough, professional defense, there was no indication they felt any warmth for their client.

And though Hunt continued to insist he had evidence that would cast doubt on Spence's involvement in the crime, he refused to share it with Vance or Reaves despite their requests.

When Sidney Smith, the fisherman who had discovered Kenneth Franks' body at Speegleville Park, testified that the body was lying stretched out flat under a tree, the legs partially in the road, Spence leaned toward Vance and said, "He's lying."

Vance turned and asked, "David, how do you know?" Spence did not answer.

Still a mystery is the fact that the letter written to federal authorities by Hunt and Fuller—long before either Gilbert or Tony told of David saying that whoever found Franks' body would "freak out" because he had left the dead youngster sitting up under the tree, still wearing sunglasses—stated "the boy's body was found leaning against a tree with his sunglasses on . . ."

How did the authors of the letter know the body had been left in a sitting position?

During the course of the trial, Vance enjoyed little support, even from staff members in his own office. His secretary, after happening on the set of crime scene photographs on his desk, told him, "If the guy you're defending did this, I hope you lose this one."

On Thursday, October 17, the jury deliberated only two hours before returning with a guilty verdict. The following day Spence again heard himself sentenced to die by lethal injection. As Judge McDonald spoke, David turned to the gallery where his father sat and whispered, "I'm really getting tired of this shit."

The aftermath of a crime such as the Lake Waco murders does not end with the tearful burials of the victims or the conviction and sentencing of those responsible. The story of the murders of Jill Montgomery, Raylene Rice, and Kenneth Franks, in fact, has not yet ended for many of those whose lives were touched by the tragedy. Scars are still evident, likely to remain for a lifetime.

What one learns after close analysis of such an event is that victims are far more numerous than the casual observer might imagine. For months after the final legal chapter was written, after David Wayne Spence had heard the Bryan jury sentence him to die for a second time, those who were intimately involved with the case suffered unexpected bouts with depression. Jan and Robert Thompson, Jill's aunt and uncle, who had been portraits of remarkable strength throughout the long months of the investigations and trials, sought psychiatric help to get through the weeks following the conclusion of the final trial. Jan's doctor expressed concern over the fact that throughout the ordeal, she had never allowed herself to cry. Three years' worth of emotion had been locked inside. For days the doctor forced her to talk about what had happened, hoping she might finally release some of the torment she had repressed so deeply. Even now, she says, there are times when she reflects on Jill's death and has difficulty separating the facts she learned while attending three trials and the "details" of Karen Hufstetler's "vision."

Jan's husband suffered severe depression following the Deeb trial and was unable to work for two months before feeling well enough to resume his normal life. He did not attend the trial in Bryan.

Friends of Russ Hunt, David Spence's Waco attorney, expressed growing concern over his continued fanatical defense of his client and his vicious attacks on District Attorney Vic Feazell. To the surprise of many in the legal community, Hunt eventually resigned from one of Waco's most prestigious law firms to open his own small law office. The last time I spoke with him (several months after the first Spence trial), Hunt said he was interested in talking with Henry Lee Lucas, the infamous drifter who once claimed to have killed 360 people before it was learned that he had duped hundreds of law enforcement officers with phony confessions. Surprised at Hunt's statement, I asked why. "I just think it would be interesting to know where Lucas was on the night of July 13, 1982," he said. Later, in a conversation with Lucas, I asked him if he had any knowledge of the Lake Waco murders. "Yeah," he said, "Bob Prince (a Waco-based Texas Ranger who was part of the Lucas Investigation Task Force) tried to get me to take them a bunch of times."

Jack Holcomb, one of Muneer Deeb's court-appointed attorneys, left Waco and is reportedly now practicing in Houston.

Assistant District Attorney Ned Butler has returned to Amarillo, Texas, where he has gone into private practice.

District Attorney Feazell became the focus of national attention when he and Texas Attorney General Jim Maddox summoned a McLennan County grand jury to investigate the bogus confessions of Lucas to two Waco murders. Ultimately, evidence was provided which indicated that numerous cases against Lucas nationwide were the result of law officers having provided him information about the crimes in order to get confessions. Soon thereafter, Feazell himself became the target of a federal grand jury probe. The Department of Public Safety, the FBI, and the Waco Police Department sought to discredit him despite the fact that his office continues to have the highest felony conviction rate in the state. Having taken on the famed Texas Rangers, who were responsible for the task force which coordinated the Lucas investigations, Feazell had stepped on some big toes. The furor resulted in his being featured on a "60 Minutes" segment which raised serious questions about the ethics and motivation of those investigating Feazell. Meanwhile, closed cases against Lucas have been reopened by embarrassed officials throughout the United States and many charges have been dropped as a result of Feazell's revelations. He is now running for a second term as McLennan County District Attorney.

In a poll recently conducted by the *Waco Tribune-Herald* asking readers to list the presently living Texans they most admired, Feazell shared company with country singer Willie Nelson, former Texas governor Bill Clements, and Baylor football coach Grant Teaff.

On March 2, 1986, Juanita White, mother of David Spence, was found murdered in the small corner house on North Fifteenth Street which she had once shared with her son. She had died from a savage beating. Lending an eerie irony to the case was the discovery of human bite marks on her body. Mrs. White's abandoned car had been found in a predominately black section of Waco. Almost immediately rumors began circulating that she had obtained new evidence that cast doubt on her son's guilt in the lake murders. While the Waco Police Department sought leads in her murder, Truman Simons, no longer working as a jailer, began conducting his own investigation from the sheriff's department. As a result of his efforts, two men were indicted for the crime in July of 1986. Neither had any knowledge of David Spence or the Lake Waco murders.

The Texas Department of Corrections refused to allow David Spence to attend his mother's funeral.

Simons was recently selected from over 450 nominees as the Texas Peace Officer of 1987.

Spence and Muneer Deeb, meanwhile, are preparing their own appeals. In a hearing in Cleburne, Judge John MacLean tried, without success, to convince Deeb to take advantage of the experience of his court-appointed lawyers, comparing his decision to that of a man who chooses "to perform his own heart surgery." Deeb ignored the judge's advice, noting that he had been studying law twelve hours a day while in prison. He and Spence never see each other but are allowed to correspond about their legal preparations.

David has again found God and now corresponds with his ex-wife June and his two sons. He continues to insist he will one day be freed and, once on the outside, will devote the remainder of his life to evangelism.

Deeb also feels he will one day be set free and says he plans to continue studying toward a law degree.

Christy Juhl, now living in another state, has begun divorce proceedings against Mahir Tumimi, who has not yet earned his U.S. citizenship. She plans to remarry in August. Karen Hufstetler now lives in a suburb of Dallas and still stays in touch with Jan Thompson.

Gilbert Melendez was recently married, by proxy, to former Methodist Home resident Penny McNutt, who testified for the defense at Deeb's trial in Cleburne. Penny had known both Jill Montgomery and Gayle Kelley while living at the Home.

Gilbert and his brother Tony are now serving their life sentences, marking time until the day they will be eligible for parole.

Jill Montgomery's mother has remarried and continues to live in Waxahachie. Her son Brad and his wife, Gloria, became the parents of a baby boy in the summer of 1985.

For Jill's aunt, Jan Thompson, the nightmare has not yet ended.

Since early September of 1985 she has received a series of anonymous phone calls which have been both frightening and infuriating.

The first time the caller indicated he thought she was Jill's mother and, in a low, menacing voice, said, "They don't got the right one . . . and we think it's funny. They (the victims) deserved what they got . . . only they should have suffered more." He then laughed and hung up.

The second call came at 2:30 on the morning of January 21, 1986. This time the caller sounded drunk. "I still think you ought to ask some questions," he said.

"About what?" Jan asked.

"About the stuff out at the lake. They're gonna kill some innocent people. That foreigner and that white guy didn't do it."

"How do you know?"

"Because I seen it," the caller answered. Then the line went dead.

He called again in February, saying he would tell her "about that stuff that happened at Koehne" if she would give him money.

"All that's over and done with," Jan replied.

"No, it ain't," he said.

On the morning of April 10, 1986, she answered the phone to hear again the same voice. "I tried to reach you all day yesterday," the man said. "I had something for you. But I guess it's not too late." With that he began to sing, *"Happy Birthday to Jill . . ."*

On the previous day Jill Montgomery would have been 21 years old. Jan, in fact, had a colorful flower arrangement prepared to place on her niece's grave but, since it had rained throughout the day, she had decided to wait until the weather cleared before taking it to the cemetery. It was sitting on the kitchen table, in full view, as she listened while the cruel song was sung.

It was after that call that she finally broke down and wept.

# Postscript

During almost 10 years of incarceration on Death Row, Muneer Deeb studied the law. Then, in 1991, largely on his own five-hour presentation before the Texas Court of Criminal Appeals, his capital murder conviction was overturned and a new trial ordered. Judges ruled that the hearsay testimony of Darryl Beckham, the former McLennan County jail inmate who had told of conversations with Spence in which Deeb's role in the crime had been discussed, should not have been admitted at the 1985 trial in Cleburne.

For families of the victims, the haunting story that had so marked their lives would have to be re-lived yet again.

None, however, were prepared for the decision of a Fort Worth jury in December of 1992. With legendary Houston lawyer Dick DeGuerin (who, ironically, would later serve as Davidian leader David Koresh's attorney) representing him, Deeb was acquitted and set free.

Gilbert Melendez, a key witnesses in Deeb's first trial, had refused to testify since prosecutors had nothing more they could offer him. Fort Worth attorney Bill Lane, assigned to the case as a special prosecutor, suggested that the passage of time had made it difficult for the jury to become emotionally involved in the case. "We did everything we knew to do and the jury obviously didn't see it our way," he said.

When the verdict was announced, Truman Simons walked toward the back of the courtroom, slowly shaking his head. "That's hard to believe," he said. Nancy Wiser, Jill Montgomery's mother, was also stunned. "When the verdict was read," she told reporters afterwards, "I said, 'God, you don't know what you've done.'"

Deeb, meanwhile, gloated. He had, he said, never lost faith that his name would one day be cleared. "I knew they were going to try and railroad me again, but this time it didn't work."

Almost immediately, Deeb was embraced by Amnesty International, the anti-death penalty organization, and quickly became a spokesman for its cause. The group even sent him to Vienna for the United Nations World Conference on Human Rights where he served on a committee with the Dalai Lama and several other Nobel laureates. He often spoke of writing a book that would, unlike what he termed the "science fiction" account you've been reading, tell what really happened in Waco years ago. Even *Life* magazine profiled him in an article it published on those wrongly convicted.

He filed a $100 million lawsuit against the McLennan County District Attorney's office and Sheriff's Department, alleging they conspired to violate his rights to a fair trial in 1985. The suit, though eventually dismissed, earned him additional headlines.

Staying out of trouble, however, seemed difficult. In March of 1993 he was twice arrested on suspicion of receiving and concealing stolen property in Dallas. In a sting operation, an undercover officer posing as a salesman of stolen merchandise was asked by Deeb to get him a television, a computer and a VCR. The undercover operation had begun as an investigation of Deeb's cousins, with whom he was living, who were suspected of buying stolen property and selling dope.

Ultimately receiving a probated sentence, Deeb found work as a cab driver, then later began his own limousine service before dropping from sight in the late '90s.

Then, on a rainy evening in April of 1997, David Spence was executed by lethal injection. Before being strapped onto the gurney, he delivered his final farewell to ex-wife June and his two sons, Jason and Steven. To the bitter end he professed his innocence.

Turning to a window where members of Jill Montgomery's family stood, he said, "I want you to understand I speak the truth when I say I didn't kill your kids. I understand your pain. I swear I haven't killed anyone. I wish I could get the rage from your hearts and you could see the truth and get rid of the hatred."

From behind the glass, Jill's brother Brad glared as Spence spoke. "Just die, just die," he responded.

Spence's death came just six days before Jill Montgomery would have celebrated her thirty-first birthday. Earlier in the day, her mother had stopped by her grave before leaving for Huntsville where the execution would be carried out. "I took fresh flowers," said Nancy Wiser, "and told her we were on our way to do our part to take care of the person who did this to her."

Nancy had requested that Spence talk with her before the execution but he refused. "I wanted to ask him what Jill's last words were," she said.

Another person who had come to witness the execution was a Waco businessman named Brian Pardo, someone David had not even known five months earlier.

Made wealthy by a business he called Life Partners which buys and re-sells insurance policies of AIDS sufferers, Pardo had been touring the Texas prison system with football player-turned-evangelist Bill Glass. Out of what he termed nothing more than curiosity, Pardo asked to meet Death Row inmate David Spence.

For two hours Pardo spoke with Spence, hearing how the Waco system had conspired to frame him for murders he did not commit. Pardo came away not only convinced David was innocent but determined to rally support that would keep him from his nearing execution.

Having once made an unsuccessful run at a Congressional seat, Pardo had contacts and knew how to generate media attention to his new cause. In the days to come he would spend countless hours and an estimated $25,000 in an effort to convince someone, anyone that David Wayne Spence was an innocent man. He contacted Governor George W. Bush, the Texas Board of Pardons and Parole, state lawmakers, and members of the media.

And, while the local newspaper and television stations gave him only brief attention, the national media quickly seized on the controversial story he was promoting. *New York Times* writer Bob Herbert jumped on the bandwagon, writing a series of columns questioning what one headline suggested was "A System Gone Mad." The network TV show "Dateline" geared up to do a piece on the case.

When a producer phoned to ask if I might appear on the show, I responded by saying that I felt certain they were planning to take the Pardo-fueled approach and asked if they had read CARELESS WHISPERS. "No," he answered, "but we plan to." I suggested they call me back after doing so.

In time I received another call. "We really need your input to make the piece we're doing balanced," I was told.

"Have you read the book?"

The answer did not surprise me: "Well, I've got it and have read parts of it. But, it is such a long book . . ."

That, I replied, told me all I needed to know about the "investigative reporting" that was being done.

Pardo, meanwhile, was relentless. He devoted the entire issue of a political newsletter he published to what he termed the "serious problems" with the investigation and prosecution of the murders. To District Judge George Allen, who had presided over the first Spence trial, he wrote, "Truman Simons, Vic Feazell, Ned Butler and Dr. Homer Campbell conspired to, and in fact did, frame all defendants for the Lake Waco murders." He went on to suggest evidence had been suppressed and witnesses had been intimidated.

And, in what was becoming something of a tradition, new lawsuits began flying. Spence's sons filed suit, alleging that "two prosecutors, an investigator and an expert witness conspired to murder Spence by framing him in the 1982 Lake Waco triple murder." Like that filed by Deeb, the suit was dismissed.

Ultimately, Simons, Butler, Feazell and Dr. Campbell would retaliate, filing suit against Pardo. At this writing, that lawsuit is still making its way through the court system.

In October of 1998, Gilbert Melendez, 43, died behind bars. The cause of death, a notification letter sent from the Texas prison system read, was "considered confidential information."

His brother, Tony, continues to serve the two life sentences which he received for the murders.

In the years that have passed since the writing of this book, relationships developed back then have been maintained, some more intimately than others. Seldom, however, are the families of the victims out of mind for long. Phone calls, Christmas cards, and an occasional face-to-face visit have seen to that.

Only recently, while in a South Texas city at a signing for a subsequent book I'd written, I looked up to see the smiling face of Sandra Sadler, Kenneth Frank's mother. We talked for some time, not about old times but, instead, of newly arrived grandchildren. Ned Butler (now an assistant district attorney in Washington County) and I recently re-lived our schoolboy track days when we attended a ceremony in Abilene where the high school track facility was named in honor of our old coach. He brought with him two grown sons whom I'd first met as children. Not once was the Lake Murder Case mentioned.

Through Waco recently, I stopped into the Sheriff's Department where Truman Simons proudly updated me on the college football playing exploits of son Jason and the fun he's having with his own grandchild. Before I left, we talked of the recent death of longtime sheriff Jack Harwell and a couple of interesting cases he was working, but there was no mention of the one which had first brought us together.

Vic and Berni Feazell have divorced. He continues to live in Austin where he maintains his law license but devotes increasing amounts of energy to producing movies. Berni and their son, Greg, live in Mexico but see Vic often.

It is rare when more than a few weeks pass without my hearing from someone wishing to talk about the tragedy that occurred in Waco so many years ago. Late in 1999, I received a long-distance call from a young woman in Wichita Falls who explained that her sister had been the victim of a multiple murderer in 1984. The case she outlined involved a 15-year search for justice that had finally ended when DNA evidence brought the killer of five young women, her sister included, to justice. As she talked, the caller explained her reason for contacting me: Her sister and Waco victim Raylene Rice had been best friends in the years immediately preceding the Lake Murders.

I'm now at work on a book on the case she alerted me to.

Just this week, I received a letter from a man in Mississippi who says he's determined to "investigate" the case himself, asking if I could provide him a transcript of David Spence's first trial. From the day I completed the writing of this book to now, I have remained firmly convinced that justice was fairly carried out. Those who committed the crimes were David Spence, Gilbert Melendez, Tony Melendez and Muneer Deeb. No new investigation, professional or amateur, is necessary.

Most recently, there came a letter from a relative of Deeb's in Saudia Arabia. The purpose was to inform me that Muneer, having moved from Texas to another state some time ago, had died of cancer.

As Ned Butler says, "This is a case that just doesn't seem to want to end. It seems like every time you think it is going to go away, something else pops up."

Indeed, it does. And so the story, like all things in real life, continues.